China Environment and Development Review: **China's Environment and Development in the Era of Globalization**

Editor-in-Chief:
ZHANG Xiao
(Chinese Academy of Social Sciences)

Translated by: JIN Jun & LIU Yusheng

中国社会科学出版社
CHINA SOCIAL SCIENCES PRESS

Paths International Ltd

Acknowledgements

We sincerely appreciate the input of China Social Sciences Press's President ZHAO Jianying and Deputy Chief editor CAO Hongju's support for this project and ZHAO shixiong, XIA Xia, YANG Yang , ZHOU Guanghuan in the department of international Cooperation & Publishing at CSSP served as the editors, making the proof-reading. They have done much work in arranging the preparation of the English version.

We also sincerely appreciate the hard work of the translators, Miss JIN Jun and Mr LIU Yusheng. Without their diligent work this English version would not exist.

Finally we especially appreciate the financial support in the publication of this book from CASS Innovation Translation Fund.

June 2015

Contents

Part III Globalization and China's Environment and Development

Part IV Trade and Sustainability

Foreword

ZHENG Yuxin

China's Environment and Development in the Era of Globalization has come out. Just as the name indicates, *China Environment and Development Review* is a comprehensive collection reviewing the coordinated development between China's environment and its economy. Based on our devoted principle to review and comment on the key and hot issues emerging in China's environment and development during recent years, this volume selects "China's environment and development under the context of globalization" as its theme.

I

Few people would cast doubts on the positive effects of economic globalization on economic development, especially when GDP is regarded as the major index to measure economic development. However, when people direct their attention to its influence on the non-economic targets such as the environment and social equity, the conclusion would be less definite and consistent.

The post reform-and-opening-up period has witnessed a rapid progress in China's industrialization. At the same time, it was also a period when economic globalization was expanding rapidly worldwide. Undoubtedly, China's remarkable economic achievements owe much to globalization and its policy of reform and opening up. One important factor is that after the implementation of reform and opening up, China, as a newly emerging country, can make better and fuller use of the global opportunities.

However, globalization poses not only opportunities but also challenges for China's development. Since China's accession to the WTO in 2001, China's economy has gradually been integrated into the world economic system. To a certain degree, China's industrial layout is a result of the multinational corporations' global distribution of resources.

China's economy relies increasingly on the international economy and is more liable to the influences of international economic prosperity. This has a direct bearing on China's economic stability, which is clearly evidenced by the enormous impact of international financial crises on China's economy in the past two years.

China has made gigantic environmental and resources sacrifices to achieve its rapid economic development. At present, China is facing severe environmental problems. Globalization and opening up exert both positive and negative influences on China's environment. China, nicknamed "the global factory", has retained its pollution discharge problems while exporting its products worldwide in exchange for foreign currencies; also, in attracting foreign investments and introducing some technologies favorable to environmental protection, China has also accepted the large scale of pollution discharge and transfer.

A significant trend abreast with economic globalization is the internationalization of environmental problems. Similar to most of the developing countries, while the severe domestic environmental problems are yet to be solved, China also has to face global environmental problems. Its rapid economic development and its coal-dominated energy structure have caught much of the world's attention due to its influence on the global environment. In particular, since China has become the largest polluter of carbon dioxide emissions, it has weathered enormous pressure from developed countries concerning this issue of greenhouse gas emissions. The influence of China's environmental problems becomes more salient in the international trade process and the development of green barriers and non-tariff barriers means China's economy is tightly sandwiched between developed countries. In December, 2009, the U. S. Environmental Protection Agency (EPA) officially listed carbon dioxide and another five greenhouse gases as harmful gases. Undoubtedly, carbon emissions would become a new rule for the international economy and politics and a hot topic for future international political diplomacy. Under such conditions, scientific problems concerning the reasons for climate warming seem to have lost their weight.

An issue of more significance is that globalization will inevitably thrust China onto the road once trod by developed countries. In China, it is an irreversible trend to look up to the developed countries' production mode, consumption mode and commercial operation mode.

The fundamental reason for China's astronomical environmental and resources pressure lies in the fact that it has followed the road of developed countries, but is unable to enjoy the resources and environmental capacity once enjoyed by developed countries in their industrialization. To a large degree, the essence of the conflict of interest between developing countries and developed countries in the issue of global warming lies in the insufficiency of the global resources and environmental capacity to upgrade the developing countries' consumption level to that of the developed countries. Instead, the developed countries maintain their unsustainable production and consumption mode and serve as the paragon in the world.

With the progress of China's opening up, especially when China acceded to the WTO, it faced more restrictions in its choices, including restrictions from WTO's regulations and more fundamental ones from traditional production and consumption modes. There is no doubt that China will face great challenges in keeping a clear mind, trying to explore new development roads on its own initiative, trying to transform its development mode and trying to establish a new sustainable production mode and lifestyle etc.

II

In September 2009, China made a commitment to reduce its carbon emissions of its own accord, which caught the world's attention. The long-term objective made by China to lower its carbon emission intensity was not only out of policy considerations but, more importantly, of strategic consideration. Currently, the world is going to experience a reformative transition in science and technology, "peaked petroleum" and global climate warming serve as a catalyst for an industrial revolution that is featured by green and sustainable energies. The essence for China to actively develop a low-carbon economy and participate in international cooperation is to grasp the opportunities amidst the transition in the international economy and to solve its own long-term development problems. The high percentage of coal in the energy structure (about 70%) and the over dependence on imported petroleum (over 50% and showing a rapidly climbing trend) have assumed prominence in China's energy problems. The former is an important reason for China's serious pollution problems and the latter concerns the nation's energy security issue. Severe restrictions on carbon emissions are an important prerequisite to develop a low-carbon economy, which will effectively decrease fossil energy consumption, promote the utilization of green technologies and the development and utilization of alternative energies such as renewable energy sources. This will lower China's dependence on imported petroleum and make the strategic objective of a green energy supply more attainable.

After China made an official commitment to lower its carbon emissions levels, these emissions undoubtedly would become another restrictive index for China's energy conservation and emission reduction. That the objective of lowering carbon emission intensity is proposed as an important strategic decision indicates that China has officially embarked on its road of developing a low-carbon economy. It can be predicted that during the period of the "12th Five-Year" Plan, China will step up its promotion of a low-carbon economy and use it as an opportunity to advance coordinated development between China's ecological resources environment and economy.

With no obligations to reduce greenhouse gas emissions, China's voluntary commitment to carbon emission intensity reduction doesn't mean China has prioritized greenhouse gases over other traditional pollutants. Because of different development stages, China reveals great differences from other developed countries in its environmental and emission reduction problems. Currently, China's environmental pollution problems still mainly center on the discharge of traditional pollutants and its emission reduction mainly focuses on the reduction of industrial pollution and domestic sewage, such as smoke, industrial dust, sulfur dioxide and other air pollutants, chemical oxygen demand, petroleum, cyanide, arsenic, mercury, lead, cadmium, hexavalent chromium and other wastewater pollutants, industrial solid wastes, hazardous wastes in particular rather than greenhouse gases.

For justice's sake, the historic responsibility for global climate warming mainly falls upon developed countries and besides, the nature of actual emissions should be categorized to the effect that the emissions from China and other developing countries are for development while those from developed countries are for luxury. Moreover, judging from the actual energy consumption per capita and carbon dioxide emissions per capita, the size of emissions from developed countries is much greater than that of China, with America being respectively 5.19 and 4.

45 times higher than China and Japan, 2. 89 and 2. 22 times higher in 2006. China and other developing countries have good reasons to refuse to undertake the obligations of emission reduction.

China is pressed by reality to treat the pollution incurred by traditional pollutants, which differs greatly with the reduction in greenhouse gas emissions in respect of responsibilities and interests. The continued rapid economic growth in China has compressed China's industrialization into a comparatively short time span. Compounded by the fact that China is still at the pollution-intensive development stage of heavy chemical industries, its environment and resources conditions are extremely grim. The discharge of pollutants is encroaching every crook and cranny of our homeland and jeopardizing our human health. For such urgent and pressing problems, the government should bear the responsibility to effectively protect and manage the environment.

III

Compared with the time when we compiled the first volume, China has undergone tremendous changes in its development concepts. From China's high-level leaders to the populace, everyone has become more aware of the need for comprehensive, coordinated and sustainable development. In the first volume, what we mainly did was to sort out and review the status of the environment and existent environmental and economic policies of China. While exposing the severe environmental conditions, we analyzed and commented on the deficiencies and inconsistencies in the policies in the hope of making more progresses in our policy integration and other more effective measures. In the second volume, we mainly focused on the deep institutional factors, ideals and value orientations relating to the environment and sustainable development, to discuss issues in key areas like the value, social surveillance of the environment and resources, and the legislation relating to this. We also concentrated on the exploration of ecological environmental resources and the public resource management system relating to the "Three Rural Issues", deepening our discussion from the policy level to the system level. The third volume was compiled and published under the context of China's advocacy of practicing a review of scientific development. We reviewed the new practical and theoretical progress secured during the new stage of our sustainable development, which involved more profound problems, such as the environmental rule of law, strategic environment, assessment of environmental policy performance, green GDP, the environment and civil society, ecological protection and humanistic development, a recycling economy, resource restrictions on regional development and innovation. The changes in the first three volumes clearly illustrate how China has matured during its development as well as how our perception is deepening.

The reform and opening up has secured China's remarkable economic clout and its international standing is improving. Although the current world international economy and politics are still dominated by developed countries, the rapid ascendancy of China and its international influence cannot be overlooked. On the one hand, China is exerting greater influence and is shouldering heavier responsibilities for the world; on the other hand, the world is exerting more and more profound influences on China. In such a context, (*Chinese edition Vol.* 4), by discussing globalization's influences on China's sustainable development, aims at making the policies more targeted and to improve our awareness through analysis and discussion to better cope with the challenges and opportunities brought to us by globalization.

The chief editor of the first three volumes of *China Environment and Development Review* is researcher Zheng Yisheng and, from this volume on, researcher Zhang Xiao will take his place. This volume consists of five parts, namely, "overview", "globalization", "climate change", "globalization and China's sustainable development" and "trade and sustainability".

Following the conventions of the first three volumes, the overview of this volume is the book's keynote report, written by the chief editor, entitled "Challenges Posed by Globalization to Sustainable Development——From the Perspective of Ecological Environment and Poverty". This article discusses, from a unique perspective, how globalization influences the underprivileged ecological environment and the poor population and points out that globalization has enlarged the gap between the rich and poor and aggravated the disequilibrium status between the ecological environment and the utilization of resources. These problems deserve our attention and only through this can we promote a real sustainable development for human beings.

The first part "globalization" is the feature report written by Researcher Zhao Jingxing "Thoughts on How to View Globalization——

The Chinese Nation and Market in its Economic Development". This article firstly gave an in-depth analysis of the essence, process and characteristics of globalization through Marx's relevant theories about capital. Also, in combination with globalization's development after the Second World War, the author clarified the basic role of the market economy in globalization and questioned the relationship between the country and the market during globalization. In discussing the actual problems before and after the reform and opening up and the current problems in our development, he made the conclusion that the country should play an active and effective role in adjusting the country-and-market relationship, which has laid a good foundation for the further discussion in this book.

The second part of this volume, consisting of seven articles, mainly centers on global climate warming. The first article is "Public Issues Requiring Man's New Wisdom——Why Cannot Man Work Hand in Hand against Global Climate Change?" by researcher Zheng Yisheng. This article reflects the author's many new thoughts on global climate warming. He gave a vivid description of the manifestations of how man cannot make joint efforts in coping with global climate warming and analyzed in depth the various reasons behind this. His multi-faceted analysis, from the respect of indefiniteness, concepts, ideals, real conflicts of interest and more profoundly, the system and ethics, can be an assistance for people to understand the complications of the climate warming problem. His proposition for "deep fairness" and new wisdom, new life values and a new civilization paradigm is very enlightening for mankind in confronting new public problems.

The other six articles in this section discussed from different perspectives are about how China should cope with global climate warming, and touch upon different aspects of this problem. There are articles discussing the current situation of greenhouse gas emissions in China and the prediction for its future prospects (Li Yuhong) and how to face international negotiations and safeguard China's rights for development from a strategic height (Chen Ying, with the Research Group of the Environment and Development Research Center, Chinese Academy of Social Sciences); there are also articles discussing how to develop a low-carbon economy in China and promote the strategic transition in China's economic society (Yang Zejun & Zhang Shiqiu) and how to motivate developed countries to transfer their advanced low-carbon technology to developing countries (Zhou Ji & Wang Haiqin). I sincerely hope these discussions can offer useful references for readers to understand and grasp the problems of global climate change.

The third part includes an article about how to improve China's energy conservation and emission reduction efforts in the context of globalization (Zheng Yuxin) and an article about the comparison and analysis of the G20 countries' economic and environmental efficiency. It is hoped these two different articles will broaden readers' horizons and deepen their understanding of some problems.

The fourth part of this volume, consisting of four articles, mainly revolves around the influence of international trade on China's environment and resources. The articles compiled in this part are highlighted by the discussion of China's environment and resources distribution in the context of globalization in professional fields, including the influences on the energy demands and environmental quality (Zhang Youguo), on the water resource supply (Zhang Xiao), on ecological forestry resources (Sun Changjin, Chen Liqiao & Chen Lijun) and on sustainable development (Fan Mingtai & Zheng Yuxin). Among these, discussions about international trade's influence on China's energy demands and environmental quality, on China's water resource supply and the connotation of corresponding policies are grounded on the input-output analysis, while discussions about free trade's influences on China's sustainable development are based on the dynamic general equilibrium analysis. Since international trade's influences on the environment and resources are very complicated, when the problem asks for accurate analysis, we will resort to sophisticated theoretic assumptions and quantitative models for our studies. To some degree, it is hoped that these academic articles may afford readers an opportunity to access the research methods of the social sciences.

Similar to the first three volumes, the compilation of this volume is co-accomplished by scholars and experts from different fields. Besides experts from Chinese Academy of Social Sciences, there are experts, scholars and managerial personnel from universities, research institutions and management departments of the government and researchers long engaged in practice at primary levels. Although having different fields of knowledge and working contexts, they share one thing in common: their long-term concern and research relating to the content of this volume. Our research center would like to extend our sincere gratitude to those who have contributed to this volume with their scientific attitudes and keen devotion.

Lastly, it should be noted that the seventeen authors in this volume have different writing styles and hold different views on certain problems. There must be inconsistencies between different parts. Also, in this volume, some are explorative researches, so some views may seem immature. It is hoped that scholars, experts and readers can offer some suggestions for this volume and we can get some feedback for discussion and exchange.

ZHENG Yuxin
Beijing, China
Jan. 10, 2015

Preface

China Environment and Development Review (*China's Environment and Development in the Era of Globalization*) was edited in an independent, objective and rigorous academic approach. We invited active scholars, experts and managers to discuss the environment and development problems in the era of globalization. The dozens of articles in this volume, with their different characteristics, embody the authors' wisdom, sense of responsibility and academic pursuit. What we offer here are not fragments of thoughts, but the crystallization of our long-term deliberation and accumulative studies. It is hoped that the constellation of our thoughts will lead China on the road to sustainable development.

The framework of this volume was designed and made by Zhang Xiao and the articles were reviewed by Zheng Yuxin, Zheng Yisheng, Zhang Xiao, Zhang Youguo, Li Yuhong from the Center for Environment and Development, the Chinese Academy of Social Sciences and Zhao Jingxing from the Institute of Quantitative and Technical Economics, Chinese Academy of Social Sciences. The Chinese version of this volume is funded by the Ford Foundation and the Key Research Laboratory of "Economic Policies and Simulations", and the Chinese Academy of Social Sciences; the English version is funded by the Innovative Program Publishing Project of the Chinese Academy of Social Sciences. Thank you all.

ZHANG Xiao
Beijing, China
January 25, 2015

Contributors

ZHANG Xiao, ZHENG Yuxin, ZHENG Yisheng, LI Yuhong, ZHANG Youguo:
Center for Environment and Development, Chinese Academy of Social Sciences

ZHAO Jingxing, FAN Mingtai:
Institute of Quantitative and Technical Economics, Chinese Academy of Social Sciences

ZHANG Shiqiu, LI Wenjun:
College of Environmental Sciences and Engineering, Peking University

CHEN Ying:
Center for Sustainable Development, Chinese Academy of Social Sciences

ZHOU Ji:
School of Environment and Natural Resources, Renmin University of China

LI Jing:
School of Economics, Hefei University of Technology

SUN Changjin:
Independent Consultant

Overview

Challenges Posed by Globalization to Sustainable Development

——From the Perspective of Ecological Environment and Poverty

By ZHANG Xiao

I. Why Do We Choose the Theme of Globalization and Sustainable Development?

It seems that globalization, the contextual theme we have chosen for this volume of *China Environment and Development Review* (hereafter referred to as the "Review"), is such a platitude. Obviously, this is not to our advantage. Undoubtedly, whether in the past or in future decades, globalization was and will be a term most frequently abused, least defined, most susceptible to misunderstanding and a term with the fuzziest connotation and the greatest political clout (Beck, 2008, p. 23). Although the discussion on globalization and sustainable development has continued for a certain period of time, we assume that in the confrontation of changeable new realities, many problems still remain untouched and need to be discussed in depth. For this reason, we have good reasons to further our discussion and research.

1. Basic Starting Points for Discussion

About the features of this round's globalization, please refer to Professor Zhao Jingxing's discussion in the first part of this book for details. In our opinion, we should especially at least grasp the following basic points:

Firstly, we should think globally in researching the current environmental and development problems in China.

A global vision and thinking is not an empty quantity concept in general, but is macro (rather than partial and micro), process-targeted (rather than result-targeted) and a dynamic observation and thinking (rather than static). The prominent feature of such observation and thinking is that there is no well-established conclusion and no blueprint for reference, which asks for our independent thinking, analysis and judgment. Global vision and thinking puts us in such a better position so that in analyzing problems, we will take a holistic strategy, placing them in a bigger framework rather than restricting them to a certain region or country, and in this way we may have better grounds to expose problems and seek appropriate solutions for them.

The by-product brought about by the large-scale worldwide cross-national capital, product and personnel flow in the context of globalization, constantly poses new security problems to human society. In today's materially abundant world, security ascends as man's major appeal after the subsistence problem has been solved. Through all those different crises, mankind feels all the more keen that the pursuit of security is ranked as one of the most important pursuits for modern nations. During globalization, ecological environment security should be regarded as the major concern. Since 1992, the World Science Organization has reiterated that most environmental systems in the world have been under severe pressure and the developed countries are the "prime culprits" (Hillman & Smith, 2009, p. 8). The *Millennium Ecosystem Assessment—Synthesis*[①] issued in 2005, pointed out that about 60% of the ecological system which sustains life on earth, such as the air, water and climate stability was degrading or could not be guaranteed for sustainable use. Water resource supply should be the central task of poverty alleviation, but according to the UNESCO-WWAP 2003, World Water Assessment Program (WWAP): *Water for People. Water for Life*[②], 1.1 billion out of the 6 billion global population had no access to safe drinking water. This problem resulted in 600 cases of water-related deaths per day and most of the victims were children under five years old. Hillman & Smith (2009, p. 65) pointed out poignantly that the present and future water resource problem of China, the poisoned major rivers in particular, was caused by the rich Western country's demand for the production of consumer goods.

---

① Millennium Ecosystem Assessment—Synthesis, www.millenniumassessment.org/en/Synthesis.aspx.

② UNESCO-WWAP 2003, World Water Assessment Program (WWAP), Water for People, Water for Life 2003—Executive Summary. http://unesdoc.unesco.org/.

Security doesn't merely lie in the avoidance or decrease in mortality, diseases and physical damage, but more importantly, it shows itself more in people's increasing emphasis on their mental condition. By participating in the globalization process characterized by the production of cheap goods and the free flowing labor force, the employee's dignity and security is flouted and his/her social status is debased (Hillman & Smith, 2009, p. 124).

How to protect the underprivileged group and the ecological environment system against disrespect and insecurity and how to improve their situation during the process of globalization should be one of the prioritized fields for global research.

Secondly, in discussing China's environmental and development problems, we should break the mold of a purely economic thinking pattern (i. e. economic growth first) and make a strategic transition to the development mode.

Superficially, there is no suspicion cast on the comprehensive, coordinated and sustainable development mode, but it should be noted that the masses are controlled by the market economy through faith in consumerism (Hillman & Smith, 2009, pp. 125-126) and the relative social poverty unceasingly fabricated by the market economy and consumerism plunges people into unalleviated status anxiety and instills into them an insatiable desire to increase their wealth. Even if they are aware of the inequity and unfairness, the chances that their dream and opportunity of making a fortune will become a reality is equivalent to that of winning a lottery. Moreover, the possession of property, which can be measured in the tangible form of money, makes some people feel so good about themselves. Therefore, people from different ladders of society, unwilling to think ahead, are preoccupied with only one thing: making money and developing the economy.

In the face of environmental and development problems, rational economists can only examine them from the perspective of economics and this is why the *Stern Report: Climate Change Economics* is probably more influential than the science report tome by IPCC (UN Intergovernmental Panel on Climate Change). Economists generally regard the world as an economic structure rather than a social one and man is a rational economic man in the sense of economics. They examine all the interpersonal relationships and man-nature relationships under the guidance of the principle of the utility maximization.

However, the reality is that the consequences of the rational behavior of the individual and country are detrimental to the public ecological environment. Some countries, for their own direct economic profits, have over exploited or polluted the "the world republic land" (the stability of such resources as lands, oceans, the air and the fresh water essential for man's health and wellbeing), which jeopardizes other countries' long-term benefits. They are exchanging their own partial development sustainability with other countries' poverty and unsustainable development. Just as Hillman & Smith (2009, p. 113) pointed out, the important crash in human society would not be the one between civilizations, but between values. The faith in a market economy and consumption reacts against the real concern for the future destiny and long-term benefits of the human world: the enterprise is becoming a system and the politician, a guardian of short-term benefits and a job hunter. The globalized market system not only destroys the "world republic land", but also the civil society.

To criticize the existing development mode and to expose and confront its innate deficiencies constitutes an important step in the exploration of China's sustainable development.

Thirdly, China's sustainable development is not singularly an urban problem, but relates more to rural sustainable development and poverty alleviation.

Concern about the rural poverty problem, poverty alleviation and ecological environmental protection and improvement are equally important in sustainable development. Although "the dual economic structure is an unavoidable stage in the economic development" (Zhao Jingxing, 2009, p. 25), in the context of globalization, the underprivileged in society are being marginalized, which is of great concern for the global society. Overall, the gap between the average rural income and urban income in China has been widening since the reform and opening up: in 1978, the per capita net income of the rural household accounted for 38.9% in the per capita disposable income of the urban household, while in 2006 the number decreased to 30.5% ①. Similar to the majority of the poor in the world, most of the over 20-million poor population in China is non-urban and their actual income

① State Statistics Bureau, ed.: *China Statistical Abstract* 2007, China Statistical Publishing House, 2007.

has no direct bearing on the agricultural production, the grain yield in particular (Sustainable Development Strategy Research Group, the Administrative Center for China's Agenda 21, 2005, pp. 47-48) . According to the statistical data (Department of Rural Social and Economic Survey, State Statistics Bureau, 2006, p. 3), the net income from household agriculture took up 45% in the total 2005 rural per capita net income. The increasing rate of the net income from household agriculture has been slowing down since the mid-1980s, which is largely attributable to the fall in the agricultural and husbandry income in the primary industry; in 2005, the rural per capita net income from the sources of industries increased and constituted the major source for farmers' income increase, taking up a percentage of 36%.

In 2005, the rural permanent residents who emigrated in search of non-farming jobs accounted for 20. 2% in the total rural labor force (Department of Rural Social and Economic Survey, State Statistics Bureau, 2006, p. 3) . The living conditions of the marginalized immigrant laborers in the cities is disconcerting as most of them are engaged in risky, filthy and taxing work in architecture, mining and service industries which is repudiated by urban citizens and their security, health and minimum subsistence are not guaranteed (Sustainable Development Strategy Research Group, the Administrative Center for China's Agenda 21, 2005, p. 48).

With the industrial transfer during the globalizing process, ecological degradation and environmental pollution have posed a serious threat to the disadvantaged agriculture and the underprivileged farmers. They are insidiously or blatantly collapsing China's agricultural foundation and causing systematic damage to farmers' livelihood (Sustainable Development Strategy Research Group, the Administrative Center for China's Agenda 21, 2005, p. 55) and even threatening farmers' health and life. In China's rural areas, ecological environmental issues aggravated the already existing poverty and rendered it even more sophisticated and demanding to solve the problem of poverty.

Care for the sustainable development of the poor and underprivileged in society is a basic measurement of a society's civilization development and its capability to pursue harmony and happiness. As a matter of fact, such care would not cost much. It only asks for the rich to save a cup of coffee or a round of golf. What really matters is the conscience and introspection of the rich as well as the political courage and managerial wisdom of the decision-makers. As long as the social consensus is established, institutional arrangements, capital and technology guarantees and surveillance during the implementation process will all be operational.

2. Basic Framework for Discussion

Besides the overview, the book is divided into four parts. The theme of the first part is "globalization", mainly discussing the influence of globalization on China, how the influence is exerted as well as the ensuing problems. In the discussion, the author, with his keen observation of both Marxist thought and China's social and economic operation in reality, has made a clear-cut and in-depth analysis of globalization, which obviously supersedes the analysis and judgment by some domestic scholars. In this part, the relationship between the nation and the development, between the government and the market, is considered in the context of globalization. The author has made observations from a strategically advantageous position, summarized many existing arguments and discerned the absurdity of the domination of the Western economics textbooks over the emerging country. This offers suggestions for us to approach the problem in its profundity and with a more objective attitude. The first part has laid a solid theoretical foundation for the following discussions.

The second part is the essence of this book. We organized scholars, experts and officials to analyze and discuss climate change, currently the major problem for the global environment and development from multi-perspectives. (1) For the central problem, the complicated contradictions and conflicts between the benefits of developed countries and developing countries, they put forward the idea of "in-depth fairness" to cope with the new public problems. Besides giving a general direction, the Research Group of the Environment and Development Research Center, Chinese Academy of Social Sciences, offered suggestions about how China, on the premise of defending its own rights of development and in dealing with climate change, should make its long-term development strategy that is far-sighted and based on its own standing. (2) Here they discuss the hot topic of a low carbon economy, mainly discussing its relationship with the transformation of China's development pattern, China's response to the regional air pollution in the context of climate change, China's response to international climate negotiations and the technological transfer based on trade. (3) Here they evaluate the research on China's greenhouse emissions.

The third part mainly discusses the understanding and reviews of China's policies on energy conservation and emission reduction and makes a comparison between some countries' economic efficiency and the new economic and environmental efficiency with the environmental factors added in.

The fourth part is also an important component of this book. It touches upon the important content of globalization, the relationship between international trade and the sustainability of energies, environment and resources. Basing its analysis on the quantitative model, this part is more academic and its conclusions are more practical for policy-making.

II. Interpretation of the Relationship between Globalization and Poverty

We agreed upon such a definition: at present globalization only occurs in the economic field. In many contexts, globalization means "economic globalization" (Zhang, 2007, p. 55). A prominent feature of economic globalization is that the flowing of such factors as goods, capital, technologies, information and labor services have crossed the boundaries of different nations (Wu, 2002). In measuring the iconic indexes of the economic globalization, we mainly examine international trade and foreign direct investment and the scale of multinational corporations.

1. Examination of the Iconic Indexes of Globalization

According to the data of the World Bank, for decades, whether the low-income, middle-income or high-income countries[①], trade (import and export) has taken up an increasingly larger share in the GDP (see data in Table 2). For example, in low-income countries, it rose from 47% in 1990 to 70% in 2007; in middle-income countries, from 39%

① Categorized according to the gross national income (GNI) of the World Bank, the same below.

to 64%. More significantly, the high-income countries have been the destination for the exports from low-income and middle-income countries. Take the year 2007 for example, 70% of the exports from middle-income economies and 67% of the low-income economies flowed into the high-income economies (The World Bank, 2009).

In 2007, 55% of the private capital flowed into the developing countries in the form of foreign direct investment (FDI). The total volume of the private capital flowing into the developing countries was on the rise: from USD 208 billion in 2003 to USD 961 billion in 2007. For many developing countries, FDI is the largest share of private capital obtainable to them, especially for those low-income countries which have the least opportunities to gain finance on the international capital market. From 2000 to 2007, the low-income countries' net inflow of FDI had doubled, with its percentage in GPD rising from 1.7% to 4.2%. What's worth mentioning is that the inflow of FDI in high-income countries was comparatively higher, taking up 75% in the global FDI inflow in 2007; the 12 largest developing countries took up 16.5% (in which China took up 26%); however, for the low-income countries it was only 1.5% (The World Bank, 2009).

Not only does the global capital flow into the high-income countries under the globalizing context, but also the global income. In 2003, the high-income countries, with their 955-million population, took up 81% of the total global income while the low-income countries, with their 2.735-billion population, took up only 1.2% (The World Bank, 2003). The poorest population accounted for one fifth of the global population, but their income share in the global total income decreased from 4% in 1960 to 1% in 1990. In contrast, the fortune possessed by the 358 billionaires exceeded the total income of half of the global population (Beck, 2008, p. 155). And the income gap in different countries is widening. Take Germany, one of the high-income countries for example, from the 1980s to 1990s, its labor income only increased by 2% while its capital income in the same period increased by 59%. Obviously, in the era of globalization, labor becomes increasingly cheaper while capital becomes more and more valuable and expensive. Correspondently, the labor income keeps decreasing while the capital income is increasing (Beck, 2008, p. 155), which not only results in a domestic gap between the rich and the poor, but also accelerates the widening of the gap internationally.

2. *Disequilibrium in Economic Development Incurred by Economic Globalization (Non-Neutrality)*

Non-neutrality of globalization means a possible asymmetry between the cost and the return (Zhang, 2007, p. 68). With globalization, the fortune (in the form of GDP) in some countries increases faster than the population. The economic prosperity seems to offer a "globalizing feast" for everyone. However, the problem calling for further deliberation is, "how is the newly increased fortune distributed?" We should further examine whether there is a serious imbalance among the share won by different parties in the so-called "win-win situation" brought about by globalization.

Here we should distinguish two kinds of disequilibrium. The first is the internal disequilibrium in the developed countries. Take America for example, the economic growth only makes the 10% richest people even richer and they have obtained 96% of the newly accumulated fortune. In Germany, the enterprises' profits have increased by 90%, but the salary has only increased by 6% and the individual income tax doubled in the past decade. At the same time, the corporation tax has been lowered by half, taking up 13% in the general tax receipts compared to the 35% in 1960 and 25% in 1980 (Beck, 2008, p. 7). Based on this, Beck (2008, p. 66) pointed out that in developed countries the enterprises' profits increased, but they failed to fulfill their obligations, refusing to provide employment and pay taxes and even transferring the cost of unemployment and economic development to others. The country and the working class have to pay for the second modernized "luxurious" life shared by the rich, for example: highly developed schools and universities, well organized transportation system, protected natural scenery, colorful urban life, etc.

The second is the disequilibrium between the developed countries and developing countries. The so-called "win-win situation" between developed countries and developing countries means that through international trade, the fierce competition leads to a cost reduction and some countries promote employment and earn revenues through exportation, while other countries consume cheaper exported goods; ultimately, both the exporting and the importing countries have been benefited. Beck (2008, p. 121) pointed out that here the two different ways of cost reduction are confused: one applies advanced technologies and organizational management to improve economic returns; the other lowers the cost through low salaries and poor working conditions to win economic returns. As a matter of fact, in some developing countries, the enterprises are competing for capital and market share by endangering the public social and environmental benefits and sacrificing the workers' health security and welfare. In face of such a brutal " win-win situation", if we continue to analyze the economics through Li Jiatu's free trade model, the conclusion will be exceptionally flimsy and self-deceiving.

To conclude, whether in terms of the internal disequilibrium in developed countries or the disequilibrium between developed countries and developing countries, the victim will always be those low-income groups or relatively poorer groups; the rich, wherever they live, will always be the beneficiary in the context of globalization.

3. Challenges Posed by Globalization to Worldwide Poverty

Economic globalization endangers the poor's benefits through the global economic rules (for example, the WTO). Borg (2009) cited an article from the *Economist* on September 25, 1999 that in the Uruguay Round of the WTO, the tax cut by the rich countries was less than that of the poor countries. From then on, the rich countries have found a new way to close their markets, the normally used one being the imposition of an anti-dumping tariff on cheap imported goods considered by them as "illegitimate". The rich countries have adopted protectionism in the most competitive areas of many developing countries, such as agriculture, textiles and clothing. As a result, according to the study of Hertel and Martin, the average tariff levied by the rich countries on the manufactured goods imported from the poor countries is four times higher than that from the rich countries. This is obviously an enormous burden on the poor countries. Moreover, according to the estimation of UNCTAD, if the rich countries could open more market share, by 2005 the poor countries could have exported another 700-billion dollars' of goods. Besides, many poor countries knew little about the content of what they had signed in the Uruguay Round: they were also disturbed by the information asymmetry. Unavailability of some information made them pay a huge price. According to the estimation of Finger and

Schuler, it was impossible for the poor countries to withstand the high cost incurred by the establishment of the complementary terms for improving trade procedures and the standards of technological intellectual property rights, since these exceeded the poorest countries' annual development budget. Not to mention that in the areas where they should have enjoyed benefits through the world trade rules, the poor countries usually enjoyed no profits. Some member countries could hardly even afford the travel fare to the WTO and therefore the agreement reached in the Uruguay Round aggravated global poverty.

Under the existent world trade system, some rich countries are enabled to continue their success in trade protectionism; the employment, income, economic growth and tax revenues in the poor countries are greatly influenced and many people in those countries are living on the margin of poverty. Under such a trade system, the market of the developed countries is more closed than open, which brings many benefits to the rich countries through free trade but stifles the development of the poor (Borg, 2009).

Today, more and more countries incline to choose the market economy system as if it is the only means to accelerate their economic development and improve their international competitiveness (Zhang, 2007, p. 23). The convergence of different countries' economic systems, global rules and regulations has become a reality. The global economic rules in current use have actually led to poverty.

With different methods to measure poverty, we will get different data. It may not be an accurate reflection of the reality. Different ways and standards to measure the condition of global poverty are shown in Table 1. According to the study of Chen and Ravallion (2008), since the beginning of the 1980s, based on the lowest measuring standard of a dollar per person per day, poverty has been alleviated to some degree. However, the absolute number of the global poor hasn't reduced fundamentally (if the standard of 2 dollars per person per day is adopted, the number, compared with that in 1981, increased by 0.8% in 2005) and even shows an increasing trend (if the standard of 2.5 dollars per person per day is adopted, the number, compared with that in 1981, increased by 12.8% in 2005). If China's data are excluded, except for the calculation based on the lowest standard, the number of the global poor shows a significant increase (with the standard of 2 dollars per person per day, the number increased by 34% in 2005 compared to 1981; with the standard of 2.5 dollars per person per day, the number increased by 48.3% in 2005 compared to 1981). Obviously, the variation of the globally poor population shows an extreme asymmetry with the global total and per capita economic growth.

Why is the new market economic global order being so harsh to the poor? The reasons are as follows: firstly, the market economic system is the result of the dominating countries' constant advocacy and promotion since they (for example: America) have to safeguard their vested interests by making international rules while other countries have no choice but to actively or passively accept the rules of the game, which deprive them of any possibilities of choosing other methods for institutional innovation (Zhang, 2007, pp. 22-23); secondly, in details, Borg (2009) pointed out that the international rules implemented in the new global order were agreed upon through international negotiations. In the international negotiations, the negotiation representatives were committed to maximizing the enterprises' benefits in making each agreement, regardless of the benefits to the global poor. Those representatives, using their excellent bargaining skills and taking advantage of the other party's weaknesses, ignorance and corruption, strived for the maximization of their own benefits. Amidst such negotiations, the rich countries may make compromises to each other, but never to the weak countries. Therefore, the accumulated results from many negotiations and agreements are biased or, in other words, the unfair and biased system arrangements will ultimately direct the flowing of the large part of economic benefits into the rich countries. Correspondently, the poorer in the world are deprived of their deserved share in the global economic growth.

Although there are many different discussions about whether the trade volume (export + import) would incur inequality, some researches (Lundberg & Squire, 2003) show that a higher trade volume trend would increase inequality. Other researches (Milanovic, 2005; Pavallion, 2001) further find that in low-income countries higher trade volume is increasing inequality, while in high-income countries the situation is the opposite. Tables 2-4 illustrate the general condition of the global import and export trade and some specific data in some countries.

Table 1 Variation in the Globally Poor Population
(100 million, Purchasing Power Parity in 2005, PPP)

Poverty Standard	Year			
	1981	1990	1999	2005
Less than 1 dollar per capita/day	15.2	12.9	11.5	8.8
Less than 2 dollars per capita/day	25.4	27.6	28.7	25.6
Less than 2.5 dollars per capita/day	27.3	30.7	33.2	30.8
Less than 1 dollar per capita/day①	7.8	7.9	8.4	7.7
Less than 2 dollars per capita/day①	15.6	18.0	21.0	20.9
Less than 2.5 dollars per capita/day①	17.6	21.1	25.5	26.1
Long-term malnutrition②	—	8.0	—	8.5

Note: ① Excluding China. ② Replaced with the data in 2004.
Data source: Chen and Ravallion, 2008; UNDP, 2005.

Table 2 World Import and Export Trade (Unit: %)

Classification of Economies①	Imports of Goods and Services (Percentage in GDP)		Exports of Goods and Services (Percentage in GDP)	
	1990	2005	1990	2005
High-Income Economies	19	24	18	24
Middle-Income Economies	21	33	22	36
Low-Income Economies	16	29	13	25
World	19	26	19	26

Note: The categorization of the global economies into high-income, middle-income and low-income groups is based on the standard of the World Bank, the same below. See www.worldbank.org.

Data source: UNDP, 2008.

Table 3 Import and Export Condition in Some Countries (Unit: %)

Country	Imports of Goods and Services (Percentage in GDP)		Exports of Goods and Services (Percentage in GDP)	
	1990	2005	1990	2005
America	11	15	10	10
Canada	26	34	26	39
Brazil	7	12	8	17
Germany	25	35	25	40
France	23	27	21	26
UK	27	30	24	26
China	16	32	19	37
Japan	10	11	10	13
India	9	24	7	21

Data source: UNDP, 2008.

Table 4 Variation in Some Countries' Share in the Global Import and Export Total (Unit: %)

Country		1983	1993	2003	2007
America	Export	11. 2	12. 6	9. 8	8. 5
	Import	14. 3	15. 9	16. 9	14. 5
Canada	Export	4. 2	4. 0	3. 7	3. 1
	Import	3. 4	3. 7	3. 2	2. 8
Brazil	Export	1. 2	1. 0	1. 0	1. 2
	Import	0. 9	0. 7	0. 7	0. 9
Germany	Export	9. 2	10. 3	10. 2	9. 7
	Import	8. 1	9. 0	7. 9	7. 6
France	Export	5. 2	6. 0	5. 3	4. 1
	Import	5. 6	5. 7	5. 2	4. 4
UK	Export	5. 0	4. 9	4. 1	3. 2
	Import	5. 3	5. 5	5. 2	4. 4
China	Export	1. 2	2. 5	5. 9	8. 9
	Import	1. 1	2. 7	5. 4	6. 8
Japan	Export	8. 0	9. 9	6. 4	5. 2
	Import	6. 7	6. 4	5. 0	4. 4
India	Export	0. 5	0. 6	0. 8	1. 1
	Import	0. 7	0. 6	0. 9	1. 6
Global Total (100 million dollars)	Export	18380	36750	73750	136190
	Import	18820	37870	76910	139680

Data source: WTO, 2008.

4. Expanding Foreign Trade Scale and Alleviating Poverty in China

Since 1980, the overall scale of China's foreign trade has obviously expanded. Figure 1 shows the variation in the percentage of the annual total foreign trade volume (import + export) in the GDP. At the same time, the implementation of the poverty reduction policies in China has yielded remarkable results: on the premise of the upgrading poverty standard, in 2005 the absolute number of the poor population in rural China decreased by 226 million compared with that in 1978 and the percentage of the poor in the total rural population reduced by 28%. The variation in the poor population in rural China is shown in Table 5. However, Pavallion's (2006) quantitative analysis shows that China's rapidly enlarging foreign trade scale has no obvious bearing on its poverty reduction. Rather, it is some other "non-trade" reform factors that have promoted the poverty alleviation in China's rural areas, for example, the relatively equal land distribution policy, the improvement in the domestic agricultural product price, the lowering of the agricultural tax, the stable macro economy, etc. Also, urbanization results in a decreasing rural population (the percentage of the rural population in China accounted for 82% in the total national population in 1978 while the number reduced to 56% in 2006①), transferring many rural labor forces into urban migrant workers, whose increase in salaries is the key factor in the decrease in the poor population in rural China.

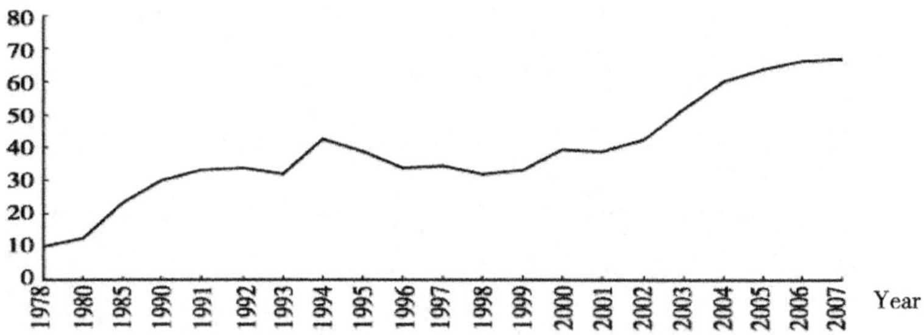

Figure 1 Annual Variation in the Percentage of China's Trade Volume in GDP (1978-2007) (%)

Table 5 Variation in the Poor Population in Rural China (1978-2005)

Year	Poverty Line (yuan per capita/year)	Poor Population (10,000)	Percentage in the Rural Population (%)	Year	Poverty Line (yuan per capita/year)	Poor Population (10,000)	Percentage in the Rural Population (%)
1978	100	25000	31.6	1983	179	13500	16.7
1980	130	22000	27.7	1984	200	12800	15.9
1981	142	15200	19	1985	206	12500	15.5
1982	164	14500	18.1	1986	213	13100	16.1
1987	227	12200	14.9	1997	640	4962	5.9
1988	236	9600	11.7	1998	635	4210	5.1
1989	259	10200	12.3	1999	625	3412	4.2
1990	300	8500	10.1	2000	625	3209	4

① *China Statistical Abstract* 2007.

(contd.)

Year	Poverty Line (yuan per capita/year)	Poor Population (10,000)	Percentage in the Rural Population (%)	Year	Poverty Line (yuan per capita/year)	Poor Population (10,000)	Percentage in the Rural Population (%)
1991	304	9400	11.1	2001	630	2927	3.7
1992	317	8000	9.4	2002	627	2820	3.6
1993①	—	—	—	2003	637	2900	3.8
1994	440	7000	8.2	2004	668	2610	3.4
1995	530	6540	7.6	2005	683	2365	3.2
1996①	—	—	—				

Note: ① Unavailability of data, the same below.

Data source: Department of Rural Social and Economic Survey, State Statistics Bureau, 2006, p. 45; *China Statistical Abstract* 2007, p. 39.

III. Gap between the Rich and the Poor in Globalization, Resources and Environment

1. Disequilibrium between Global Resource Consumption and Ecological Environmental Degradation

Resource consumption and ecological environmental degradation has become an issue of global concern, which is in turn closely intertwined with globalization. There are two forces influencing resource consumption and the ecological environment: one is the omnipresent force which consumes resources and harms the ecological environment in the seeking of fortune; the other force mainly gathers in the poverty-stricken areas where people, because of poverty, have been exploiting resources and the environment until they are exhausted (Beck, 2008, pp. 44-46).

According to the *Human Development Report* 2006 (UNDP), there was a disequilibrium of water resource use between the rich countries and poor countries, which can be captured by making a simple comparison between their daily domestic water use. The average daily water consumption in most of the European countries is 200-300 liters while in some developing countries, for example, Mozambique, it's less than 10 liters. According to the international water consumption standard, the lowest standard of water consumption in a household of five members is 100 liters (including drinking water and water used for basic personal hygiene). When considering the need for bathing and washing clothes, the bottom line for personal water use would upgrade to 50 liters per day. There is a population of 1.1 billion worldwide whose daily water consumption usually falls below 5 liters.

Those who make a fetish of globalization rely heavily on the world market and even believe that ecological environmental protection can also be strengthened through free trade. But the reality is that not only the widening of the gap between the rich and the poor and the increase in the poor population are moving at the same pace with globalization, but so are resource consumption and ecological environmental degradation in the developing countries and middle-income and low-income countries.

Anderson and Lindroth (2001) suggested that the current international trade model actually had confused the responsibility of the producer and the consumer for the ecological environment.

(1) Depiction and review of the unequal utilization of global resources and environment between rich and poor countries with the "ecological footprint"

Table 6 shows the overall assessment of the global ecological footprint[①] and Table 7 shows the data of some countries' ecological footprint and water footprint[②].

The quantity index of the ecological footprint is the land area, but it only reveals the goods and services provided by the natural ecological system and consumed by a certain group in a certain lifestyle and the environmental capacity for the wastes produced in the consumption process. The ecological footprint measures man's need for the natural

---

① "Ecological footprint" is an index marking human society's sustainable development (Rees, 1992, 1996; Rees & Wackernagel, 1994). It refers to the average "biological production space" owned by individuals or communities (may be villages, cities or countries). Its measurement unit is the "hectare" and the overall ecological footprint consists of six parts: areas of arable lands, grasslands, forestry, constructive lands, productive ocean and forests which can take in man's carbon dioxide emissions (Hoekstra, 2009).

② "Water footprint" refers to the water resource volume consumed by individuals or communities in their goods and service production process (Hoekstra & Hung, 2002; Hoekstra & Chapagain, 2007).

resources. It depends on the population scale, material standard of living, technical condition and ecological productivity. The method used to calculate the ecological footprint and its result show explicitly how many natural resources a country or a region has used. An examination of the overall data of economies with different incomes (Table 6) can reveal that in 2005 the high-income countries boasted the highest ecological deficit[①], 4.5 times higher than the global average and 27 times higher than the low-income countries; the middle-income and low-income countries have low or even no ecological deficit. This shows that the gap between the incomes has a profound influence on the utilization of the global ecological resources. Some countries' ecological footprint data are greater than others' (Table 7), which shows the degree of inequality in resources and environment (White, 2007). According to the data in Table 7, America, Australia, Canada, UK, France, Japan and Germany have larger ecological footprints; further data show that the resource consumption per capita in North American countries is 2 times higher than that in European countries and 4 times higher than that in Asian and African countries. Western society is consuming natural resources at an unsustainable rate. According to the estimation of *Living Planet Report* 2008[②] (Global Footprint Network, 2009), in 2005, among the 74 countries with a population exceeding 1 million, China's ecological footprint per capita ranked the lowest, being 2.1 global hectare/capita.

What should be noted is that the ecological footprint is only one means to measure man's need for a global ecological system and natural resources. If a country's resource consumption exceeds its own resource reproduction capacity, it will definitely lead to environmental degradation in the country or the world. However, it can transfer its ecological crisis to other countries by importing raw materials or manufactured goods through international trade; through industrial transfer, the pollution will also be transferred to other countries. Therefore, with globalization, a country's consumption of resources and environmental capacity does not necessarily occur in the country's own

---

① Ecological surplus = biological production capacity-ecological footprint. If ecological surplus < 0, it means there appears the ecological deficit (unit: global hectare or global hectare/capita).

② "Living Planet Report" may also be translated into "Planet Life Report".

territory, but can always be imported from other countries. All this has already stretched beyond the narrow connotation of trade.

Through the variation in the ecological footprint and import trade volume, Anderson and Lindroth (2001) discussed in depth how a nation can protect its national natural resources (capital) through international trade. We summarized Anderson and Lindroth's discussion into a table (shown in Table 8) to get clearer findings through logic analysis. According to the categorization in Table 8 and in reference to the data from different countries in Table 7, we can make the judgment that Canada (13.0gha/cap), Australia (7.6gha/cap), Brazil (4.9gha/cap) and Russia (4.4gha/cap) whose ecological surplus is over zero and higher than the global average are ranked as the countries with the best ecological resource preservation; as for America (−4.4gha/cap), UK (−3.7gha/cap) and France (−1.9gha/cap), although with an ecological deficit and an ecological surplus higher than the global average (−0.6gha/cap), we still have good reasons to believe that in the three countries, as net importers of goods and services, their import trade is advantageous to increasing their ecological capital, if we examine the data in Table 3; according to other research by Anderson and Lindroth, some North European countries, such as Sweden (4.9gha/cap) and Finland (6.5gha/cap), have an over-zero ecological surplus and are also net importers of biomass, which means that these countries boast sound ecological capital, having avoided overusing their national ecological resources and at the same time made a proper use of external ecological resources.

Further analysis of the components of the ecological footprint by White (2007) shows that in the global average, energy (including wood burning fuel, fossil fuel and lands for nuclear power) takes up 54% in the ecological footprint and environmental land, 4% (see Table 9 for details). White (2007) replaces the ecological footprint with Gini coefficient, concentration ratio and the inequality of estimated income, as shown in Table 10. The data in Table 10 show that in the four categories, energy, food, forests and the environment, which make up the ecological footprint, the greatest inequality in the global ecological footprint distribution occurs in the energy utilization, followed by food consumption.

(2) Depiction of the unequal utilization of global resources and environment between rich and poor countries with the "water footprint"

The water footprint reflects the water resource volume needed for man's consumption of all the goods and services in a certain lifestyle. This includes the water needed for the consumption of man's subsistence, food and daily goods as well as domestic water use and water for the environment. Similar to the concept of the ecological footprint, the water footprint refers to the water use index relevant to consumption. It is made up of two parts: domestic water resource usage (internal water footprint) and overseas water resource usage (external water footprint). The latter is produced for the consumption of imported goods. The water footprint in Table 7 has excluded the water resource volume in the exported goods.

Data in Table 7 show that developing countries such as China and India have a lower water consumption footprint; developed countries have a higher water consumption footprint, among which America ranks the top in the world, with an annual average per capita consumption of about 2,500 cubic meters, 3.5 times higher than that in China. According to the estimation of *Living Planet Report* 2008 (Global Footprint Network, 2009), there were 27 countries worldwide that have their external water footprint exceeding 50%, which include North European countries such as Norway, Denmark and Sweden, West European countries such as the UK and Holland, Asian countries such as Japan and Korea. If a country's external water footprint share is large in the total water consumption footprint, it means the country has an effective external resource use strategy, but it also indicates it has a great influence on the other countries' environment. The global virtual water trade is subject to the influence of the global product market and agricultural policies, and for the virtual water export countries, the virtual export trade may bring environmental, economic and social costs.

(3) International trade expanding the sustainable gap between rich and poor countries

The analysis of both the ecological footprint and water footprint involves international trade. Therefore, international trade is closely tied to the utilization and consumption of the ecological environment and natural resources and becomes an integrated part of the non-economic income. Take the ecological footprint as an example, rich countries are capable enough to pay for the protection or improvement of their national ecological resources (capital) and one of the ways is to import biological production capacity from the poor countries. High-income countries, by importing products from middle-income and low-income countries, are actually importing the virtual land resources, water resources and environmental capacity from the relatively poor countries. They lower or eliminate their own "ecological deficit" by possessing and consuming more of the global resources. In contrast, the middle-income and low-income countries serve as global factories in the globalized international division of labor. Through exporting products they sell more of their own natural resources and environmental capacity and, at the same time, carry the ethical blame for accelerating their ecological environmental degradation and environmental pollution.

Under such a global trade model, rich countries regard their lifestyle and development model as sustainable for sure because their ecological resources (capital) haven't shown signs of degradation or exhaustion and instead they are protected and improved; however, their sustainable development is at the sacrifice of the poor countries' ecological resources and based on the unsustainable development of the poor countries.

Under this round's model of the globalized trade division of labor, the gap in the ecological environment between the rich and poor countries is widened and the middle-income and low-income countries' ability for future sustainable development is weakened.

Table 6 Variation in the Global Ecological Footprint

Economies	Ecological Footprint (I) (global hectare/capita) ①		Biological Production Capacity (II) (global hectare/capita)		Ecological Deficit (II-I) (global hectare/capita)	
	1961	2005	1961	2005	1961	2005
High Income	3.6	6.4	5.3	3.7	1.7	-2.7
Middle Income	1.8	2.2	4.1	2.2	2.3	0
Low Income	1.3	1.0	2.4	0.9	1.1	-0.1
Global	2.3	2.7	4.2	2.1	1.9	-0.6

Note: ① Global hectare/capita: abbreviation in English (gha/cap).

Data source: Global Footprint Network, 2009.

Table 7 Some Countries' Ecological Footprint (2005) and Water Footprint Review

Country	Ecological Footprint (global hectare/capita)	Biological Production Capacity (global hectare/capita)	Ecological Deficit (global hectare/capita)	Consumed Water Footprint (m^3/capita/year) (1997-2001)
China	2. 1	0. 9	-1. 2	702
India	0. 9	0. 4	-0. 5	980
Japan①	4. 9	0. 6	-4. 3	1153
Australia	7. 8	15. 4	+7. 6	1393
Brazil	2. 4	7. 3	+4. 9	1381
America	9. 4	5. 0	-4. 4	2483
Canada	7. 1	20. 0	+13. 0	2049
France	4. 9	3. 0	-1. 9	1875
Germany①	4. 2	1. 9	-2. 3	1545
UK	5. 3	1. 6	-3. 7	1245
Russia	3. 7	8. 1	+4. 4	1858
Global Average	2. 7	2. 1	-0. 6	1243

Note: ① Data in 2004.

Data source: Global Footprint Network, 2009.

Table 8 Review of Countries' Natural Resource Protection with the Ecological Footprint and Import Trade

	Ecological Surplus > Net Import Biomass①	Ecological Surplus < Net Import Biomass
	I-1: Ecological resources (capital) are well preserved or increased	II: Ecological resources (capital) are decreasing
Ecological Surplus > 0	I-2: When the net import biomass > 0, improve national ecological resources	
Ecological Surplus < 0	III: Ecological resources (capital) are decreasing	IV: Ecological resources (capital) are increasing

Note: ① Net Import Biomass: converted into the net import goods of the quantity of the ecological production lands.

Data source: Anderson and Lindroth (2001).

Table 9 Global Ecological Footprint and its Constitution in 2003

Constitution	Total Ecological Footprint (million global hectare)	Ecological Footprint per Capita (global hectare/capita)	Percentage in the Total Volume (%)
Energy	7315.3	1.18	53.7
Food	4691.5	0.76	34.4
Forest	1058.3	0.17	7.8
Environment	553.8	0.09	4.1
Total Volume	13619.0	2.20	100.0

Data source: White (2007).

Table 10 Gini Coefficient and Concentration Index of the Global Ecological Footprint Distribution

Constitution	Gini Coefficient	Concentration Index	Unequal Share
Energy	0.553	0.545	0.655
Food	0.272	0.260	0.201
Forest	0.663	0.641	0.112
Environment	0.390	0.349	0.032
Total Volume	0.446	0.446	1.000

Data source: White (2007).

2. Global Climate Change is Challenging Poverty

Talking of global environmental problems, we cannot evade global climate change. In the confrontation with the threat posed by climate change, all tiers of human society are facing different challenges. The basic challenge is that climate change casts suspicion on what human society deems as "progress": creating economic wealth and achieving economic growth. As a result, the rich become richer and the poor become poorer and the planet we are living on is plunged into disasters. Is this human society's progress or retrogression? Therefore, economic growth and the accumulation of wealth do not correspond to social progress. Under current economic and energy policies, the more developed the economy is, the more threats and risks will be posed to man's development.

(1) Two forces for development: maintaining luxury versus getting rid of poverty

We should distinguish two different motivation models in the pursuit of economic growth: one is carbon-intensive economic growth led by the Western industrialized countries for several centuries: under the current economic development model for promoting economic growth, the rich countries, in order to maintain their luxurious lifestyle, are lavish with the use of resources and harm the environment. This is not only ecologically unsustainable, but also an important reason for the widening gap between rich and poor countries. The other motivation force is the high-carbon growth model inherited by the emerging countries. They try to get rid of poverty and seek prosperity through the transfer of the production of the major commercial goods in the world market. Such motivation to escape poverty and attain prosperity also results in a low efficiency in resource utilization and environmental pollution as well as widening the gap between the rich and the poor inside the country. Therefore, how to combine man's economic activities and his consumption behavior with global ecological realities constitutes the biggest challenge for human society.

(2) Reverse relationship between the discharge responsibilities and risks

A clear distinction between the historic responsibilities of countries with different income levels (poor countries and rich countries) in carbon dioxide emissions will help in urging industrialized countries to provide capital and technology support for the emerging countries in the global action to reduce carbon dioxide emissions, so as to ensure scientific and reasonable progress in this regard. Table 11 shows the variation in the carbon dioxide emissions of economies categorized according to their income level. Table 12 shows the variation in the total carbon dioxide emissions of some countries and the accumulative emissions of carbon dioxide per capita from 1850 to 2004.

Since 1990, although the total flow of carbon dioxide emissions in some developing countries has been on the rise (the data of China, Brazil and India are shown in Table 12), so have emissions from some developed countries, such as America, Canada, Japan, France and Italy (see Table 12). However, in examining the stock of the carbon dioxide emissions, we may get important findings. Rich countries have a large share of the total accumulative emission. Since the industrialization era, the emissions of the developed countries has accounted for 70% of the total accumulative emission, among which the historic accumulative emission per capita in America and the UK is 20 times higher than that in China (see Table 12). Obviously, high-income developed countries are held accountable for the present accumulation of carbon dioxide in the air and it is the accumulative emission of carbon dioxide and greenhouse gas that leads to climate change. Also, the usable ecological "space" for future emissions depends on actions in the past (UNDP, 2008). The "enormous contribution" the developed countries have made to the accumulative emissions also reflects their corresponding "carbon debt" (UNDP, 2008): for a long time, their abuse of the earth's atmosphere not only results in today's global climate change, but also occupies and seizes developing countries' emission space. They should repay their debts.

The fact is that the population of rich developed countries takes up 15% of the global total, but their carbon dioxide emissions take up 45%; the population of low-income countries takes up 33% of the global total, but their carbon dioxide emissions take up only 7%. This indicates a serious imbalance. The poorest global population is most susceptible to the threats of climate change since they live in rural areas and slums in urban areas which have the poorest resistance to nasty weather. However, they are the least to blame for inciting such threats (whether in terms of stock or flow) (UNDP, 2008). This is how the reverse relationship between discharge responsibilities and risks occurs.

(3) Emission reduction and poverty alleviation

At a glance, there is an increasing convergence between the carbon dioxide emission flow in developed countries and developing countries (see Table 12). As a result, based on the convergence of the total emissions, the developing countries are required to take rapid actions to reduce the emissions. However, except for the fact that such a convergence is overestimated (UNDP, 2008), we should also be aware of the fact that, in most of the developing countries, many people are still struggling to get rid of poverty and have basic energy services① (for example, electric light and television). This constitutes an important component of poverty reduction and is a totally different aim from that of the developed countries, which hope to maintain a high living standard

① For example, in India where the total carbon dioxide emission flow is increasing, there are great differences in its energy service usage. About 500 million people have no access to electricity and some households even have no lighting bulbs. They depend on wood and animal manure for cooking (UNDP, 2008).

and a luxurious lifestyle. When the development is extremely uneven inside the developing countries, the requirement for them to take rapid actions for emission reduction is likely to slow the social equity process to promote basic energy demands and further widen the gap between the rich and the poor. This will cause new unfairness and ultimately hinder the emission reduction progress.

Table 11 Variation in Global Carbon Dioxide Emissions

Economies	Carbon Dioxide Emissions (100 million ton carbon)		Annual Change (%) 1990-2004
	1990	2004	
High-Income	105721 (46.6%)[1]	129751 (44.8%)	1.6
Middle-Income	89715 (39.5%)	121629 (42.0%)	2.5
Low-Income	13234 (5.8%)	20839 (7.2%)	4.1
Global	227025	289827	2.0

Note: ① The number in the bracket is its percentage of the global emission.

Data source: UNDP, 2008.

We believe that when the carbon dioxide emission reduction plan and action involves economies by those with different economic incomes, priority should be given to the benefits of the underprivileged poor group and the group which is in search of basic social services so as to avoid plunging them into eternal poverty and weakness in our action to alleviate climate change. To do this, we should conduct studies from different perspectives to make preferential institutional arrangements and corresponding preferential capital and technical plans.

Table 12 Some Countries' Carbon Dioxide Emission Conditions

Country	Carbon Dioxide Emission Flow (million-ton carbon dioxide)		Accumulative Carbon Dioxide Emission Volume per Capita (1850-2004, ton carbon/person)
America	4818.3	5696.8	586.54
UK	579.4	536.5	476.16
Canada	415.8	528.8	406.24
Germany	980.4	823.5	280.61
France	363.8	377.5	211.17
Russia	1984.1	1587.2	167.12
South Africa	331.8	342.0	159.90
Japan	1070.7	1212.7	125.72
Italy	389.7	448.0	102.39

(contd.)

Country	Carbon Dioxide Emission Flow (million-ton carbon dioxide)		Accumulative Carbon Dioxide Emission Volume per Capita (1850-2004, ton carbon/person)
Mexico	313.3	270.3	46.27
China	2398.9	5605.5	22.89
Brazil	209.5	332.4	22.46
India	681.7	1249.7	10.30

Data source: Pan Jiahua, et al., 2010, p. 15; Chinese Academy of Science, et al. 2009, p. 3.

References:

[1] [German] Ulrich Beck, translated into Chinese by Chang Hefang and reviewed by Wu Zhicheng. *What Is Globalization? Misunderstanding of Globalism——Coping with Globalization*. East China Normal University Press, 2008.

[德]乌尔里希·贝克 :《什么是全球化? 全球主义的曲解——应对全球化》,常和芳译,吴志成校,华东师范大学出版社 2008 年版。

[2] [American] Thomas W. Borg, Redesigning global economic security and justice, in: [British] David Held & Anthony McGrew ed., *Globalization Theory: Research Methods and Theoretical Arguments*, translated into Chinese by Wang Shengcai, Social Sciences Academic Press, 2009, pp. 242-264.

[美]托马斯·W. 博格:《重新设计全球经济安全与正义》,见[英]戴维·赫尔德、安东尼·麦克格鲁编:《全球化理论:研究路径与理论争论》,王生才译,社会科学文献出版社 2009 年版,第 242—264 页。

[3] Department of Rural Social and Economic Survey, State Statistics Bureau. *China Yearbook of Rural Household Survey (2006)*. China Statistical Publishing House, 2006.

国家统计局农村社会经济调查司:《中国农村住户调查年鉴(2006)》,中国统计出版社 2006 年版。

[4] [American] Layna Mosley, Globalized Political Economics, in: [British] David Held & Anthony McGrew ed., *Globalization Theory: Research Methods and Theoretical Arguments*, translated into Chinese by Wang Shengcai, Social Sciences Academic Press, 2009, pp. 116-140.

[美]莱纳·莫斯利:《全球化的政治经济学》,见[英]戴维·赫尔德、安东尼·麦克格鲁编:《全球化理论:研究路径与理论争论》,王生才译,社会科学文献出版社 2009 年版,第 116—140 页。

[5] Pan Jiahua, Chen Ying, Zhuang Guiyang & Yang Hongwei. 2008-2009 Situation analysis and prospects of the global efforts to cope with climate change. *Academic Trends (Research Report Version)* by the Research Bureau of Chinese Academy of Social Sciences, 2010 (2 or 1265 <total volume>).

潘家华、陈迎、庄贵阳、杨宏伟:《2008—2009 年全球应对气候变化形势分析与展望》,中国社会科学院科研局主办:《学术动态(研究报告版)》2010 年第 2 期(总第 1265 期)。

[6] Wu Hongying. Characteristics of the times for the development of the Third World, in: Tan Shizhong, Wang Yaoyuan & Jiang Shixue ed., *Economic Globalization and Developing Countries.* Social Sciences Academic Press, 2002, pp. 50-58.

吴洪英:《第三世界发展的时代特征》,见谈世中、王耀媛、江时学编:《经济全球化与发展中国家》,社会科学文献出版社 2002 年版,第 50—58 页。

[7] [Australian] David Hillman & Joseph Wayne Smith. *Challenges Posed by Climate Change and Dysfunctional Democracy*, translated into Chinese by Wu Xishen & Li Nan. Social Sciences Academic Press, 2009.

[澳]大卫·希尔曼、约瑟夫·韦恩·史密斯:《气候变化的挑战与民主的失灵》,武锡申、李楠译,社会科学文献出版社 2009 年版。

[8] Zhang Yuyan. *Globalization and China's Development.* Social Sciences Academic Press, 2007.

张宇燕:《全球化与中国发展》,社会科学文献出版社 2007 年版。

[9] Zhao Jingxing. Past, present and future of China's economic development, in: Wang Tongsan & Li Xuesong ed., *Analysis of Macro Economic Effect and Prospects.* Economic Management Press, 2009, pp. 1-26.

赵京兴:《中国经济发展的过去、现在和未来》,见汪同三、李雪松编:《宏观经济效应及前景分析》,经济管理出版社 2009 年版,第 1—26 页。

[10] Sustainable Development Strategy Research Group, the Administrative Center for China's Agenda 21. *Globalization and China's "Three Rural Issues".* Social Sciences Academic Press, 2005.

中国 21 世纪议程管理中心可持续发展战略研究组:《全球化与中国"三农"》,社会科学文献出版社 2005 年版。

[11] Andersson, Jan O. and Mattias Lindroth. 2001. Ecologically unsustainable trade. *Ecological Economics* 37 (2001), pp. 113-122.

[12] Chen, Shaohua and Martin Ravallion. 2008. The developing world is poorer than we thought, but no less successful in the fight against poverty. *The World Bank Policy Research Working Paper*, Report No. WPS4703. http://go.worldbank.org/NJNRF6AJX0.

[13] Chinese Academy of Sciences, Chinese Academy of Social Sciences, Development Research Centre of the State Council, National Climate Centre, Tsinghua University. 2009. *Carbon Equity: Perspective from Chinese Academic Community.* Dec. 10, 2009.

[14] Global Footprint Network. 2009. Living Planet Report 2008. www.footprintnetwork.org/.

[15] Hoekstra, A. Y. and A. K. Chapagain. 2007. Water Footprints of Nations: Water use by People as a Function of Their Consumption Pattern. *Water Resource Management* 21 (1), pp. 35-48.

[16] Hoekstra, A. Y. and P. Q. Huang. 2002. Virtual Water Trade: a Quantification of Virtual Water Flow between Nations in Relation to International Crop Trade. *Research Report Series* 11, UNESCO-IHE, Delft.

[17] Lundberg, M. and L. Squire. 2003. The Simultaneous Evolution of Growth and Inequality. *Economic Journal*, 113, pp. 326-344.

[18] Milanovic, M. 2005. Can We Discern the Effect of Globalization on Income

distribution? *World Bank Economic Review.* 19 (1), pp. 21-44.

[19] Pavallion, Martin. 2001. Growth, inequality and poverty: Looking beyond averages. *World Development* Vol. 29, No. 11, pp. 1803-1815.

[20] Pavallion, Martin. 2006. Looking beyond averages in the trade and poverty debate. *World Development* Vol. 34, No. 8, pp. 1374-1392.

[21] Rees, W. E. 1992. Ecological footprint and appropriated carry capacity: what urban economics leaves out. *Environment and Urbanization* 4 (2), pp. 121-130.

[22] Rees, W. E. 1996. Revisiting carry capacity: area-based indicators of sustainability. *Population and Environment* 17 (3), pp. 195-215.

[23] Rees, W. E., M. Wackernagel. 1994. Ecological footprint and appropriated carry capacity: measuring the natural capital requirements of the human economy. In Jansson, A. M., M. Hammer, C. Folke, and R. Costanza (eds.) *Investing in Natural Capital: The Ecological Economics Approach to Sustainability.* ISEE/Island Press, Washington, D. C., pp. 362-390.

[24] The World Bank. 2003. *World Development Report* 2003. New York: Oxford University Press.

[25] The World Bank. 2009. 2009 *World Development Indicators.* http://web. worldbank. org/.

[26] UNDP. 2005. *Human Development Report* 2005. http://hdr. undp. org/.

[27] UNDP. 2006. *Human Development Report* 2006. http://hdr. undp. org/.

[28] UNDP. 2008. *Human Development Report* 2007/2008. http://hdr. undp. org/.

[29] White, Thomas J. 2007. Sharing resources: The global distribution of the Ecological Footprint. *Ecological Economics*, 64 (2007), pp. 402-410.

[30] WTO, 2008. *World Trade Development* in 2007. www. wto. org/.

Part I
Globalization

Thoughts on How to View Globalization

——The Chinese Nation and Market in its Economic Development

By ZHAO Jingxing

The purpose of this article is to contribute my own thinking about how China is influenced by globalization and the major problems brought about by this through discussions on how to view globalization. Since the 1990s, plenty of research has been conducted on globalization and the relationship between globalization and China, with voluminous essays and monographs published which have touched upon various problems. This article selects this topic mainly for the reason that it is close to the theme of this book——"China's Environment and Development in the Context of Globalization". ①

To achieve my aim, the article will discuss the following three questions: 1. The Nature of Globalization; 2. Globalization and Nations; 3. The Chinese Nation and Market in its Economic Development.

The basic thinking and views of this article are as follows: it is deemed that the general nature of globalization is the expansion of capitalism in the world and its intrinsic drive originates from capital movement. I have applied Marx's relevant theories about capital to give a simple illustration about this. At the same time, globalization also marks a special stage for the expansion of capital worldwide. Among its different characteristics, the core one is that it is based on the establishment of the market economy worldwide, which poses challenges to the nation's traditional sovereignty, thereupon incurring problems

---

① The editor of this book invited me to write an article about globalization probably because, in recent years, I have participated in the project "Globalization and China" chaired by Wang Luolin and therefore perused some relevant literature. I just crossed the threshold of this field and in writing this article I aimed to raise some problems and share my reading experience with readers. I hope I can get some suggestions from readers.

between globalization and the nation. I assume that the concentrated manifestation of this problem is the relationship between the nation and the market. Following this line, I have explored possible policies for China to adopt against this problem in the context of globalization.

I. Globalization Marks a New Stage for the Expansion of Capitalism Worldwide

As far as I am concerned, among Western academics, dominating views have conceded that globalization is a matter of capital. Contrariwise, it is the Chinese academics that are evasive about this. They argue that globalization, as an objective process, cannot be defined as the globalization of capital. Such a claim is obviously unfounded although it has its own rationality (theoretically, the relationship between socialist China and capital globalization cannot be coordinated). Even from the formal logic, the objectivity of globalization and its capitalistic characteristics are not in an antagonistic relationship. Globalization, as an objective social phenomenon, may also show characteristics of capitalism.

Whether in terms of history, reality or theoretical analysis, we can easily come to the conclusion that globalization is one of capital. There are plenty of books in this regard, so there is no need for further elucidation. However, to deepen this understanding, we still need to make a simple review of Marx's capital theory, especially theories about the impetus for capital movement and the features of its form. Maybe this can provide a new theoretical framework for deepening our understanding of globalization. Pitifully, up to now, it hasn't been fully discussed in theory or in a combination of theory and practice.

As early as 1848, Marx and Engels pointed out the universality of capital and the inevitability of its expansion worldwide in *The Communist Manifesto*. "The need to expand the product marketing motivates the capitalist class to go around the world. They settled everywhere, started business everywhere and established contacts everywhere .... For the rapid improvement of the instruments of production and the great convenience of transportation, the capitalist class draws all the nations, even the most barbarian, one into civilization. Their cheap products are a powerful leverage to destroy all the fortresses and conquer the barbarians. They force all the nations to adopt the capitalist lifestyle if they don't wish to perish; these nations are forced to implement their so-called civilized systems, namely to become the capitalist class. In one word, they have created a world for themselves by imitating their own. "①

The above verdict and prediction by Marx embody the unique insight of Marx's theory, the insight of which originates from his understanding of capital.

In Marx's opinion, the movement of capital is boundless and borderless by its very nature: capital is the value which increases by itself. Described with a modern complicated theoretical jargon, it is a self-maintaining, self-developing and self-organizing system. It is exactly for such self-organizing capability that it is able to develop from a corner of Europe to such a global-scale capitalist world system.

Marx not only pointed out the motivation for the expansion of capitalism in the world through the concept of capital, but also provided a methodological foundation for understanding the practice mechanism for the motivation of capital expansion and its various contradictions through the analysis of capital circulation. In this way, we can not only analyze the features of capital in its form and functions, the conflict between capital and labor therein, but also the different relationships between capital and the movement of its contradictions. These contradictions, while promoting the expansion of capitalism worldwide, also give rise to socialist theory and practice. In a word, socialism has emerged and developed as the product of the contradiction movement in capitalism. The vitality of socialism originates from the contradiction unable to be solved by capital and this is exactly why it can emerge and develop in a world dominated by capital. This point is significant for us to expound how China should view the relationship between the nation and the market in the context of globalization.

The basic capital circulation formula proposed by Marx is:

$$G - W < \begin{matrix} A \\ P_m \end{matrix} \cdots P \cdots W' - G' \Big|$$

① *Selected Works by Marx and Engels (Volume I)*, People's Publishing House, 1972, pp. 254-255.

In this formula: G represents currency, W goods and here they respectively represent currency capital and goods capital. G′ and W′ represents respectively value increment of currency capital and goods capital. P production and here production capital. A and P_m represent labor and means of production respectively.

The secret of capital's constant expansiveness lies in its rotation. Since it's a rotation, the end of the round symbolizes the beginning of another round and thus it is incessant; since every round brings value increment, which is again capitalized during the new round, it is expanding.

From the modern view, we will immediately notice the profound conflict between capital's limitless rotation and its corresponding productivity. As agriculture is the foundation for the emergence and development of feudalism, manufacturing industry (earlier handicraft industry) is the foundation for the emergence and development of capitalism. Here occurs such a question, "can the rotation of capital at the level of productive relations exist at the same time in its corresponding productivity?" The answer given by modern science and technology may be affirmative. However, this requires the establishment of a rotation process at the productive level during the material exchange between man and nature. To make such a rotation possible, modern industry should not only build the product's production and consumption system, but also the recycling and reuse system for the wastes (including solid wastes, liquid wastes and gas wastes) produced during production and consumption. However, up to now, the latter has not been built even in the most developed countries, which are said to enter the post-industrial society. Without such systems, human society, resembling a patient with his kidney failing, is not able to survive soundly and will be inundated by its excrements. Then the question is "even if we can build such a system, can it function well in capitalist production relationships which regard profits as the supreme aim?" With the development of the capitalist production mode, the reality presses us to reflect upon the conflict between the limitation of the resource and environmental capacity and the boundlessness of the capital rotation. This is in urgent need of an answer and solution.

Of course, in the era of Marx, people didn't have to think over this problem. What Marx analyzed was the conflicts facing the capital which was included in the rotation.

First we see the different forms of the existence of the capital G, W, P, while difference in itself means contradiction. Different forms of capital are mutually exclusive, namely the existence of one form excluding the possibility of the existence of another. However, at the same time, they are interdependent. To realize the self-increment value, capital must constantly adopt the three forms to accomplish its rotation. This stipulation decides that capital and the conflicts in its form are symbiotic. Since different capital forms serve for different functions, they have different ways of action and each capital form requires different conditions. In their personification form, they represent different institutions and groups and thus form different conflicts of interest between different capital blocs. Also, capital increment, namely the surplus value should be distributed among different forms of capital and different capital individuals. This means competition between capitals and also the conflicts of interest between capitals. In addition, the antagonist distribution relationship between profits and salaries during the production will incur conflicts of interest between capital and labor. Lastly, the basic condition for capital rotation is the realization of the goods' value including the value after increment, which means we need an expanding market. Absence of the market symbolizes the disruption of the rotation and in depth, the loss of the capital's vitality. Consequently, for one thing, we cannot serve the basic function of any economic organization and realize the combination of production factors, which means that workers are unemployed, with no production to go into. For the other, it will lead to the idling of capital, namely the loss of its value increment function. Further analysis shows that such a conflict originates from capital itself.

Capital is a value increment by itself, a concept of contradictive relationships, both value and added value. Its movement is subject to dual laws, both value laws and surplus value laws. The former means laws of general goods production or the market economy. Capital, as a value increment by itself, grows in the fertile land provided by the market economy. According to Marx, capitalism is a universalized commodity economy. However, there is an intrinsic conflict between the capital monopolizing method aimed at value increment and the market economy. This article believes that this conflict is exactly the concrete manifestation of the conflict between socialization of production and the private ownership of capitalism, the basic capitalist conflict as said by classical Marxist writers. A detailed analysis of this conflict will aid us to understand the basic contradiction of capitalism.

The market economy, as a way to organize human production, is of historical significance to promote the division of labor, by which to improve production efficiency. In this sense, the market economy is an historic form to promote socialization of production. It not only increases the interdependence between different components, but also tends to distribute all the social labor to various production areas as a whole. This is what is called the basic meaning of socialization of production. Obviously, this method of social labor distribution requires the labor to be distributed proportionally to each production area. This is how the law of value functions. It adjusts the supply-demand relationship through price fluctuation in order to regulate the distribution of production factors (more often than not, it's the labor, including direct labor and materialized labor) in every production area. However, the law of the capital monopolizing method is the surplus value law, aiming at reaping the maximum surplus value (the so-called profits maximization). Therefore, here it is the surplus value law rather than the value law in a general sense that governs the production adjustment method. The pursuit of the surplus value dominates the distribution of production and production factors in each area. This has two serious implications: one is the imbalance between the production scale and the consumption scale with payment capacity; the other is the disproportion between each production sector. The reason is that first, to obtain more surplus value, capital tends to be driven by its own nature to press down the payment of labor, which makes the first implication possible. Also, although the natural law of the productivity development is unbalanced, once encountering the capitalist production mode it will lead to disproportion between every production sector. What has caused this is the prevalent law of surplus value maximization. Its basic mechanism is that owing to the unbalanced production development, the productivity of every producer or every department is, in fact, different. Superficially, we can say that different productivities will inevitably incur different costs. When their products are sold at the same price in the market, they will bring different profits. Such differences are not necessarily the reflection of the supply-demand relationship, but it means the same thing for capitalist producers. So it drives capital to flood into those production areas based on the supply-demand law and ultimately leads to disproportion between products and even departments. Both the above-mentioned two implications are manifested in production surplus and result in the disruption of the capital rotation. In Marx's era or the early period of capitalist development, the first of the manifestations of these contradictions in a nation was the escalation of the conflict between capital and labor.

However, capitalism, since its birth, has been a global production mode which bases its development on the premise of the world market. ① Therefore, it has to cross over national boundaries. The driving force and form spurring the global development of capital varies in different historic periods in that although they originate from the contradiction movement in the capital itself, as is mentioned above, the capital's contradictions are manifested in different ways and there are intrinsic relations among these manifestations. When the contradiction shows as the escalation of the contradiction between the domestic capital and labor, to solve the domestic contradiction through the global market becomes an important driving force to promote the international expansion of capital. As an imperialist in Lenin's *Imperialism Is the Pinnacle of Capitalism* said, "if you don't want the civil war, you should become an imperialist!" Here, as usual, the externalization of the contradiction becomes the form for its solution. Together with the mercantilism which promoted the global expansion of capital at the early stage of capitalism, it involves the precapitalist countries in the global system of capitalism.

This has externalized the internal contradiction in the capitalist countries, escalating it to a global contradiction, one between the imperialism of the 19th century to the beginning of the 20th century and the colonized or semi-colonized countries. It should be said that this contradiction, by its very occurrence, shows an antagonism between capital and labor. It is this contradiction that develops socialism in a way unexpected by Marx. The so-called "unexpected" has two

① The abrupt commercial expansion and the formation of the new world market exert an overwhelming influence on the decaying of the old production mode and the prosperity of the capitalist production mode ... the world market in itself constitutes a basis for this production mode", Marx. *On Capital (Volume III)*, People's Publishing House, 1975, p. 371.

implications: first, socialist reform doesn't break out in advanced countries, but instead in backward countries; second, the proletariat, in combating the capitalist class, models their fight and struggle on those of colonized and semi-colonized countries against imperial host countries. Therefore, the original appeal of socialist theory and practice for the working class to revolt against the domestic capital suppression turns into one for the oppressed nation and country to fight against global capital suppression. The appeal evolves into the methods and policies for society to organize and practice fighting, which means it is no longer merely a social movement, but real social and economic life in some countries. It develops into a system at the national organization level and becomes a force to manipulate the state apparatus. Such a result has a profound impact on the current globalization.

According to different main roles, this article, in reference to Wallerstein's world system theory[①], divides the historic process of the global expansion of capitalism into two stages. The first stage begins from the birth of the capitalist world system in 1500 to the end of the Second World War, for convenience it being called the imperialist stage in the global expansion of capitalism; the second stage spans from the end of the Second World War to the present, namely the so-called globalization stage. Of course, each stage can be divided into different sub-stages but for the purpose of this article the division of two general stages is sufficient for clarification and we will not discuss further division of each stage.

In the first stage, the nation is the forefront force to promote capital to flow worldwide, whether in the earlier mercantilism or the later imperialism. It has played a central role.[②] The so-called nation system is formed at this stage. The positive achievements of this stage are as follows: to scatter capitalism in every corner of the world and bring the precapitalist countries into the global capitalist system and to have produced a group of socialist countries.

In the imperialist stage, in walking towards the world, what capital faces are many precapitalist countries and their social production mode,

---

① [American] Wallerstein. *Modern World System (Volume I-III)*. Higher Education Press, 2004.

② [Britain] David Harvey. *New Imperialism*. Social Sciences Academic Press, 2009.

social structure and ruler. The capital mainly in play here is commercial capital and financial capital built upon it.[①] Because of the special operation mode of commercial capital, while preserving the precapitalist countries' backward production mode, it can also suck their blood. Although having destroyed and collapsed the precapitalist mode, it will not bring a new production mode and is not revolutionary. By dividing territory as its sphere of influence, it has not only led to wars between imperialist countries, but also resistance from the colonized and semi-colonized countries. Ultimately, this form of imperialism will collapse with the decline of its leader, Britain.

In the second stage, the nation is still in play, but has become a background supportive force. The actors on the stage are the multinationals. Hence, a series of new features are formed during the global expansion of capital in the world and it ushers in a new stage for capital to go global, namely the globalization stage.

In the globalization stage, the global expansion of capital is based on the generalized market economy. The stage the multinationals rely on is the global market, which is established on the premise that every country follows the same rule of the market economy. The rule of the market economy provides an institutional guarantee for the multinationals' activities and enables them to survive without the violence provided by the host country. As multinationals, they are a part of the industrial capital, namely the capital based on production capital, which will directly influence the host country's industrial structure and production mode. The multinationals have promoted the new system of the division of labor featured by the value chain, thus resulting in a micro-effect of the capital on the nation-to-nation relationship.[②]It seems that the micro-effect of capital has deprived the function of the nation and the national border has blurred. In this sense, people visualize this round of the expansion of capital worldwide as globalization; the world is a social concept corresponding to the nation while the globe is a geographical concept. The use of the globe is to accentuate the

---

① See [Australian] Linda Wiss & John M. Hobson, *Nation and Economic Development——A Comparative and Historical Analysis.* Jilin Publishing Group Co., Ltd. 2009, pp. 243-246.

② See Jin Fang. *Globalization Business and Contemporary International Division of Labor.* Shanghai People's Publishing House, 2006.

geographical nature rather than the national nature. Therefore, the concept of nation seems to have lost its tenability.

II. Globalization and the Nation

There are two misunderstandings about globalization: one is the overemphasis on the uniqueness of globalization and the overlooking of the generality of the globalization of capital. Globalization is viewed as a singular historic event, which severs itself from all the historical ties; the other is the emphasis on its generality and the ignorance of its uniqueness, equating globalization with the general worldwide expansion of capital. These two misunderstandings make it difficult for us to grasp the features, significance and consequences of globalization.

As a social phenomenon of our concern, globalization, emerging in the 1980s, developed on a large scale in the 1990s. However, nearly the same phenomenon rapidly developed between developed countries as early as post-Second World War. In particular until the 1980s, most of the development of the multinationals, the mark of globalization, was between developed countries. Because of China's reform and opening up, developed countries' investment in developing countries has grown significantly. The division of the value chain, as a new form of international division of labor, emerged in the 1960s and 1970s. [①] Their commonality lies in their adoption in the market economy countries. And such a market economic operation is based on the international economic system established and headed by America after the Second World War and also called the Bretton Woods System. [②] America's GNP after the Second World War accounted for over half of the world GNP, with its manufacturing output taking up 40% of the global total and 70% of the gold reserves. It has established a developed market economic system with enterprises, especially large enterprises as the main market players, during America's economic development process. The post-war capitalist international economic system shows exactly such a competitive

---

① See Jin Fang. *Globalization Business and Contemporary International Division of Labor*. Shanghai People's Publishing House, 2006; [Japanese] Michael Y. Yoshino, [Indian] U. Srinivasa Rangan. *Strategic Alliances——Shortcuts for Enterprises towards Globalization*. The Commercial Press, 2007.

② [Australian] Lou Holden. *Globalization and National States*. World Affairs Press, 2006.

edge of America. In 1973, when the Bretton Woods System collapsed and a post-Bretton Woods System was established, America's competitive edge was not weakened, but strengthened, which has created conditions for America to use the dollar standard to gain global fortune. China's reform and opening up and the disintegration of the Soviet Union and eastern European socialist alliance pushed this market system worldwide and thus gave rise to the globalization wave in the 1990s.

The market economic system in the process of globalization is the expansion of the post-war international capitalist market system in the world. In this sense, globalization is one dominated by America and it can also even be called Americanization.

As mentioned above, the market economy is actually an historic form to promote the division of labor and production socialization. The establishment of the global market economy motivated production socialization worldwide. During this process, a new form of division featured by the division of the value chain is formed. Thanks to this division of the value chain, China's exports, mainly based on labor-intensive products, grew rapidly and accelerated the development of the whole national economy. In this sense, China became one of the major beneficiaries in globalization.

China's success in becoming the beneficiary of globalization was, of course, not possible without China's market-oriented reforms. Such reforms have not only made it institutionally possible for China to participate in globalization, but also are an important driving force for globalization. Hence, it becomes a basic factor influencing the relationship between globalization and China and challenges the nation's active ability.

Such challenges come from two aspects: firstly, the globalization of the market rule means the weakening of the nation's economic sovereignty; secondly, the existence of multinationals results in a micro-international economic liaison, with the cross-national economic activities becoming more and more general in the enterprises' internal communication, with the discarding of national surveillance. At the same time, the international financial system has limited the nation's ability to regulate and control the national macro-economy, which is crystallized in the so-called "Mundell's impossible triangle" theory. ①

From the above-mentioned impacts of globalization on traditional national state sovereignty, some people draw the conclusion that globalization will lead to a country's extinction. ②

That the country will be doomed is the core opinion of Marx's theory of Scientific Socialism. However, the extinction of a country claimed by Marx is predicated on the extinction of class, which is totally different from the theory of a country's extinction directly caused by globalization.

Facts show that although, superficially, globalization seems to have weakened the nation's sovereignty and even given rise to a national alliance like the European Union, in fact it hasn't and isn't possible to make a country perish. A look at the arguments between different countries at the Copenhagen Climate Conference is sufficient to prove my point.

One of the fundamental reasons for a country's existence is the present hierarchical national order in the international arena. This is not only a reflection of the uneven development of capitalism, but also the heritage of the worldwide expansion of capital in the form of imperialism in the above-mentioned first stage.

---

① In 1960s, Robert A. Mundell and J. Marcus Flemins proposed the Mundell-Fleming Model and gave an analysis of the ISLM Model under an open economy. This model pointed out that in the absence of capital flow, the currency policy is effective in influencing and changing a country's income under the fixed exchange rate and is more effective under the floating exchange rate; under the condition of limited capital flow, the whole adjustment structure and policy effect is basically the same with that in the absence of capital flow; however, under the condition of totally free capital flow, the currency policy is totally incapable to influence and change a country's income under the fixed exchange rate, but is effective under the floating exchange rate. Hence originates the famous "Mundell's impossible triangle" theory, namely, the three policy aims: the independence of the currency policy, the free flow of capital and the stability of the exchange rate cannot be achieved at the same time. In 1999, an American economist, Paul Krugman drew a triangle based on the above theory and called it "the eternal triangle" which clearly clarified the internal principle of the "impossible triangle". In this triangle, there are the independence of the currency policy and the free flow of capital, the fixed exchange rate and the free flow of capital, the independence of the currency policy and the fixed exchange rate. The three aims cannot be coordinated and at most only two can be achieved. This is the famous "The Impossible Trinity".

② [Britain] Clive Crook. Globalization and a Country's Future. *Marxism and Reality*, 1988 (2).

Although the identical rule of the market economy has provided a stage with nominal fair competition, the actual unfairness caused by the unfair competitiveness is unable to be overcome. Such unfair competition will harm the benefits of the newly emerging countries in globalization. Under such circumstances, on the one hand there will be different national interests and, on the other hand, such a competition pattern cannot be reversed by mere market forces. Besides the state, developing countries have no other weapons to fight against developed capitalist countries. Therefore, globalization would not lead to a country's extinction, but aggravate the antagonism between the profits of different countries and thus strengthen the country which represents the national interest.

The historical development of capitalism in different countries shows that it always relies on the support of the country. From the earliest in Britain to the late-comer Japan, which ascended as one of the developed countries, all of the countries have offered different forms of support for capitalist development. Modern national states themselves are the products of capitalist development. According to this historical experience, later developing countries' development also relies on the country's support. However, globalization based on the identical market rule comes at the same time and imposes rigid restrictions on the role of the country.

Therefore, although it cannot be said that globalization will lead to a country's extinction, globalization is indeed a challenge for developing countries.

III. The Chinese Nation and Market in its Economic Development

China, as a developing country, is also facing the same challenge in the relationship between the state and the market. Moreover, since in the past stage we were the major beneficiary of globalization, we may incline to look at globalization in a positive light and overlook the challenge it has brought. To deal with the challenges brought about by globalization, we must make it a top priority to properly tackle the relationship between the state and the market.

Firstly, we should recognize that the reason why China is able to benefit from globalization is that it has laid a good social and economic foundation before joining in the globalization process. The concentrated manifestation of such a foundation is the establishment of a modern country and the comparatively comprehensive industrial system at its service and the social progress advanced by the country.

In summarizing the achievements of the reform and opening up, some people, consciously or unconsciously, incline to debase the achievements scored by the New China in its first 30 years and overlook the great significance of the 30-year achievements in the development of the whole country. They usually adopt a simplified economic standard index to measure the development achievements of this era. As a matter of fact, such an assessment is one-sided. If we have a proper understanding of the 30 years' development objective, we will find that although the development of this era is beset with obstacles, the achievements obtained are not necessarily inferior to those since the reform and opening up.

A country, as an organization, has many functions. The fulfillment of such functions is based on certain material conditions. During different periods of economic development, the production modes to ensure the provision of these material conditions are different.

Since modern massive industrial production, the nations which have already realized their industrialization have built the material conditions for the realization of such functions of the state as national defense, transportation and communication on the basis of the massive industrial production.

Until 1949, China, as a newly emerging country, lacked the support of massive industry in the infrastructure in both national defense and domestic transportation and communication.

Because of the international and domestic environment known to us all, after 1949 the pressing task facing the new-born sovereignty is to establish the material foundation of massive industry to safeguard the nation's independence and unity, meaning the nation's basic functions. To realize this aim, on the one hand we should build the basic national defense industry and, on the other hand, build the transportation and communication system connecting the railway, highway, post and telecommunications and communication nationwide. For a large country like China, to finish these tasks we need to build an independent and comparatively comprehensive industrial system, especially a basic heavy industry system.

The development achievements during this period reflect clearly the features of industrialization at that time. Since the 1960s, China has not only transited from imitation to self-development in conventional weapons, but also secured remarkable achievements in sophisticated weapons marked by the "atomic and hydrogen bombs and man-made satellites". In basic industry, steel and iron and coal output have grown significantly and a comparatively comprehensive industrial machine industry, with the national defense industry as its main customer, has been established. In the construction of the railway and highway infrastructure, the growth also doubled or was even dozens' of times higher. The most representative example is the construction of the Sichuan-Tibet Highway and Qinghai-Tibet Highway. Before 1949 there were no accessible highways in Tibet and the transportation between Tibet and the rest of China was extremely inconvenient. Whether in the period of the Republic of China or at the beginning of the 1950s, the delegates designated by the central government to Tibet had to detour from India to Lhasa. In the four-year construction from the end of 1950 to December 1954, the Sichuan-Tibet Highway connecting Sichuan and Lhasa and the Qinghai-Tibet Highway connecting Xining and Lhasa were concurrently put into use, which has provided important material conditions for the safeguarding of national unity.

At the same time, with the strengthening of the state capacity, various social undertakings have made significant progress and great improvements were made in people's education and medical and health services. As an overall indicator reflecting the economic and social progress, the average life expectancy of the Chinese population increased from 35 in 1950 to 67. 7 in 1981. The founding of the New China put an end to the humiliating history when China was subject to the oppression of foreign countries and the time when it was in the midst of incessant fighting between warlords.

Such achievements have provided sound social environmental and infrastructure conditions for the reform and opening up. Also, thanks to the industrial foundation laid during the first 30 years, China boasts a better capacity for self-development and product packaging than developing countries in general.

Just as stated in the book *Adam Smith in Beijing*, "contrary to the general view, the attraction of the People's Republic of China holds for foreign countries is not its rich and cheap labor resources. There are plenty of such resources worldwide, but no place can invite so much capital like China." In discussing the successful experience of China's reform and opening up, I found that "to a large degree, the success of the reform is based on the achievements made at the early stage of China's revolution", "compared with India, China's labor force including immigrant workers from rural areas are better educated, more inquisitive and disciplined ... which has nothing to do with the later market reform". ①

In addition, since the reform and opening up, China's successful experience in dealing with the Asian financial crisis in 1997 and the international financial crisis in 2007 lies in the country's enormous economic clout. During the Asian financial crisis, to maintain the rapid economic growth, from 1998 to 2003 China invested hundreds of billions of yuan in infrastructure and technology reform by increasing the issue of treasury bonds from its average annual revenue. At the end of 2008, to maintain an economic growth of 8% during the international financial crisis, the Chinese government again implemented stimulus measures with an investment of 4 trillion yuan from the national revenue to ensure economic stability.

Lastly, the market reform itself is an act adopted by the nation on its own initiative. China's reform is a gradual one from the top down to the bottom. How to transit from the planned economic system to the market economic system is in itself a global puzzle. The difficulty lies in how to cross over the "river" between the two systems. According to Western economists, people cannot cross over the river in divided steps. In China, by relying on the country as the support for the system before and after, such a gradual reform becomes successful. As a matter of fact, the country has played the role of mediator during the process.

Facts also prove that the so-called reform guideline of "small government, large society (actually large market)" will result in the failure of the reform, for example, the reform of the medical care system. Actually the developed countries which advocate this are not small governments at all, which is strongly evidenced by their fiscal expenditure being over 35% of their GDP. However, this doesn't mean that their market is underdeveloped. This fact shows that the

---

① [Italian] Giovanni Arrighi, *Adam Smith in Beijing*. Social Sciences Academic Press, 2009, pp. 354-373.

relationship between the government and the market is not governed by an inverse relationship, the empowering of one leading to the weakening of the other. Instead, strong government and strong market can make a perfect combination.

For our country, which is still at the stage of industrial development, many social and economic problems we are facing require the forced intervention of the country. They cannot be solved by merely relying on the market, but by collaboration between the state and the market. Only in this way can we maintain a sustainable and rapid economic development. The most pressing problems include the macroeconomic disequilibrium, the income gap and the relationship between resources and the environment. The solution of all these problems depends on the active intervention of the state rather than the market alone. In fact, some problems are exactly a reflection of the problem of the market itself, like the income gap problem and the environment problem.

IV. Conclusion

This paper, in combination with how to view globalization, first discussed the nature of globalization and explained the driving force and mechanism of the globalization of capital from Marx's capital theory; then it analyzed the market economy's basic role in globalization by referring to the development of globalization after the Second World War and raised the problem of the relationship between the state and the market during globalization; finally, it made the conclusion that the state should play an active role and properly deal with the relationship between the state and the market by discussing the realities before and after the reform and opening up and the current problems facing our development.

Although it may seem to go beyond my scope of discussion, I deem it necessary to point out that, although currently the globalization is one of capital, it doesn't mean that it can create a millennium kingdom of capitalism. A deep research on China's revolutionary history and the economic history of the New China may reveal that the secret of the success of China's revolution and the development of the New China lies in its adoption of a socialist method to solve and accomplish the historical task required by the capitalist revolution and development (including globalization). I believe that the developing countries' practice during globalization will continue to prove the effectiveness of this development road. With the modernization of developing countries in which half of the global population reside and the recurrence of the class contradictions inside the capitalist countries (they are actually the two sides of the same coin and are emerging in globalization in recent years), the dialectics of history will definitely push the globalization of capital towards its opposite direction and the globalization of socialism is sure to replace the globalization of capitalism. Such a process is pacified and gradual, representing the tolerance shown by an ideal and a system for one another, but in essence it is still revolutionary.

References:

[1] [Australian] Linda Wiss & John M. Hobson, *Nation and Economic Development——A Comparative and Historical Analysis.* Jilin Publishing Group Co., Ltd., 2009.

[澳] 琳达·维斯、约翰·M. 霍布森:《国家与经济发展——一个比较及历史性的分析》,吉林出版集团有限责任公司 2009 年版。

[2] [Italian] Giovanni Arrighi, *Adam Smith in Beijing: Lineages of the Twenty-First Century.* Social Sciences Academic Press, 2009.

[意] 乔万尼·阿里吉:《亚当·斯密在北京——21 世纪的谱系》,社会科学文献出版社 2009 年版。

[3] [Australian] Lou Holden, *Globalization and National States.* World Affairs Press, 2006.

[澳] 罗·霍尔顿:《全球化与民族国家》,世界知识出版社 2006 年版。

[4] Marx. *Capital (Volume I-III)*, People's Publishing House, 2004.

马克思:《资本论》1—3 卷,人民出版社 2004 年版。

[5] [American] Wallerstein, *Modern World System (Volume I-III)*. Higher Education Press, 2004.

[美] 沃勒斯坦:《现代世界体系》1—3 卷,高等教育出版社 2004 年版。

[6] [American] Willian Greider, *The Manic Logic of Global Capitalism.* Social Sciences Academic Press, 2003.

[美] 威廉·格雷德《资本主义全球化的疯狂逻辑》,社会科学文献出版社 2003 年版。

[7] [American] Barbara Stallings, *On the Regional Effect of Globalization.* Chongqing Publishing House, 2002.

[美] 芭芭拉·思多林斯主编:《论全球化的区域效应》,重庆出版社 2002 年版。

[8] [French] Francois Chesnais, *Globalizing Capital.* Central Compilation & Translation Bureau, 2001.

[法] 弗朗索瓦·沙奈:《资本全球化》,中央编译局 2001 年版。

[9] [French] Francois Chesnais, *Financial Globalization.* Central Compilation & Translation Bureau, 2001.

[法] 弗朗索瓦·沙奈等著:《金融全球化》,中央编译局 2001 年版。

[10] Zhao Jingxing, Past, present and future of China's economic development, in: Wang Tongsan ed. , *Globalization and China: Analysis of Macro Economic Effect and Prospects.* Economic Management Press, 2009.

赵京兴:《中国经济的现在、过去和未来——中国的分层工业化道路》,载汪同三主编《全球化与中国:宏观经济效应与前景分析》,经济管理出版社 2009 年版。

[11] Wang Zixian, ed. *China's Reform and Opening Up and its 30 Years' Foreign Trade.* Economic Management Press, 2008.

王子先主编:《中国改革开放与对外经贸 30 年》,经济管理出版社 2008 年版。

[12] Wang Yizhou, ed. 30 *Years' Transition of China's Foreign Relations.* Social Sciences Academic Press, 2008.

王逸舟主编:《中国对外关系转型 30 年》,社会科学文献出版社 2008 年版。

[13] Mei Junjie, *Legend of Free Trade——Research on the Way for Britain and America's Prosperity.* Shanghai Joint Publishing Press, 2008.

梅俊杰:《自由贸易的神话——英美富强之道考辨》,上海三联书店 2008 年版。

[14] Jin Fang, *Globalization Business and Contemporary International Division of Labor.* Shanghai People's Publishing House, 2006.

金芳:《全球化经营与当代国际分工》,上海人民出版社 2006 年版。

[15] Qiu Zunshe, ed. *Research on Marxism and Contemporary Economic Globalization.* Peking University Press, 2006.

邱尊社主编:《马克思主义与当代经济全球化问题研究》,北京大学出版社 2006 年版。

[16] Zhang Zhenjiang, *From Pound to Dollar: Transfer of the International Economic Hegemony (*1933-1945*).* People's Publishing House, 2006.

张振江:《从英镑到美元:国际经济霸权的转移(1933—1945)》,人民出版社 2006 年版。

[17] [American] Robert Gilpin, *Global Political Economics——Interpretation of the International Economic Order.* Shanghai People's Publishing House, 2006.

[美]罗伯特·吉尔平:《全球政治经济学——解读国际经济秩序》,上海人民出版社 2006 年版。

Part II
Climate Change

Public Issues Requiring Man's New Wisdom

——Why Cannot Man Work Hand in Hand against Global Climate Change?

By ZHENG Yisheng

Introduction

If a Martian descends on the earth, he/she will definitely be shocked at how inactive the earthman is when they have already realized their shared crisis. Although more and more people acknowledged the risk of climate change, up to now human society still fails to work together in the real interests of the community. Whether actively or passively, they still devote much of their wisdom to vying against each other, thus making the problem more and more complicated. Man tends to vacillate on the problem of climate change and is cunning and self-contradictory in dealing with it. Judging from the surface, international cooperation affords no optimism, proceeding intermittently and with one step forward and two steps backward.

Why is it so hard for man to change his existing lifestyle? Why is it so hard for international cooperation on climate change? Is there a mismatch between the features of climate change itself and the current thinking pattern?

This article focuses on analyzing the problem from the economic perspective. It will discuss in turn the following views: (1) Global climate change is a new public issue and poses unprecedentedly profound challenges to human society. (2) Currently, the methods adopted by human society against climate change are not enough to tackle these challenges. (3) Human society needs to exert its wisdom to solve the long-term problem.

I. Global Climate Change is a New Public Issue

From the perspective of economics, climate is a Global Public Good. There are two especially disturbing features about climate change: the first lies in all its uncertainty in the relationship between nature and man; the second is that it greatly upsets the tradition of the relationship between "non-homogeneous" societies, like between developed countries and developing countries. Up to now, man's determination to change his behavior in tackling climate change and his sincerity in working with others is bogged down in the severe challenges posed by the above-mentioned two features. We call them respectively the first challenge and the second challenge.

1. The First Challenge: Indefinite Disaster

(1) Features of the indefiniteness in the problem of climate change

In considering the climate change policy, every link in the train of our thoughts will face uncertainty. For the complexity of climate change, some mechanisms for the change are not made clear. Besides, scientists can only tell us that the global average temperature rise since the middle of the 20th century is probably largely (more than 90% probability) attributable to the observed increase in the man-made greenhouse gas intensity (IPCC, 2007). Although some scientists deny or doubt this conclusion, their supportive evidence (different explanations or assumptions) fails to convince most of the scientists. "Scientific uncertainty" first appears in the emission conditions, reaction of the carbon cycle to the emissions, the climate's sensitivity to the changes in the carbon cycle, the regional implication of every global climate situation etc. Even if we can accurately predict what the climate in 2050 will be, we still have to face its uncertain impacts. Besides, the policies man selects to adapt to and alleviate the impact of climate change are another source of indefiniteness (Heal and Kristrom, 2002).

Some may say with dismissal, "the indefiniteness of future costs, profits and discount rate is nothing new because the financial text (about investment policy) has proposed the 'standard method' long ago to deal with the indefiniteness: only to set an 'expected value'. However, here the degree of the complexity of the indefiniteness varies greatly. First is the nonlinearity of the cost of climate change and the height of the benefit function. This matters much under the circumstances of ' the trigger point' of the environmental mutation, but we have no idea of the accurate function shape. The second is the entrenched irreversibility of the environmental policy, which interacts with the indefiniteness in a complicated way. Such a condition baffles the policy makers: if the policy investment is irreversible, namely the deposit cost or opportunity cost is too much, then it's better to wait. If the environmental damage is irreversible, for example, it takes years for the influence of the greenhouse gas accumulated in the air to take effect, then it's better to take actions earlier. The problem is that the two conditions are uncertain. The traditional cost effectiveness analysis is incapable of doing this or even giving the opposite guidance. The third is the prolonged time span of climate change. The prolongation exacerbates the uncertainty between the cost and effect of the policy and makes it hard to predict the long-term influence. For this, the uncertainty of the discount rate becomes particularly important. In a word, the above-mentioned features of climate change make the indefiniteness much more complicated and are regarded as the central problem of the climate policy (Pindyck, 2007)."

Weitzman believes that the uniqueness of the economic problem of climate change lies in that today's decision has irreversible long-term impact. It is not that the result of the random process is hard to affirm, but that when we are analyzing the expected effect with the discounted present value, we also face the indefinite deep structure of the science of global warming and the incapability of the current economic analyzing methods to deal with it. Climate science informs people that the probability of the occurrence of disastrous collapse in a certain system cannot be overlooked, even if we are not very familiar with such a meager probability.

The implication of the indefiniteness of the structure generalized by "Heavy-Tailed Distribution" for the understanding of the climate change problem is as follows: small probability and great disaster (Weitzman, 2008).

(2) Profundity of the indefiniteness of the challenge

"The risks we are facing are untraceable, but they are disastrous" (Giddens, 2009). On the one hand, global climate change has brought with it disastrous risks, but on the other hand its infiniteness makes man vacillate in his determination to take action. Such a dual nature plunges human society into a dilemma. Under such circumstances, whether we should take action or not and how to take action remain the problem. The politician Gore and the sociologist Giddens respectively use "the frog in the lukewarm water" and "Giddens' paradox" to describe the decision-making dilemma brought about by such indefiniteness: when there is an opportunity to take action, there is no consensus reached among people. When the problems begin to emerge, it is too late to take action.

The climate change problem reminds us repetitively that we must make decisions on significant issues against all the indefiniteness. Strictly speaking, this is an important issue which is non-linear, irreversible and requires long-term dedication and concerns human beings' destiny. The decision of such a "big issue" goes beyond the competence of our habitual control over the individual, short-term, linear, reversible and definite thinking pattern. The heated argument on the tackling of climate change and the confused and self-contradictory action just reflect the challenge posed by the "big issue" to our thinking pattern.

Challenges to methodology——take the argument on the discount rate as an example

In October, 2006, the "Stern Review Report" supported by the British government, through the calculation of cost effectiveness, showed that climate warming had caused enormous loss to the future of human society (at the beginning of the 22nd century, it will reach 5% - 20% of GDP) and it was only rational and worthwhile to take early action (an expenditure of 2% of GDP). The report elicited great repercussions and argument. Some economists criticized this report based its conclusion of "early action" not on the new economics, new science or model, but on the arbitrary parametric hypothesis, namely a time discount rate approaching zero. It was not that easy to support the radical action by replacing the actual interest and savings rate in today's market with it and the central problem (how much should we do and what is the appropriate speed and cost?) of the climate change policy is not thus solved (Nordhaus, 2007). However, what should be noted is that this argument "catalyzed a deep reflection of the economic consideration on the climate change action" (Heal, 2008). Some economists pointed out that there were no simple guiding principles and applicable tools for understanding these profound indefinite problems (Pindyck, 2007): for example, under some circumstances, we need rapid and strong action while under other circumstances, such action is not applicable. Even some conditions render it perfectly reasonable for us to take a firm and strong stand on climate change, but it is not that simple to find support in relevant economics (Heal, 2008). Weitzman's remarks that "the conclusion of taking early action required by the Stern Review Report is justified, but is based on the wrong methods" (this refers to our assumption of the extremely low discount rate in the aggregative model, but little understanding of which discount rate should be used in the climate change problem under the uncertainty) is to remind people that an important thinking pattern in dealing with the great uncertainty (hard to be quantified) is to give an intuitional reasoning through the understanding of the problem (Weitzman, 2007). Later, he further proved that the original cost-effectiveness analyzing method cannot cope with the problem of "small probability and great disaster". ①

A brief summary: another implication of the argument on the discount rate: some existing economic methods and concepts no longer fit when coping with the challenges posed by the new problem of climate change. Some scholars are pragmatic and sagacious about this: considering the indefinite profundity of the problem, we should care more about the features of the problem rather than force the current methods and concepts upon the problem to twist its reality. However, up to now, there are still no effective new methods. This is obviously not satisfying, but may be a stage for the incubation of a new thinking pattern.

Conflicts with the current popular concepts

Behind the argument of methodology are different concepts. Ackerman summarized new concepts required to cope with global

① Weitzman pointed out that the "heavy-tail disaster" economics offered some conceptual difficulties and the analysis it elicited is more "subjective", unlike the "scientific conclusion" given by the cost-effectiveness analysis. However, if there is indeed such an ungraspable thing in the world, we have no choice but to admit it. We cannot put the cart before the horse and tackle it in the way we tackle the problem of the "thin tail" probability distribution (just because by doing this, we can apply the cost-effectiveness analysis with assumed importance) (Martin L. Weitzman, 2008).

warming and they were obviously different from the currently popular thinking pattern. He emphasized: firstly, you should no longer consider that our posterity's life is inferior to yours. The market interest rate only applies to the middle-term or short-term private investment. If like some economists, we apply it in the climate change problem (higher discount rate, for example, 10%), we actually assume that our future generation is undoubtedly richer than us and needs no help from us. If you really think our future generation is equally wealthy as us, do we still have to discount for the future? Is your granddaughter less valuable than your daughter just because she is among the later generation? As long as their life value is equal, we don't have to discount for our future at all (the discount rate should be zero). Climate change thrusts this choice before our generation. We find that in the face of the next generation (ineffective to us), we are jeopardizing the planet when we try to maximize our economic luxury at the sacrifice of our future generation's life value. Secondly, transform from the "profit-oriented mindset" to "safety mindset" (for our own planet). Economists make the "optimized" decision based on the average (disaster breakout) probability while those who worry about being plagued by the disaster guard against the worst condition (adhering to the security mindset). In dealing with the disaster problem possibly incurred by climate change, what we should consider is how to deal with the overall disaster problem intelligently rather than how to secure expectant maximum utility or profit. Although we should consider the pros and cons both in chasing profits and avoiding disasters, they are two different issues. The transition from the former to the latter requires us to overcome our predilection to blindly pursue the profit. Thirdly, the cost caused by climate change is so tremendous that it should not be evaluated at a certain price. The mindset to estimate everything from the market's perspective should be restricted to a certain scope. The cost-effectiveness analysis requires us to designate a unified price for things both good and bad. However, in this world, some things have their relative value or price while other things are innately precious, such as dignity. When what we face is life, is man's dignity (stressed by Kant), is nature, should we say their value can be measured by a certain price? Furthermore, if we notice that almost all such estimates seem to hinge on man's income, can we reasonably assume that the life of the rich is more precious than that of the poor? The incompetence of the cost-effectiveness analysis here lies in its attempt to designate a price for human dignity and nature. Therefore, with the rationality of a market economy man, the mission to save our planet cannot be accomplished. Fourthly, our cost-income consciousness should be expanded. Investment in the alleviation of global warming can not only save more losses, but also create new technological methods. Gains and losses here cannot be compared with the short-term and partial commercial profits in the same breath (Ackerman, 2009).

Perplexity breeds internal changes

Although factors contributing to global warming may be man-made, this doesn't exclude the possibility of the intervention of other factors. Although those scientists against "the man-made claims" are not in the mainstream, sometimes truth is in the hands of the minority. Unprofessional as we are, we feel more perplexed and hand-tied. Facing such a "big issue" featured by indefiniteness, besides placing hope on further studies on the understanding of the mechanism for climate change and the knowledge accumulation of how to alleviate and adapt to the change, we may also need to make progress in how to appropriately review the relationship between man and nature (from traditional Chinese culture, a separate understanding of these two is problematic) and man and man. As is mentioned above, in the confrontation of the climate change problem, even the economists who are very insensitive to this have made more reflections on the option value and policy's flexibility and adaptability and most of their thoughts have touched upon the basic value. Challenges posed by the indefiniteness of climate change, of course not only climate change, have shaken the world outlook of some sensitive persons, making them doubt the justification of the current dominating behavioral norm and its order. Perhaps this is man's "intensive evolution" (Laszlo, 2002). Perhaps such an in-depth perplexity is ultimately beckoning a more harmonious and compatible world.

2. *The Second Challenge: A Requirement to Change the Relationship between Developed Countries and Developing Countries*

The first challenge is mainly about the relationship between man and nature (may also be understood as the relationship between generations). While grounded on the first, the second is about the relationship between different groups. On the climate change problem, man is not an interests community——the existence of different countries and groups in possession of different fortune has greatly complicated the problem——Lao-tzu said, "one begets two, two begets three and three begets everything." The game playing on the climate change problem has two features: firstly, the focus is not between the citizens in a country, neither between the countries of the same type or in the same developmental stage. Rather it is between developed countries and developing countries. Secondly, such a "cross-type" relationship is new in its content: namely, human society must cooperate for its common interest.

(1) "Shared but differentiated principle" implies a daunting challenge for the relationship between developed countries and developing countries

A basic fact is that the historical accumulative emissions by developed countries are the major factor contributing to today's global warming while nowadays more and more emission sources are attributable to developing countries, like China and India. Based on developed countries' acknowledged "ecological debt" to developing countries and the gaping void between the competence of the two, the international society has reached a consensus on climate cooperation between countries in different developmental stages——"shared but differentiated principle". In terms of the development opportunity, developing countries should be given more emission space; in terms of competence, developing countries should be provided with technical and economic endorsement. It should be noted that the cooperation under the new principle is not only different from market exchanges, but also from philanthropic assistance. Instead, it is to fulfill climate responsibility and obligation. While developed countries, as the more capable entities, are "shouldering more responsibilities" and "repaying their historic debt", developing countries should also restrict or reduce the emissions. Perhaps those who proposed and agreed on the "shared but differentiated principle" didn't realize what a great and profound challenge this has posed to tradition and reality: in retrospect, the relationship between developed countries and developing countries was only one of the conqueror and the conquered and non-market trade and market trade; there was no such technical and economic cooperation relationship to speak of, designated by public responsibility. Overall, up to now, the above-mentioned relationship usually brings benefits to developed countries. Even if there are win-win situations, it is the developed countries which gain more profits. This is because, generally speaking, whether resorting to violence or trade, developed countries had all the initiatives and made the rules most familiar to them for the game. Otherwise, why are developed countries controlling more and more global resources (including the environmental capacity) and reaching an increasingly higher living standard? Considering this backdrop, for many people from developed countries, the "shared but differentiated principle" is indeed producing unprecedented "mandatory concessions". In their opinion, under this principle, developed countries, in "transferring" their development opportunities (the distribution of carbon emission space) and commercial profits (technology transfer) to developing countries, have received no returns and in the profit and resource theory it may even lead to a "reverse flow", namely from developed countries to developing countries. That such an "irrational" thing should happen under the pretext of "saving our planet through joint efforts"——this is really unbelievable!

(2) "Free riding paradox"

We have noted that based on lessons from practice, in much of the literature studying the international cooperation on climate change, stemming international "free riding" behavior is critical in the institutional arrangement and mechanism design (Wang, 2008). "Some countries, while reducing their emissions, transfer their greenhouse gas-intensive industry to other countries, increasing their emissions. From the perspective of entrepreneurs, this means 'competitiveness' loss; from the perspective of environmentalists, this means 'carbon leakage'. From either perspective, to avoid free riding or leakage, we need to establish corresponding international agreements" (Barrett, 2009). "Free riding" indeed jeopardizes cooperation, but broadly speaking it is easily confused with the "shared but differentiated principle". We should be aware that the preferential treatment for developing countries under the "shared but differentiated principle" is not the market trade failure familiar to us or the loophole of public affairs management (namely "free riding"), but the necessary adjustment to the premise of the historical unfairness and unequal competence between developed countries and developing countries. To afford more emission space for developing countries and affirm that "developing countries secured technological advances that are more preferential than commercial trade"——this is in itself a cost-effective policy elbowing the world onto the road of low carbon development. It is the due obligation of the "shared but differentiated principle". Disregarding the fact that the basic competence of developing countries to improve their low-carbon technology is inseparable from the emission effect will confuse their responsibility with developing countries' "free riding", insubstantializing the "shared but differentiated principle".

Therefore, a practical paradox occurs in international cooperation on climate change: if the "differentiated treatment" is given to developing countries on the condition that "they are not allowed to improve their economic competitiveness", then there are only two possibilities: either "differentiated" is only a lip service, which means the developing countries will be plunged into more difficulties on account of their weak economic clout or developing countries are not able to reduce their emissions. This will send the substantial cooperation between developed countries and developing countries into an endless tug of war, which is doomed to be a problem with no solutions.

In a word, a random and abusive use of the "free riding" concept reminds us that many people are not mentally prepared for the practice of the "shared but differentiated" new principle and some, consciously or unconsciously, pluck the new cooperation principle back to the old track of "commercial + charity" (which will be discussed in the following part).

(3) The climate change problem touches the "hard core" of the relationship between developed countries and developing countries

We have seen more inconvenient facts than the movie alerting people of climate change promoted by Mr. Bigorre, namely, under uncertain circumstances, some people have more fear of "the reverse flow of profits" (referring to the tangible benefits provided by developed countries to developing countries, especially to those rapidly developing countries) than the global shared disaster. The misfortune encountered by the "shared but undifferentiated principle" shows that the climate change problem has touched upon the in-depth reason hindering the "cross-type" cooperation: here there is a tacit bottom line for the international relationship: rich countries can do anything good, like charity, but cannot bridge the gap between the competitiveness between developed countries and developing countries. This indicates that there is actually a demarcation line of identity in the minds of people from developed countries. For the citizens inside the demarcation line, they are committed to all the just legislations and obligations, regardless of the nature of the problems they are facing; for the countries and people outside the demarcation line, they are strategic adversaries to them, even if in economic cooperation they still try to make them their resources and manual labor provider or the host of the parasitic economy. Of course, their "own" interest community or the membership of their club can stretch beyond the national boundary and expand. It can be the countries at the same developmental stage as them, be their descendents, but it can never be the developing countries and their citizens. They ask you to be clean, but unnecessarily healthy and the most ideal situation is to realize low-carbonization without development momentum. As for what difficulties those underdeveloped countries will be beset with, it's none of their business. "Their first priority is to maintain their own advantages rather than to protect the global public interests. " The dual principle applied by the rich countries is probably the hard core hindering the cooperation on climate change and is the source of all the vacillation and simulation on the climate change problem. The challenge posed by climate change is actually an historical interrogation which is directly targeted at rich countries——they remind us of the slaveholders and colonizers of villagers from other parts of the world over time——whether you acknowledge people from developing countries as your "brothers on the planet" in the same boat.

3. A New Public Issue

Compared with other public issues, the climate change problem challenges some established thinking patterns of human society more blatantly, bearing upon the deepest side of the relationship between generations and contemporaries and resulting in a confusion of thoughts and the "Giddens paradox" and "free riding paradox". In this sense, we assume the global climate change problem to be a new public issue. Many phenomena clustering around the climate change problem are responses to the old thinking pattern and its material benefit structure to this new public issue. In the following part, we will review the features of the efforts made by human society so far.

II. Efforts Made by Human Society to Cope with Climate Change and the Results So Far

1. Dream and Reality: "Working Together Plan" and "No Regret Policy"

It is hard to refuse the "working together plan" if we truly acknowledge the serious threat posed by climate change to man and are thinking of the benefits for the human race. The thinking pattern is rather simple: take actions that are most favorable to save our planet. There are four principles: firstly, the principle of priority areas, namely areas where intense greenhouse gas emissions are increasing rapidly and the cost is low, like developing countries including China; secondly, start from the solution to key problems. Because technological backwardness is the key reason, then we should consider how to make the advanced and applicable energy technologies available to them; thirdly, solve the problem of new technology applications and renewed sustainability in developing countries. If a country fails to develop overall economic and technological capabilities (including professional talents and healthy economic structures), even by "transfusion-like" technological introduction, it can only alleviate the situation over a short span of time and may even trigger new and difficult problems because of the side effect produced. Besides, the development of such overall competence should be based on a more healthy economic structure, which requires an adjustment in the current international economic relations to ensure there is no economic disequilibrium in developing countries; fourthly, make explicit requirements so that human society will be transformed towards sustainable lifestyles and decisively stifle luxurious consumption. Developed countries must take the lead to transform their lifestyles to reduce energy and resource consumption and the rich group in developing countries should never imitate the luxurious lifestyle of developed countries. We should encourage a diverse, happy and high quality, but a low-carbon lifestyle.

This thinking pattern has two features: firstly, under current technological and economic conditions, it is absolutely applicable; secondly, it will not repeat the "partial improvements but overall degradation" global environmental governance which cures the symptoms, not the disease. A reminder for those who immediately accuse it of "utopia" is that most thoughts in the "working together plan" have been expressed more or less at some relevant international conventions and in manifestos and I just make them more explicit and clear here.

Then, why is such a seek-truth-from-facts plan so remote to us? Are there more urgent necessities, greater difficulties or sacred reasons for man to refuse those thinking patterns (including this plan) which lead to more effective solutions? The reason lies in our current thinking pattern mentioned above, which mismatches the challenges we are facing.

On the one hand, people's understanding of the indefiniteness of climate change is still stuck at pragmatism[①], and on the other hand, developed countries and developing countries have not broken the traditional commercial—charity cooperation mode. The two forces together have resulted in the features of the policy for human society to cope with climate change during this period— a popular and short-term "no regret policy". To put it simply, "no regret policy" is not only favorable to the environment, but also to the economic returns, which makes it a perfect and natural policy choice. However, when it comes to the solution of global climate change, it doesn't seem that easy.

---

① For example, the drafter for President George W. Bush told the president, "we find that the climate change problem is one of the most complicated problems in the prospect of decision-making. ...the emissions should be reduced by over a half in the new century. Many experts think that to realize the compulsory objective to stabilize man's pressure on the climate system means such a convincing policy is required: today's society should pay a price for the benefits of the indefiniteness that man will see in the remote future. However, the time spanning generations exceeds that for the government to take most of its actions. This problem is not only extremely complicated, but also facing extremely opposite views... " Therefore, the drafter suggested to the president, "the great perplexity of the public to the views on the risk and conflict of climate change not only increases the odds of the policy dysfunction, but also provides an opportunity——it can direct the public's view towards your most favorable policy direction" (Victor, 2004). Another overly pragmatic attitude is the opposite: some politicians adopted the "cherry picking method" to stress the necessity for man to take action, namely, using exaggerated and simplified methods to dodge the indefiniteness of science or other fields. Serious scientists think it is risky to "hoodwink" the public in the long run (Muller, 2009).

2. Features of the Ways to Cope with Climate Change in Reality

The popular and short-term "no regret policy" is endowed with some characteristics of the responsibility assignment of the greenhouse gas emission reduction at the current stage and the selection of the methods to alleviate climate change.

(1) Bargaining on the responsibility of emission reduction strays far away from the "shared but differentiated principle"

Since the 1970s, different global environmental agreements have appeared. Similar to the destiny of some global environmental cooperation agenda, the climate change problem begins to show the tendency of "rising first and declining later". In 1997, *the Kyoto Protocol* stipulated developed countries' emission reduction responsibility, an embodiment of the "shared but differentiated principle". Afterwards (2001), America announced its retreat in that "it cannot finish the index① in the protocol with acceptable costs and forcing American industry to compete in the global economy where other countries are not required to duly reduce their emissions is unfair" (Victor, 2004). However, a decade after *the Kyoto Protocol* was signed, most of the countries in the Annex 1 hadn't accomplished their tasks. Practices show that it is the consideration of the cost effectiveness that dominates and decides whether the task of greenhouse gas emission reduction is accomplished or the emission has increased (this is the "no regret policy"). The "shared but differentiated principle" is destined to gradually fade out when its proponents are seemingly unwilling to fall into the circle "making promises-breaking promises-changing promises" and when the richer America is firmly against these promises and insists on comparing its total emission volume (not "emission per capita" or "historical accumulative emission") with that of China and refuses to admit its "historical responsibility". Besides, whether to shake off or nullify the emission reduction principle in *the Tokyo Protocol* binding them, some developed countries need to preset their scapegoat and regard the emission problem in China as the major subject. Therefore, although the Copenhagen Summit in 2009 was very lively, capricious and unprecedentedly chaotic, its disappointing result is within our

① Emission reduction in 2012 was 7% less than that in 1990.

expectations. We have already said that the specious "free riding" concept is repeatedly employed to exploit the "shared but differentiated principle". It should be noted that this is the forever excuse updated and used by the rich countries for their repudiation to pay more money under the differentiated principle. Following this logic, as long as there are gaps and deficiencies in developing countries, they always have reasons to point fingers at you and suppress you into submission while escaping their major responsibilities. Another phenomenon is the fancy vista of emission reduction but little short-term commitment and even the long-term vision and proposal seems not that generous. For example, in the Copenhagen conference, some developed countries suggested that by 2050 the global emissions should be reduced by 50%, but for the developed countries 80%. Some scholars noticed that before achieving this objective, the emission per capita in developed countries is still higher than that in developing countries, even excluding the consideration of historical emissions and the reduction of local emissions by developed countries' purchase of their emission rights.

Then we had, the idea of "domestic losses to be compensated abroad". A carbon border tax was passed in America while other scientists proposed a unified global carbon tax. The former attempts to seek developing countries to compensate their possible losses from fulfilling their emission obligations while the latter (the unified carbon tax) actually is contradictory to the "shared but differentiated principle", which objectively helps to blur the "differentiation" (Shen, 2010). History revolving around emission reduction demonstrates that people's understanding of the "shared but differentiated principle" is poles apart and there is invariably a force suffocating the promising new principle to death. It is the "zero-sum game" rather than the cooperation that dominates.

(2) Preferable ways and actions

Besides the emission reduction, people, in selecting ways to alleviate climate change, have a predilection to explore ways through market trading and technological innovation rather than ways to change their lifestyles.

1) Actively exploring and trying out the carbon exchange market

Since the emergence of the undertaking to tackle the challenge of climate change, there are always people wishing to replace it with commercial plans. Some developed countries, America in particular, wish to incorporate the emission reductions into the international market trade (we should note that the market mechanism is not only in play domestically). They stress that the establishment of the global carbon trade market can introduce the direction of the capital flow to those emission reduction sectors with optimized "cost effectiveness", decreasing the emission reduction costs and strengthening the incentive for emission reduction. However, there are some critics arguing that for a series of features of carbon emissions, such as the difficulty in its supervision and price setting, the global carbon trade market is likely to provide a new opportunity for the speculators and it is hard for people to monitor its environmental effect. Therefore, the combination of the transaction arrangement with different rules will actually encourage "competing for the worst" behavior: transfer the capital to those emission reduction activities with the worst environmental protection and laxest surveillance. They aim to include the "carbon derivatives" in the global trade market like "financial innovation" in the past. Once the country defines the carbon emission quota, this will be the largest trade market, valued at about 10 trillion dollars. In consideration of the little effect of the carbon trade on environmental protection and the disheartening lessons from the recent financial crisis, some may worry that, by doing this, ultimately only the banks on Wall Street will benefit while the world will be put at another risk①. Such a problem is worth our careful observation and deliberation.

2) Attempts to get rid of the tug-of-war"pure technology method"

In contrast to the hesitation and vacillation on emission reductions, the competent countries, developed countries in particular, are extremely generous and decisive on large-scale investment in the development of new technologies because it is a "no regret policy" choice, not only of charitable significance, but also a part of the national competition, occupying new strategic areas for new energies and technologies. President George W. Bush's refusal to sign *the Tokyo Protocol* runs parallel with his decision to strengthen investment in the development of new energies and technologies. President Obama's *Clean Energy Act* aimed at changing the situation of America's energy dependence on petroleum and aimed at dominating the global high

---

① Chan, Michelle, Carbon Markets and Financial Risk, Briefing Paper, 2009, pp. 12-16.

technology search for new renewable energy. However, the act for greenhouse gas emission reduction has suffered great hindrance and is still in discussion. Different countries and companies have fully prepared for the age of new energies, indeed like an unprecedented arms race. Also, in recent years, many disputable "climate projects" have been proposed and won acclaim by some economists (Levitt and Dubner, 2009) . The great technological advances are undoubtedly essential in alleviating the influences of climate change. We expect that we can use limited investment in new technologies to find a direct solution to the problem, but we wonder whether under commercial manipulation such hopes will fall through: is it possible to avoid the trouble of "changing lifestyles" and "making concessions to developing countries" and directly solve the problem of climate change? Or can it only create the miracle of realizing the commercial monopoly of new technologies rather than fulfilling the great mission of saving the planet? Another issue is that it is possible for developed countries to regard developing countries as powerful experimental sites for their new technologies. Some think tanks in America look at technological cooperation with developing countries in this way: "in the international technological cooperation, we have important reasons which you (President) cannot announce in public: some new highly risky technologies which will mar our reputation cannot be developed in the advanced industrialized world. " (Victor, 2004)

3. Summary of the Phased Achievements

"No regret policy" is the preliminary product of the interaction between new public issues and current popular human society and its vested profits. At this phase, both the old and new thinking patterns are effective, but more powerful people, in seeking an outlet, still restrict themselves to the old commercial rationality space, fearing to jeopardize the rich countries and people's vested profits.

It is understandable that under such restrictions, it is hard for them to yield any results in their tackling of climate change. Firstly, the actual greenhouse gas emission reduction in those countries is not optimistic. Since a change in production style and lifestyle was not put on the agenda, the situation at the 2009 Copenhagen conference was that developed countries hardly fulfilled their promises in *the Tokyo Protocol* to accomplish the index for emission reductions. Although the rapidly developing countries, such as China and India, are not designated with such responsibilities by the international agreement, they should also consider changing their development mode on account of their fast increasing emissions. Secondly, the " shared and differentiated principle" has always been the eyesore of some developed countries and they are trying every means to get rid of it, for example, by making "the differentiated principle " empty, blurring the difference between developed countries and developing countries, adding conditions for assistance, market replacement and technological patents. The prospects for this principle are put to rigorous test.

The predicament comes from the contradiction between narrow-minded commercial wisdom and the new public issue. Practices prove that the efforts made by human society so far haven't decreased the risks brought about by climate change. Instead, they make us realize all the more the limitation of our conventionalized thinking pattern. The contradiction between narrow-minded commercial wisdom and the new public issue is that at first it invariably requires transforming the long-term, overall and indefinite problem into a short-term, partial and definite problem. We have stressed that the cost-effectiveness analysis suitable for simple questions lacks the vision and ambition required to solve the new public issues. Also, the narrow-minded commercial wisdom always requires substituting the interpersonal relationship with the relationship of profit exchange where the market price is the value criterion. It not only makes transactions of the existent things in the market, but also those not in the market or that should not be sold at a certain price (such as the dignity of life, the value of the environment and the co-existence of human beings). It is unable to understand and tolerate those global villagers who are different from them. In addition to exploiting them for profit, it has no substantial responsibilities for them and has no relationships with them. Compared with new public issues, the dominating narrow-minded commercial wisdom is too limited. This is the reason why we are inactive in respect of our long-term and overall benefits.

III. Greater Wisdom Needed for Tackling the Climate Change Problem

New wisdom is needed to change the situation in which we remain inactive in our long-term and overall benefits. It should be helpful to lift the narrow restriction of the commercial wisdom and re-establish the relationship between man and nature and man and man.

1. We Need to Understand a More Expanded Causal Relationship

A strange phenomenon is that on account of the complicated reasons which cause climate change, the natural scientist's conscientiousness is in stark contrast with the politicians and economists self-assurance: we have seen many economic reports detailing the condition of the emission increases in developing countries, but few have explored the causal chain behind this phenomenon and less are interested in the interactive relationship between the climate and each country. Therefore, we might as well hear the advice of an environmentalist. In summarizing the vain efforts made by human beings to save the environment in recent years, Mr. Strong realized that when considering the environment, we cannot overlook the influence of "man's complicated progress". He said that the reason why he followed the progress related to "globalization" is that "we should view these (environmental) problems from a broader causal relationship"[①]. Obviously, we cannot study the carbon emission

---

① Mr. Maurice Strong, General Secretary of the United Nations Conference on the Human Environment (1972) and the United Nations Conference on Environment and Development (1992), the former vice general secretary of the United Nations and an environmentalist, noted that accompanying the process of "globalization" which created much wealth for civilization was "the expanding of the gap between the winner and the loser". For those who are solicitous about the environment of human society and sustainable development, this is particularly important because "we must view these problems from a broader causal relationship". "We haven't accepted such a fact: globalization in its nature is systematic while our management mechanism and system are not." As for the necessity to adopt more systematic, comprehensive and interdisciplinary methods in management and decision-making, there are many discussions in this regard and some useful but limited progress. Even so, the current management and decision-making process is seriously disjointed with the causal system of the real world (Zhang, 2008).

condition of each country separately, but should understand the production of emissions and solution of the climate change problem in the context of economic globalization.

(1) The relationship between carbon emissions and international trade shows that production and consumption should not be split in their understanding

In recent years, many scientists have studied and calculated the "carbon transfer" problem in international trade and studied the asymmetrical status of the producer and the consumer in the problem of carbon emissions. This is a new case of the "pollution paradise assumption": in international trade, industrialized countries transfer the highly polluting products and industries to developing countries, making them bear the dual harm brought about by environmental pollution (including reputation) and importing for themselves pollution-free products. Zhang Youguo's (2009) study shows that since 2004 the energy consumption and carbon emissions resulting from China's exportation have significantly exceeded that of imports and the gap is rapidly expanding. In 2006, it approached one tenth that of the whole production sector.

Considering that China is a country with comparatively limited environmental capacity per capita, it has paid great sacrifices to exchange its own environment for foreign exchange. The accusation that China is the "global factory" on account of its large amount of emissions is one-sided, which is as hard as encouraging the trade in Tibetan antelope cashmere while banning poaching. Therefore, from the perspective of effectively alleviating the greenhouse gas emissions and distributing an equal share of carbon emission rights, the responsibility of the consumer's carbon emissions is a problem worth discussing.

(2) Greenhouse gas emissions are a product of global industrialization

The greenhouse gas emission growth of the rapidly developing countries such as China and India is a result of their active imitation of the Western countries' industrialization. Superficially, the greenhouse gas emission increase is slowing down in developed countries, as a gradually mitigating and descending wave, while in China and India the wave is surging. However, this is the same "vibration motion" process. The vibration source from which a series of shock waves are stirred resembles an intangible hand tremulously brandishing a long whip into the distance——this is the unrestricted economic globalization. In the advances of economic globalization, most countries have been or are partially or even wholly being incorporated into the international system of the division of labor. Capital can allocate the resources of different countries (especially developing countries), including environmental capacity, for value appreciation in its free flow and in various degrees locking imperceptibly the economic and environmental situation of these countries during this "optimization" process. The global environmental problem, in the dynamic transference of "partial improvements but overall degradation", agglomerates increasingly in developing countries. Emission reduction is not simply a matter of technology updating: to a large degree, it hinges on its relationship with the external environment①. For example, since 2006 China has begun to levy taxes on the exportation of high energy consuming products, but the reduction in exports slowed down the economic growth and incurred a series of employment problems. As a result, it had to recover the tax reimbursement for exports.

(3) Consumerism also originates from the cross-national capital flow

It is sarcastic that developed countries are never willing to make their luxurious high-carbon lifestyle a subject for discussion, but what their environmentalists blatantly accuse, and their companies and governments promote, is that such a style is an increasingly favorable target for developing countries. Behind this dual standard lurks the "privileged villager" consciousness (in the global village). The development of consumption seems to be the consumer's right, but to a large degree it's a product of the production companies' incitement and their successful domination (even monopoly) in the market of developing countries. "In today's global economic order, developed countries are

① A foreign study on China's greenhouse gas emissions can more or less show the interaction between factors at home and abroad. It shows that the technological advances are the long-term choice for emission reduction, but this should be endorsed by another condition: social development equality which is related to the incorporation of globalization: in the two situations in which the economy overly depends on the global market and economic efficiency (S2 and S4), greenhouse gas emission reduction fares the worst (the accumulative carbon emissions in the 21st century is 111 billion tons. Compared to the situation in which emphasis is given to the investment in the domestic demand and the gap-bridging between different development levels, it increases respectively by 58% and 23%) (Wang and Watson, 2008).

indeed the dominator in the economic development trend of globalization. That is to say, if developed countries don't take the lead in the transformation of the economic consumption model, it is hard for developing countries to solve the environmental problem single-handedly because they are suffering greater social pressure (the poverty problem etc.) and international competition pressure" (Baudrillard, 2000)[①].

In summary, globalization in its nature is systematic. Strictly speaking, a country cannot accomplish the transformation of the production mode alone. At least a country has no reason to accuse others while it is one of the major factors causing these problems itself. Since climate change is the product of the global system, the causes of these problems cannot be comprehended by severing the causal relationship. If you admit that there is something wrong with human society at large, logically we are unlikely to find who is responsible for the failure to find a right solution to the problem. If we admit the reality that although climate change is caused by the decision-making of different countries, its motivation comes from the global system, why can't we find a solution by starting from here? Why shouldn't we first understand the relationship and history between climate change and the global social mechanism and, based on this, share out the work and cooperate with one another to find the most effective solution to the problem?

To refuse to respect the real causal relationship with the lawsuit concept in the narrow commercial wisdom is superficial and hypocritical. It is not a suitable method to solve the great problem caused by global climate change risks. No matter what a fanfare it has made, the consequence can only be "curing the symptoms, not the disease", just as Einstein said, "You cannot use the ways which cause the problem to solve the problem."

2. *We Need to Further Understand the Relationship between Equality and the Environment in the World*

(1) Maintenance of the global environmental system requires a worldwide "in-depth equality"

The incompetence in stemming the greed of the minority and the

---

① Zhang Rongnan & Lu Feng, Consumerism and Consumption Ethics. *Thinking*, 2006 (2).

possessive economic political system are the source of instability and the worldwide environmental degradation and are also the systematic loophole which induces a few people to mistake the global climate change problem for an evil act so as to have more in their possession and to suppress others. Absolute power produces absolute corruption. The world financial crises show that the richest countries are not necessarily the ones with ethics because we cannot depend on them to be self-disciplined. In the Copenhagen conference, China and other developing countries were criticized by Western public opinion for resisting developed countries' discharging of their responsibility. As a matter of fact, such a kind of resistance is absolutely necessary for the formation of a healthy international relationship.

There may be two possibilities: a pattern in which the developing countries, with their large population, are a far cry from developed countries in terms of economic development. They cannot easily get rid of the current economic growth mode under present international economic relationships and are facing the pressure of an imbalance between the environment, society and the economy. Some developing countries have already lost the balance amidst the global and domestic polarization; the other pattern is that the development of different countries is more balanced. In the long run, which one is more favorable for global peace and the equal utilization and co-governance of resources and the reversal of the current "partial improvements but overall degradation" environmental situation? We believe the latter is better because a clean global environment asks for a healthy global economic structure. Therefore, as a basic capability development of human society, we should support every effort made to curb, alleviate and change the imbalanced development worldwide so as to fundamentally alleviate the global environmental crisis (including the climate change problem). No matter how tortuous the road to "in-depth equality" is and how those "privileged villagers" (from the global village) divert their attention, we should not forget that to constrain willful and reckless privilege is not only the condition for the majority to improve their living conditions, but also the necessity for solving the world environmental protection problem.

Climate change requires more nation-to-nation systematic cooperation and less vicious competition, which actually has initiated a new-type relationship between developed countries and developing countries——endowing developing countries and their people not only with assistance, but also capabilities and freedom for development. "Do unto others as you would be done by" rather than "go on one's own way and leave no room for others". In the confrontation of such a potential disaster as climate change, so fickle and disconcerting, how much vicious competition would be avoided in a more peaceful world with more balanced development! Under any circumstances, doesn't a human society which "shares weal and woe" enable the majority to "tactfully manage the unforeseeable to live a better life" at ease and with delight?... Are the "privileged villagers" in our global village dodging such considerations? Does not history teach them that only by emancipating more of the slaves can they themselves be helped out and saved?

The "shared but differentiated principle" being impaired is exactly the first bridge for man to promote healthy social evolution and walk toward in-depth equality.

(2) In-depth equality needs to break the restriction of some old conceptions about equality

1) Relinquish the logic of the solidified and vested interests——doubting the Pareto Principle

Compared to some philosophical concepts, the justice concept of traditional welfare economics based on the principle of utility is more influential. Its standard in judging the justice of the action lies in the outcome——whether it can bring the maximum "social total utility" (namely efficiency). Such a justice principle in connection with the outcome also exerts an important impact on the justice discussion in climate change (IPCC, 2007). The "Pareto Equilibrium" is defined as the justice (also efficient) status: after a thing is done, no one's welfare decreases (the loser gains compensation from the winner) and the total social welfare is maximized (the winner wins more). The standard of the "Pareto Improvement" is: no matter what happens, the original benefits (welfare and utility) can only increase rather than decrease. Although combining the Pareto efficiency (namely justice) with the reality will trigger many theoretical problems (such as the aggregation problem and whether it is right to measure the welfare with the market value), what matters is "the vested profits cannot decrease" (this means that in the cost-effectiveness analysis, the net proceeds must surpass zero), which has become a presupposition of the justice belief in the real world. By the justice principle of climate cooperation——according to the logic of the Pareto efficiency——the overall alleviation effect should reach its pinnacle and, at the same time, no parties' original benefits should decrease. This seems to be perfectly justified. Actually it is also the presupposition of some international cooperation designs, but this is exactly what should be suspected: if we are beset with the same urgent risk, the complexity of the climate change problem cannot ensure that, while alleviating the crisis, every member is able to improve their own benefits and then whether we should still stick to the principle of "no decrease in the vested benefits". If all the countries and all the people participated in the negotiation with this principle as their non-negotiable "hard core" to implement the "no regret policy" both in the long run and in the short term, then is there actually no solution for such a "climate cooperation equation set"? "No solution" here is exactly the consequence of the domination of the "no changes in the vested benefits" over the justice principle.

2) The view of justice based on rights should keep pace with the times

The justice principle based on rights comes from a moral value, which judges the justification of social actions with the criterion of a "social contract". Modern philosophers believe that what matters is not utility but more fundamental things (namely, besides the income, it should include rights, freedom, opportunity and other social foundations which support human dignity). Rawls further stresses that we should allow for the weak, believing social justice should be evaluated based on the living standard of people living in the worst social conditions. Such superficial "injustice" is aimed at the realization of justice and is a view of justice supporting the "shared but differentiated principle".

Scholars at home and abroad once regarded the emission per capita or historical accumulative emission per capita as the manifestation of the equal rights of man to develop his own space (Pan & Chen, 2009). From the performances in the actual climate negotiations, the fair rights principle advocated by them is extremely conservative and rigid, which is far from satisfactory according to Rawls' requirements. For example, the country with high energy intensity uses the concept focusing only on property rights to advocate the emission quota distribution plan based on the "Grandfather Principle", which affords the historically high-emission countries more emission permits. Such a thinking pattern is criticized, but there are many ramifications of the "Grandfather Principle", for example, the intellectual property rights problem.

One of the stalemates in the negotiation is that developed countries are unwilling to make commitments to provide low-carbon technology to developing countries. The intellectual property right is the major reason. In the face of the climate change problem threatening global environmental security, it is natural for people to change or reform the current "leaving one to sink or swim" intellectual property rights system. For example, some scholars want to legalize the public nature of "knowledge about climate change" (Qiang, 2009)[①]. In consideration of the source-opening of the IT area and the experience of the free software movement, some scholars proposed that "facing the severe threat of climate change to human civilization, the emission reduction technology area or sustainable development technology area is also in urgent need of a source-opening movement" (Wen, 2009).

3) Make the view of justice based on capabilities promote the realization of "in-depth justice"

Amartya Sen stressed that we should pay attention to the capability with which an individual chooses his or her own worthy lifestyle. Capabilities refer to the subjective conditions for the arrangement of the optional lifestyle, especially when the freedom to choose and engage in the social and market trade activity is what that right embodies. Therefore, Sen criticized not only the utility principle for its flouting of the process and stressing the result in judging every view, but also the inconsideration of the justice maintenance method based on rights to "individual's diversity". He pointed out that even if the weak were provided with privileges (according to Rawls' maximum and minimum principle), the real consequences would still vary. Therefore, rights should be understood in the context of capabilities. To my understanding, the justice principle based on capabilities, although proposed from the different perspectives of social beings, it is of great relevance to the global social justice that is extremely imbalanced in terms of its development level and competence. Climate change asks us to pay concurrent attention to the macro-environmental result and the existent and development problem brought about by "low carbon" in

① Qiang Shigong. "Carbon politics": new-type international politics and China's strategic choice. 2009, www. wyzxwz. com.

different countries——as a guarantee for the two, we must solve the "capability bottleneck" problem fundamentally rather than temporarily. This requires a new-type relationship between different economic zones——the freedom of choice, egalitarian education and generally similar living standards——just like the developed countries which settle properly their regional development problems. Although there are differences, there is no yawning gap between regions and people are allowed to move freely rather than just the capital. In-depth justice is to expand the scope of the interested community. This is a reasonable historical trend.

(3) New wisdom needs a new outlook on life

If we are to achieve the objective of a more proper distribution of the global basic resources, we have no choice but to reform our economic system. However, without a change in the value and orientation of the key majority of society, there would be no reform to speak of (Laszlo, 2002).

1) Sustainable consumption needs new life morality

In-depth justice is ultimately the form of consumption. It relates to the lurking "privilege complex": many people from developed countries regard their lifestyle as sacred and inviolable①, which, to a large degree, is the unwillingness to give up the privilege and to be unaware that it is outdated and is unfair possession and consumption of world resources. Laszlo Ervin pointed out that in the new civilization transition, we must find in the already polluted environment a lifestyle suitable for the 6 billion population in order to promote a new behavior mode. This is the application of the new morality principle "let us live in the way which also allows others to live", which can replace the principle of today's rich people "live and let live (as long as I am not interfered with)" and the poor people's aspiration "let me live as a rich man". The key lies not in the number of people using the global

---

① Mr. Blair said, "one of the important challenges in the 21st century is to make great efforts to change our lifestyle and make it a sustainable one. The reality of climate change tells us in the best manner what consequences will ensue if we disregard these challenges." It should be noted that this view was proposed in *China's Agenda* 21 as early as 1992, "the major reason for the constantly degenerating global environment is the unsustainable production and consumption methods, especially those of the industrialized countries." (Chapter Four) However, during the past 17 years, the voice, rather than coming into the mainstream, is fading out.

resources, but in how they use them. Just as Gandhi has said, the world can provide what man needs, but cannot quench their greed. "Live a simple life only to allow others to live" (Laszlo, 2002).

2) The premise of many studies should be changed

Since the environmental movement in the 20th century, human beings have been gaining more and more new understandings of their relationship with nature. Many achievements have been scored in the evolution of environmental ideas, which may be gathered into an impressive wave. "Planet consciousness", the developing B model...all advocate re-evaluating the value of nature. Economists for global climate change also proceed from the scenario of "small probability and great disaster" and raise again these thoughts. Some economists realized that for new issues like global climate change, people should no longer deal with such big problems by the cost-effective method used to judge small matters. Other scholars even tried to seek wisdom in traditional Chinese culture to find an outlet from the misunderstanding of Western civilization or to explore from a higher level the way for the world to walk towards harmony.

3) Demand for new wisdom, namely the omen for the approaching of a new civilization paradigm

"Living in the era of profound transitions, we can easily find the imprints and symptoms of a civilization transition. In fact, it is owing to the continual emergence of updated thoughts that a rational human culture and civilization can continue to exist and evolve ... no extinguished ancient civilization has been sacrificed for its inability to adapt itself to the increasingly changing environment (Laszlo, 2002)." The industrial and commercial wisdom bringing economic prosperity and a series of profound problems is not enough to tackle a series of challenges including the new public issue and should be replaced with the new civilization.

IV. Epilogue

The view of this article is that at present human society has only embarked on the first stage in dealing with the climate change problem. The "one step forward and two steps backward" situation, the little progress made and other obstacles in international cooperation, to a large degree can be attributed to the adoption of the old thinking pattern in solving the new public issue, global climate change. Narrow-minded commercial rationality dominates the progress of the climate change problem at this stage, but facts show that it lacks the penetration and complexity to deal with this problem. Unfortunately, people remain inactive in face of the impending disaster and those with the greatest share of the vested interest don't have the most advanced thinking pattern. It is inevitable for us to choose the "easy first and hard next" thinking pattern. People tend to choose partial, controllable and superficial methods in areas which may need changes, such as diplomacy, project investment, technological updates, economic structure, production mode, lifestyle, benefit structures and social norms. A convention and system, before its potential and adaptability is drained, will not be easily discarded. Before a profound reform, there will be many attempts to try to get round it. This is exactly the significance of these unsatisfactory practices so far: they are exhausting current society's potential to cope with public disaster risks and allow the creativity of science and technology. They show the need for the creation of a new stage.

Although we know that to get to the "working hand in hand plan" mentioned above in one go is unrealistic, we should hasten to bridge the gap between the method to cope with climate change and the profundity of the problem because scientists have warned that we don't have much time left.

"The current problem is that the future is different from today"—— it is hard for us to pretend that we are aware of the trajectory of the future changes with all this indefiniteness. What matters is not to get stuck in the mud. As long as people find out that some means can only "address the symptoms" and the climate change problem is aggravated, then man will come to the second stage to cope with climate change. This marks a stage in man's retrospection from the level of civilization as well as a stage towards in-depth justice: here, in-depth justice is the condition for sustainable development, which ensures the freedom for the development of each country, community and individual. Should we welcome or refuse such a transition?

Perhaps in some sincere and kind people's view, God, with a penetration of man's weaknesses, is using climate change as a tricky problem to perplex them and educate them to walk on the right track. Just as a Japanese scholar said after seeing the unsatisfactory results of the practices of the Kyoto Conference in 1997, "seen from today, the reason for such a result from *the Kyoto Protocol* is that we have completely ignored the 'ethic' problem and put the priority on weighing the pros and cons." (Sasaki Takeshi, Kim Tea-Chang, 2009) A dozen years have elapsed and we feel all the more about this.

This article has mainly discussed the problem in developed countries which dominate the climate change process and this is the important premise for us to discuss the problem in developing countries like China: China should make great contributions to help the world cope with global climate change, which includes the change in some of its conceptions and habits as well as a change in the imbalanced global relationships.

References:

[1] [British] Anthony Giddens, trans. Cao Rongxiang. *Politics of Climate Change*. Social Sciences Academic Press, 2009.

[英] 安东尼·吉登斯:《气候变化的政治》,曹荣湘译,社会科学文献出版社 2009 年版。

[2] [American] R. A. Muller, trans. Li Yong. *Physical Lessons for Future Presidents*. Hunan Science and Technology Press, 2009.

[美] 穆勒理:《未来总统的物理课》,李泳译,湖南科学技术出版社 2009 年版。

[3] [American] Ervin Laszlo, trans. Du Mo. *Radical Changes*. China Citic Press, 2002.

[美] 欧文·拉兹洛:《巨变》,杜默译,中信出版社 2002 年版。

[4] Pan Jiahua & Chen Ying, Carbon budget proposal: a fair, sustainable international climate system framework. In: Wang Weiguang & Zheng Guoguang ed. *Reports to Cope with Climate Change*. Social Sciences Academic Press, 2009.

潘家华、陈迎:《碳预算方案:一个公平、可持续的国际气候制度框架》,见王伟光、郑国光主编《应对气候变化报告》,社会科学文献出版社 2009 年版。

[5] Shen Keting, Carbon tariff conflicts and its influence on China's manufacturing industry. *China Industrial Economics*, 2010 (1).

沈可挺:《碳关税争端及其对中国制造业的影响》,《中国工业经济》2010 年第 1 期。

[6] Wang Jun, Literature review on climate change economics. *World Economy*, 2008 (8).

王军:《气候变化经济学的文献综述》,《世界经济》2008 年第 8 期。

[7] Wen Jiajun, Unilateral carbon tariff and intellectual property right: two obstacles for global climate cooperation. *Green Leaf*, 2009 (10).

文佳筠:《单边碳关税与知识产权:全球气候合作的两大障碍》,《绿叶》2009 年第 10 期。

[8] Zhang Haibin, *Environment and International Relations: Rational Thinking on the Global Environment.* Shanghai People's Publishing House, 2008.

张海滨:《环境与国际关系:全球环境的理性思考》,上海人民出版社 2008 年版。

[9] Zhang Youguo, *Environmental Cost in China's Foreign Trade——Evaluation and Policy Study.* Research Report of the Institute of Quantitative & Technical Economics, Chinese Academy of Social Sciences, 2009.

张友国:《中国对外贸易中的环境成本——评估与对策研究》,中国社会科学院数量经济与技术经济研究所研究报告,2009。

[10] [Japanese] Sasaki Takeshi, [Korean] Kim Tea-Chang, trans. Han Lixin & Li Xinrong. *Global Environment and Publicness.* People's Publishing House, 2009.

[日]佐佐木毅、[韩]金泰昌:《地球环境与公共性》,韩立新、李欣荣译,人民出版社 2009 年版。

[11] Ackerman, Frank, *Can We Afford the Future—The Economics of a Warming World*, Zed Books, 2009.

[12] Heal, Geoffrey and Bengt Kristr M. , Uncertainty and Climate Change, *Environmental and Resource Economics*, Vol. 22 (1-2), 2002.

[13] Heal, Geoffrey, Climate Economics: A Meta-Review and Some Suggestions. *NBER Working Paper* 13927, April, 2008.

[14] IPCC-Working Group 1, *Climate Change* 2007*: the Physical Science Basis.*

[15] IPCC-Working Group 3, *Climate Change* 2007*: Mitigation of Climate Change.*

[16] Levitt, Steven D. and Stephen J. Dubner, What do Al Gore and Mount Pinatubo Havein Common? In SuperFreakonomics, Chapter 5, 2009.

[17] Nordhaus, William, A Stern Review on the Economics of Climate Change, *Journal of Economic Literature*, Vol. XLV, September 2007.

[18] Pindyck, R. O. , Uncertainty in Environmental Economics, *Review of Environmental Economics and Policy*, 2007 1(1).

[19] Victor, David, *Climate Change: Debating America's Policy Options*, Council on Foreign Relations Press, 2004.

[20] Weitzman, Martin L. , A Review of the Stern Review on the Economics of Climate Change, *Journal of Economic Literature*, Vol. XLV, September 2007.

[21] Weitzman, Martin L. , On Modelingand Interpreting the Economics of Catastrophic Climate Change, *the Review of Economics and Statistics*, Vol. 91 (1), June, 2009.

Opportunities and Challenges Posed by a Low Carbon Economy to China's Sustainable Development [①]

By YANG Zejun

Climate change is influencing and changing the current situation of the planet. We are facing such a reality: the icebergs are disappearing, the sea level is rising, the bottleneck constraint of energy resources is strengthening, natural disasters break out frequently with increasingly devastating force, animal and plant epidemics are "changing with each passing day", the living condition of man and other living creatures is facing challenges and threats. Climate change has become a focus of global concern. Since human society entered the industrial era, the global average temperature has risen by approximately 0.7℃ (1.3 ℉) and with the progress in globalization, industrialization and urbanization, the global average temperature is rising at a speed of 0.2℃ per decade[②]. With the warming up of the planet, to develop a low-carbon economy has become the universal trend worldwide. According to the calculation of the International Energy Agency (IEA), since 2008 China has become the largest country in global carbon emissions and with the rapid and continual economic growth China will undoubtedly become the focus of international society. To maintain our sustainable economic growth while making contributions to the global greenhouse gas (GHG) emission reduction, one of our priorities in the future is to develop a low-carbon economy.

---

① This article comes from my studies and practices at the low-carbon economy training symposium at the University of Edinburgh, Scotland, from January to April, 2009. Combining the reality and the future development of our economy and society, I made a brief introduction to my learning experience and basic views. I'm looking forward to getting some feedback from readers.

② UNDP Human Development Report 2007/2008, Sven Lindqvist: *Climate Changes in the* 21st *Century*.

I. Developing a Low-Carbon Economy Has Become a Universal Theme

To alleviate the threat posed by global warming to human existence, since the beginning of the 1990s different countries have actively made a series of steps to cope with climate change. In December 1990, the 45th United Nations General Assembly decided to draft *the United Nations Framework Convention on Climate Change* (UNFCC) (hereinafter referred to as the *Convention*), which was passed on May 9, 1992 and became a basic reference for countries in dealing with climate change. In December 1997, the Third Conference of the Parties to UNFCC was held in Tokyo, Japan. Representatives from 149 countries and regions agreed upon *the Kyoto Protocol*, aiming at restricting the greenhouse gas emissions of developed countries to stem global warming. They also established three flexible cooperation mechanisms for greenhouse gas emission reduction, namely, International Emission Trading (IET), Joint Implementation (JI) and Clean Development Mechanism (CDM). This conference has formed a basic system guarantee for the alleviation of global warming and the establishment of a low-carbon development mechanism.

In the 21st century, Britain has proposed the low-carbon economy concept, taking the lead in the research on climate change and the development of the low-carbon economic technology. It explicitly declared its strategy to develop a low-carbon economy. The low-carbon economy means that human economic activity is measured by carbon emissions, which is an economic model based on low energy consumption, low pollution and low emissions. Speaking from the viewpoint of economic activity, the carbon emission problem involves different sectors of the national economy and different areas of human activity. Therefore, in talking about the development of a low-carbon economy, we're actually referring to the development of a national economy based on the principle of strengthening carbon emission reduction. Some low-carbon economists pointed out that there are three new methods to establish a low-carbon economy: firstly, changing the traditional lifestyle, including people's luxurious model regarding food, shelter, clothing and transportation; secondly, optimizing the traditional extensive industrial structure, especially the development of energy-conservative and environment-friendly high technology industries and modern service industries; thirdly, improving the energy utilization efficiency and the development and utilization of new energies, mainly focusing on developing energy-conservative industries and accelerating the development of renewable energy sources[①].

In July 2007, America also promulgated *the Low Carbon Economy Act* and made the development of a low-carbon economy their new strategy to lead the future world economic trend. The Japanese government explicitly proposed its strategy to construct a "low-carbon society" and, in July 2007, passed the "Low-Carbon Social Act Plan", aimed at ushering in the wave of a global low-carbon revolution. The Korean government also made *the Low-Carbon Green Growth Basic Law* in 2009 and established an international image of green development. Russia promulgated *Russia's Energy Development Strategy before 2020*, aimed at incorporating the implementation of its ecological security policy as an important component of its energy strategy.

As global warming has become aggravated, the human living environment has been degenerating. The international climate organization stepped up its organization of global coordinated activities and countries also began to take active countermeasures.

1. Enforcing System Construction

The British government passed *the Climate Change Act* in 2008, under which the former Department of Energy and Department of Climate Change were merged into the Department of Energy and Climate Change (DECC). It established the Committee on Climate Change (CCC), independent from the government and with authority on policy making. Its main functions are: making independent suggestions for government to set its carbon budget and achieve its expected objective; monitoring the process of emission reduction and objective realization; conducting independent studies on, and analysis of, climate change; communicating with the parliament to share its research results and analyzing relevant information. At the same time, it established the

① Speech by Lord Turner, chairman of the Britain's Committee on Climate Change (CCC) in the Economic Forum on Developing a Low-Carbon Economy in the University of Edinburgh, on February 9, 2009.

climate change coordination mechanism across different governmental sectors and set up its climate change office at DECC. According to the actual emission conditions of different regions and enterprises, the country made a scientific carbon budget, explaining that in 2050 the emissions would be reduced by 60% compared with 1990. According to some relevant analyses[①], the accomplishment of the 50%-60% emission reduction objective means that the carbon dioxide emission per capita is 2.1-2.6t. Based on this level, Britain should reduce its emissions by 80% by 2050. To realize this objective, the British government proposed a series of countermeasures: to develop new materials and improve energy efficiency in architecture and industry; to implement low-carbon development in the power sector (with the focus on the year 2030); to mitigate the carbon emission intensity by the transport department; to promote low-carbon measures in the thermal industry; to implement low-carbon technology in various industries (especially to increase the investment in carbon capture and storage technology in the concrete and steel industries).

2. Establishing and Improving the Carbon Trade Market

The first one is the EU Emissions Trading Scheme (EU ETS). Under the world's largest cross-national-border emission trading scheme, different members make a commitment to realize corresponding emission objectives under *the Kyoto Protocol* and establish the current trading market and long-term trading market with a corresponding carbon emission quota. The enterprises with a good emission reduction effect can reap more economic profits by selling their emission quota on the market within its own quota. Contrarily, for those who cannot achieve the emission objective, they should purchase a certain quota from the market to seek a balance. Since the scheme was implemented in 2005, although some problems still exist, including the unreasonable distribution of the quota between regions and countries, the overall achievement is remarkable, which has promoted enterprise technology and strengthened the emission reduction intensity. Britain has also established the domestic Carbon Reduction Commitment (CRC) plan parallel with EU ETS, which stipulated that, from 2009, the

---

① The analysis report, finished by Britain's CCC research institute.

organizations which spent more than 6000 megawatts of electricity in 2008 must purchase the carbon emission quota, and further strengthened the pressure and motivation for British enterprises to reduce their emissions.

The second one is Joint Implementation (JI). It mainly refers to the mechanism for emission rights trading among the contracting parties under *the Tokyo Protocol* (see Annex I Countries), namely, a country obtains its corresponding emission quota by investing in effective emission reduction projects in another country and at the same time enters the market trade. Such a measure actually transfers the same emission quota between industrialized countries and designates the dominating power to the investors.

The third one is the Clean Development Mechanism (CDM). This mainly refers to the fact that developed countries obtain the emission quota by implementing emission reduction projects in non-Annex I countries and seek approval from the relevant institutions of the United Nations. The projects include the construction of such renewable energies as wind energy, water energy, solar energy and bioenergy; the improvement in energy efficiency; afforestation, wetland construction and carbon capture and storage (CCS). Currently, China has implemented the most CDM projects in the world since our economy is soaring and the relative investment cost is low.

Also, some countries cross-national regional carbon trade market is under construction and development. For example, the American sulfur dioxide emission trade market realized a 43% emission reduction from 1990 to 2007. With an increasing emphasis on the construction of the carbon emission trade market worldwide, a global carbon trade network will be gradually formed.

3. Stepping up the Method to Restrict Emissions and the Policy Support

The first one is to levy carbon taxes. Some countries including the European Union studied and levied the carbon tax to decrease carbon dioxide emissions. The carbon dioxide emission calculation is very complicated for every kind of fuel has its own carbon content and its tax rate should be based on the heat content calculated by the "British thermal unit". For the convenience of operation, some countries levy taxes based on the corresponding tax rate by the consumption of fuel (or volume of purchase) classified with different specifications. In the actual research and operation of taxation, there are some different voices in the international arena, arguing that levying carbon taxes will legalize some entities with high carbon emissions and this is detrimental to the reduction of global carbon emissions.

The second is the marketization of the government's action. The government implements its policies through marketized operations, namely some policies and projects to conserve energy and reduce emissions by the government are not necessarily directly operated by the government; instead, the government invested to establish corresponding emission reduction companies entirely independent from the government and they promoted the social and enterprise emission reduction through marketized action. For example, the British government founded two entirely independent non-profit private companies (Carbon Trust and Energy Saving Trust) through the DECC. Their function is to promote the energy conservation and emission reduction of some relevant enterprises and public sectors through the support of technological improvement and the study and management of carbon footprints or some project cooperation. From this there will appear some commercial opportunities for the development of low-carbon technology and investment opportunities for a low-carbon economy. From the practices during recent years, through the companies' marketized action, the implementation of the government's policy and the guidance of the social investment orientation, there have been remarkable achievements in energy conservation and emission reduction.

The third one is to standardize the Voluntary Market. The Voluntary Market is where the enterprises trade in the carbon emission based on the principle of mutual benefits and voluntariness outside the carbon trade market dominated by the government. Such an outside trade market is characterized by low trading cost, expansive scope and flexible trading ways, which plays an active role in energy conservation and emission reduction. With the gradually expanding trading scope, it has caught the attention of different social sectors. While fully affirming its positive effect, the government is also conducting studies on how to make policies to support and encourage its healthy development.

The fourth one is to establish an adaptation mechanism. The country should make it a priority to establish adaptive countermeasures against the natural disasters triggered by climate change, such as drought, flood, ice and snow and even landform change and rise in sea level. For example, it can carry out long-term monitoring, policy study, system construction, technology investment, space planning and defensive measures in water resources and the ecological environment and strengthen the construction of a corresponding monitoring management system.

The fifth is to adopt various incentive measures. This is to afford various forms of financial support or tax reduction support in the renewable energy and clean energy development, carbon emission reduction research projects, enterprises' low-carbon technology development and carbon footprint management, low-carbon technology and market services, etc. It means providing fiscal and financial services for the small enterprises' development of a low-carbon economy, especially to encourage and support the financial investment service industry which promotes the development of the low-carbon economy. The supportive methods include direct capital injection, indirect tax reliefs and cooperation through the projects of trust companies.

The sixth one is to exert the influence of the non-governmental organizations. In climate change and the low-carbon economy, Britain has established non-governmental organizations in policy research, information development, market guidance and financial intermediaries, which are important complementary additions to the governmental sectors. The Carbon Disclosure Project (CDP) is a typical non-governmental organization to cope with climate change, which is closely tied to the government's climate change management sector and has provided a carbon emission information exchange platform for investors or enterprises. CDP has founded worldwide enterprise carbon emission data-bases and played an important role in monitoring key enterprise carbon emissions and their influence on climate change.

II. Severe Challenges for China to Promote a Low-Carbon Economy

Accompanying the era of industrialization and urbanization is the consumption of large amounts of energy resources and even harm to the natural environment. In the 1950s, both Europe and Japan underwent difficult processes. Our country is right at the stage of the rapid development of its industrialization and urbanization. Facing the same subject as the Western developed countries, we cannot follow their industrialized "exploitative" and devastating road, but we must also face the reality, proceeding from the reality to seek a new development road. To develop a low-carbon economy is the new ideal formed in international society and is also the important trend for the world's future economic development. Developed countries have equipped themselves with capacity and advantages in developing the low-carbon economy while developing countries, China in particular, are comparatively backward. Especially in the 21st century, resource and environmental restrictions in China's economic development have strengthened, plunging China into many dilemmas, such as whether to continue the development, what kind of development and how to promote the development. It can be said that to develop a low-carbon economy has posed pressure and challenges to China's economic development in many areas.

Firstly, there is China's comparatively low-level stage of rapid economic development at present. As a developing country, China's GDP per capita is still very low and development is still the priority. On the one hand, China still maintains an extensive economic development model. During the thirty years since the reform and opening up, China has gone for rapid economic growth with a high investment in energy resources and at a high cost of the ecological environment. As a matter of fact, some costs have to be paid for at the stage of economic development, but some costs can be avoided. However, for a limited overall national economic and technological development level, the economic growth mode dependent on high input cannot be fundamentally transformed in a short span of time. How to tread on a road with low consumption, low emissions and high growth constitutes an important subject for our future. On the other hand, China is also a "global factory". During recent years, our foreign trade has maintained a rapid growth and the trade surplus has increased significantly. In 2008, the processing trade accounted for 41.1% in the total volume of foreign trade and 47.3% in the total volume of exports. This fully demonstrates that, as a global factory, China's standing is increasing and China has made contributions to the global economy by exploiting its land and through energy and resource consumption. However, the original extensive global factory mode cannot be sustained. The transition of the "global factory" has posed new challenges to China's economy and social development. At the same time, our regional economic development is extremely imbalanced, with a huge gap between the western and eastern regions. Shanghai's GDP per capita, ranked the highest in China, is 8 times higher than that of Guizhou, the lowest. Under such circumstances, different regions must have different economic and social development goals and policy orientation. In accepting the eastern developed regions' industrial transfer, some underdeveloped western regions still regard economic growth as their objective and ignore the protection of resources and the environment. Some even boast of their large space to accommodate carbon emissions and continue to invest in large-scale industries with high energy consumption and emissions, tending to follow the old extensive growth road of the eastern region at the beginning of the reform and opening up. Therefore, we still have a long way to go in transforming our economic development mode and improving the quality and efficiency of our economic growth.

Secondly, there is overdependence in energy consumption on coal resources. Our energy structure basically features the dominance of coal resources, with over 70% of coal resources used in energy production and the consumption structure (see the table below) of all fossil fuels, over 90%. Such a feature in our energy structure is a key factor contributing to the rapid increase in the carbon emissions amidst our economy prosperity. The abundant coal resources are one of the advantages to ensure our economic development and making full use of this resource advantage is essential to the realization of sustainable development. Therefore, how to optimize the energy structure and significantly improve the energy efficiency constitutes an important subject for the development of our low-carbon economy.

China's Energy Production and Consumption Structure

Project	1978	2000	2008
Energy Production (million ton)	62.77	129.0	260
Coal (%)	70.3	72.0	76.7
Petroleum (%)	23.7	18.1	10.4
Natural Gas (%)	2.9	2.8	3.9
New Energy (%)	3.1	7.2	9.0
Energy Consumption (million ton)	57.14	138.55	265.48

(contd.)

Project	1978	2000	2008
Coal (%)	70.7	67.8	68.7
Petroleum (%)	22.7	23.2	18.7
Natural Gas (%)	3.2	2.4	3.8
New Energy (%)	3.4	6.7	8.9

Note: New energy mainly includes hydropower, nuclear power and wind power, etc.
Data source: *China Statistical Abstract* 2009.

Thirdly, there is a comparatively weak ability in scientific and technical innovation. With the trend to internationalization in the low-carbon economic development, there will be increasingly fierce competition over carbon emission rights between different countries. However, the key link to improve the effect of energy conservation and emission reduction lies in technical innovation, which is still a weak link for our country. Although in recent years China has implemented a strategy for national innovation and improved technical the innovation competence and level, currently our macro-environmental incentive mechanism and enterprise innovation motivation mechanism are yet to be formed. In particular, the immaturity of the corresponding low-carbon economic market will inevitably become the "Achilles' heel" for the current development of our low-carbon economy and also pose higher demands to its future development. Also, it will suffer long-term restrictions on the economic technology and development strategy by developed countries.

Fourthly, there is a strengthened international technology trade barrier. Strengthening international exchange and cooperation for low-carbon technologies is an important way to cope with climate change and develop a low-carbon economy, and also a fundamental foothold for a mutual understanding and cooperation between different countries in their shared global objectives. The continual deepening of the international financial crisis has enhanced the global technology trade barrier under the pretext of carbon emissions, which begins to exert a deep influence on international trade. During recent years, in some countries and regions, there have been some studies and proposals about measures concerning the implementation of a "carbon tariff" to intervene and enforce the rules of the import and export trade, which has gained the world's concern. They are aimed at occupying the "moral high ground" and consolidating developed countries' control and clout in the international economic area. Overall, such a predilection is unfavorable to international technical exchange and cooperation and, in particular, it will inevitably exert a profound influence on the development of a low-carbon economy in developing countries and also may trigger a new round of trade-wars from a new angle. The technology trade barrier has obviously become a heated topic in strengthening cooperation and negotiation in the area of climate change between developed countries and developing countries.

Fifthly, there is a growing external pressure and more challenges. China, as one of the world's largest carbon emission countries inevitably suffers various pressure from developed countries. On the one hand, as the representative of developing countries, the Chinese government is pushed to the forefront and flattered as the "savior"; China is forced to shoulder the responsibility that is inconsistent with its reality. On the other hand, developed countries have strengthened the barriers in trade, technology and capital to China and often make irresponsible commitments in capital and technical assistance. Besides, developed countries raised more concrete demands on China in the field of climate change, enforcing the pressure and challenges in China's low-carbon economy field①.

(1) They hope the Chinese government should be more dedicated to its commitment to emission reduction. The British government assumes that at the end of 2009, the UN Climate Change Conference held in Copenhagen marked an important transition for the planning of international climate change during a certain period. The Chinese government's attitude will play a critical role. Some high officials from the British government, institutions and organizations have fully recognized the contribution the Chinese government has made in the area

① The opinions mentioned above were proposed by the senior consultant of the British Prime Minister, the senior officers in relevant governmental sectors (including DECC, CCC and the Ministry of Finance) and senior managers of the carbon emission industry during my exchanges with them and participation in the low-carbon economy training symposium in Britain from January to April, 2009. These views and demands were raised unilaterally and some were objective while some were one-sided and unrealistic, but they offered in-depth solutions for China to cope with climate change and develop a low-carbon economy on a global stage.

of energy conservation and emission reduction and they hope the Chinese government will continue to take an active part in various activities in international climate change and play a more important role in this field, especially to show a more active attitude in its commitment to emission reduction.

(2) The consultation about the technology transfer between countries should be strengthened. The senior officials of the British government made it explicit that Britain is willing to provide capital and technical assistance to support China's energy conservation and emission reduction, but the capital is often in a package with the technology. Since it involves intellectual property rights protection, on the one hand it should enhance its communication with enterprises equipped with relevant technologies and realize the technology transfer through market action; on the other hand, it hopes China will make more detailed and explicit demands in the technology transfer, for example, outlining in which areas and in which kinds of technology. In this way, unnecessary misunderstanding will be avoided and the technology transfer can be completed effectively. In particular, it should be made explicit that the technology transfer cannot be used for other motives.

(3) The construction of the emission monitoring system should be enhanced. Some high officials believe that currently there is corruption in China's carbon emission monitoring for both objective and subjective reasons. Such a situation is not helpful to international cooperation and assistance. Some government high officials noted that they hope the Chinese government would step up its all-dimensional construction of a systematic monitoring mechanism over carbon emissions, adhere to the transparent and fair rules of the game and ensure objectivity, justice and accuracy in the emission monitoring process.

(4) More pragmatic policies should be implemented in the CDM management. Some high-level enterprise managers and investors proposed that China boasted a large investment market in the field of emission reduction and developed countries leading in the carbon emission reduction technology area, like the European Union, had motivation to invest in the CDM project in China. Due to the low prices in the international carbon trade market and inflexible price management in China, the investor assumes that the suppressed profit space may influence the passion for investment.

In December 2009, before and after the UN Climate Change

Conference in Copenhagen, the Chinese government fully expressed its determination to cope with global climate change and explicitly made it its objective to reduce the emissions per GDP in 2010 by 40%-45% compared to those in 2005, having set a good example for developing countries as well as developed countries to follow. China's emission reduction objective is down-to-earth and also requires hard efforts to accomplish. To achieve this, we should actively confront various challenges and fulfill the sacred mission that history has endowed on us.

III. Important Opportunities for Us to Promote Low-Carbon Economic Development

The low-carbon economy, a new economic area, marks a new historical revolution and leap for economic and social development as well as an inevitable trend in the world's progress. It has brought new opportunities for man's sustainable development. During the 30 years since China's reform and opening up, remarkable achievements have been achieved in social and economic development. The era of a low-carbon economy has arrived at the right time. A new round in the economic revolution will provide new development opportunities for China to realize leapfrogging economic and social development.

To actively promote the development of a low-carbon economy will create better development opportunities and space for us in the following key links and areas.

Firstly, it is helpful to our institutional innovation. The development of a low-carbon economy will make it inevitable to transform the system and mechanism. To begin with, we should promote the value transformation. We should fully recognize that a low-carbon economy is the trend leading the world's future development and to keep up with the trend we must make it a national strategy to develop the low-carbon economy and include it as an important part in the long-term national planning. Also, we should improve the legal system construction. The development of a low-carbon economy requires the guarantee of an improved legal system. Reversing the transmission of the pressure to promote a low-carbon economy, a highly efficient market guarantee system and operation mechanism will be gradually formed. In addition, we should improve the policy incentive mechanism. We should make an organic combination between macro-economic policy and low-carbon economic development strategy, gradually establishing a sound policy environment and space and forming a motivation mechanism in which society is the main force to promote the development of a low-carbon economy.

Secondly, it is good for the adjustment and optimization of the macro-economic structure. The low-carbon economy has posed challenges to the extensive development model, especially those production modes, circulation modes and lifestyles which are unsuitable for the requirements of the low-carbon development. The transformation of the traditional lifestyles including the consumption concept and structure, the optimization of the extensive industrial structure, including production and sale methods, and the significant improvement in the energy efficiency and the development and utilization of new energies have promoted the transformation of the macro-economic structure and social activities towards a low-carbon economic model.

Thirdly, it is good for the enterprise's technical innovation. Innovation is the inexhaustible source for a country's development and technical innovation is the lifeline for an enterprise's survival and development. The enterprise's technical innovation should be guided by the government's policy and driven by the benefits for the market. With the development and maturity of a low-carbon economic society, higher demands will be made on the enterprise's technical innovation and the intensification of the reform of the state-owned enterprises will be made more urgent. In particular, the establishment of the carbon emission trade market and its international development will speed up the competition among enterprises and improve the enterprise's self-innovation ability.

Fourthly, it is good for the prosperity and innovation of the financial market. The British government employed its sound financial innovation monitoring system to promote and participate in the development of the global carbon trade market and carbon financial market and established a comparatively healthy current and long-term trading market and network for carbon emissions. It supported and encouraged the carbon financing of the private sector and promoted the prosperity of the financial market and enriched the financial products, having established its leading position in the global carbon financial market. Our financial market is comparatively weak. The development of a low-carbon economy and the gradual establishment of a comparatively independent carbon trade and financing market have brought good opportunities to improve our financial market and the innovation of our financial services. At the same time, during the process of innovating the carbon trade market, we can expand our exchange and consultation with developed countries, increase the depth and breadth of the negotiations and fight for developed countries' technology and capital support.

Fifthly, it is helpful for China to take the initiative in coping with global climate change. As one of the engines of the global economy, the Chinese economy has made enormous contributions to the development and prosperity of the global economy. In doing research on climate change, developed countries have neglected the cheap and good products China has provided them and the resources and environmental sacrifice China has made and instead accused China's production and trade practices. Indubitably, we should also further reflect on the import and export trade strategy since the beginning of the reform and opening up and improve the quality and level of our foreign trade. By implementing the low-carbon economic development strategy, we can not only improve our international competitiveness, make the social and economic development more sustainable and improve people's living standards, but also allay the bottleneck restrictions of energy resources on economic and social development and strengthen the national energy security development strategy; at the same time it can also effectively assuage the pressure from different sectors of the international community and enable China to take the initiative in international strategy.

IV. Reflections on Our Development of the Low-Carbon Economy

In the 21st century, especially since the financial crisis, developed countries have been seeking a new development strategy to sustain their leading and controlling role in the process of global economic development. Currently, a new economic pattern featuring the development of new energies and materials as the core industry in leading the development of the world's low-carbon economy has emerged. The European Union, with Britain as its head, has been leading the field of the low-carbon economy since the 1990s and since

President Obama came to power it has been the shared orientation of both Europe and America. Japan is also ranked among the top countries in the field of energy conservation and emission reduction. It can be predicted that future low-carbon economic development, especially the development of the core industry, will dominate the trend in global economic development.

The Chinese government is riding the wave of this trend and it must have a clear understanding and a definite strategy. On the one hand, we should be fully aware that there is an objective gap between our country and developed countries and the new trend dominated by developed countries may bring new impacts and unfavorable factors to our country. Therefore, we should actively adopt international countermeasures and brave the possibly great challenges from different fields. On the other hand, we should adapt ourselves to the mainstream of international development, grasp the important opportunities brought about by the current development of a low-carbon economy, catch up with the pace of the global advanced technical innovation and promote the realization of China's sustainable development and leapfrog development.

It is a shared responsibility and obligation for different countries to cope with global warming. China should realize that, as a developing country, it should regard it as a top priority to establish a moderately prosperous society and realize the objective of socialist modernization. Also, it should be aware that the development objective is to improve people's life quality and bring benefits to future generations and it should play an active role in alleviating global warming and developing the low-carbon economic progress. Firstly, as a developing country, China must stick to the "shared but differentiated principle" and oppose decisively developed countries' mixing the carbon emission "stock" contradiction with the "increment" change, their unanimous emphasis on the current carbon emission "increment" condition and their inclination to transfer their historical responsibilities to developing countries, so as to protect developing countries' right to development. It should be made explicit that developed countries must take responsibilities for the large amount of greenhouse gas emissions since the industrial revolution and must show their sincerity rather than point the finger at others in the process of global greenhouse gas emission reduction. They bear responsibilities and obligations to provide essential assistance and support to developing countries in terms of technologies, capital and services. Also, as a large economy, China should build an image of a strong country and should have a sense of responsibility, actively promoting energy conservation and emission reduction and developing the low-carbon economy worldwide. It should be said that through more than three decades' of reform and opening up, China's economy has come into a new development stage. Since the traditional extensive development model is unsustainable, it is inevitable for us to transform our economic development mode and contribute to a low-carbon development and scientific development.

Entering the 21st century China has secured remarkable achievements and made great progress by making long-term development strategies and guidelines in energy conservation and emission reduction and the promotion of scientific development, clarifying its periodical objectives and implementing a series of policy measures. In the "11th Five-Year Plan" made in 2005, the Chinese government made it explicit that by 2010 the GDP energy consumption per capita should decrease by about 20% compared to 2005, with the total discharge of the major pollutants decreasing by 10%. The ambition of these objectives and tasks is incomparable to those of any other countries in the world and there must be great difficulty in accomplishing them. In the first three years' accumulation of the "11th Five-Year Period", our GDP energy consumption per capita decreased by 10.1%, with the emission decrease in chemical oxygen demand and sulfur dioxide reaching 66.1% and 89.5% of the target respectively①. Overall, international society has fully acknowledged China's efforts and achievements in the field of energy conservation and emission reduction. At the same time, we should also learn from developed countries their useful experience and practices from the perspective of implementing our scientific development outlook and promoting the progress of our energy conservation and emission reduction work.

1. Enhancing the Research on the Development Strategy of a Low-Carbon Economy

Since the "11th Five-Year Plan" proposed establishing a resource-

① Sina Finance: *National Development and Reform Commission: the Objective of the Eleventh Five-Year Plan Is Expected to be Completed.*

conserving and environment-friendly society, the Chinese government has made a series of policies and measures to step up energy conservation and emission reduction. In 2008, China put forward a clear strategic guideline[①] in developing a low-carbon economy and caused much repercussion in the international community, to which some developed countries showed their strong support and acclaim. Energy conservation and emission reduction is the core requirement of the low-carbon economy. From the long-term development strategy, China needs to further enhance the systematic research on the low-carbon economy, including the international strategy for a low-carbon economy and domestic overall development. At present, we should focus on the overall demand for scientific development, gradually press forward relevant legislation on low-carbon economic development, and enhance the clean development mechanism characterized by low energy consumption and low emissions, so as to form a low-carbon development model with Chinese characteristics.

2. *Research and Exploration of the Establishment of a Low-Carbon Trade Market*

The key in developing a low-carbon economy is to make full use of the market means, regarding "carbon emissions" as a "product" for trade. If the emission actors can obtain economic benefits during the emission reduction process, energy conservation and emission reduction will become the enterprises' conscious activity and innate motivation. At present, our carbon emission private market is in formation and some regions have begun to establish the regional trade market. The Chinese government should step up the corresponding market research and tracking, encourage and support the private organizations' bold exploration and practices, summarize experience from different aspects and explore from the experience how to establish a domestic carbon emission trade market system that is in accordance with our own development demand. This is beneficial to promoting the formation of our low-carbon economic mechanism and the sound development of the

---

① President Hu Jintao explicitly put forward the strategic thinking to develop a low-carbon economy in his speech at the Central Economic Working Conference at the end of 2008.

low-carbon economy while accelerating the transformation of our economic development mode and the construction of a resource-conserving and environment-friendly society. On the one hand, it is helpful to improve the enterprise's self-innovation ability and optimize the industrial structure; on the other hand, it can also develop relevant new service industries, including the intermediary services and market in the form of low-carbon finance, low-carbon technologies and low-carbon information and form new economic growth points.

3. Developing Clean Energy and Renewable Energy Sources

In a short span of time, it is not possible for China to change its energy consumption structure featured by the domination of coal, but we must focus on establishing a long-term secure energy development strategy. On the one hand, we need to enhance our technical innovation in coal energy production and consumption and improve the energy efficiency, especially discover new development advantages in the elaborate processing of the coal and its recycling, storage and reuse to form a new high-tech industrial agglomeration; on the other hand, we should improve the incentive policy for such renewable energies as wind energy, solar energy, tidal energy and bioenergy and gradually form an incentive mechanism to promote the development of new energies. We also need to improve our energy structure and provision guarantee and promote the establishment of an energy security guarantee system. At the same time, to promote its healthy development, we must enhance the overall industrial and regional planning of the development of new energies, ameliorate the market price mechanism and establish a corresponding information network system, guide the investment direction and industrial layout and prevent new overinvestment and reconstruction.

4. Improving the Emission Monitoring System

We should regard the improvement of the emission monitoring system as an important content in our low-carbon economic development and gradually form the index system, standard system and assessment system for emission monitoring and the corresponding enforced punishment system. At the same time, we should establish an effective emergency management system targeted at the pollutant discharge and try hard to assure a fair and just market monitoring mechanism and create a sound operating environment for the low-carbon economic market.

5. Hastening to Levy Environmental Taxes

Although the carbon tax has a significant positive influence on emission reduction, its implementation is not possible during a short span of time. We should conduct research on the timing and conditions for levying carbon taxes based on the reality of domestic development and the great backdrop of international development. At present, we should accelerate the process of tax reform, put forward the environmental tax at the right time and promote legislation for environmental protection. This is not only an effective means for the implementation of the strategy to conserve energy and reduce emissions, but also an important measure taken by China to actively cooperate with the international community to tackle climate change.

6. Improving the Regional Transfer Payment and Compensation Mechanism

According to the layout of different function zones, we should categorize the restricted development regions in need of environmental protection, such as Sanjiangyuan Conservation Region, energy resource protection region and ecological and nature protection region. We should establish a corresponding ecological compensation mechanism to promote a coordinated development between regions on the principle of guaranteeing an egalitarian basic public service and with scientific methods. Firstly, we should improve the financial transfer payment system and step up the support of the central Chinese government for ecological compensation; secondly, we should establish an effective market operation mechanism and policy orientation, fully exerting the positive factors in the private and social sectors; thirdly, promote regional dialogues and coordination to form a positive interaction mechanism for regional biological compensation.

7. *Developing the Energy Conservation and Emission Reduction Service Industry*

We should encourage and support different private enterprises to promote energy conservation and the emission reduction process with various market operation methods such as a project sales model, facility service model, BOT model, energy-cost trust or contract model, so as to gradually develop the "voluntary market" of energy conservation and emission reduction and make the overall social energy conservation and emission reduction effective. In recent years, China has made some progress and obtained some achievements in this area, but there is still great potential to be tapped, which needs the government to create a more positive environment and conditions, especially to form good incentive mechanisms in the tax policy and financial policy. It should mobilize positive factors in different areas and gradually improve and promote the prosperity of the low-carbon service market and network to form another important growth pole to promote healthy and sustainable economic development.

8. *Establishing a Scientific System to Tackle Climate Change*

We should gradually change the traditional "anti-disaster" concept of "battling against nature" into a "disaster-avoidance" mind-set which respects the development and changes in the natural world and ecological environment issues and is consistent with the situation. We should establish various systems, make overall planning and take corresponding defensive measures to cope with climate change, enhance capacity building to cope with climate change and promote a harmonious co-existence between man and nature and a virtuous cycle of the natural environment.

9. *Strengthening and Improving the International Cooperation Coordination Mechanism*

At present, China has become the focus of international emission problems and this also brings a good opportunity for us to implement international cooperation strategies. We should strengthen international cooperation in the climate change area. We should change our passive stance into an active one, start from energy conservation and emission reduction, fully prepare different international cooperation plans on the premise of guaranteeing economic security, proactively seek international capital and technical support, make full use of global resources to promote our industrial upgrading and structure adjustment, as well as promoting a fundamental transformation of our economic development mode.

10. Promoting the Publicity and Education for a Low-Carbon Economy

At present, there are some misunderstandings about a low-carbon economy in society, such as the confusion between the carbon industry and carbon emissions and the antagonism between the development of a low-carbon economy and a national economy. Through publicity and education for a low-carbon economy, on the one hand, it can remove different misunderstandings and promote the idea of developing a low-carbon economy; on the other hand, it can promote a sense of social responsibility in energy conservation and emission reduction, encourage active actions and surveillance in society to protect the environment and conserve energy and form a healthy social ambience. At the same time, education should start from the elementary and middle school by popularizing low-carbon economic knowledge to improve the overall quality of the public's energy conservation and emission reductions and their code of conduct to form a social environment in which everyone is promoting low-carbon economic development.

Overall, at the current stage, we face both opportunities and challenges in developing the low-carbon economy and the former is greater than the latter. For a large developing country like us, challenges will be channeled into compulsion and motivation. Only if we grasp the opportunity tightly, brave the challenge and change it into an opportunity can we step up our development amidst the global competition in the 21st century and maintain an overall coordinated and sustainable development. It should be said that China has fully recognized the environmental problems and the conditions facing its economic development and is fully prepared to accelerate the transformation of its economic development mode, promote the green economy and low-carbon economic development. We believe that under the guidance of the important "Thought of Three Represents" (http://en.wikipedia.org/wiki/Three_Represents) and Deng Xiaoping Theory and through the learning and implementation of the Scientific Outlook on Development, we can indubitably promote the transformation of our economic model, meet the great target of realizing China's modernization and a moderately prosperous society and realize the great rejuvenation of the Chinese nation.

A Low Carbon Economy: Coping with Climate Change and Air Pollution

By ZHANG Shiqiu

I. Introduction

The two subjects to improve air quality and allay climate change are inseparable. Firstly, China is facing severe air pollution problems as well as enormous pressure from the climate change problem; air pollution and climate change constitute the dual challenge for China; secondly, air pollutants have influences on the climate and people's health. Because of the differences in the pollutant and its physiochemical process, air pollutants may aggravate or alleviate the climate change. The climatic effects of air pollution will become the top subject in future international climate negotiations; thirdly, because of the closeness in their sources and the control technology, and because measures taken are relevant to the policy, the control of air pollutants and the climate change problem have symbiotic effects and shared methods for a win-win situation; fourthly, we have conducted studies on the climate effect, climate change, the Asian brown cloud and black charcoal in regional pollution, but the studies are not systematic and recognized internationally. In-depth and systematic studies on the relationship between regional pollution and climate change and its healthy, social and economic effects, the integrated basic research and control policy research in particular, will help China to know both itself and its adversaries in the negotiations and to take the initiative.

II. Interaction and Innate Relation between Air Pollution and Climate Change

Firstly, large parts of the conventional air pollutants and the greenhouse gas represented by carbon dioxide come from a common emission source. The climate is influenced by greenhouse gas like carbon dioxide, emitted from fossil fuel through the greenhouse effect, which is the major driving force for the global warming caused by human activities; at the same time, sulfur dioxide, nitric oxide, volatile organic compounds and particulate matter emitted from the burning of fossil fuels are major pollutants influencing the quality of the air environment. The energy structure propping up China's current economic development is mainly characterized by coal and such a trend will continue for decades in the future. The burning of coal will emit large amounts of air pollutants such as sulfur dioxide and particulate matter, causing serious pollution. China is the country with the most sulfur dioxide emissions worldwide and one third of its territory is influenced by the pollution of acid rain. At the same time, rapid urbanization and the increase in car usage cause combined pollution (coal-smoke pollution and vehicle emission pollution) in Chinese cities and urban agglomerations. Besides, although the greenhouse gas emission per capita is low in China, it has already been one of the largest greenhouse gas emission countries in the world in terms of its total emission volume.

Secondly, conventional air pollutants have a dual effect on climate change: they can both increase and decrease the temperature. Although it is uncertain scientifically whether human activities will increase or decrease the temperature of various aerosol concentrations in the air, the result from the newest studies shows that the changes in the surface reflectance caused by the black charcoal sediment on the surface of ice and snow has accelerated the glacier melting process. During recent years, the international community has given special attention to the problem of black charcoal's irradiation effect. Take black charcoal for example, the black charcoal particulate matter endangers human health and at the same time, similar to carbon dioxide, it will increase the temperature. However, their difference is that the black charcoal survives a shorter time than the greenhouse gas. There are also studies showing that during the prolonged climate transformation on the planet, the greenhouse gas (leading to the global warming) and the aerosol (leading to the global cooling) remain the two major factors. The difference lies in that during the early era of climate change on the geological time scale, these two factors originated from nature while now on account of human beings (see Figure 1).

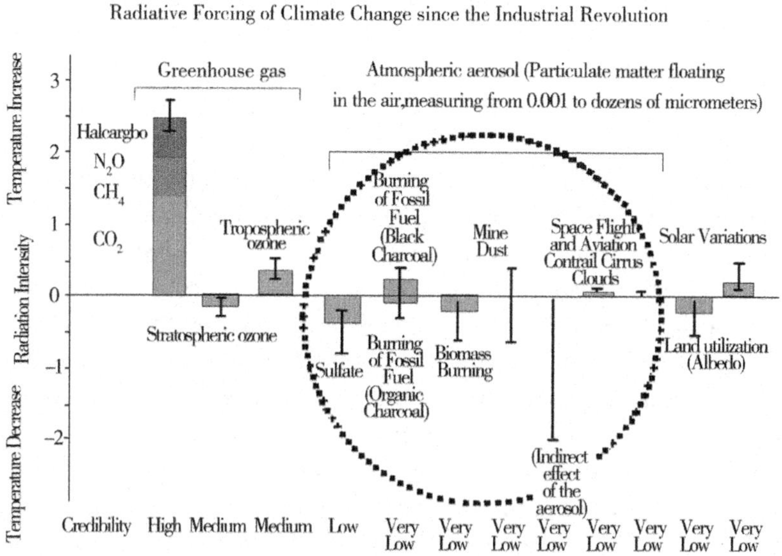

Figure 1 Interaction between Climate Change and Air Pollution

Thirdly, control strategy and measures have symbiotic benefits and costs. Current studies clearly show that there is an innate relationship between air pollution and climate change. Air pollution control and greenhouse gas emission reduction bears an obvious relationship with each other in the strategy, policy and technology respects. For example, whether in coping with the climate change or improving air quality, generally we will take measures such as adjusting the energy structure and industrial structure, improving energy efficiency and transportation structure and control, which have obvious symbiotic benefits. The carbon emission reduction effect at the Beijing 2008 Olympic Games shows that the series of measures aimed at improving the air quality during the Beijing Olympic Games not only reduced large amounts of air pollutants, guaranteed the fulfillment of the green Olympic commitment, but also reduced greatly the carbon dioxide emissions. Our research findings show that in hosting the Olympic Games, the carbon dioxide emissions in Beijing increased by 650, 000 to 1. 98 million tons owing to the construction and operation of the Olympic venues, urban transport and domestic and international air travel. However, at the same time, to fulfill its green Olympic commitment and with various measures to control air pollution, such as adjusting the energy structure, controlling industrial pollution, improving the energy efficiency and controlling the transport pollution emissions, we have decreased by about 8. 37 million tons' carbon dioxide emissions, with the net emission reduced by 6. 38 million to 7. 72 million tons. Such a result shows the objective existence of the symbiotic benefits. However, at the same time, we should also recognize that the technologies, measures and policies for different objectives may also have a negative effect on the realization of another objective. For example, the application of desulfurizing and denitration technologies for coal-fired power plants may increase the comprehensive energy consumption; although the combustion efficiency of the diesel engine may be higher than that of the gasoline engine and increasing the percentage of diesel engines may decrease the emission of carbon dioxide, carbon monoxide and hydrocarbon, without effective exhaust treatment technologies, it may increase the emission of oxynitride and particulate matter, and especially may produce severer fine particle pollution and cause greater health costs. Also, in the area of solar power generation and electric bicycle, although they use clean energies, without life cycle assessment, the actual energy consumption may be even higher. This requires innovation and improvement of the electricity generation technology from the perspective of the life cycle. At the same time, we should make effective and bio-safety disposal of the battery, enabling it to satisfy the requirements of greenhouse gas emission reduction and promote, or at least not increase, the emission of air pollutants and vice-versa.

In consideration of the innate relationship between air pollution and climate change, it is necessary for us to integrate climate change and the air pollution effect and make a unified policy system from the perspective of a synergistic effort to seek win-win methods, establish a comprehensive air quality management system and policy system that is climate-change-friendly and promote a win-win situation in the effective development of the economy, climate change and air quality.

III. Strategy Adjustments Are Needed in the Face of the Severe Domestic Environment and Development Problems and Climate Change Pressure

During the 30 years since the reform and opening up, the Chinese economy has developed rapidly but its environmental problems and crisis have assumed prominence; the environmental and social issues, economic development, social stability and global environmental political relations have become increasingly interconnected and the trend to integration is more pronounced. In January 2010, the executive meeting of the State Council chaired by Premier of the State Council, Wen Jiabao, emphasized that although our environmental protection work is effective, the overall condition of environmental pollution is not stemmed, the environmental surveillance capability still lags behind and the situation remains grim.

According to our research on China's environment and development issues①, China has to face several basic contradictions: (1) while creating employment opportunities and improving income to promote economic growth, we should realize the development-environment-society harmony and stability; (2) while alleviating poverty, we should strengthen the environmental protection and improve the environmental quality; (3) under the situation of imbalanced regional development, we should avoid the transfer of polluting industries and promote a fair and efficient distribution and allocation of environmental resources in different groups and regions; (4) in international trade, we should exert the comparative advantage of the economy while improving the "sustainability" of the export problem, namely to change the problem of exporting products abroad but retaining pollution domestically; (5) the intertwinement of the intensification of environmental resource agglomeration and the expansion of the income gap has exacerbated social contradictions and conflicts; (6) the environmental protection work is strengthened, but the old problem is yet to be eliminated while new problems keep cropping up. We must cut the stock while controlling the increment; (7) the overlapping of the local-regional-global environmental problem, the combined and synergistic effect, the synergy cost and the effect problem are pronounced, requiring us to select methods for environmental protection from an integrated perspective.

Also, China's own economic development and diplomatic pressure from the international community have also posed essential demands on the transformation of China's industrial structure and growth mode. The following factors inevitably force us to make strategic adjustments: (1)

---

① Refer to some relevant articles by the author.

the predicament of China's export-oriented economy must be faced; (2) industrial changes and adjustments of developed countries and regions like America and the European Union and possible and relevant policy orientation are likely to result in the new trade order; (3) the new pattern of climate change will impose pressure on China, the largest potential energy consumption country and greenhouse gas emission country; (4) the influence of America, the European Union and the international environmental policy on China, especially the possible implementation of the carbon dioxide emission trade/transaction and carbon tax will compel us to consider how to avoid possible trade barriers.

Considering the society-economy-environment evolution and the changes in the pattern at home and abroad and pressure from global economic crises and the global environment, can China predispose "crisis" towards "opportunity", seek and establish a development model that is sustainable and with Chinese characteristics? This will not only directly influence China's standing, but also set up an example for developing and fast developing countries. It will also inevitably influence the global economic trend, the environment and resource conditions in the future and even a new global management model and the relationship of checks and balances, as well as the transformation of the economic development model.

IV. China Is Facing Dual Pressure from Air Pollution and Climate Change

Owing to China's rapid urbanization and industrialization, many pollutants are released into the air and their interplay causes serious compound air pollution in our urban agglomeration areas. The compound air pollution is characterized by the increase in the intensity of the oxidizing species in the air and fine particulate matter, the dropping of visibility and the degradation of the regional atmospheric environment. In essence, the pollution is represented by the interplay of many species which are the sources of each other and the interconnection of various processes in their transformation in the air.

During three decades of the reform and opening up, China has secured continual and rapid economic growth at the sacrifice of energy consumption and the environment, which unleashes concentrated atmospheric environment pollution problems in China which existed in developed countries for nearly a century. In 2000, about 63.5% of the urban air quality exceeded the national secondary standard, with the smog and fine particulate matter produced from coal burning in 11 big cities causing 50,000 adolescent deaths and 40,000 new cases of chronic bronchitis annually. Until 2007, about 40% of the prefecture-level cities and cities above the level failed to reach the secondary level, days of hazy weather in mega cities increased and 60% of urban citizens have no access to clean air. In the 500 monitored cities, 56.2% had acid rain and about 10% suffered severe acid rain (pH < 4.5). The traditional pollutants (index) such as sulfur dioxide and TSP were controlled overall. In 2008, China's sulfur dioxide emissions decreased from 26 million tons in 2007 to less than 25 million tons (see Figure 2). However, the pollution of oxynitride, ozone and inhalable particles is still grim and is even exacerbating. At present, China's regional air pollution is expanding across different regions. Owing to the interaction of patches of emissions and the overlying effect of transference, the combined effect of different factors in the pollution source, process and mechanism of action transforms air pollution into a combined pollution which has a wider effect.

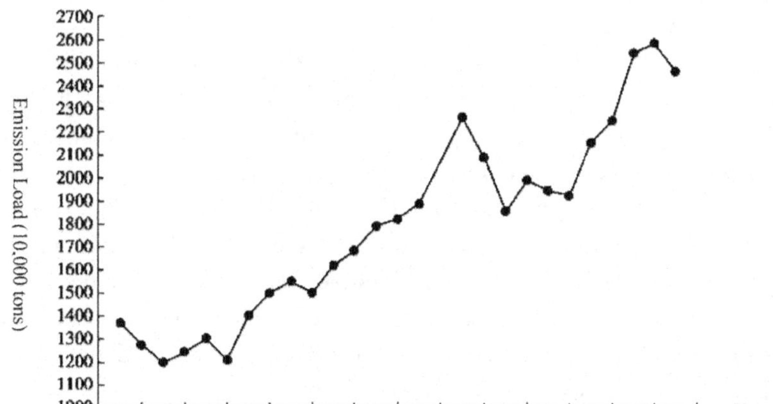

Figure 2 Variation in China's Sulfur Dioxide Emission Load from 1980 to 2008 (Summary from China Statistical Yearbook on the Environment)

China became the world's largest greenhouse gas emission country in 2009. At present, our emission per capita is still comparatively low, an equivalent of 87% of the global average and 33% ① of the countries in the OECD. However, currently China is still at the stage of rapid economic development and urbanization and its carbon emissions will keep increasing in the future. In 2009, China made the objective to decrease its per capita GDP greenhouse gas emissions by 40%-45% by 2020, which will effectively control the increase rate of the total carbon dioxide emissions. On the one hand, it is predicted that China will make greater efforts to achieve its carbon dioxide emission performance objective and on the other hand, China, as a large country, will still be burdened with blame and pressure from the international community for its constant greenhouse gas emission increase.

V. The Low-Carbon Way is the Strategic Choice to Cope with Air Pollution and Climate Change

Should China make the transition into a low-carbon economic development mode? Considering the tackling of the complicated and intertwined relationship between current international economic, political and environmental diplomacy, this is not a problem of tactics, but a strategic choice.

In recent years, the discussion on China's economic structure adjustment and the transition of its growth pattern has mainly been conducted against two backdrops. One is China's low resource utilization efficiency, acute environmental problems and energy security; the other is the international pressure to tackle climate change. The Chinese government emphasized the adjustment of the economic structure and the transition from an extensive and resource-consuming economic growth pattern into an intensive and energy-conserving one. During this process, the "low-carbon economy" also plays a part in the decision-making and comes into the limelight.

China has become a rapid developing economy winning the world's biggest attention; however, China still faces grim environmental problems, high energy consumption and greenhouse gas emissions. One

---

① *China's Plan to Cope with the Climate Change*, climate change information website, http://www.ccchina.gov.cn/website/ccchina/putile/file189.pdf.

of the most common driving factors (or pressures) behind environmental problems is the energy problem. China's energy structure is based on coal and its important energies such as petroleum depend on imports. Under such circumstances, we have to enforce our politics and military affairs to guarantee safe energy provision. Since basically we rely on rapid industrial growth for our rapid economic growth, harm to natural resources and the environment is mainly caused by the traditional industrial economic growth pattern, especially the energy structure characterized by fossil fuel. Considering the close relationship between regional air pollution and climate change, efforts made to improve regional pollution and environmental problems will produce the secondary effect of global greenhouse gas emission reduction. Similarly, control over greenhouse gas emissions will also produce the secondary effect of local and regional pollution control and environment improvement. At the same time, whether climate change or local and regional environmental problems, they all belong to development problems. China is facing key challenges to alleviate poverty, bridge the income distribution gap and improve the fairness of economic achievements and the environmental burden, while improving the environmental quality, protecting nature and satisfying people's increasing material needs and environmental quality needs in developing its regional and national economy.

For China, the transition to a low-carbon economy that is characterized by a low-consumption, low-emission and high-output growth pattern is helpful to change the industrial structure and reset the industrial allocation and to balance the relationship between economic growth and environmental protection during the development. For China, which is facing severe regional pollution problem and pressure from greenhouse gas emission control, low carbon will indubitably become a highly concerned choice of development mode.

Taking all the above factors into consideration, to allay the domestic pressure from environmental problems, guarantee energy security, improve the resource utilization efficiency of economic growth and cope with climate change, the transformation of our economic growth pattern and the adjustment of the economic structure are inevitable and the transitioning into a low-carbon economy or the promotion of the low-carbonization of economic development has become an inescapable strategic choice for China. Only through this can China take the initiative to confront the future changes in international trade and the environmental pattern.

This global financial and economic crisis has also provided important opportunities for China's low-carbon transition. During past years, for China's large investment in high-energy-consuming industries, the technological life expectancy was usually two or three decades. That is to say, generally speaking, it takes two or three decades for us to adjust these enterprises or industries. However, this economic crisis has great impacts on the industry with excessive production capacity. If we take this opportunity to seek new economic growth points and develop a new investment direction, then the economic crisis is very likely to become an opportunity for China to remove the lock-in effect of high-energy-consuming industrial technology.

China's voluntary transition into a low-carbon development mode will produce a dual effect on its tackling of international pressure and breaking away from the domestic economic development bottleneck. It should be especially stressed that in pursuing the low-carbonization it doesn't mean that we can soon realize a low-carbon economy because it takes time for the adjustment of the industrial structure and growth pattern; however, we should be prepared for the strategic transition, including establishing a powerful political will, making effective policies, revolutionizing the environment-development governance model, effectively exerting the enterprise's role and improving the public's awareness and action.

Although there are different conceptions of a low-carbon economy, the core is a growth pattern characterized by low consumption, low emissions and high output, which includes all the processes from the exploitation, processing, utilization and consumption of raw materials, especially the development and application of low-carbon technology, production and consumption of low-carbon products and development and utilization of low-carbon energy. For China, the low-carbon economy will not only help to change the industrial structure, reset the industrial allocation, but balance the relationship between economic growth and environmental protection and reduce environmental pollution. At the same time, it also helps to increase China's international competitiveness in coping with the global "new industrial revolution" in the face of a new round of climate change talks.

Firstly, the promotion of low-carbon economic practices helps to change China's late-starting disadvantage into a late-starting advantage, and realize the leapfrog development and its energy conservation and emission reduction objectives. China is devoted to improving people's livelihood, life quality and alleviating poverty. It is also facing a series of problems such as severe energy and resource shortages and environmental pollution. Especially as the world's second largest greenhouse gas emission country, China is sure to face tremendous pressure to achieve greenhouse gas emission reductions in the future. In globalization, as an emerging developing country, it cannot follow the development and growth pattern of developed countries and can only choose leapfrog development to realize economic development while protecting the environment. China's rapid economic growth not only needs sufficient environmental capacity resources but also the resource-conserving and environment-friendly technologies and development modes to maintain sustainable and stable economic growth. China's future economic development can only depend on the decrease in energy consumption, the improvement of energy efficiency and the development of renewable energy sources. Only through these low-carbon economic practices can we realize China's economic growth objective and improve people's livelihood. The low-carbon economic practices are indubitably important opportunities for China to realize its late-starting advantages and leapfrog development.

Secondly, the low-carbon economy and its corresponding environmental protection industries are new economic growth points and a win-win solution for China to realize its transformation of the energy consumption structure while protecting its regional environmental quality and coping with international challenges. The core factor of a low-carbon economy is the development of a series of low-carbon technologies and industries. Take the clean development mechanism (CDM) for example. In 2006 the global carbon trade and CDM carbon trade reached 30 billion dollars. By February 2008, the certified emission reduction credit designed by China's CDM projects reached 36.37 million tons, 31.33% of the global total. If the CDM mechanism is fully applied, it is expected that there will be 100 billion dollars' investment flowing from developed countries to developing countries. The low-carbon economy, in essence, is an issue of energy technology innovation and energy structure adjustment. To promote low-carbon economic practices, it means to develop and utilize various energy utilization technologies and renewable energies. Such practices will indubitably help China to implement a series of measures to coordinate the economy and environment, including conserving energies, improving resource and energy utilization efficiency, adjusting the energy structure and transforming the growth pattern and industrial structure.

Thirdly, the incentive for low-carbon economic practices helps to promote China's technical innovation process and break through the existent and possible technology and trade barriers in the future. At present, in the face of the pressure from climate change, major developed countries have introduced many practices in technology development and storage. Facing such an international economic and technological development pattern, Chinese enterprises must improve their core competitiveness through technical innovation in a new round of competition. At the same time, it can avoid the possible influences of technology and trade barriers on the development of Chinese enterprises and economy.

Through low-carbon economic practices, it can help to reduce the risk of pollution transfer from developed countries to developing countries.

VI. Major Problems in the Low-Carbon Strategy to Cope with Air Pollution and Climate Change

To make and adjust strategies and propose policies, we should know both ourselves and our adversaries and have a clear understanding of the pros and cons of every possible action and strategy. Therefore, we need to clearly identify the essence of the scientific, technological, social and economic influences of the international environmental problems; to analyze other countries' possible measures and their impacts; more importantly, to analyze deliberately China's possible role in international politics, economy and trade pattern.

Firstly, improve our scientific awareness, including the relationship and synergistic effect between China's local-regional pollution problem and climate change and the possible influence of climate change on China; we should focus on the research on how China's efforts to improve the local and regional environment influence climate change and greenhouse gas emissions and how the efforts to cope with climate change may influence local and regional environmental problems; we should distinguish the areas with symbiotic benefits, the symbiotic benefits of different improvement measures and rank the cost; we should further identify China's strategic preferential areas and preferential strategic choices, study and analyze the influence of emission reduction and the adaptive strategy choice.

Secondly, we should study and analyze the possible changes in the international environmental political pattern and its influence on China, especially the climate change policies in the European Union, America and Japan and their domestic environment-climate policy changes. Track and observe the changes in the new global environmental political pattern possibly caused by climate change, discern and analyze the new interest groups and the competition and balance between them. Follow and study the changes in Europe-America-Japan and their respective environmental diplomacy and cooperation with China, in the competition and balance between them as well as in the diplomatic ties between China and other developing countries. Study the influence of every possible attitude in China's climate change on the orientation of the international environmental political game and check the relationship and the positioning of China's overall international politics and diplomatic ties.

Thirdly, study how other countries' possible policies to cope with the environment-climate change can influence China. We should concern ourselves with the global carbon emission trade, carbon tax, carbon label system and possible influences of "products and the carbon content during the production process" trade rules on China's industrial and economic development and trade.

Fourthly, we should promote technical change, innovation and industrial upgrading through institutional innovation and policy reform. If we agree that the low-carbon economy means a new development mode and corresponding technical innovation and industrial development, then we must make clear the incentive mechanism for innovation and industrial development. First of all, the market demand will lead the direction of industries and technical innovation. Although at present there are certain market demands for low-carbon products and technologies, we still need to renovate and standardize this market. Therefore, the government's relevant policy orientation, including relevant laws, legislation and technical standards, will have a direct bearing on the market capacity and the direction and speed of technical development. Also, we should establish economic incentives and give market price signals to improve the low-carbon economy and industrial competitiveness. Only in this way can we create profit margins for low-carbon economic practices, promote substantial investment in such practices, accelerate technology development and utilization and improve relevant production and consumption actions. In the reform of the environmental system, we should particularly emphasize the transition from terminal management to whole process management, namely the whole process of surveillance and adjustment from pollution control and treatment, to economic and social development strategy, industrial structure and layout, and the control and renovation of the environmental damage. From the perspective of life circle assessment, we should conduct overall greenhouse effect and air pollution effect assessment of various policies and technologies. In addition, we should shift the focus of our strategy from a single pollutant to the co-controlling of several pollutants, not only paying attention to sulfur dioxide, particulate matter and oxynitride, but also making controlling strategies over diversified pollutants according to other pollutants such as greenhouse gas and heavy metals. Through the controlling of various pollutants, it helps society to make long-term environmental management strategies and through the implementation of such strategies, in the long run, we can obtain possible common benefits from pollutant co-controlling, including the global environmental benefits of local pollution control and the local pollution control benefits of global environmental protection.

Fifthly, in promoting the transition into a low-carbon development model, we should construct government-enterprise-public liaison and a balanced relationship. To make a transition into the low-carbon economic development mode, firstly we need to make clearly identified strategies. Once the strategy is made, we should give relevant policy signals and through institutional improvement we should lead fair competition in the market and enable the government, the enterprise and the public to check and reinforce each other. Among them, the government should have a perfect understanding of its position, to be devoted to constructing a sound institutional environment and, more importantly, to providing the policy guidance.

The problem in China is that we have too many policies at hand, but cannot implement one policy to fully serve our purpose: when a problem gets serious, the policy may be too rigid; when the problem is gone, the policy becomes invalid. Here are many objective reasons, such as China's current developmental stage, China's vast territory and abundant resources and the complexity of its problems. However, whether for subjective or objective reasons, the direct consequence is a drop in the credibility of the governmental and administrative sectors which promulgate relevant policies. Whether in terms of enterprises or individuals, they all construct their behavioral model under specified and expected circumstances. If there are slight changes in the external policy leverage signal provided by the government, especially a competent government like in China, or the adjustment is made when the majority of people are unprepared, the cost of the adjustment will become extremely high. More probably, it may result in the abandoning of adjustments and the non-interference of each other. Therefore, we should be devoted to transforming the dynamic management model to a long-effective policy incentive mechanism.

Also, under many circumstances, a competent Chinese government will show its advantages especially in the face of crises. However, a competent government doesn't necessarily mean that the government's policy should be imposed by force. It should fully consider the characteristics and demands of its policy subjects and devote itself to behavioral changes and incentives (including negative incentives and positive incentives) rather than merely resort to behavioral restrictions. In this way there can be positive interactions between the policy maker, the policy executor and the policy subject.

The enterprise is both the policy subject and the main player in the market. For the enterprise, the government's regulation is exceptionally important. There are various types of enterprises, such as the average type (operating strictly according to the policy direction), adventurous type (or pioneering type, which likes exploring new problems and new areas), rent-seeking type (which can exploit an advantage in any policies) etc. A good policy or institutional environment should provide nourishment for the enterprises with insight, which are able to shoulder more social responsibilities. If we, on the one hand, encourage or demand the enterprise to shoulder social responsibilities and make contributions to energy conservation and emission reduction while, on the other hand, fail to strictly enforce environmental policies and allow some enterprises to escape deserved punishment for their continual sewage emissions, a market environment in which bad money drives out good money will be formed in the long run.

An effective exertion of the public's right is the best way to lower the government's surveillance cost. The public enjoys the basic rights of the environment, such as the rights to get clean air and clean water. To these rights, we should afford support and guarantees. At the same time, the public also shoulders relevant responsibilities for improving the environment. To fulfill the public's environmental responsibilities, the government should give them the corresponding " bundle of rights": the appropriate rights of receiving environmental information, the rights to claim when the environment is damaged, the rights of environment supervision etc.

In tackling problems in climate change and the improvement of air quality, the maturity and development of the civilian society plays a very important role. The civilian society requires each individual to be a capable, active and responsible civilian and it is the agglomeration of the civilian's rights and power, responsibilities and obligations. Civilian participation and responsibilities for environmental protection are multi-faceted, which can be summarized by one sentence "do not give up things though they may be insignificant and do not do things carelessly even if they are in a mess". (1) Emphasize self-consciousness, namely, to promote the awareness of environmental protection and take action in every detail of daily life. (2) Try to persuade others to join in your environmental protection activities in various ways and by your own action. (3) Exert the consumers' power and adhere to the concept of "consumption being responsible for the environment". Influence the enterprise's production behavior through product purchase and various consumption habits. (4) Exert the civilians' power, namely their rights of knowing the environmental information including public affairs like environmental protection, the rights of environmental surveillance and the rights to claim when the environment is damaged.

New Progress in International Climate Negotiations and Challenges Facing China's Low Carbon Economic Development

By CHEN Ying

Introduction

The United Nations Climate Change Conference held in Copenhagen, the capital of Denmark during 7-18 December, 2009 was a feast of unprecedented scale, which had a stake in the destiny of all human beings and was full of fierce competition between different political powers. Copenhagen, a tucked-away city in the North of Europe, home to the Little Mermaid, had never been the focus of the whole world until the conference was held, holding the breath of millions of people. Some are extremely disappointed or even furious at the achievement of this Copenhagen conference, merely several pages of agreements, while some say it is what they expected. However, the international climate process will not cease and the general trend for the whole world to transit into a low-carbon economy will not change and China, adhering to its old saying, "practicing what you preach and striving for a result", will remain adamant in fulfilling its commitment to international society.

This article will make a comprehensive analysis of the newest progress and future development trend of international climate negotiations before and after the aforesaid Copenhagen conference, and mainly focus on exploring China's transition into a low-carbon economy in the future, especially the challenges and the strategies for China to decrease its carbon emissions per unit of GDP by 40%-45% in 2020 compared with that in 2005.

I. New Progress in International Climate Negotiations

1. Historical Significance of the Copenhagen Conference

As early as the 1970s and 1980s, scientists alerted human beings about the threat climate change would bring to the environment and human society. To cope with climate change, international climate negotiation between countries was initiated in the 1990s, marking the climate change problem's inception into the international political agenda. Reviewing about a dozen years' process in international climate negotiation, we can see it was beset with twists and turns.

The United Nations Framework Convention on Climate Change (UNFCCC) passed in 1992 and *the Kyoto Protocol* signed in 1997 are two important milestones. Up to now, they have been the important legal foundation for international climate negotiation. However, the first round of commitment of *the Kyoto Protocol* expired in 2012. To make institutional arrangements for the international society to cope with climate change after 2012, a conference on climate change was held in Bali, Indonesia, in December 2007, which pinned down the "Bali Road Map". According to the relevant stipulations of this map, a new negotiation process will start to promote long-term cooperation under the convention and together with the second round of commitment to emission reduction by developed countries in the protocol, a "double track" pattern will be formed with the aim of reaching a comprehensive, valid and effective international agreement on international climate regime after 2012 by the Copenhagen conference at the end of 2009.

Climate change has endangered human society in various aspects and will continue to pose direct threat to man's future survival and development. We should lose no time in coping with the climate change. Therefore, the Copenhagen conference shouldered an important historical mission and was even described as "the last chance to save humanity". About 40, 000 representatives from governmental, enterprise, non-governmental and international institutions in 193 countries and journalists from news presses attended the conference. More than 100 heads of state or leaders gathered at the last moment to engage in the highest level of political consultation in Copenhagen. It was very rare to see a conference with so many attendees and on such a large scale.

2. International Climate Political Competition

Climate change is not only an environment matter, but also a development matter. With the intertwinement of complicated scientific, political, economic, technological, legislative and ethical factors, the Copenhagen conference was a fierce game between different political powers and its negotiation was extremely tricky and complex. The negotiation process of the Copenhagen conference was beset with obstacles and gripped everyone's heart.

Bali Action Plan, the core of "Bali Road Map" identified five key subjects for the negotiation under the convention[①], namely the "shared aspiration", the core being the global long-term objective of emission reduction and alleviation, adaptation, technology and capital. All these have constituted the key factors and basis for the international climate regime after 2012. In the alleviation part, the clauses about developed countries and developing countries stipulated different details. Developed countries should fulfill their greenhouse gas emission reduction that is measurable, reportable, verifiable and corresponds with their own national conditions, including quantified emission reduction targets. At the same time, we should ensure the comparability of the efforts by developed countries to reduce emissions. On the premise that developed countries provide sufficient support in technologies, capital and capacity building for developing countries, the developing countries should take appropriate actions to allay their domestic emissions. Developed countries' support and developing countries' alleviation actions should be measurable, reportable and veritable. As a matter of fact, the first clause was especially made for the USA because it didn't approve the protocol and was unable to participate in the negotiation during the second round of commitment as a contracting party. However, as a developed country, the efforts made by the USA to reduce emissions were comparable to other developed countries.

Overall, the core issues for the Copenhagen negotiation were as follows: 1. The legalization of the achievements of the conference. 2. The emission reduction target. What the global long-term target is and what the middle-term emission target by 2020 is. 3. The capital

① Bali Action Plan, unfccc. int.

problem, including the financing scale and the revolutionization of the capital management method. 4. The international report and verification mechanism concerning the emission reduction and capital, namely the issue of increasing transparency. On the key issues mentioned above, the south-north antagonism between developed countries and developing countries was still sustained and layers of contradictions permeated inside the two groups. There were conflicts between Europe and America, disputes between developing countries and the competition between different political powers was extremely fierce.

There was no definite stipulation in the "Bali Road Map" about the legalized achievement of the conference. Judging from the "double track" negotiation pattern, two different legalized achievements should be scored through the "double track" negotiation. However, some developed countries, headed by the European Union, out of the consideration of their own benefits, have integrated the double track into a singular one in international climate negotiation and formed a unified legal document. In fact, this is an attempt to stray away from *the Kyoto Protocol*, especially the series of principles such as the "shared but differentiated principle" stipulated in the protocol. During the conference, Denmark, as the sponsor, even drafted the "Danish Text" jointly with other major developed countries besides the negotiation draft, which has channeled the opinion of various parties. The Text went beyond the authorization of the "Bali Road Map" and reinforced the developing countries' obligation to achieve emission reductions. This indubitably incurred vehement opposition from developing countries and the "Danish Text", leaked before its implementation, was aborted. Developing countries emphasized that *the Kyoto Protocol* was a long-binding legal document and was the only international treaty that made quantified emission reduction targets for developed countries and had legally binding schedules and a default penalty system. Abandoning the protocol not only meant a serious retrogression in the international climate regime, which was deprived of the contract enforcement mechanism, but also a loss of carriers in the important principles such as the "shared but differentiated principle". Under such circumstances, we faced enormous risks and uncertainties in establishing a new and more improved legal document.

Emission reduction targets are the core of the international climate regime. In terms of the long-term target, the G8 Summit held in Italy in

June, 2009 discussed how to control the global temperature rise to within 2℃ and had reached some consensus. At that summit, the European Union emphasized the legalization of the 2℃ target and ultimately brought it into the achievements of the Copenhagen conference. If the fulfillment of the long-term target showed the concern of politicians from different countries and their moral support of the climate change problem, in comparison the middle-term target directly decided the emission reduction cost distribution among different countries and concerned their immediate economic returns, thereupon leading to increasingly fierce interest disputes among countries.

Before the Copenhagen conference, different countries had revealed their intention, nearly all Annex I countries (developed countries and transitioning countries) having proposed their middle-term emission reduction targets. For example, the European Union promised to reduce the emissions by 20%-30% by 2020 compared with those in 1990. The US President, Barack Obama, announced a reduction in emissions by 17% by 2020, compared with those in 2005. Japan promised to reduce the emissions by 25% by 2020 compared with those in 1990. Canada promised to reduce the emissions by 20% by 2020 compared with those in 2006. Australia promised to reduce the emissions by 5%-25% by 2020 compared with those in 2000. Russia proposed to reduce the emissions by 15%-25% by 2020 compared with those in 1990.

Actually, these emission reduction targets had underlying implications. Firstly, each country had chosen a base year that was favorable to them. For example, if America's target was converted into the one in 1990, the emissions were only reduced by around 4% while Canada, only around 2%. Russia currently has reduced the emissions by about 34% compared with those in 1990 on account of its economic depression. Actually, compared with the emission reduction target in 1990, it still had large room for improvement. Also, they were ambiguous about whether the emission reduction target included forest carbon sink and made no clear demarcation between domestic emission reduction and overseas emission reduction. For example, America planned to offset as much as 1 billion tons' carbon dioxide emission quota through domestic forestry management and overseas emission reduction, which would greatly alleviate the pressure on domestic emission reduction. It was hard for the originally comparatively low emission reduction target to be effectively binding for domestic emissions. Some countries' emission targets are conditional, such as the European Union's 30% emission reduction target required other countries to make comparable efforts on emission reduction; Japan and Australia required major emission countries to participate in international agreements and the latter even raised more complicated conditions for its 25% emission reduction target. If the conditions were not fulfilled, developed countries would discount their efforts in their committed emission reduction target. Besides, America's emission reduction target had still to be approved by the Congress and was uncertain whether it would come into force. According to some institutions' analyses and estimations, if excluding forest carbon sink, the overall emission reduction percentage of the Annex I countries in 2020 would hang around 12%-18% compared with that in 1990①, far away from the minimum 25%-40% target in the conclusion of the IPCC science assessment and further away from the over 40% target required by most developing countries.

Table 1 Middle-Term Emission Reduction Targets Promised by Annex I Countries

	Base year	Emission Reduction Target (%)
European Union 27	1990	20-30
America	2005	17
Japan	1990	25
Australia	2000	5-25
Canada	2005	17
Russia	1990	15-25
The Republic of Belarus	1990	5-10
New Zealand	1990	10-20
Norway	1990	30-40
Iceland	1990	30

① WRI: Interactive Chart: Analyzing Comparability of Annex I Emission Reduction Pledges, http://www.wri.org/publication/comparability-of-annexi-emission-reduction-pledges/chart; Climate Action Tracker, http://www.climateactiontracker.org/.

(contd.)

	Base year	Emission Reduction Target (%)
Croatia	1990	5
Monaco	1990	30
Liechtenstein	1990	20-30

Note: There are additional conditions attached to some countries' emission reduction targets.
Data source: unfccc. int.

Some non-Annex I countries (developing countries) also proposed their detailed targets in emission reduction. If we see Table 2, we can find that China was committed to reducing the carbon intensity per unit of GDP by 40%-45% by 2020 compared with that in 2005 and India by 20%-25%. Brazil promised to reduce its emissions by 36%-39% by 2020 compared with Business As Usual (BAU) emissions and its important measure is to decrease the deforestation emission by 80% by 2020 under the support of international capital, compared with that in 2005. South Africa was committed to reducing its emissions by 34% by 2020 compared with BAU emissions and most developing countries' targets were related to the corresponding international technical and capital assistance they would receive. However, it was explicitly stipulated in *the Bali Action Plan* that the nature of such targets is domestic alleviation action, which is different from that of the quantified emission reduction obligation developed countries must shoulder. The alleviation action target proposed by developing countries will cause some international pressure on developed countries and was of great significance to the promotion of the Copenhagen conference.

As for the capital problem, all parties have acknowledged that under the current climate convention there is a serious shortage of public funds provided by such capital mechanisms as GEF. Developed countries and developing countries have serious disagreements on the expansion of capital channels, the scale of investments and the capital management. Developing countries emphasized that it is developed countries' obligation under the convention to provide technology transfer and capital assistance to developing countries while developed countries have been making slow progress and shown little sincerity in this regard, merely regarding the capital problem as a leverage to bargain with developing countries. On the one hand, it stressed the role of the investment by the private sector and the market mechanism, toned down the government's role and, on the other hand, tried to make use of the future's Official Development Assistance (ODA) to avoid their deserved capital obligations and even direct the capital obligations to developing countries. The Copenhagen conference initially made a short-term plan for developed countries to provide 30 billion dollars at the rapid starting stage during 2010-2012 and the long-term capital assistance plan to increase their support to 100 billion dollars by 2020. However, compared with the 0.5%-1.0% of developed countries' GDP proposed by developing countries, this was far from enough, and the detailed implementation was still uncertain. Anyhow, this marked a step forward.

Table 2 Middle-Term Alleviation Action Targets Proposed by Major Non-Annex I Countries

		Target Year	Emission Reduction Target
Carbon Intensity Target	China	2020	40%-45% decrease compared with 2005
	India	2020	20%-25% decrease compared with 2005
Emission Reduction Target	Brazil	2020	36.1%-38.9% decrease compared with BAU emissions
	Indonesia	2020	26%-41% decrease compared with BAU emissions
	Mexico	2020	30% decrease compared with BAU emissions
	Singapore	2020	16% decrease compared with BAU emissions
	South Africa	2020	34% decrease compared with BAU emissions
	Korea	2020	30% decrease compared with BAU emissions
Carbon Neutral Target	Costa Rica	2021	-100%
	Maldives	2019	-100%

Note: BAU refers to the yardstick emission based on the unchanged current development trend. Some countries' alleviation action target is in need of corresponding international technical and capital assistance.

Data source: unfccc. int.

The problem of transparency assumed prominence at the last moment of the Copenhagen negotiation. America proposed that it could join in the annual financing of 100 billion dollars by 2020 on the condition that developing countries' emission reduction action should be subject to international verification and increase the transparency. However, developing countries assumed that it was unreasonable to subject all of their emission reduction actions to international verification and they believed that only those who received international capital and technology support needed international verification. Developing countries could increase transparency according to the international need, but they would mainly depend on the domestic mechanism for statistics and assessment. The measurable, reportable and verifiable (MRV) mechanism stipulated in the "Bali Road Map" not only applied to the emission reduction action by developing countries, but also included the capital and technology support by developed countries. Therefore, when developed countries did not make clear financing plans, they shifted the focus to developing countries which ran counter to the requirement of the "Bali Road Map".

3. The Ultimate Result of the Copenhagen Conference and its Assessment

Through two-weeks of harsh negotiations in the Copenhagen conference, a resolution was passed at the last moment to record the *Copenhagen Accord* reached between America and major developing countries like China, India, Brazil and South Africa as well as those countries which agreed with the Accord. It also decided to prolong the authorization to the two specially designed working teams under the Convention and the Protocol and reach legal agreements at the 16th Conference of the Parties to UNFCC in Mexico in 2010.

The above achievement made in the Copenhagen conference was a legally non-binding political agreement reached with limited scope. Although it failed to live up to the expectations of some international environmental organizations, objectively it basically corresponded to the composed analysis and expectations before the conference. We could not expect to reach a comprehensive, binding and ambitious international legal agreement at just one conference. To express the political willingness of different parties to cope with climate change in the form of political agreements and to focus on some consensus and achievements constitute the first step in the right direction. Therefore, the achievement of the conference was positive and its meaning was far-reaching. Its positive significance could be captured in the following three aspects:

Firstly, it firmly maintained the "shared but differentiated principle" established in *the United Nations Framework Convention on*

Climate Change and *the Kyoto Protocol.* Denmark, the sponsor of the conference, drafted the "Danish Text" with major developed countries in an attempt to "unify two tracks into one", abandon *the Kyoto Protocol* and impose emission reduction obligations on developing countries. With the unremitting efforts made by contracting parties, the contracting developing parties in particular, the direction of the "Bali Road Map" was ultimately confirmed.

Secondly, it took new and firm steps in enforcing developed countries to reduce emissions and encourage developing countries to take the initiative to alleviate emissions. Up to now, all the developed countries have proposed their middle-term emission reduction targets and most developing countries also proposed their alleviation action targets. These targets are an important foundation to promote follow-up negotiations although some developed countries have no clear aims in utilizing forest carbon sink and overseas emission reduction and have additional conditions; besides, according to the assessments by relevant international research institutions, the emission reduction percentage of developed countries will be merely 8%-12% in 2020 compared with that in 1990, far below the 25%-40% in the scientific conclusion of IPCC and the minimum 40% required by most developing countries.

Thirdly, it reached broad consensus on the focus problems such as the global long-term objective, capital and technical assistance and transparency. *The Copenhagen Accord* agreed on the scientific conclusion as the long-term objective for global cooperation to control the global temperature rise to within 2℃; form an initial short-term capital assistance plan for developed countries to provide 30 billion dollars at the rapid starting stage and a long-term capital assistance plan to increase the number to 100 billion dollars annually by 2020; the two camps made their own interpretations of developed countries' obligation to emission reduction and developing countries' transparency in their alleviation actions.

It should be said that China, as a large developing country, played a positive and constructive role in promoting the negotiation. It not only showed its sincerity by proposing its concrete and ambitious objective of alleviation action at the beginning of the negotiation, but also made great efforts to bring the negotiation to a fruitful ending during the negotiation process. Standing with developing countries, China, on the one hand, showed no compromise to developed countries on matters of principle and tried hard to guarantee developing countries' interests and, on the other hand, made it explicit that the most underdeveloped countries enjoyed privileges in capital assistance, which effectively ensured the solidarity among developing countries. At the last moment of the negotiations, Premier Wen Jiabao declared that to fulfill the emission reduction target, China must "do what it preaches and strive for results", which were acclaimed by the international community. To ensure some political agreements were reached at the Copenhagen conference, China also showed flexibility in its policies. Together with the USA and other large developing countries, China, through active communication and maneuvers, ultimately contributed to *the Copenhagen Accord*. Although different parties still disagreed on this accord, the political agreement framework was far from enough to solve the climate change problem. The agreement itself meant a consolidation of the achievements and progress. China should win credit for this.

II. Challenge for China to Develop a Low-Carbon Economy①

1. Developing a Low-Carbon Economy Is China's Own Voluntary Choice

Although the political agreement reached at the Copenhagen conference was not legally binding, the global transition to a low-carbon economy was irreversible. Compared with the 20% energy intensity reduction target during the "11th Five-Year" Plan by 2010 with 2005 as the base year, China's objective to reduce its carbon intensity per unit of GDP by 40%-45% by 2020 with 2005 as the base year was more directly targeted at carbon emissions and more ambitious in emission reduction. At the same time, this objective was without any attached conditions and was not related to any countries' emission reduction targets. It showed China's choice of a low-carbon economy. Although there was international emission reduction pressure, more importantly it originated from the internal demand to transform China's economic growth pattern.

---

① The research report based on the energy environment sub-project of the "Tracking Research on China's Major Economic Problems", Chinese Academy of Social Sciences.

Firstly, China's energy security problem has assumed prominence. With the rapid economic growth, the demand on energy is also burgeoning. In 2008, China's total energy consumption reached 2. 85 billion tons of standard coal equivalent, nearly doubling the 990 million tons in 1990. According to the statistics of the General Administration of Customs of the People's Republic of China, China's accumulative imported crude oil reached 183 million tons in the first 11 months of 2009, having exceeded the 179 million tons in the whole year of 2008. 2009 marked China's dependence on imported crude oil that exceeded 50% of consumption for the first time.

Secondly, the resource shortage problem is deteriorating. With a large population, China's per capita hold on resources is relatively insufficient. With its economy stepping into the development stage of a heavy chemical industry, China's demand for energy and raw materials is also increasing. It is predicted that by 2020, among the 45 mineral resources required for China's economic development, only 24 can be guaranteed and 2 basically guaranteed while 10 are in short supply and 9 in serious short supply. It relies on importation for such important mineral resources as petroleum, iron, copper, lead and zinc. The extensive growth mode is hard to sustain. In strengthening the domestic resource development and the utilization of foreign resources, the development of a low-carbon economy is favorable to transform the economic growth pattern and reduce resource consumption.

Thirdly, the environmental pollution pressure is increasing day by day, especially the miscellaneous environmental problems concerning energy utilization, such as air pollution, acid rain, industrial wastewater and solid wastes and the economic operation costs and social costs are expanding. Through developing a low-carbon economy, we can alleviate the harm brought about by the above-mentioned environmental problems while reducing greenhouse gas emissions, which shows obvious "synergistic effect".

Lastly, global warming has become an indisputable fact. The registered representatives of the Copenhagen conference reached as many as about 40, 000 and more than a hundred heads of state or leaders attended, which shows that the global concern for climate change is unprecedented. China, as a large greenhouse gas emission country, has a relatively low historical emission level and less per capita emissions, but it is also burdened with increasing international pressure.

To conclude, a low-carbon economy, a trend marking the global development, poses both challenges and opportunities to China. The carbon intensity objectives raised by China reflected the new feature and mainstream of international and domestic social development. It served not only as a positive response to the expectations of the international community, showed China's image as a large responsible country, but also was China's own voluntary action.

2. The Energy Conservation Target of the "11th Five-Year" Plan is Expected to be Accomplished

China's "11th Five-Year" Plan was made in 2005. Judging from the condition of the target fulfillment from 2006 to 2008, the national energy consumption per unit of GDP increased by 0. 8% on a year-on-year basis in the first half of 2006 and then the increasing trend was quickly reversed. In the whole year of 2006, it decreased by 1. 79% ① on a year-on-year basis, coming to the turning point from increase to decrease. Afterwards, the energy intensity index decreased rapidly. In 2007, it decreased by 3. 66% on a year-on-year basis and in 2008 it exceeded the 4% energy conservation target for the first time, decreasing by 5. 2% on a year-on-year basis. It accumulated to about 12. 45% in three years, accomplishing 62. 5% ② of the target of the "11th Five-Year" Plan . Although work on energy conservation made some achievements, it was still below the planned expectation.

Regionally speaking, as is shown in Table 3, the target of 20 provinces, municipalities and autonomous regions has been on a par with the national target. The target of Shanxi, Inner Mongolia Autonomous

① After adjusting GDP, the data about energy intensity per unit of GDP should also be adjusted: in the base year 2005, from 1. 22 tons of standard coal equivalent/10,000 yuan to 1. 226 tons of standard coal equivalent/10,000 yuan and in 2006, from 1. 21 tons of standard coal equivalent/10, 000 yuan to 1. 204 tons of standard coal equivalent/10,000 yuan, with the decrease rate from -1. 33% to -1. 79%.

② According to the result of the *Second National Economic Census* published on December 25, 2009, after the adjustment of GDP and energy consumption data, the energy consumption per unit of GDP in 2008 decreased by 5. 2% than the previous year, with an accumulation of 12. 45% accomplished during three years. Compared with the previous three years before the adjustment of the data, it accumulatively fulfills 10. 05% and the pressure from fulfilling the objective in the last two years has been allayed. http: //finance. sina. com. cn/review/fxzs/20091225/16447156657. shtml.

Region, Jilin and Shandong was around 22% to 30%, which was higher than the national level, with Jilin being the highest, 30%[①] while the target of Fujian, Guangdong and another five provinces and autonomous regions was around 12% to 17%, obviously lower than the national level, with Tibet and Hainan being the lowest, 12%.

In the practical implementation, for different regional social and economic development levels, industrial and energy structures and different policy making and implementation based on various regional conditions, the ultimate implementation effect varies greatly. Among the regions, Beijing ranked first during three consecutive years from 2006 to 2008, with an accumulative decrease of 17.53%, taking up 86.37% of the 20% energy conservation target. The progress in Qinhai, Hainan, Xinjiang and Sichuan was relatively slow, such as the accumulative decrease during the three years in Hainan was 4.46%, only 35.70% of the 12% and Sichuan, 9.76%, only 46.04% of the 20%.

It is absolutely necessary to analyze the reasons behind the regional differences in accomplishing the targets. For example, the obvious achievement in energy conservation and emission reduction in Beijing is attributable to the local government's efforts and the unique advantages it enjoys as the national capital, especially the contribution from a series of infrastructure construction projects, pollution treatment and environmental protection work carried out in hosting the 2008 Olympic Games[②]. For example: to improve the environmental quality, Beijing transferred the high energy-consuming and highly polluting industry of the Shougang Group to Caofeidian, Hebei, reduced the use of automobiles by adopting vehicle restriction rules, replace the coal-fired boilers with natural gas transmitted from Shaanxi and renovated the public lighting system to save energy. All these measures were helpful in

---

① According to the data calculation of *The Energy Conservation Objective Fulfillment Condition in Provinces, Autonomous Regions and Municipalities in* 2008, the 2009 No. 13 Decree published by the National Development and Reform Commission on October 9, 2009, the objectives of Jilin, Shanxi and Inner Mongolia which are much higher than the national energy conservation objective are lowered, from the original 30%, 25% and 25% to around 23%. http://www.sdpc.gov.cn/zcfb/zcfbgg/2009gg/t20091013_306579.htm.

② The energy conservation and emission reduction work in Beijing has made remarkable achievements and fully completed its target, the Official Website of the People's Government of Beijing Municipality, January 5, 2009.

reducing the energy consumption intensity and greenhouse gas emissions in Beijing. Take the energy conservation work in Sichuan for example. It was influenced by the earthquake and although there was support from other provinces in China, the demand on local high energy-consuming products such as construction materials, cement, iron and steel will promote the industry, enabling the survival of some small high energy-consuming factories planning to close in such special circumstances. Take Hainan Province for another example, with uniquely local features in its economy. It has less industries but a prosperous tourism industry, so its emission reduction potential is small.

Table 3 Regional Energy Conservation Targets and Target Accomplishment Conditions from 2006 to 2008

Region	2005 (tons of standard coal equivalent/ 10,000 yuan)	2010 emission reduction target (%)	2008 compared with the previous year (%)	2006 - 2008 accumulation (%)	Target fulfillment (%)
National	1.226	20	-5.2	12.45	62.25
Beijing	0.80	20	-7.36	-17.53	86.37
Tianjin	1.11	20	-6.85	-14.94	72.53
Hebei	1.96	20	-6.29	-12.83	61.54
Shanxi	2.95	25 *	-7.39	-13.32	57.52
Inner Mongolia	2.48	25 *	-6.34	-12.79	55.09
Liaoning	1.83	20	-5.11	-11.83	56.44
Jilin	1.65	30 *	-5.02	-12.22	52.47
Heilongjiang	1.46	20	-4.75	-11.43	54.37
Shanghai	0.88	20	-3.78	-11.67	55.60
Jiangsu	0.92	20	-5.85	-13.04	62.60
Zhejiang	0.90	20	-5.49	-12.64	60.51
Anhui	1.21	20	-4.52	-11.59	55.2
Fujian	0.94	16	-3.70	-10.05	60.77
Jiangxi	1.06	20	-5.53	-12.20	58.32
Shandong	1.28	22	-6.47	-13.81	59.80
Henan	1.38	20	-5.10	-11.71	55.82
Hubei	1.51	20	-6.29	-12.98	62.3

(contd.)

Region	2005 (tons of standard coal equivalent/ 10,000 yuan)	2010 emission reduction target (%)	2008 compared with the previous year (%)	2006 - 2008 accumulation (%)	Target fulfillment (%)
Hunan	1.40	20	-6.72	-13.88	66.95
Guangdong	0.79	16	-4.32	-10.05	60.74
Guangxi	1.22	15	-3.97	-9.47	61.21
Hainan	0.92	12	-2.55	-4.46	35.70
Chongqing	1.42	20	-4.97	-12.30	58.82
Sichuan	1.53	20	-3.55	-9.76	46.04
Guizhou	3.25	20	-6.11	-11.51	54.78
Yunnan	1.73	17	-4.79	-9.97	56.36
Tibet	1.45	12	-2.50	7.13	57.88
Shaanxi	1.48	20	-5.92	-13.23	63.61
Gansu	2.26	20	-4.53	-10.82	51.34
Qinghai	3.07	17	-4.18	-4.79	26.37
Ningxia	4.14	20	-6.79	-10.98	52.12
Xinjiang	2.11	20	-3.15	-7.13	33.16

Data source: 2006-2008 Statistical Bulletin of the National Bureau of Statistics, regional statistic bulletins on energy consumption per unit of GDP published by the National Bureau of Statistics. No. 13 Decree of the National Development and Reform Commission published on October 9, 2009. The national GDP adjustment data published on December 25, 2009.

Note: According to the calculation of the accomplished index accumulated during the three years published by the National Development and Reform Commission, the original target is adjusted obviously, with the energy conservation target of the three provinces adjusted to about 23%, which is different from the original published one.

Different sectors have made different contributions to the national energy conservation target. Generally speaking, high energy-consuming industries and manufacturing industries are the priority areas for energy conservation and emission reduction. From 2006 to 2007, the continual rapid growth in iron and steel, cement and other high energy-consuming industries was the major reason for the failure to complete the annual task of national energy intensity per unit of GDP index. In the first half of 2006, the national energy consumption per unit of GDP increased by 0.8% on a year-on-year basis. The per unit energy consumption increase of high energy-consuming industries was higher than the national average, for example, the increase in coal being 5.5% and petrochemicals 8.7%. In 2008, with the strengthening of the energy conservation and emission reduction policy targeted at key high energy-consuming industries and the influence of the global financial crisis, the energy consumption of major energy-consuming industries decreased significantly. According to the statistics, the national energy consumption per unit of GDP from January to September 2008 decreased by over 3% on a year-on-year basis and the decrease rate of high energy-consuming industries exceeded the national average. For example, the decrease rate for coal, building materials and the textile industry was 6.74%, 9.98% and 9.61% respectively.

Influenced by the financial crisis, the overall economy in 2009 grew more slowly than previous years, with the economic growth in the first quarter being 6.1% on a year-on-year basis and the second quarter, 7.1%. The high energy-consuming heavy industries suffered the most serious blow and the pressure from energy conservation and emission reduction was a temporary alleviation. According to the data published by the National Bureau of Statistics in June 2009, the energy consumption per unit of GDP decreased by 3.35% in the first half of 2009. However, with the rapid economic rebound in the fourth quarter, the energy consumption grew rapidly again. In 2009 it was expected to fulfill the 4% decrease target. With persistent efforts in 2010, the energy conservation target of the "11th Five-Year" Plan was expected to be basically completed. This owed much to the enormous efforts made by China to fulfill its commitment to the international community and its contribution to the alleviation of climate change.

3. Severe Challenges for China to Transit into a Low-Carbon Economy

During the roughly 4 years' implementation of the "11th Five-Year" Plan, China took important steps on the road to a low-carbon economy. This was mainly manifested in three aspects: firstly, in the powerful policies. For example, the government invested in ten key energy conservation projects, audited and managed the energy conservation of a thousand high energy-consuming enterprises, "developing large units and suppressing small ones" sifting our outdated production facilities. It made preliminary achievements in energy conservation and emission reduction. Until the first half of 2009, the energy intensity per unit of

GDP had decreased by 13% compared with 2005, an equivalent of a reduction of 800 million tons' of carbon dioxide. It aimed at the 20% energy conservation target of the "11th Five-Year" Plan; secondly, the development of renewable energies: in 2008, the total utilization of renewable energy reached 250 million tons of standard coal equivalent. Only 30 million rural households used methane, which reduced 49 million tons' of carbon dioxide compared with using coal; thirdly, in its great efforts to return the wheatfields to forestry and afforestation, it scored remarkable achievements. At present, China boasts 54 million hectares' of artificial afforestation, ranking it the first in the world. Also, China has made great contributions to the alleviation of global greenhouse gas emissions through population, resource, ecological and environmental protection policies.

In spite of these achievements, it doesn't mean that China's future low-carbon economic development will be devoid of difficulties. We must be clearly aware of the fact that it takes pain to realize the target of reducing the carbon intensity by 40%-45% and we face severe challenges in our low-carbon economic transition.

At present, we are in the stage of rapid industrialization and urbanization. The economic development places a high demand on heavy chemical industries. Such a developmental stage will at least be sustained for two or three decades. In 2006, the heavy industries increased to 17.9%, in 2007 to 19.6% and in 2008 decreased to 13.2% (influenced by the financial crisis), but all higher than the increase rate of the domestic industries in the same period. At this special developmental stage, to promote a low-carbon economy is indeed an enormous challenge. To promote the local economy, the local government usually puts the economic growth target in first place. At the current stage, our economic growth is typically motivated by investments. More new projects will bring more pressure on energy, resources and the environment. The development of a low-carbon economy, in the final analysis, should depend on the breakthrough of low-carbon technology R&D and its large-scale promotion and application. However, the improvement in the technological level should be backed up by a strong overall national strength which takes time to develop.

Studies show that to decrease the energy consumption per unit of GDP, the contribution rate of technology advancement is 30%-40%

while that of the structural adjustment is 60%-70%. Some institutes, by assessing the middle term of the "11th Five-Year" Plan, made the conclusion that the contribution rate of industry to the decrease in energy consumption per unit of GDP was above 80%. It is inevitable that the structural adjustment is important, but it is by no means easy to handle this. At the current stage, our industrial structure is unscientific in several aspects: firstly, it is to be seen in the production structure, with low level, regional overproduction, high energy consumption and costs of production; secondly, in the problem that the industrial organization structure is inefficient: the industry is too scattered, with little concentration; thirdly, in the problem that the industrial technology structure is also inefficient: there are few large enterprises with advanced technologies but many medium and small-sized enterprises with backward technologies; there are data showing that during the three years from 2006 to 2008, there were 34.21-million-kilowatt small thermal power generating units, 60.59-million-ton outdated puddling capacity, 43.47-million-ton outdated steelmaking capacity and 140-million-ton outdated cement capacity that were eliminated nationally and the greenhouse gas emissions were cut down significantly. However, China has paid a high social and economic price for all this. Besides, closing backward production facilities is not a sustainable way for energy conservation, the continuity of which will incur more difficulties and higher cost. Fourthly, it is to be seen in the backward tertiary industries, especially the emerging industries such as the high-tech industry and environmental protection industry. The added value in our service industry takes up around 40% of the GDP, not only lagging far behind the average 64% of developed countries, but also lower than the average 55% of the middle and low income countries. Also, the marked difference between different economic and social development made it more difficult to adjust the structure. Even if many control measures are adopted in policy implementation, it takes a comparatively longer time for them to take effect.

As a matter of fact, in recent years the effect of our industrial structure adjustment has been very limited. The percentage of the secondary industry is basically flat; the optimization of the energy structure also progresses slowly; even under pressure from the rapidly increasing demand on energy, coal consumption increases faster than other energies. The energy structure, instead of being improved, shows signs of deterioration. In recent years, China has developed vigorously its new energies, among which the photovoltaic power generated by solar energy reached 120,000 kilowatts and the utilization area of solar energy was 130 million square meters, ranking it first in the world (2008); the installed hydro and wind power capacity were ranked respectively first and the fourth in the world and the installed nuclear power capacity increased to 9.1 million kilowatts, with 20 million kilowatts under construction (2008). By the end of 2007, there were more than 26.5 million rural households using methane in China, which can substitute about 16 million tons of standard coal equivalent annually, an equivalent to 44-million-tons of carbon dioxide emission reduction. However, new energies and renewable energies still occupy a low percentage in the total energy consumption, unable to play a key role. Objectively speaking, the target was better fulfilled during the period 2008-2009 than the period 2006-2007. This has benefited from the strengthening of the implementation of energy conservation and emission reduction policies and the construction of key energy conservation projects. Also, the economic downturn caused by the global financial crisis in the second half of 2008 greatly influenced the high energy-consuming industry. Some high energy-consuming industries were forced to reduce and cease production and thus the energy demand decreased. This was also an important reason.

With the global economic recovery, China's economy has been turning for the better and the energy demand and emissions will rebound. During 1997, when the Asian financial crisis erupted, the growth of China's total energy consumption was negative during the three consecutive years from 1998 to 2000, a respective decrease of 4.9%, 9.3% and 0.3% compared with the previous year. The decrease in the coal consumption was the most obvious, four consecutive years' negative growth from 1997 to 2000, namely a respective decrease of 3.0%, 7.8%, 15.7% and 5.2% compared with the previous year. However, since the economic recovery from the financial crisis in 2001, there was historically rapid growth in China's energy consumption, with an increase of 9.4% and 14.8% in the total energy consumption respectively in 2001 and 2002 compared with the previous year. The consumption of coal increased 10.5% and 19.5% respectively in the same period and the elastic coefficient of energy consumption approached or even exceeded 1. Learning from the lesson provided by the 1997 Asian financial crisis, we should adhere firmly to energy conservation and emission reduction amidst economic recovery.

III. Prospect of International Climate Negotiations and China's Countermeasures

Facing the present grim situation in the international and domestic efforts to cope with climate change, China should allow for both the international and domestic conditions, on the one hand, continuing to maintain and fight for its development rights in international negotiation and, on the other hand, actively fulfill its 40%-45% carbon intensity target in the country. It should make great efforts to promote its transition into a low-carbon economy.

1. Promote International Climate Cooperation at the New Starting Point

The Copenhagen conference was a milestone of historical significance during the international climate process. It marked not an end, but a new start for international climate cooperation. Since the political agreement made in the Copenhagen conference was not binding, we cannot exclude new changes in the follow-up negotiations. There even may be partial repetition or retrogression and the follow-up negotiation process is doomed to be difficult and tortuous.

In maintaining and fighting for its development rights in international climate negotiation, the international pressure will increase in the following three aspects:

Firstly, the suppression of the global emission reduction target on our future emission space. The Copenhagen conference made the long-term target that the global temperature rise should be controlled to within 2℃ and for some small island countries, the target was even more radical, which was within 1.5℃. The focus in the follow-up negotiation would be be the materialization of the long-term target. As a matter of fact, the 2℃ target has delimited the global emission space. In 1990, the global emissions were about 21 billion tons' of carbon dioxide and in 2009 it was 29 billion tons. Around 2015-2020 it will reach the peak and afterwards there will be a significant decrease. If by 2050 the global emissions are cut by half with 1990 or 2005 as the base year, the global emissions will be about 10.5 billion to 14.5 billion tons. However, in

2009, the overall emissions of the developing countries had reached 13.7 billion tons, with China's contribution being about 6 billion tons and showing sign of climbing. Although the conference did not agree on the 50% global emission reduction target by 2050, obviously China is facing increasingly strong international pressure, not only from developed countries, but also from developing countries.

Secondly, international consultation and analysis has placed higher demands on our relative statistics, monitoring and assessment system. *The Copenhagen Accord* stipulated that there should be international consultation and analysis of developing countries' voluntary alleviation action and future negotiations will discuss some details. Developed countries hoped to include developing countries in the global emission reduction system through this opportunity and even require them to shoulder greater emission reduction obligations. Concerning this, China's relative statistics, monitoring and assessment system have yet to be improved and it has been pressing to enhance relative capacity construction.

Thirdly, the carbon tariff and other trade measures proposed by the developed countries in Europe and America posed a threat to our exports in the future. Although the Copenhagen conference did not take the trade problem as a negotiation topic, developed countries, especially the European Union, were in active preparation for the promotion of carbon tariffs. Later negotiations touched upon this sensitive issue. Foreign trade is one of the "three carriages" for China's economic growth, but as the "global processing factory", the low added value in China's exports and its energy-intensive products still take up a large proportion. China will bear the brunt if the carbon tariff is implemented.

The 16th Conference of the Parties to UNFCC was held in Mexico in 2010, and the parties continued their consultations on such key issues as emission reduction targets, the capital mechanism and transparency. The major tasks facing international climate negotiation are: firstly, *the Copenhagen Accord* itself. It should strive for more international support for the consensus embodied in it while making clear distinctions in describing and recording different countries' emission reduction commitments; secondly, sticking to the "double track system". On the basis of the chairman's text of two working groups, negotiations should be conducted on the problems yet to be agreed upon, including defining the emission obligation of developed countries in the second round of commitment under the Protocol and urging developed countries to fulfill their commitment of a 30-billion-dollar capital timely and to implement the long-term capital target. It is hoped that the international climate negotiation process will advance head-on amidst difficulties. All the parties will strive for consensus by seeking common grounds while reserving differences so as to bring a brighter future for human society.

2. *Policies Adopted by China to Promote the Transition to a Low-Carbon Economy*

Although the Copenhagen conference did not fulfill its historical mission, the low-carbon economy has become the general trend in global economic development. Although academic circles have started in-depth discussions on the basic concept and theory of the low-carbon economy, just as the concept of sustainable development, which was gradually put into practice and won people's concern, to develop a low-carbon economy there is no need to excessively concentrate on its accurate definition and theoretical elaboration. More importantly, it is necessary to accumulate experience from practices and keep moving forward. "A journey of one thousand miles begins with one step". China should learn from the present and strive to explore a low-carbon development road that is suitable for its national conditions.

To gear itself towards the general trend of the global transition to a low-carbon economy, China must establish an overall strategy for the development of a low-carbon economy, not only including hardware construction, for example, the construction of key energy conservation projects and energy infrastructure, but also including software construction, such as the construction of relative legislation, policy systems and mechanisms; we should not only exert the government's dominate role, but also motivate the enterprises and encourage the broad participation of the public; not only promote the development and application of the low-carbon technology in the production area, but also the importance of low-carbon emissions in our lifestyle and consumption patterns.

Firstly, from the operational level, to realize or even exceed the target whereby the carbon intensity per unit of GDP decreases by 40%-45% in 2020 with 2005 as the base year, China, on the basis of summarizing the experience from the "11th Five-Year" Plan, should enhance its energy conservation and emission reduction policies and more importantly, improve its policy-making and implementation. For example:

To a large degree, the energy conservation target of the "11th Five-Year" Plan was made from "the top to the bottom", and lacked sufficient scientific studies to support the decision-making. The annual and regional breakdown of the energy conservation target was very casual. Judging from international practice, for example, Britain, in making its national emission reduction target, employed a specialized independent consultant agency to make an overall "bottom-to-top" assessment of different departments' emission reduction potential so as to make sure the breakdown of national, regional and departmental emission reduction targets was more rational. From 2001 to 2005, China's energy intensity was on the increase and to reverse the increasing trend, it should first be stabilized before its decrease. It is obviously over-simplified to break down the 20% target of the energy intensity decrease during five years on average into an annual 4%. From the implementation of the "11th Five-Year" Plan energy conservation target, some provinces and municipalities failed to finish the energy conservation target for different reasons and this should be analyzed under specific circumstances. For example, Sichuan, for its reconstruction after the earthquake, had a high demand for high energy-consuming building materials like cement and some of the small high energy-consuming factories still have room for survival. Although the 12% emission reduction target of Hainan Province is the lowest compared with other provinces, it has its own economic development features, with less industries but prosperous tourism, so its energy conservation and emission reduction potential is limited. All in all, we should make more scientific decisions on the basis of in-depth and careful investigation.

Secondly, before the implementation of the target, it lacked an integrated implementation plan and policy design. We could only try to make improvements during the implementation and increase the policy coordination. It was only after the energy conservation target was nailed down in 2005 that different policy measures were made and promulgated. When the energy conservation target failed to be completed as planned in the first two years, the policy measures were further enhanced. Hence, the policy-making process takes up the time of policy implementation. Considering that the effect of the policy implementation may show up at a later time, actually the time for the policy to take effect is further shortened. In making the "12th Five-Year" Plan target, we needed to consider the consistency of the policies and although it was not a ripe time for implementation, we also needed to conduct research on the policy instrument (for example, the carbon tax or the emission trade system) which was possible to introduce and put on trial at an earlier time for necessary policy storage. At the same time, we needed to view the situation overall, enhancing the coordination between the policy of different departments and avoiding fragmentation or subjecting the policy implementation to the influence of departmental benefits.

Thirdly, energy conservation and environmental protection is an overall problem concerning the overall social and economic situation. In mobilizing local, enterprise and social strength, we should not only involve the local government, enterprises and the public in policy implementation, but also encourage more stakeholders into the decision-making. The city is densely populated and the center of economic activities. It is the major source of energy consumption and greenhouse gas emissions. At present, different regions are enthusiastic about the construction of low-carbon cities, but some regions have no clear understanding of the low-carbon economy and city. They have no guidance and the country should protect the local enthusiasm while providing guidance and regulation through appropriate policy measures. The enterprise, as the main player in economic activities, is a large entity of energy consumption and emission and also the implementer of energy conservation and emission reduction, which plays an extremely key role in the realization of the energy conservation target. The government should establish broader channels, hear from the enterprises and mobilize the enterprises. Energy conservation and emission reduction can not only depend on policy orders, but also should establish economic incentives in the enterprise's interest, enabling them to obtain economic returns from energy conservation and emission reduction.

Fourthly, we should stress the differentiation in different region's distribution of labor and industrial transfer. The energy consumption per unit of GDP is an overall index, concerning many factors such as economic growth, economic structure, energy structure, technological level and resource environment. Different regions should make different energy conservation targets based on their own conditions. Also, the regional high energy-consuming industrial transfer is very general, showing the trend from the relatively economically developed regions in the eastern area to the middle and western area. We should pay attention to its influence on the energy conservation target in the western area and different regions should also make adjustments to the energy saving policy based on actual conditions. For example, since Beijing transferred the industrial enterprises like the Shougang Group to other areas, the economic structural change is now favorable to energy conservation and emission reduction. At the same time, the priority of energy conservation is shifting from production utilization to consumption utilization. And the regions accepting the industrial transfer must weigh the economic benefits and environmental effects thus incurred and make proper adjustments to the industrial transfer through policies.

Fifthly, the establishment and improvement in energy, carbon emission statistics, reports, evaluation and assessment system is a basic step for the promotion of energy conservation and emission reduction and the development of a low-carbon economy, which plays a very important role. During the "11th Five-Year" Plan period, national and regional bulletins on energy consumption per unit of GDP were established. According to the State Council's requirement, the National Bureau of Statistics will publish national and regional bulletins on energy consumption per unit of GDP index every half a year and the middle-term assessment results of different provinces' "11th Five-Year" Plan targets were announced. The *Second National Economic Census* launched at the end of 2008 included an energy consumption census as one of the seven major censuses. From the energy intensity target to the carbon intensity target, it involved larger areas, more data and faced more difficulties. This required the statistical system to make corresponding adjustments.

To conclude, China must be prepared to take the challenges of a low-carbon economy. Especially at present, we should combine the short-term target to cope with the financial crisis with the long-term task to promote energy conservation and emission reduction, taking the financial crisis as a good opportunity to change the economic growth pattern and accelerate the structure adjustment, guide the overall situation with the Scientific Outlook on Development, applying the scientific development conception in every aspect and the whole process in the implementation of the "11th Five-Year" Plan and the making of the "12th Five-Year" Plan, and construct a relatively well-off society that is resource-conserving, environment-friendly, economically developed, self-innovative and socially harmonious.

Effect Evaluation and Influential Factor Analysis of the International Transfer of Low Carbon Technology Based on Trade

——Revelations for Post-Copenhagen

By ZHOU Ji & WANG Haiqin

Introduction

Currently, the international community is in urgent need to establish an innovation mechanism for low-carbon technology development and transfer to promote the circulation of advanced technologies around the world, especially the wide application and dissemination of those from developed countries to developing countries, thus improving the developing countries' capability to deal with climate change under the sustainable development framework. To this end, some scholars began to focus their studies on the innovation mechanism of technology development and transfer in the field of climate change (Zhou, 2008; Michael Hubler & Andreas Keller, 2008), among which an important research project is the effect of the scientifically assessed technology transfer method based on the market mechanism in promoting the international transfer of low-carbon technology. A research on this problem will help us to better understand the argument of the policy of the international transfer of a low-carbon technology from developed countries to developing countries: namely, whether the large-scale transfer of low-carbon technology is largely driven by the market mechanism or the government.

The international technology transfer method, in its broad sense, mainly includes international trade, foreign direct investment (FDI), official development assistance (ODA) and the global environment fund (GEF), among which the first two are mainly driven by the market while the latter two by the government or international public organizations.

This article selects international trade, a typical international technology transfer method as the research object to assess the effect of the traditional market-driven mechanism in promoting the international transfer of low-carbon technology and its corresponding influencing factors. Relevant studies show that in international trade, the traditional technology transfer method carries over 75% technology transfer in its broad sense from developed countries to developing countries (Lile & Toman, 1997). However, when considering the uniqueness of low-carbon technology and low-carbon technology transfer (Zhou & Wang, 2007), further studies should be conducted to explore whether international trade can effectively promote this technology transfer and whether it's enough to improve the developing countries' competence to cope with climate change.

Considering this, this article selects China's gas turbine technology① introduced from developed countries as a case study to investigate in depth the process for China's enterprises to import this technology under the analysis framework structure-conduct-performance (SCP). It has observed and analyzed the conduct of major relevant stakeholders under the specified market structure during the introduction and absorption process and through interviews and investigations, obtained the first-hand materials of the Chinese enterprise's introduction and absorption of the technology so as to assess the effect of the technology transfer and its influencing factors. This case study has evaluated the active role international trade has played in promoting the international transfer of low-carbon technology and its limitations and influencing factors. It has provided research support for the establishment of low-carbon technology development and a transfer innovation mechanism in the post-Copenhagen era.

I. Case Introduction

This section will introduce in detail the case of how China's enterprises import developed countries' gas turbine technology for future

① Gas turbine technology is an advanced and mature low-carbon technology in the power sector. For the coal-fired power plant, the SO_2 emission and solid wastes emission from the natural gas power station are nearly zero. The greenhouse gas emission reduced by half, NO_X emission by 2/3 while TSP by 3/4.

analysis.

1. Technology Import Process

During the "10th Five-Year" Plan period, China's energy policy took an important turn, the implementation of the project "West-East natural gas transmission" has provided an opportunity for the development of heavy gas turbine technology. In 2001, it was pointed out in the *Suggestions on the Development and Introduction of Gas Turbine Technology* published by the National Development and Reform Commission that with the large-scale development and utilization of China's natural gas resources and the progress in the offshore natural gas development and liquefied natural gas project, the national energy structure adjustment has been put into practice. The development of the gas and steam combined cycle for electricity generation constitutes an important part of the strategic adjustment.

Against such a backdrop, the National Development and Reform Commission proposed "to make a unified organization of national resources, centralize the invitation for bidding, introduce technologies and promote the development and manufacturing level of the domestic gas turbine industry", namely, to implement "a market in exchange for technology" through bundled bidding and the combination of technology and trade and to purchase foreign gas turbine facilities while introducing the manufacturing technology of heavy-duty gas turbines.

After mutual selection and negotiation between major domestic and foreign electricity generation facility manufacturers, ultimately a famous American power station equipment manufacturer (hereinafter referred to as "American manufacturer") and a domestic Heilongjiang power station equipment manufacturer (hereinafter referred to as "Heilongjiang manufacturer") combined into a consortium for bids, a famous European power station equipment manufacturer (hereinafter referred to as "European manufacturer") and a domestic Shanghai power station equipment manufacturer (hereinafter referred to as "Shanghai manufacturer") combined into a consortium for bids and a famous Japanese power station equipment manufacturer (hereinafter referred to as "Japanese manufacturer") and a domestic Sichuan power station equipment manufacturer (hereinafter referred to as "Sichuan manufacturer") combined into a consortium for bids. In every consortium, the foreign enterprise and the Chinese enterprise are both the technology provider and the technology acceptor and they are companions in the manufacturing process of the contracted equipment. This project, with the market demand of China's gas turbine power station owners as the leverage, demanded the foreign investors' commitment to transfer the gas turbine manufacturing technology to Chinese enterprises. If foreign investors failed to do so, they could not participate in the bidding for the gas turbine equipment purchase. At the same time, foreign investors used the market share as the precondition for the gas turbine technology transfer. The larger the share, the more gas turbine technologies the foreign investor would transfer to Chinese enterprises.

2. Major Stakeholders

According to the classification standard of the stakeholders during the international transfer process of the low-carbon technology by Metz & Davidson (2000), this article identified the major stakeholders during the gas turbine technology import process as follows:

Technology provider: the "American manufacturer", "European manufacturer" and "Japanese manufacturer";

Technology purchaser: this is the most important stakeholder during the international technology transfer. In this case, this refers to the "Heilongjiang manufacturer", "Shanghai manufacturer" and "Sichuan manufacturer";

The government: including both the technology exporter government and the technology importer government. In this case, the main focus is on the government sectors such as National Development and Reform Commission and Ministry of Science and Technology, which have provided different policy support for the import of the gas turbine technology;

Gas turbine user: refers to the power station using gas turbines produced by the three consortiums, and they are the important stakeholders in the technology import process. Although the power station owner hasn't participated directly in the gas turbine technology import process, however, their use of the gas turbine would emphatically influence the importer's digestion and absorption of the gas turbine technology.

Besides these major stakeholders, the import of the gas turbine technology involved many market media and relevant enterprises linking the process, such as the component supplier, the wielding business, the material provider etc.

Based on the research need, this article will mainly analyze the major interest focus and the behavioral features of the government, the technology importer and the technology exporter during the gas turbine technology transfer as well as the effect thus incurred.

II. Framework of the Case Study

This article adopts the "Structure-Conduct-Performance" (hereinafter referred to as the "SCP Analysis Paradigm") in the industrial organization theory as the framework for analysis (Figure 1) to study the effect of the gas turbine technology transfer and the influencing factors.

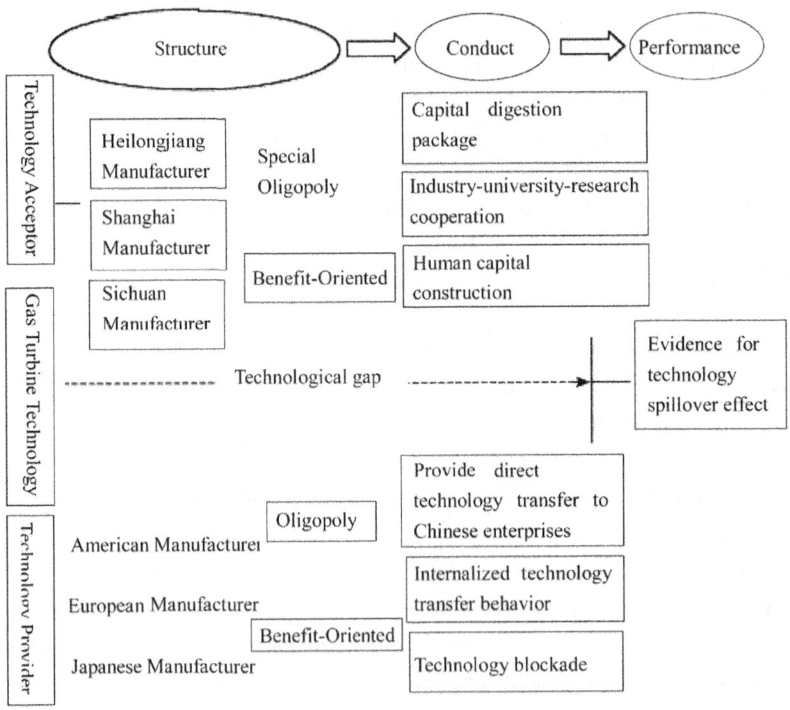

Figure 1 Analytical Framework for the Case Study

1. Introduction to the SCP Analysis Paradigm

The SCP research model was proposed by an American scholar named Bain of Harvard University. By inheriting the predecessors' research findings, he broke down the industry into a specified framework consisting of structure, conduct and performance through empirical studies, a three-phase industrial organization analysis paradigm with logical system and which can be used for detailed analysis.

The market structure refers to the competition or monopoly relations between market players including the provider and the demander. Generally speaking, based on the monopoly level (the number of enterprises), the scale of the manufacturer, the differentiation of products and the in-and-out barrier, it can be structured into perfect monopoly, oligopoly, monopoly competition and perfect competition (Aghion, 2001). The enterprise conduct refers to a series of strategic activities adopted by enterprises to maximize their profits in the market and win larger market share, including the enterprise's price strategy and product strategy. The market performance refers to the industry's resource distribution efficiency and profit distribution resulting from or formed by the market conduct of the major enterprises in the industry under the established market structure. It reflects the overall concept of the detailed industrial operation efficiency and, through studying the industry's market performance, it can accurately judge the rationality and effectiveness of the market structure and conduct.

To some extent, the SCP paradigm will establish a causal relationship between the market structure and the economic performance, so in the relationship that the market structure influences/decides the economic performance, it is easy to simplify the former as the reason and the latter as the result in empirical studies. This is the hot topic of industrial organization theory.

Since the deciding factors and measurement indexes for the structure and performance are different, the results of the empirical studies concerning the relationship between the two are markedly different. Even so, most studies view competition and monopoly, the enterprise scale and the centralization level as important manifestations of the market structure and the productivity, profit rate and technology advancement as the core content of the economic performance. In this way, the structure-performance relationship evolves into different function relationships (Wang, 2001).

2. Selection of the SCP Index in the Case Study

In the case study of the gas turbine technology transfer in this article, we still adopt the factors reflecting competition and monopoly to measure the market structure, such as the number of enterprises, the enterprise scale, the differentiation of products and the in-and-out barrier.

Under the specified market structure, different enterprises will reveal different conduct to improve their competitiveness and this article will focus on the technology transfer conduct of the stakeholders. The technology exporter's conduct is to adopt different technology exporting strategies to maintain its competitive edges; the technology importer's conduct is in response to the Chinese government's strategy of "market in exchange for technology", to import advanced gas turbine technology and enhance its own technical innovation ability through its digestion and absorption.

This article chooses the technology spillover effect as an index to measure performance. The so-called spillover effect refers to the embedded economic growth incurred by the technology transfer in the host country. Chen Xiaofeng (1999) believed that the spillover effect referred to the advanced technology exported in trade or other economic activities, the technology advancement brought about through digestion and absorption of the importer and the economic growth during the technology transfer in the importer's country. Zhang Jianhua (2005) assumed that developing countries' technology import was the international technology spillover from another angle. In the case study, the technology spillover effect is embodied in the enhancement of the enterprise's manufacturing capability and the exporting capability and the increase in the import substitution rate. In assessing the technology spillover effect during the gas turbine technology transfer process, we observed the "mechanism for the occurrence of the technology spillover effect" and sorted out the "evidence of the technology spillover effect" to analyze "whether the stakeholders' conduct has promoted or prohibited the technology spillover effect" and make a qualitative analysis of "the level of promotion or prohibition".

III. Market Structure Analysis of the Technology Provider and Acceptor

1. Market Structure of the Oligopoly Technology Provider

After sixty years' research, development and competition, the world heavy-duty gas turbine manufacturing industry has been currently highly monopolized, with dominating companies as the core, such as the "American manufacturer", "European manufacturer" and "Japanese manufacturer" mentioned in this article and other manufacturers as their partners. The product share of these large transnational corporations and their partners occupies 80% in the total number of the world's gas turbines. Their technical performance and structural features represent the major characteristics and development trend of the heavy-duty gas turbines in today's world.

The technology providers, as the major monopolizing force in today's global gas turbine market, are facing fierce competition from other oligopolies. To obtain China's large market share of the gas turbine, they have to export their technologies. The research finds that the "unwilling" technology transfer of the "American manufacturer", "European manufacturer" and "Japanese manufacturer" to their Chinese partners is an enterprise conducted to suppress their competitors. For example, in studying American manufacturers, relevant personnel expressed that although the American manufacturer's gas turbine market share had been ranked the first emphatically in the global gas turbine market share, yet it still had to transfer its gas turbine technology to Chinese enterprises so as to suppress other multinationals' fierce competition.

2. Market Structure of the Technology Acceptor under the Division of Diverse Government Subjects

At present, China has ten major large and small steam turbine manufacturers, among which the "Heilongjiang Manufacturer", "Shanghai Manufacturer" and "Sichuan Manufacturer" mentioned in this article are the major ones to be equipped with the ability to design and manufacture large steam turbines as well as the ability for the research and development of nuclear power, supercritical units and gas turbines. They have taken up nearly 90% of the domestic market share. Superficially, China's three power facility manufacturers are situated in the oligopoly market structure, but such an oligopoly pattern is not a simple one illustrated in the industrial organization theory, but the "market structure of the technology acceptor under the division of the diverse government subjects" formed under the manipulation of the administrative power and it has the following features:

Firstly, there are diverse government investment subjects in the market. The central government, local government and relevant departments at different levels can all become the market investment subjects. However, these subjects have diverse interest demands, especially under the divided governance of China's power generating equipment manufacturing industry and such demands are hard to coordinate.

Secondly, the enterprise's investment is under soft budget constraint. Since the enterprise bidding for power generating equipment is not the real investor, the enterprise may not hold authentic responsibilities for the investment benefits——for example, the voice "importing gas turbine technology is the country's task" was heard in investigating China's three major manufacturers——and instead, driven by local interest and the requirement of the upper level, it may adopt an extensive development model featured by a disregard of the cost and competition for resources and investment and has little awareness of the enterprise market and the investment risk. This will lead to a general lack of motivation for innovation among enterprises, which will be at a disadvantageous position for competition.

The oligopoly market structure under the intervention of the administrative power, where the technology importer is involved, decides both their active and passive performance during the technology import process. On the one hand, China's three manufacturers will actively import advanced technologies from foreign countries and hold technical innovation activities in the face of the fierce competition; on the other hand, the country's administrative intervention and soft budget constraint also impair the enterprise's motivation for technical innovation to some extent.

IV. Analysis of the Conduct of the Technology Provider and Acceptor

After getting to know the market structure of the technology provider and acceptor, I will discuss major stakeholders' conduct motivated by their own interests during the gas turbine technology transfer process.

1. Analysis of the Technology Provider's Conduct

For an oligopoly market structure, the "American manufacturer", "European manufacturer" and "Japanese manufacturer", as the provider of advanced technologies for China's power facility manufacturers, are facing fierce competition between each other. To fight for China's market share and maintain their own competitive edge, the multinationals have to adjust their own gas turbine technology transfer strategy under the Chinese government's "bundled bidding".

For the gas turbine technology transfer, the " American manufacturer", "European manufacturer" and "Japanese manufacturer" have selected different technology transfer methods based on the technology quality. The conventional gas turbine manufacturing technology is directly exported to Chinese enterprises; as for the core technology like the manufacturing of the gas turbine's high-temperature components, considering that these core technologies are more important than the market share and, once they are spread or transferred to Chinese enterprises, it may possibly cultivate a competitor against themselves in the international market as they transfer these technologies to their joint ventures; besides, for most core technologies, for example, the manufacturing technology of the first stage blade of the gas turbine, the three foreign enterprises basically adopt a technology blockade strategy.

(1) Directly transfer the conventional technology to Chinese enterprises

The conduct of the direct technology transfer to the Chinese enterprise refers to the three multinationals' direct transfer of their technology to China's power generation facility manufacturers based on the stipulation of the contract. According to the investigation, the three foreign enterprises are active in transferring this technology and adopt corresponding measures to help Chinese enterprises to digest and absorb the transferred technology, including adopting different training measures to help Chinese enterprises to digest various technology materials and graphics and establish specialized gas turbine project service groups to help Chinese enterprises to overcome various problems in digesting and absorbing the gas turbine technology at any time.

The three foreign enterprises are active in the transfer of the conventional gas turbine technology which, compared to the core gas turbine technology, has lost its leading and advanced position. Therefore, the technology provider has loosened the grip on its transfer and expansion.

(2) Establish joint ventures and transfer the core gas turbine technology internally

Although the conventional gas turbine manufacturing technology is what the Chinese enterprise lacks, for multinationals it is not the core technology. The three foreign enterprises are conservative about the transfer of the core gas turbine manufacturing technology, or what they are doing can also be called internalized technology transfer conduct.

According to the internalized theory of technology transfer, for the deficiency in the market, the high trade cost and the great risk of international technology transfer have led to the predilection to internalize the technology transfer. In other words, only the internal transfer between the parent company and sub-companies will not pose a threat to the company.

During the gas turbine technology transfer process, the three multinationals all adopted the internalized technology transfer measure as far as the core gas turbine technology is concerned, namely the high-temperature component manufacturing technology. They transfer the core gas turbine technology by establishing joint ventures with Chinese enterprises and as the holding company. Such a conservative conduct has reflected their motive to strictly control the core technology and prevent the leaking of the secrets of the technology.

The "American Manufacturer", "European Manufacturer" and "Japanese Manufacturer" have respectively established joint ventures in China to manufacture the core components of the gas turbine. The foreign enterprises transfer the core technology in an internalized way, which shows their blockade of the core technology.

(3) Blockade the most core components of the gas turbine manufacturing technology

By the time of the investigation, the three foreign enterprises had blockaded the technology for manufacturing the most core components of the gas turbine, such as the first stage blade and nozzle. Besides the technology factor that the manufacturing technology of the first stage blade is far too complicated for the Chinese enterprise to absorb, there is also a non-technology factor, such as the technology exporter's wish to obtain higher monopoly profits by maintaining their technology monopoly and the foreign government's blockade policy on its core gas turbine technology.

2. Analysis of the Technology Acceptor's Conduct

The specific market structure the three Chinese gas turbine technology importers are involved means they have decided that while being active during the importing, digesting and absorbing process, they also cannot avoid being passive.

(1) Take various measures and actively absorb the gas turbine manufacturing technology

The active measures the technology importer has adopted include establishing the specified gas turbine technology import project group, responsible for the management and coordination of the gas turbine technology import; at the same time, the technology importer has amassed a large amount of capital for the absorption of the gas turbine technology by striving for national support and local government's financial support; the establishment of the industry-university-research consortium is an important measure to enable the enterprise to digest and absorb the gas turbine technology. The three foreign enterprises all participated actively in channeling local and national academic resources from institutes of higher learning and the research institutes to cooperate in the digestion and absorption of the gas turbine technology and the secondary research and development work. Other active measures adopted by the technology importer also include the strengthening of human capital construction and the overall theoretical and practical training for the gas turbine technology personnel in various ways.

(2) Passive conduct of the technology acceptor

Since China's power generation facility industry is in the oligopoly market structure under the administrative intervention of a diverse government, besides the active conduct shown in the import process, the technology importer is also passive in digesting and absorbing the technology.

In our investigation into the technology import enterprise, we found that because of the long return-on-investment cycle of the research and development of the gas turbine technology and the existence of relevant substitute technologies, the enterprise didn't deem it as a priority development strategy to import the gas turbine technology, but regarded it as "a task designated by the central government". At the same time, the nation's capital investment was far from satisfactory in supporting the enterprise in finishing this national mission. Therefore, the enterprise had to invest a large amount of capital on its own. However, as far as the achievements made by the technology import and the secondary research and development of the gas turbine technology, the enterprise cannot have them in its own exclusive possession. All this has impaired the innovation motivation of the enterprise through importing, digesting and absorbing the technology.

V. Assessment of the Effect of the Gas Turbine Technology Transfer and Its Influencing Factors

In importing the gas turbine technology, China has obtained a certain technology spillover effect, namely by having improved the enterprise's technological level and the gas turbine manufacturing labor productivity, which has filled the gap in China's heavy-duty gas turbine technology and cultivated a group of technical personnel. This has laid a foundation for the realization of the secondary innovation of China's gas turbine technology. However, as the case study shows, various factors have stemmed the spillover effect and the effect of the gas turbine technology import.

1. The Overall Assessment of the Technology Spillover Effect

In importing the gas turbine technology, China's three major power facility manufacturers digested and absorbed the gas turbine manufacturing technology and testing technology transferred from the foreign enterprises in the form of graphics, technology documents and computer software. They were learning while practicing and improved their own gas turbine manufacturing ability, the export capability of some products and the import substitution rate of the gas turbine. The concrete manifestations are as follows:

Proof 1——Skills Improvement

During the investigation, we found that China's technology importers have made some improvements in their skills, based on the digestion of the graphics. For example, some enterprises made innovative adjustments to the assembly sequence of the transition period of the gas turbine's combustor to cut the assembly period for each piece of equipment by 4-6 days, which improved the gas turbine's productivity; also, some units used the component produced domestically to replace some parts of the gas turbine, which saved large amounts of capital for the enterprise. This is what the enterprise has done to make reasonable improvements in the technology based on the actual local production conditions and its understanding of the gas turbine manufacturing technology. In this way, the technology spillover effect ensues.

Proof 2——Improvement in the Product Export Capability

During the investigation, we found that through the long-term cooperation with the technology exporter and on the basis of understanding and mastering the gas turbine assembly and testing technology, the technology importer has developed an independent ability to produce some important components and to become the supplier of some components for the technology exporter. For example, the assembly of the air cylinder of the gas turbine is a fine skill of high sophistication. The Chinese enterprise's technical personnel, after countless adjustments of the revolution and feed methods, overcame the difficulty of accuracy control and realized quantity production of the air cylinder. At present, they can annually produce 8-12 sets of air cylinders of the gas turbines up to the standard of the technology exporter and become the eligible supplier of the air cylinder for the technology exporter. Such a virtuous "importing-digesting-absorbing-exporting" technology introduction model shows that the enterprise is capable of self technical innovation and product exportation after digesting and absorbing foreign technologies, which is also an important manifestation of the enterprise's attainment of the technology spillover effect.

Proof 3——Improvement in the Import Substitution Rate

Another index to reflect the enterprise's technology spillover effect is the import substitution rate. It shows the percentage of the enterprise's understanding and mastery of the gas turbine manufacturing technology. The higher the rate the more manufacturing technologies the enterprise has mastered and the more likely will be the secondary innovations of the gas turbine technology. According to the latest investigation into the technology import enterprise, as the number of the gas turbines manufactured by the enterprise increases, the enterprise will master more gas turbine manufacturing technologies and the import substitution rate will be improving during the process. According to relevant statistics, a Chinese company had its overall gas turbine import substitution rate improved from the original 46.5% to 77%. The gas turbine import substitution rate of the other two Chinese companies has also increased to some degree.

Indubitably, Chinese enterprises have obtained a certain technology spillover effect. However, it should be noted that the spillover effect China has obtained is still weak. According to the "proof of the technology spillover effect" gathered in the investigation, the three power generation facility manufacturers which import the gas turbine technology are still at the primary stage of learning and imitating foreign enterprises' advanced gas turbine technologies. That is to say, the three manufacturers can accomplish the general assembly and the testing based on the graphics and, during the process, they will improve the technology of manufacturing some conventional components. However, for now they are unable to improve the core components of the gas turbine with high technical content, such as the rotor, the blade and the combustor. In the short run, they can only import such components from foreign countries. The three power generation facility manufacturers also lack the facility for sophisticated processing of the core components and lack highly competent technical personnel, which has, to a certain degree, hindered the technology spillover effect.

2. *Influencing Factors on the Gas Turbine Technology Spillover Effect*

The technology transfer conduct of the technology acceptor and provider directly leads to the technology spillover effect. Besides such conduct factors, we also examined other factors influencing the technology spillover effect.

(1) The gap between foreign and Chinese gas turbine technologies

helps the Chinese party to absorb the conventional technology of gas turbine manufacturing, but prohibits the import of the core technology

Undoubtedly, the technological gap will have an influence on the technology spillover effect. However, there is no definite answer as to whether a large gap or a small gap helps to bring about the technology spillover effect. Current literature only assumes that there is a certain "technological gap threshold value" that is most favorable to bring about the technology spillover effect.

The case study in this article shows that for the conventional gas turbine technology, it is not obvious that the technological gap will prohibit the technology spillover effect because the Chinese manufacturers have basically absorbed the manufacturing technology transferred from foreign enterprises; however, for the core gas turbine technology, or the high-temperature component manufacturing technology, the technological gap has obviously stemmed the technology spillover effect. Up to now, the three power facility manufacturers are unable to manufacture the rotor and turbine blade on their own. The main gap between the Chinese and foreign gas turbine lies in the manufacturing ability of the high-temperature components such as the rotor and blade. Obviously, besides the fact that the foreign enterprise has blockaded its core technology, an excessive technological gap also stems the technology spillover effect to some degree.

Judging from China's gas turbine technological level at present, we believe that at the current stage the gap between Chinese and foreign gas turbine technology is favorable for the import of the conventional gas turbine technology. Right now, China needs to firstly import the conventional gas turbine manufacturing technology and then the core manufacturing technology step by step.

(2) The inherent shortage of China's natural gas reserves reduces the technology spillover effect

As a country "abundant in coal but short in oil and gas", China's natural gas takes up less than 3% in the one-time energy consumption structure, far lower than the global average. According to the statistics of the IEA (2008), China's 67.7-billion-cubic-meter natural gas production accounted for only 2.2% of the world's 3,031.4-billion-cubic-meter total natural gas production in 2007.

An excessively low natural gas reserve will make Chinese enterprises less motivated in the development, digestion and absorption of the natural gas utilization technology, which will influence the technology spillover effect. To begin with, if there is a shortage in the natural gas supply, it may lead to a dwindling demand by Chinese power station owners for gas turbine facilities, making it hard for China to adopt the "market in exchange for technology" strategy and unable to obtain more advanced technologies. Additionally, China's power facility manufacturers may also be pessimistic about the prospect of the application of gas turbine technology because of a shortage of natural gas and become less motivated to digest and absorb the gas turbine technology already imported. It should be conceded that the reason why Chinese enterprises fail to adopt the import of the gas turbine technology as a priority for their own development lies, to a certain degree, in the inherent shortage in China's natural gas reserves.

(3) The effect of China's relevant policies on the technology spillover effect

Here are two kinds of policies: one is the environmental protection policy, mainly referring to the discharge standard of the power plant; the other is the electricity generation policy of natural gas.

Compared with the coal-fired power plant, the natural gas power station discharged almost no sulfur dioxide (SO_2) and solid wastes, reduced the greenhouse gas emission by 1/2, nitric oxide (NO_X) by 2/3 and Total Suspended Particulates (TSP) by 3/4. The more rigorous the discharge standard made by China is, the more motivated the owner becomes to adopt the gas turbine technology. However, at present China's environmental legislation is comparatively lax, which is unfavorable for the promotion of natural gas as a way to generate electricity and for the manufacturer to strengthen their import, digestion and absorption of the gas turbine technology. This has curbed the effect of the import of the gas turbine technology.

Another policy influencing the gas turbine technology import effect is the electricity pricing policy of natural gas. Although generating electricity through natural gas is a typical low-carbon and environment-friendly technology featured by high efficiency and low emissions, its cost is higher than generating electricity from coal. Without the support of some relevant preferential policies, generating electricity from natural gas lacks a competitive edge. Currently in China, whether the price of power plant natural gas or the retail electricity price using gas, there are no corresponding preferential policies. The absence of such policies hinders the popularization of gas turbine technology in China.

VI. General Conclusions of the Case Study

This article analyzed the case in which China imported low-carbon technology through trade at the beginning of the 21st century and observed the process of the technology transfer and spillover. Under the analysis paradigm of "Structure-Conduct-Performance", it studied the interests involved and the technology transfer conduct of the technology exporter and importer during the gas turbine technology transfer process as well as their influence on the technology spillover effect; at the same time, it analyzed the influence in the gap between Chinese and foreign gas turbine technology, the natural gas provision and China's environmental policy on the technology spillover effect. The general conclusions of the case study include:

1. Trade, the traditional technology transfer method can promote the international transfer of low-carbon technology to a certain degree

The case study shows that trade is an important channel for developing countries like China to share developed countries' technology development achievements and obtain a foreign technology spillover effect. The three major Chinese manufacturers, in importing the gas turbine technology, digested and absorbed the gas turbine manufacturing technology transferred by foreign enterprises, improved their production skills and the export capability of some products and the import substitution rate of the gas turbine. At present, when most developing countries are under the dual pressure of alleviating climate change and accelerating their economic development, it is necessary to make full use of the trade channels to promote the transfer and expansion of low-carbon technology to developing countries on a large scale.

2. The import of low-carbon technology requires the intervention of the government

In essence, the multinational corporation in pursuit of profits is under no obligation to willingly export its technology to improve the environment and technology of developing countries like China. As a matter of fact, advanced technologies are the arm for the multinational to maintain its global competitive edge. Under such circumstances, to break through the blockade of advanced technologies by the technology provider becomes one of the obstacles during developing countries' import of advanced energy technologies.

In the case study, we can find that the intervention of the Chinese government can change the conduct of the technology provider and acceptor through policy methods so as to promote the expansion of low-carbon technology in developing countries and encourage the technology acceptor to actively digest and absorb the imported technology. To be more specific, the Chinese government combined "market in exchange of technology" and "competition in exchange of technology" in its strategy to break through a foreign enterprise's blockade of advanced gas turbine manufacturing technology. It used China's domestic gas turbine market share as the leverage and forced the three multinationals, the gas turbine facility and technology providers, to export technologies to Chinese enterprises for the attainment of China's gas turbine market share.

3. It is unrealistic to depend on trade for the realization of a large-scale international low-carbon technology transfer

Trade, the traditional technology transfer method, can indeed promote the international transfer of low-carbon technology and its influence cannot be ignored. However, we should note that influenced by factors like the market, policy and technology, the technology spillover effect obtained by China is weak, unable to meet China's urgent need for advanced low-carbon technologies at present. This shows the limitation of trade as a traditional method in promoting the international transfer and expansion of low-carbon technology and further proves that it is unrealistic to depend merely on the market mechanism to realize the large-scale international transfer of low-carbon technology.

4. The host country's policy coordination is an important factor influencing the transfer effect of low-carbon technology

Studies show that China's environmental regulation policy has prohibited the transfer effect of low-carbon technology to some extent. Whether the environmental policy and regulation concerning the power plant's discharge standard or the electricity generation through a natural gas policy, both of them are unfavorable in guiding and motivating power plants to adopt the electricity generation method through natural gas. This will jeopardize the enterprise's incentive to digest and absorb the gas turbine technology and reduce the technology spillover effect. This shows that China's environmental regulation policy fails to be consistent with the low-carbon technology import strategy, which has influenced the technology transfer effect.

VII. Policy Connotation

Based on the above research, to promote the international transfer of low-carbon technology and help developing countries, including China, to improve their capability to cope with climate change, this article proposes:

1. Domestically, to enhance the mechanism, system and capability construction that is favorable for the international transfer of low-carbon technology

Firstly, establish new mechanisms for technology import based on the selection of the market under the government's intervention and make full use of technology import strategies to realize the leapfrog development. The aim of the government's intervention is to establish a reasonable system and policy framework for the import of low-carbon technology, create a market environment that is favorable to the transfer and expansion of low-carbon technology and play an appropriate role in selecting, digesting, absorbing and promoting the technology. At the same time, we should be cautious of the government's over intervention in the import of low-carbon technology, mitigate the prohibition of the market structure under the diverse government's intervention in the enterprise's self-innovation, enable the enterprise to combine the import strategy of low-carbon technology with its self-development strategy on its own initiative and make it highly motivated to import, digest and absorb advanced low-carbon technology that is consistent with China's basic national conditions. Next, we should coordinate the strategic relationship between the low-carbon technology import and self-research and development. The import of low-carbon technology should be grounded on the digestion, absorption and innovation followed by the promotion of the national technology as the ultimate aim. We should avoid the prohibition of repetitive and excessive technology imports and allow Chinese enterprises' the ability to do self-research and development and encourage the enterprises to establish themselves gradually as the major players in the innovation of low-carbon technology.

Secondly, enhance the construction of the environmental regulation policy and coordinate the low-carbon technology import strategy and climate policy. To begin with, in consideration of the externality of the climate change problem, the government should internalize the external cost through a policy method like taxation. In addition, we should improve relevant legislation on climate change and motivate the enterprise to actively import and absorb low-carbon technology by setting an energy efficiency standard and emission standard and establishing statistics, monitoring and assessment system. At the same time, for the high cost of the low-carbon technology utilization, we should also foster a sound market environment by making such preferential policies as subsidy provision and tax reduction and exemption to improve the demand for low-carbon products and technologies and ultimately promote the digestion, absorption and expansion of the imported low-carbon technology, enhance the enterprise's capability of digesting and absorbing imported technologies and enable the enterprise to obtain greater technology spillover effects.

Thirdly, strengthen capability construction and improve the technology importer's absorption ability. To begin with, we should enhance the enterprise's research and development capability and increase the investment in their fund, make effective and reasonable distribution of human resources, improve the enterprise's internal technical innovation mechanism and strengthen its self-innovation capability; also, we should establish a cooperation mechanism for the enterprise, university and research institute to jointly digest and absorb the technology. In the case study, it can be found that the three power generation facility manufacturers, in importing, digesting and absorbing the gas turbine technology, have all established cooperation mechanisms with universities and relevant research institutes. Through such mechanisms, the digestion and absorption of the gas turbine technology will be accelerated; lastly, we should realize that human capital is an important factor to improve the technology import effect and we should take measures to attract excellent personnel in science and technology.

To conclude, the Chinese government should scientifically manage and properly direct the import of low-carbon technology. It should take the import of low-carbon technology as an opportunity to realize China's leapfrog low-carbon development and, at the same time, enhance the enterprise's self-innovation ability, promote the construction of an innovative nation, make the technology import strategy more coordinated with the climate policy and ultimately realize multi-purposes in economy, society and environment.

2. *At the international level, establish a new mechanism for the international transfer of low-carbon technology*

In the post-Copenhagen era, an innovative international transfer mechanism for low-carbon technology should remove the limitation of the traditional international transfer mechanism in promoting the low-carbon technology transfer. From the case study in this article, we can find that the developed countries' export policy of some technologies has restricted the expansion of their low-carbon technology to China. Under such circumstances, the governments of developed countries and developing countries should reach further consensus on the urgency of the technology development and transfer. Developed countries should realize that some of their foreign policies are blocking the real-time transfer of low-carbon technology to developing countries. Another obstacle is that the enterprises from developed countries, in order to maintain their technology monopoly advantages, constantly enhance their blockade of low-carbon technology. Such kinds of problem should be solved through the corresponding arrangements made by the international technology transfer innovative mechanism in the post-Copenhagen era.

As a product of the political competition and compromise between major stakeholders in international climate negotiation, the new mechanism of the international low-carbon technology transfer should be a brand-new one based on the existent mechanism and improved through the existent mechanism. Its aim is to accelerate the speed of developed countries in transferring low-carbon technology to developing countries, expand the coverage of the international cooperation of low-carbon technology, enhance international technology cooperation and deepen low-carbon international cooperation without jeopardizing the enterprise's profit-seeking and rapid economic growth (Sustainable Development Strategy Research Group, China Academy of Sciences, 2009). The mechanism should fully integrate the import channels of low-carbon technology, including the utilization of the traditional international technology transfer mechanism based on trade and the existent international technology transfer method driven by the government's public fund. It should also make the cooperation between governments the major driving force for the low-carbon technology transfer while combining the market mechanism.

Firstly, establish specialized agencies and funds to coordinate different countries' stakeholders, promote the exchange and sharing of the information and knowledge between different countries, and constantly predispose the policy environment in the aspects of taxation, financing, technology and standard towards the international transfer of low-carbon technology.

Secondly, motive the private enterprises in developed countries to participate in the international transfer of low-carbon technology. The governments of developed countries should adopt policy measures to issue positive signals to the private enterprises in their countries and encourage them to actively participate in the technology transfer to developing countries. This includes: exempt taxation for the enterprises from developed countries in exporting low-carbon technology; provide subsidies to encourage the development and transfer of low-carbon technology; offer preferential conditions for export credit concerning low-carbon technology, such as providing trade guarantees and export subsidies; lift the restriction on the export of low-carbon technology and other relevant policies and measures (Sustainable Development Strategy Research Group, China Academy of Sciences, 2009).

References:

[1] Chen Xiaofeng. Occurrence of the technology spillover effect and its influencing factors. *Journal of Fuzhou University (Social Sciences Edition)*, 1999: 13(2).

陈晓枫:《技术溢出效应的产生及影响因素》,《福州大学学报(社会科学版)》1999 年第 13 卷第 2 期。

[2] Cui Ping, Lin Rumei, Jin Hongguang & Xu Yujie. Manufacturers in the global gas turbine market and the properties of products. *Gas Turbine Technology*, 2004 (2).

崔平、林汝谋、金红光、徐玉杰:《世界燃气轮机市场厂商与产品性能》,《燃气轮机技术》2004 年第 2 期。

[3] Wang Weiguang & Dong Ruhe. The marketstructure and technical innovation: a view of the industrial organization theory. *Journal of Shenyang Normal University (Social Sciences Edition)*, 2001(6).

王伟光、董如合:《市场结构与技术创新:一种产业组织理论的观点》,《沈阳师范学院学报(社会科学版)》2001 年第 6 期。

[4] Wu Xianfu. Research on the Technology Improvement Investment Project of Dongfang Steam Turbine Works [MA]. University of Electronic Science and Technology of China, 2003.

吴贤富:《东汽厂燃气轮机技改投资项目研究》,电子科技大学硕士学位论文 2003 年版。

[5] Zhang Jianhua. Theoretical analysis and empirical research of technology improvement and China's sustainable economic growth. *Nanjing Business Review*, 2005 (6).

张建华:《技术进步与中国经济可持续增长的理论分析和经验研究》,《南京大学商学评论》2005 年第 6 期。

[6] Sustainable Development Strategy Research Group, China Academy of Sciences: China Sustainable Development Strategy Report 2009. Science Press, 2009.
中国科学院可持续发展战略研究组:《2009 中国可持续发展战略报告》,科学出版社 2009 版。

[7] Zhou Ji. Innovation in the international mechanism of technology development and transfer in the field of climate change. *Environmental Protection*, 2008(5a).

邹骥:《气候变化领域技术开发与转让国际机制创新》,《环境保护》2008 年第 5a 期。

[8] Zhou Ji & Wang Haiqin. A tentative study of the uniqueness of the international technology transfer against the backdrop of multilateral environmental agreements. *Environmental Protection*, 2007(4b).

邹骥、王海芹:《浅谈多边环境公约背景下国际技术转移的特殊性》,《环境保护》2007 年第 4b 期。

[9] Aghion, P., C. Harris, P. Howitt and J. Vickers, Competition, Imitation and Growth with Step-by-Step Innovation, Review of Economic Studies, 2001 (3).

[10] Hubler, M., and A. Keller. Energy Savings via FDI? Empirical Evidence from Developing Countries, 2008, Working Paper.

[11] International Energy Agency (IEA), Key World Energy Statistics, 2008, Paris.

[12] Lile, R. and M. Toman. Promoting International Transfer of "Clean" Technology, Prepared for Mutually Beneficial Opportunities for Technology Transfer to Promote International Greenhouse Gas Reduction Workshop, Beijing, November 14-17, 1997.

[13] Metz, B., O. R. Davidson, J. W. Martens, S. V. Rooijen and L. V. W. McGrory. Methodological and Technological Issues in Technology Transfer, A Special Report of IPCC Working Group III, Cambridge University Press, 2000.

China's Greenhouse Gas Emissions and Evaluation of Scenario Research

By LI Yuhong [*]

Institute of Quantitative & Technical Economics, Chinese Academy of Social Sciences; the Environment and Development Research Center, Chinese Academy of Social Sciences

Introduction

Since the reform and opening up, China's economy has developed at an annual rate of 9.5%, which has caught worldwide attention. At the same time, China's energy consumption featured by coal is increasing year by year, with its carbon dioxide emissions repetitively surpassing the expectation of the international organization, which becomes a highly concerned problem for the international community. In 2007, the *World Energy Outlook* published by the International Energy Agency (IEA) focused on the scenario research on China and India's future energy supply and demand and carbon emissions. Relevant public and private organizations in Europe and America are highly concerned about China's energy demands and greenhouse gas emissions and have constantly published their research findings (EIA, 2009; PBL, 2009; Wang and Watson, 2008, et al.).

The scenario refers to the description of current circumstances, possible or favorable future circumstances and a series of events that could take place under future circumstances. The three factors of the scenario can be captured as follows: the description of current conditions, various future conditions and the method connecting the

---

* The author is grateful for the suggestions of Zheng Yisheng, Zhang Xiao and Zhang Youguo in the Environment and Development Research Center, Chinese Academy of Social Sciences on the first draft. Many views in this article come from the discussion with Researcher Zheng Yisheng. The author takes sole responsibility for his views.

present and the future. An understanding of the current scenario is the basis for the research on China's future greenhouse gas emissions. This article firstly estimated China's carbon dioxide emissions during the industrial production process and the burning of fossil fuels; then reviewed the baseline scenario and mitigation scenario research on China's greenhouse gas emissions and lastly assessed these scenario researches and made possible predictions about their future development.

I. Connotation of Scenario and Origin of the Scenario Research

Scenario originally had the following meanings: the plot outline of a play, the plot prompt used by the actor in the improvisational performance in the 16th or 17th century in Italy and the film script, which extended to mean the scheme and event. As a tool's scenario method, it is a description of the current situation, the possible or favorable future situation and a series of events eliciting the future situation. This has three connotations: firstly, the description of the current situation includes two factors: the innate inertia and the probability of changes; secondly, the future situation; thirdly, the development method from the present to the future. If these two factors are excluded, there can be no justified description of the present situation, thus easily resulting in a scientific fiction. Also, if the development method cannot be depicted, the result may be a utopian description (F. R. Veeneklaas and L. M. van den Berg, 1995). The three factors of the scenario can be summarized as: the description of the current state, different future situations and the method connecting the present and the future.

To establish a scenario we have to make a series of consistent and coherent assumptions linking the research phenomenon, the decisive factor and the expected development. Sometimes the premise is based on scientific knowledge and theories, but sometimes it may be subjective judgments. The consistency and coherence required in the premise makes the scenario analysis different from the variable analysis and the sensitivity analysis, with the latter illustrating the influence of the variable on the future development merely through the change of one or several parameters. Under the premise of consistency, we need to make a systematic and selective description of the current situation and identify the most important external factor in deciding future processes. The joint impact of the internal assumption and the external factor of the scenario give rise to different incident combinations and ultimately leads to different future situations. Both quantitative model and qualitative reasoning can be adopted. The bottom-up method starts from the partial analysis of the key factor, while the top-down one from the all-encompassing concepts.

Scenario, as a tool to identify the problem and aid the decision-making, can be traced to the time around the Second World War when the nuclear physicist used computational simulation to deal with the probability and uncertainty. Since the early 1970s, the enterprise and governmental organizations used the scenario tool in making strategic decisions and planning. One of the reasons why the scenario research surpasses the expert's judgment and other planning tools lies in that it can elaborate the future's uncertainty (I. J. Schoonenboom, 1995).

The climate change assessment concerns the highly complicated mechanism of the interaction between human beings and the natural system and climate change itself is a phenomenon that has been long accumulating in history. To assess such a highly unstable phenomenon, the scenario method has its incomparable advantages. It can utilize both science and imagination, clearly clarifying a series of possible future situations and development methods. A long-term view with many possibilities in the future is required to examine the basic risk of climate change, evaluate the interaction between climate change, human beings and the environmental system and guide the policy response (IPCC, 2001).

In 1990, the intergovernmental IPCC developed its first greenhouse gas emission scenario, which was used as the input parameter of the global general atmospheric circulation to assess the impact of climate change. In 1992, IPCC updated and expanded its original scenario, abbreviated as IS92 Scenario, which spanned from 1990 to 2100, including such greenhouse gases as CO_2, CO, CH_4, N_yO_x and SO_2. In 1995, IPCC evaluated the IS92 model and believed that it cannot be used to evaluate the result of the emission reduction policy because these scenarios lack sufficient detailed departmental and regional information.

The aim of the scenario study lies in the diversity of the process and outcome. In consideration of the diverse future possibilities, it may involve one or many scenarios. An alternative scenario means different interpretations of the current situation and the possible occurrence of future events. The greenhouse gas emission scenario is divided into the baseline scenario and the mitigation scenario, with the latter based on the former and to alter the greenhouse gas emissions through policy intervention by man. However, the difference between the two is lesser than the gap between different baseline scenarios. In the IS92 Scenario, there is only one baseline scenario, which has limited the description of many future possibilities.

Since 1996, IPCC has begun to establish a set of new baseline scenarios. In 2000, IPCC issued the Special Report on Emission Scenarios (SRES). Based on the evaluation of over four hundred scenarios from 171 different documents, the panel of experts from IPCC proposed 40 baseline emission scenarios of four types and six models (IPCC, 2000). Compared with IS92, SRES added many baseline scenarios by combining a qualitative description and quantitative model and expanded the scope of the key variables. However, excessive baselines increased the complexity of the mitigation scenario research. In 2001, IPCC issued the Third Assessment Report (TAR), having examined the progress of the scenario research since the Second Assessment Report (SAR). The research literature touches upon three aspects: the mitigation scenario since the second assessment report, the descriptive scenario in the research of futurology and the mitigation scenario based on the SRES baseline scenario (IPCC, 2001). After SRES was issued, IPCC no longer developed new baseline scenarios and only reviewed the already existent emission scenario researches (Jiang, 2005).

In scenario researches, both qualitative and quantitative methods are used. Futurology research usually adopts a qualitative method which aims at depicting the overall situation in the future and provides convincing interpretations for a series of events happening in the future. Such a method boasts advantages in describing systematic evolution, such as the changes in value, culture and system, while the qualitative research is unable to describe such systematic variables. The quantitative standard model adopts tools from mathematics to depict the key features of human beings and the environmental system to show the systematic evolution based on different premises. These features include population, the economic growth, technological advances and the environmental sensitivity. It is advantageous in predicting the future situation driven by inertia while the qualitative research is too assertive in this regard (IPCC, 2001).

According to different reasoning directions, the scenario can be categorized into two types, projective and prospective, the former from the past to the present and to the future, which offers the motivation mechanism for the present and predicts how things will progress in the future, while the latter is the opposite, tracing back from the expectant future, which offers the future possibility or the idealized scenario to analyze how to realize the target (I. J. Schoonenboom, 1995) . A baseline scenario is generally projective while a mitigation scenario may be both projective and prospective.

It is worth noting that the scenario tool is different from prediction. The latter attempts to predict what the future is like rather than explore possible future or expected future possibilities. It is to describe the most likely future. These two are different philosophically. If the development of the phenomenon is deemed to be dominated by the important innate inertia, prediction is the most preferred choice; however, if the future holds great uncertainty, or we are unsatisfied with the current situation and its trend and hope that idealized situations may occur, then the scenario tool is more applicable. Chronologically speaking, prediction is better to be used in the short term because, in the short term, the factor manipulating the progress of the event can be deemed as stable, which is already known, while in the long run the scenario analysis is needed since it is likely that the trend and action relationship has undergone critical changes. In reality there is no big difference between the two. The baseline scenario in the scenario analysis usually adopts the method of prediction. In prediction, the uncertainty of the key parameter is usually set as a group of variables, teaming into a creditable scope for future possible outcomes and giving rise to a high scenario and a low scenario.

II. An Estimation of the Total Carbon Oxide Emissions in China

The calculation and the research into our present carbon dioxide emissions are mainly done by foreign institutions, such as the United Nations Framework Convention on Climate Change (UNFCCC), Intergovernmental Panel on Climate Change (IPCC), International Energy Agency, Netherlands Environmental Assessment Agency and DOE Carbon Dioxide Information Analysis Center etc. Chinese scholars estimated China's carbon emissions in 1990s, but few have estimated the national carbon emissions in recent years, especially since the first round of economic growth. In *China's National Program to Cope with Climate Change*, some experts made a preliminary estimation that until

2004 the total carbon dioxide emissions in China would be 5.07 billion tons. In the Copenhagen UN Climate Change Conference, China showed the whole world its determination and aim to reduce carbon dioxide emissions. It will be China's international obligation to calculate and report the carbon dioxide emissions in coping with climate change. This section will estimate the carbon dioxide emissions from China's burning of fossil fuel and China's industrial production since 2000 by using the energy balance sheet and output of industrial products, adopting the reference approach proposed in *the* 2006 *IPCC Guideline for National Greenhouse Gas Inventories* and integrating the discharge coefficient of the carbon dioxide emission source issued by the domestic and international institutions. This helps to deepen our understanding of the present transformation of economic development model and enhance our capability to cope with the challenges posed by global climate change.

1. Estimations from the Existing Literature

Since the 1990s, relevant sectors of the Chinese government have organized much research about China's greenhouse gas. For example, *Research on China's National Strategy towards Global Climate Change* jointly by the State Scientific and Technological Commission and Asia Development Bank, *Problems and Strategies in Controlling China's Greenhouse Gas* by the State Environmental Protection Administration and the World Bank, 1990 *China's Greenhouse Gas Control Source and Sequestration Estimation* by GEF project analysis, *Research on National Climate Change* and *Research on the Strategy with Minimal Cost for Asia to Reduce Greenhouse Gas Emissions* organized by the State Scientific and Technological Commission and *Integrated Analysis of China's Greenhouse Gas Source Emission and Absorption Research Findings* and *Current Situation and Future Conception of China's Greenhouse Gas Emissions* by the National Climate Change Coordination Group Office. Relevant experts from the Energy Research Institute of the National Development and Reform Commission, Tsinghua University, Institute of Atmospheric Physics, Chinese Academy of Sciences, Chinese Academy of Agricultural Sciences and Beijing Municipal Environmental Monitoring Center have participated in these researches (Zhang, 2001).

Gao Shuting, et al. (1994) estimated China's greenhouse gas emissions in 1990. They adopted the carbon emission coefficient of the fossil fuel by the Energy Research Institute and estimated China's carbon dioxide emissions at 2. 12 billion tons in 1990. Since the emission source of the industrial production process that was calculated only included the cement industry, therefore the estimated result was less than the official release, 2. 4 billion tons. They predicted that by 2010 China's carbon dioxide emissions would be 3. 96 billion tons and by 2020, 4. 9 billion tons. However, China's carbon dioxide emissions had already reached 5 billion tons in 2004①.

Zhang Renjian, et al. (2001) adopted the emission coefficient in the 1996 *IPCC Guideline for National Greenhouse Gas Inventories* and calculated China's carbon dioxide emissions as 2. 22 billion tons in 1990, among which 92. 5% came from fossil fuels, with 47. 2% of the industrial emission source coming from the cement industry. In 1994, the carbon dioxide emissions increased to 2. 79 billion tons, an increase of 25. 6% over 1990.

In 2005, the most authoritative UNFCCC published China's greenhouse gas emissions in 1994, about 4. 06 billion tons' carbon dioxide equivalent (excluding the changes in land utilization and forestry), taking up 34. 6% of the 122 Non-Annex I contracting countries. The greenhouse gas included carbon dioxide, methane and nitrous oxide, among which the carbon dioxide emission was 3. 073 billion tons, accounting for 74% of the three greenhouse gas emissions. The energy sector had the largest amount of greenhouse gas emissions, followed by agriculture and industry. These data were sorted out based on the *IPCC Guideline for National Greenhouse Gas Inventories* and were comparatively comprehensive.

Table 1 China's Greenhouse Gas Emissions in 1994
(Carbon Dioxide Equivalent)

	Energy	Industry	Agriculture	Wastes	Total
Emissions (100 million tons)	30. 08	2. 83	6. 05	1. 62	40. 58
Percentage (%)	74. 1	7. 0	14. 9	4. 0	100. 0

Data source: UNFCCC, The 6th compilation and overall report of the 1st national information bulletin by the contracting parties in the Non-Convention-Annex I: Greenhouse Gas Emissions through Man-Made Source and Sequestration Removals Inventory, 2005.

① National Bureau of Statistics: *International Statistics Yearbook (2005)*, China Statistics Press, 2007.

The Carbon Dioxide Information Analysis Center (CDIAC) of the Oak Ridge National Laboratory (ORNL), USA, estimated China's carbon dioxide emissions based on energy consumption and cement production. According to their calculation, China's carbon dioxide emissions in 1990 and 1994 were respectively 2.41 billion tons and 3 billion tons①, a percentage of 10.7% and 13.1% in the total global carbon dioxide emissions. In 2006, China's carbon dioxide emissions were 6.1 billion tons, a percentage of 20% of the total global emissions.

Table 2　CDIAC's Estimation of China's Carbon Dioxide Emissions

Year	Total Emissions (100 million tons)	Annual Average Increase rate (%)	Percentage in the Global Emissions (%)
1990	24.1	—	10.7
1994	30.0	—	13.1
2000	34.1	2.6	13.8
2001	34.9	2.4	13.8
2002	37.0	6.1	14.5
2003	43.5	17.6	16.3
2004	51.0	17.1	18.1
2005	56.3	10.3	19.2
2006	61.0	8.5	20.2

Data source: website of the Carbon Dioxide Information Analysis Center (CDIAC) of the Oak Ridge National Laboratory, America, cdiac.ornl.gov/trends/emis/meth_reg.html.

In 2007, the IEA reported that in 2005 China's carbon dioxide emission from fossil fuels was 5.1 billion tons (IEA, 2007) and 5.6 billion tons in 2006, 6 billion tons in 2007, accounting for 21% of the global total, 300 million tons more than that of the USA (IEA, 2009).

In 2007, the Netherlands Environmental Assessment Agency (PBL) announced for the first time to the world that in 2006 China's carbon dioxide emissions ranked 1st in the world, estimating that China's carbon dioxide emissions in that year were 8% more than that of the USA (in 2009, they updated the number to 6.59 billion tons, 13% more than that of the USA) and they included fossil fuels and cement in their calculation②. In 2009, the U.S. Energy Information Administration (EIA, 2009) reported that in

① http://cdiac.ornl.gov/trends/emis/meth_reg.html.

② http://planet.nccucs.org/2009/01/25/434/.

2006 China's carbon emissions had exceeded that of the USA. Some scholars disagreed with this verdict, who estimated China's carbon dioxide emissions at 5. 67 billion tons in 2006, which were lower than America's 5. 955 billion tons (Guan, et al. , 2008).

Table 3 Collection of Research on China's Carbon Dioxide Emissions (unit: 100 million tons)

Research Institution/ Author	Publishing Year	Calculation Scope	1990	1994	2004	2005	2006	2007	2008
Gao Shuting, et al.	1994	Fossil fuel, cement	21. 2						
Zhang Renjian, et al.	2001	Fossil fuel, industrial process	22. 19	27. 88					
UNFCCC	2005	Based on the inventory guideline of IPCC		30. 73					
ORNL	2009	Fossil fuel, cement and waste gas burning	24. 1	30. 0	51. 0	56. 3	61. 0		
IEA	2008, 2009	Fossil fuel	24. 11		47. 61	51	56. 45	60	
EIA	2009	Fossil fuel	22. 62		47. 07	52. 49	60. 18		
PBL	2007	Fossil fuel, cement				58. 9	65. 9	71. 3	75. 5
Guan, et al.	2008	Fossil fuel, cement, metallurgy, chemical engineering					56. 7		

Data source: Gao Shuting, Zhang Huiqin & Yang Lirong, et al. : A tentative study of China's greenhouse gas emission estimation, *Research of Environmental Sciences*, 1994(6).

Zhang Renjian, Wang Mingxing & Zheng Xunhua, et al. : Analysis of the current situation of China's carbon dioxide emission source, *Climatic and Environmental Research*, 2001(3).

UNFCCC, The 6th compilation and overall report of the 1st national information bulletin by the contracting parties in the Non-Convention-Annex I: Greenhouse Gas Emissions through Man-Made Source and Sequestration Removals Inventory, 2005.

http: //cdiac. ornl. gov/trends/emis/meth_reg. html.

IEA, CO_2 Emissions from Fuel Combustion 2009; EIA, International Energy Outlook, 2009.

EIA, International Energy Outlook, 2009.

Dabo Guan, Klaus Hubacek, Christopher L. Weber, et al. The Drivers of Chinese CO_2 Emissions from 1980 to 2030, Global Environmental Change, 2008, 626-634.

2. Emission Source and Calculation Method

Economic activities such as the burning of fossil fuel and the industrial production process are the major source of carbon dioxide emissions from human activities. This article estimated the emission of these two activities. Undoubtedly, there are other human activities which also discharge carbon dioxide, such as the burning of biomass and garbage, the changes in land and forest utilization etc. However, compared with the two mentioned above, their emissions are comparatively less. The energy sector of developed countries generally takes up over 90% of the carbon dioxide emissions (IPCC, 2006) and the burning of fossil fuels and the industrial production process took up over 90% of China's carbon dioxide emissions in 1994. Compared with the requirements for different emission sources in *the* 2006 *IPCC Guideline for National Greenhouse Gas Inventories* (abbreviated as "2006 IPCC Guideline"), this article only makes a rough estimation.

(1) Emission source of fossil fuel

The energy sector is usually the most important department for greenhouse gas emissions. The carbon dioxide emissions of the energy sector in developed countries generally takes up 95% of the total greenhouse gas emissions in the sector, the remainder being methane and nitrous oxide. The burning of fixed sources usually contributes to 70% of the greenhouse gas emissions in the energy sector. About half of the emission is related to burning in the energy industry, mainly in the power plants and the oil refineries. The burning of moving sources (cars and other transportation means) accounts for 1/4 of the emissions of the energy sector. During the burning process, the carbon and hydrogen in the fossil fuel (irrespective of sulphur) turns into carbon dioxide and water. There are two ways to calculate the carbon dioxide emission of the fossil fuel: reference approach and sectoral approach. Generally speaking, the former is a top-down approach based on different types of fuels; the latter, a bottom-up approach based on different techniques. These two approaches can have their findings inter-examined (IPCC, 2006).

According to the 2006 IPCC Guideline and in consideration of the availability of the data, this article uses the Tier1 method, a reference approach to calculate the carbon dioxide emission, but in selecting the emission coefficient, I will compare how different emission coefficients influence the estimation of the carbon dioxide emission. The emission of the fossil fuel burning source can be calculated based on the amount of the fuel burned and the average emission factor. As for carbon dioxide, its emission factor mainly depends on the carbon content of the fuel. The burning condition (burning efficiency and the carbon residue in the slag and stove ash) is, comparatively speaking, irrelevant. Therefore, the carbon dioxide emission can be estimated on the basis of the total amount of the fuel burned and the average carbon content in the fuel.

Many countries have calculated the carbon dioxide emission coefficient. If calculated at per unit coal equivalent in the burning of the fossil fuel, the carbon emission coefficient of the coal, petroleum and natural gas is respectively 0. 651-0. 755, 0. 5-0. 585 and 0. 395-0. 447. In 2006, the IPCC Guideline offered the carbon emission coefficients per unit heat value of different fossil fuels as the reference value for the estimating country when there is no relevant data available. When converted into per unit standard coal equivalent, the anthracite coal emission coefficient is 0. 785, the crude oil, 0. 586, the natural gas, 0. 448 and the coke, 0. 856.

Table 4 Estimated Coefficients of the Carbon Content in Different Types of Fuels (per unit standard coal equivalent)

Institution/Product	Coal	Petroleum	Natural Gas	Coke
Energy Research Institute of National Development and Reform Commission	0. 651	0. 543	0. 404	
ORNL	0. 733	0. 596	0. 411	
IPCC	0. 785[1]	0. 585[2]	0. 449	0. 856

Note: 1. Anthracite coal; 2. Crude oil.

Data source: Gao Shuting, Zhang Huiqin & Yang Lirong, et al. : A tentative study of China's greenhouse gas emission estimation, *Research of Environmental Sciences*, 1994(6).

Qian Jie & Yu Lizhong. Research on the contribution of the fuel fossil emission to carbon dioxide in Shanghai. *Shanghai Environmental Sciences.* 2003(11).

IPCC. 2006 IPCC Guideline for National Greenhouse Gas Inventories, 2006.

The carbon emission coefficient of the coal, petroleum and natural gas calculated by the Energy Research Institute of National Development and Reform Commission is respectively 0. 651, 0. 543 and 0. 404 (Gao, et al. , 1994).

The carbon emission coefficient of the fire coal, fuel oil and gas proposed by the ORNL is respectively 0. 733, 0. 596 and 0. 411 (Qian & Yu, 2003).

It can be seen that the carbon dioxide emission coefficient in different countries varies. The emission coefficients of different fuels in China are comparatively low while those issued by foreign institutions are high, the coal emission coefficient in particular, with the coefficient of the IPCC 20. 6% higher than that of the Energy Research Institute. That of the petroleum and the natural gas is 7.8% and 11.1% higher respectively. This problem will be discussed in the following part.

(2) Emission source of industry

The emission source of industry refers to the greenhouse gas emissions produced during the industrial production process, not including the greenhouse gas produced from using fuels in the production process. The major emission source comes from the industrial process in which the material has undergone chemical or physical conversion. For example, the silicate cement commonly seen uses limestone and clay as the main ingredients, made first through grinding and calcining and then through levigating by adding gypsum and synthetic materials. In calcining the limestone, $CaCO_3$ emits carbon dioxide after being heated and decomposed. Also, the about 1% $MgCO_3$ in the limestone, after being heated and decomposed, also emits a small amount of carbon dioxide. From China's realities, the production of cement, lime, iron and steel, aluminum and fertilizers has gone to a sizable scale; therefore, the carbon dioxide emission during the industrial process is large.

Here I only calculate several major industrial products discharging carbon dioxide, and the calculation formula is:

Carbon dioxide emission = the output of products discharging carbon dioxide * the carbon dioxide emission coefficient per unit of output

Take cement production for example, according to the calculation of Chinese scholars, one ton's cement will emit 0.365 ton of carbon dioxide (Zhu, 2000). In the regional investigation, the number is 0.41 (Wu, 2006) and the experience emission coefficient by the ORNL is 0.4987 (Qian & Yu, 2003).

There are two factors deciding the emission coefficient: the first is the percentage of the calcium oxide content in the clinker, which decides the carbon dioxide emission. The higher the content, the larger the emission coefficient; the second is the percentage for the clinker to turn into cement. In the IPCC (2006) estimation inventory, the emission coefficient of the clinker is 0.5071 while different types of cement share different percentage relations with the clinker. If the cement production cannot be calculated respectively based on different types and if there are doubts that a large amount of blending cement and/or architecture cement is produced in the Portland cement, then the favorable acceptable calculation is to assume the overall clinker content as 75%. If the known cement production is nearly all Portland cement, then the favorable calculation is to use clinker with a default value of 95%. Generally, if calculated according to the equation that 0.75 ton of clinker produces 1 ton of cement, the IPCC estimated that the cement emission coefficient is about 0.3803. Similarly, the emission coefficient of the lime, glass and other industrial products is shown in Table 5.

Table 5 Carbon Dioxide Emission Factor in the Production Process of Major Industrial Products

Product	Cement	Lime	Glass	Ammonia Gas	Sodium Carbonate	Virgin Aluminum
Emission Coefficient	0.3803	0.75	0.20	3.273	0.138	1.6

Data source: IPCC, 2006 IPCC Guideline for National Greenhouse Gas Inventories, 2006

3. Elaboration of the Data

Fossil fuel can not only be used as energy, but also for non-energy use, for example, chemical materials, which discharge no carbon dioxide. Therefore, we should distinguish the function of fossil fuel.

If it is used for industrial raw materials (fuel for raw materials for short), in the processing process it will undergo various physical and chemical transformations, by which carbon content is stored in different products rather than discharged in the form of gas. The plastic, synthetic rubber and fiber are all chemical raw materials and products from the chemical manufacturing industry, as the preliminary material for chemical fibers, plastic products and rubber products. The amount of the fuel for raw materials is not directly accessible. There are researches indicating that the percentage of the non-fuel use in the raw coal, petroleum and natural gas consumption is respectively 2.5%-3.5%, 21%-25% and 32%-38% (Gao, et al., 1994).

This article calculated the fuel for raw material from the coal and petroleum balance sheet. Take the coal balance sheet as an example and assume that its ultimate consumption is all for burning and during the intermediate consumption, excluding the consumption used for electricity generation, heat supply, coking and gas production, the remainder is all used for industrial raw material. This proportion of the fuel takes up about 2%-3% of the coal consumption and 3%-4% of the petroleum consumption. Such a percentage is very small mainly because fossil fuel is used for multiple purposes, but statistically these are generalized as one type. For example, coal, while used for coking and gas production, can also be used for producing carbon-content by-products. However, in statistics, all these are generalized into one type: coking and gas production.

The fossil fuel consumption data come from the coal and petroleum balance sheet published by *China Statistical Yearbook* over the years. The natural gas data come from the consumption of chemical raw material and the chemicals manufacturing industry. The energy consumption data in 2008 came from *China Statistical Abstract (*2009*)*. The amount of the fuel for raw material was obtained based on the prediction of the average increase rate in the first two years.

If the burning fossil energy has no loss in its carbon content in whatever secondary energy it has transformed into, then the ultimate carbon dioxide emission is equivalent to the emission calculated through the primary energy. However, the secondary energy for net export should be excluded. The secondary energy usually exported to China includes the coke and petroleum products (which are also frequently imported). The import and export of the petroleum product has already been included in the import and export of petroleum, while that of the coke is not included in that of the coal. Therefore, only the import and export of coke are considered. These data are obtained from *China Statistical Yearbook* over the years.

Except for lime, the data on output of industrial products, like cement, come from *China Statistical Yearbook* and *China Industry Economy Statistical Yearbook* over the years. The data in 2008 came from *China Statistical Abstract (*2009*)*, *China Monthly Statistics* (January, 2009) and 2008 *National Economic and Social Development Statistical Bulletin.* There are no direct data available for the lime output and it can only be estimated in an indirect way. According to the data from China Lime Association, the limestone is mainly used in the industrial intermediate input, such as in construction; the lime (cement) takes up 70.4% and the remaining 30% is used for such industrial manufacturing as metallurgy, calcium carbide, caustic soda and paper making[①]. If this percentage is sustained and the limestone for other purposes also discharges carbon dioxide, then the percentage of the carbon dioxide emitted by the lime in the cement and other industries is about 7: 3. We use the carbon dioxide

① China Lime Association: Analysis and prospect of the development situation of China's lime industry in the first half of 2004, *China Building Materials*, 2004(7).

emission discharged by the cement industry to calculate the carbon dioxide emission from the lime in other industries.

Table 6 Basic Data of China's Carbon Dioxide Emission Sources

	Unit	1994	2000	2004	2005	2006	2007	2008
Energy Consumption								
Coal	10,000 tons	128532.3	124537.4	193596.0	216557.5	239216.5	258641.4	274000.0
Petroleum	10,000 tons	14024.6	21232.0	28749.3	30086.2	32245.2	34031.6	36000.0
Natural Gas	100 million cubic meters	173.4	245.1	396.7	479.1	561.4	695.2	807.0
Exported Coke	10,000 tons	404.0	1520.0	1501.0	1276.0	1447.0	1530.0	1213.0
Industrial Raw Material Consumption								
Coal	10,000 tons	0.0	3117.0	3878.3	4818.9	5500.3	6175.4	6991.1*
Petroleum	10,000 tons	0.0	721.9	1195.1	1166.7	1277.3	1282.1	1345.3*
Natural Gas	100 million cubic meters	65.9	90.3	130.6	154.4	193.9	223.4	269.0*
Industrial Product Output								
Electrolytic Aluminum	10,000 tons	146.2	279.4	669.0	778.7	926.6	1234.0	1317.6
Sheet Glass	10,000 tons	596.3	917.6	1851.3	2010.5	2328.7	2695.9	2759.3
Synthesis Ammonia	10,000 tons	2436.8	3363.7	4135.1	4596.3	4936.8	5171.1	4995.2
Sodium Carbonate	10,000 tons	581.4	834.0	1334.7	1421.1	1560.0	1765.0	1881.3
Cement	10,000 tons	42118.0	59700.0	96682.0	106884.8	123676.5	136117.3	140000.0

Note: * indicates predicted value.

Data source: *China Statistical Yearbook*, *China Industry Economy Statistical Yearbook*, *China Statistical Abstract* (2009), *China Monthly Statistics* (January, 2009) and 2008 *National Economic and Social Development Statistical Bulletin.*

4. Estimated Result and Analysis

Based on the above-mentioned method and data, we can get the preliminary estimation of China's carbon dioxide emissions during recent years. This article mainly uses the estimated result from the coefficient by the Energy Research Institute and that from the coefficient by the IPCC for reference. It should be specially noted that, according to the former, China's carbon dioxide emissions during the burning of fossil fuel and the cement production were 5. 3 billion tons and that of the USA was 5. 75 billion tons (CDIAC) , with China's carbon dioxide emissions less than those of the USA. Of course, if according to the latter, China's carbon dioxide emission were 6. 19 billion tons, which indeed surpassed that of the USA, it can be seen that the selection of the coefficient has some influence on the estimated result.

Table 7 Preliminary Estimation of China's Carbon Dioxide Emissions

Unit (100 million tons)	1994	2000	2004	2005	2006	2007	2008①
Fossil Fuel Burning							
Calculated with the coefficient by the Energy Research Institute							
Coal	21.91	20.70	32.35	36.10	39.85	43.05	45.53
Petroleum	3.99	5.83	7.84	8.23	8.81	9.32	9.86
Natural Gas	0.02	0.03	0.05	0.06	0.07	0.08	0.10
Deducting Coke	-0.12	-0.46	-0.46	-0.39	-0.44	-0.47	-0.37
Total:	25.80	26.10	39.77	44.00	48.28	51.98	55.11
Calculating with the coefficient by IPCC							
Coal	26.44	24.98	39.03	43.56	48.08	51.94	54.93
Petroleum	4.13	6.30	8.46	8.88	9.51	10.06	10.64
Natural Gas	0.02	0.03	0.05	0.06	0.07	0.09	0.11
Deducting Coke	-0.12	-0.46	-0.46	-0.39	-0.44	-0.47	-0.37
Total:	30.64	30.84	47.08	52.11	57.22	61.62	65.30
Production Process							
Electrolytic Aluminum	0.02	0.04	0.11	0.12	0.15	0.2	0.21
Sheet Glass	0.01	0.02	0.04	0.04	0.05	0.05	0.06
Synthesis Ammonia	0.8	1.1	1.35	1.5	1.62	1.69	1.63
Sodium Carbonate	0.01	0.01	0.02	0.02	0.02	0.02	0.03
Cement	1.6	2.27	3.68	4.06	4.7	5.18	5.32
Lime (excluding cement)	0.69	0.97	1.58	1.74	2.02	2.22	2.28
Total:	3.13	4.42	6.77	7.5	8.55	9.36	9.53
All②	28.93	30.52	46.54	51.49	56.83	61.34	64.64

Note: ① the data in 2008 were predicted figures. ② calculated with the coefficient by the Energy Research Institute. ③ calculated with the coefficient by the IPCC.

In 2007, China's carbon dioxide emissions were 6. 13 billion tons, among which 5. 2 billion tons from the burning of fuel, accounting for 84. 7% of the total emission and 940 million tons from the industrial process. The three emission sources with the largest emissions are coal, petroleum and cement, respectively, accounting for 70. 2%, 15. 2% and 8. 4% in the total emission. In 2008, the expected carbon dioxide emission was 6. 46 billion tons and the carbon dioxide emission per capita was 4. 9 tons. From 2000 to 2008, the average annual increase rate of China's carbon emissions was 9. 8% while that of the GDP was 10. 5%. The average elastic coefficient of the carbon emission was 0. 9. From 1994 to 2004, the average annual increase rate of China's carbon emission was 4. 9% and the average elastic coefficient of the carbon emission was 0. 6. China's economic structure is predisposed towards industry with high carbon emission intensity.

Judging from the increasing trend, in 2007 China's carbon dioxide emissions increased by 112% more than those in 1994, among which there was an increase of 199% in the production process and 101% in the burning of fossil fuel. Although the increase rate in the coal emission is lower than the average level, with a large cardinal number, its 96. 4% increase rate contributed 65. 2% to the total carbon dioxide emissions, becoming the greatest contributor to the increase in carbon dioxide emissions. Petroleum and cement rank second and third.

Coal is China's largest carbon dioxide emission source. In primary energy, the carbon content of the per unit heat value of coal is the highest. Since coal takes the largest share of our energy structure, the amount of our carbon dioxide emission is considerable. In 2007, just the burning of coal discharged 4. 31 billion tons' of carbon dioxide, an increase of 96. 4% over 1994. Coal is the major fuel to generate electricity. In 2007, half of the coal was used for electricity generation, while in 1990 the figure was a quarter. The rapid growth in electricity generation is the major reason for the increase in coal consumption. Just during the "11th Five-Year" Plan period, when the electricity generation nearly doubled, the coal used for electricity generation also doubled. The increasing demand on electricity mainly originates from metal smelting, electricity generation, chemical raw material manufacturing, excavation and non-metal mineral products manufacturing, all of these industries having consumed 52% of the power.

Petroleum is mainly used for final consumption. China's increasing demand on petroleum mainly comes from the rapid increase in transportation. By the end of 2007, China's civilian vehicle holdings had increased to 43.58 million, 14 times higher than that in 1985. The number of private cars increased particularly fast, with the number in 2007 being 101 times higher than that in 1985 and the number of passenger service vehicles, featured by the minibus, being 1200 times higher than that in 1985. The petroleum consumed by the transportation industry grew from the 9.12 million tons in 1980 to 122.97 million tons in 2007, the percentage of the total petroleum consumption from 10.4% to 33.6%.

Table 8 China's Private Car Ownership

Year	1985	1990	1995	2000	2005	2006	2007	Average annual increase rate from 1985 to 2007 (%)
Total Vehicle Number ① (10,000)	28.5	81.6	250.0	625.3	1848.1	2333.3	2876.2	23.3
Passenger Service Car (10,000)	1.9	24.1	114.2	365.1	1383.9	1823.6	2316.9	38.0
Truck (10,000)	26.5	57.5	131.8	259.1	452.1	494.9	539.4	14.7

Note: ① "Total vehicle number" includes other types of vehicles.

Data source: *China Statistical Yearbook* 2008.

With the development of our heavy industry, the percentage of the carbon dioxide discharged during the industrial process in the total emission is increasing. In 1994, that was 310 million tons with a percentage of 10.8%; in 2007, it increased to 940 million tons with a percentage of 15.3% of the total emission. We should particularly pay attention to the contribution of our large-scale and rapidly increasing cement industry to the increase in carbon dioxide emissions. The percentage of the carbon dioxide emissions from the cement industry in the total emission grew from 5.5% in 1994 to 8.4% in 2007. Since the reform and opening up, the large-scale urban construction has promoted the development of the building materials industry. Our cement output ranked first in the 1980s. In 1990, China's cement output reached 210 million tons, taking up 18.4% in the global total. Since the late 1990s, to stimulate domestic demand, China has expanded infrastructure construction, launched housing reform, expanded the construction of universities and implemented the "connecting villages with highways" project, all of which have increased the consumption of cement. Since 2000, the cement output has increased at the rate of over 10% and by 2007 China's cement output reached 1.36 billion tons, 6.5 times higher than that in 1990, taking up 59% in the global total. From 1980 to 2007, China's average annual cement output increased by 11.1% and by 16 times. In the global cement output increase of 1.44 billion tons, China contributed a share of 89.2% . During China's rapid industrialization and urbanization, cement consumption will inevitably grow and at the later period of industrialization and urbanization the demand on cement will become stable and ultimately decrease. However, it cannot be denied that to some extent some cement is wasted in the consumption; a building in China is designed to last for 50 years but in fact is only used for 30 years[①], and there is premature consumption like the blind expanded construction of universities. In the management of the demand on cement, China has room for emission reduction.

Table 9 China's Cement Output and Its Global Percentage

Year	1980	1985	1990	1995	2000	2005	2007
China's output (10,000 tons)	7986	14595	20971	47560.6	59700	106884.8	136117.3
Average annual increase rate (%)	—	12.8	7.5	17.8	4.7	12.4	12.8
Global output (10,000 tons)	87201	94997	114125	141960	132799	179720	230874
Global percentage (%)	9.2	15.4	18.4	33.5	45.0	59.5	59.0

Data source: *International Statistical Yearbook* 2008.

① Zhong Zhe & Hu Fang: The average life of China's architecture is 30 years, *Xinhua Daily Telegraph*, June 27, 2006.

5. Analysis of the Reliability of the Calculation

This article takes the top-down reference approach and has calculated the carbon dioxide emission in 1994 at about 2.89 billion tons, including the burning of fossil fuels and the carbon dioxide emission from the production process of six industrial products. UNFCCC announced that China's carbon dioxide emission was about 3.07 billion tons in 1994, an authoritative report turned over to the UNFCCC by the Chinese government. The calculated result in this article is 5.9% lower than that of UNFCCC because I only calculated the emission source of six industrial products, not including the burning of biomass and garbage. This is why there is such a gap. Overall, the estimated result is highly reliable.

This book may have two factors overestimating the carbon dioxide emission: firstly, it underestimates the amount of the fuel for raw material and thus overestimates the amount of the fuel for burning. There are two ways to obtain the consumption of the fuel for raw material, one being the energy balance sheet and the other the energy consumption based on the division of industries. These two ways have their own pros and cons. For example, from the coal balance sheet we can estimate that the coal as the intermediate product for the raw material is about 2%. The coal balance sheet is made-up based on the single use of coal while coal serves for multiple purposes, for example, the byproduct from coking can be used as a chemical raw material. Therefore, such a number has underestimated the coal consumption for raw materials. From the energy consumption based on the division of industries, we can find that the coal consumption in chemical raw materials and the chemicals manufacturing industry has approached 5%. However, this proportion of coal may not be used wholly for raw materials, part of which may be used for energy burning. Therefore, this approach will overestimate the coal consumption used for raw materials. With the development of China's coal chemical industry, non-fuel-use coal chemical products will store more and more carbon content, the research of which depends on obtaining more detailed energy use data and the recycling data of the coal chemical product. There is the same problem in the petroleum for non-energy use. For example, existent literature says the petroleum for non-energy use accounts for about 21%

to 25%, but in this article it's only 3% to 4%.

Secondly, during the smelting process in the metallurgy industry, steel and cast iron products have a certain proportion of carbon. This may overestimate the carbon emission from the coal burning. The percentage of the carbon content in steel ranges from 0.04% to 2.3%, which, although a small one, cannot be overlooked for a large steel and iron production country. If calculated at the average 1% content, in 2007 our steel production was 566 million tons. If the carbon content in the steel was converted to carbon dioxide, an excessive 20 million tons' carbon dioxide was included, accounting for 0.3% in the total carbon dioxide emission in 2007.

In the carbon emission sources, the fossil fuel takes the largest share and the selection of the carbon emission coefficient of the fossil fuel has an obvious influence on the calculated result. In calculating China's carbon dioxide emission from the fossil fuel burning in 2006, foreign institutions came to different conclusions, with that of the US Energy Information Agency the largest, as high as 6.02 billion tons while that of the US Carbon Dioxide Information Research Center the least, 5.5 billion tons and that of the International Energy Agency being 5.65 billion tons. Using the coefficient of the Energy Research Institute, the result in this article is only about 4.83 billion tons while with the coefficient of the 2006 IPCC Guideline, it is 0.9 billion tons higher, 18.5% higher than the result calculated with the coefficient of the Energy Research Institute. The reason for such a gap lies in a higher emission coefficient of the IPCC and a lower one in China. This has a bearing on the feature of China's coal resources. Although China has a complete list of coal resources, the high-quality ones are scarce, with a large proportion of lignite and low-metamorphic soft coal, a percentage of 55% in the identified resources storage while high-metamorphic meager coal and anthracite coal only takes up 17% in the identified resources storage (Zhang, 2009). China's per unit heat value of coal is lower than that of foreign countries, so is its carbon content. If we adopt the coefficient provided by the IPCC or foreign institutions, China's carbon dioxide emissions from coal will be overestimated.

III. Review of China's Greenhouse Gas Emission Scenario Research

1. Baseline Scenario

Baseline scenario, is also called reference scenario or non-intervention scenario. Baseline scenario is an essential part of scenario research and usually it refers to the future scenario of greenhouse gas emissions based on the innate motivation of the past and present development and without the adoption of new policies or projects on emission alleviation or increase in the carbon sink (Jayant Sathaye and Stephen Meyers, 1995). In 1990, the estimation report issued by the IPCC was a baseline scenario while, since 1992, a mitigation scenario has been added in the report. Many small projects' researches on a mitigation scenario are generally based on a baseline scenario by large institutions. Since the relationship between greenhouse gas and climate change gripped scientists' attention, China, as a large greenhouse gas emission country, should join with developed countries and international institutions to regard the greenhouse gas emission problem as its hot research topic.

Auffhammer and Carson (2008) predicted China's carbon dioxide in 2010 with the waste air emissions in different Chinese provinces as the proxy variable of carbon dioxide and through the estimation of China's environmental Kuznets line. They used the historical data from 1985 to 2004 and set four types of population increase scenarios. From 2000 to 2010, the population increase rate was respectively 0.91%, 0.40%, 1.03% and 0.51%; there were three scenarios of economic growth, with the GDP increase rate being 3.02%, 5.02% and 7.02%. In this way, there were 12 scenario combinations in total. It was predicted that in the short run, the population change had a small influence on the increase in carbon emissions, while the economic growth played an important role. From 2000 to 2010, the average annual increase rate of China's carbon emissions ranged from 11.05% to 11.88%, with an increase of 4.4 billion tons in the carbon dioxide emission, higher than the emission reduction amount stipulated in *the Kyoto Protocol*. Such an amount is much higher than the results of other research, but is more consistent with the reality, mainly in that during the investigation the trend in China's economic growth has not reversed since 1998 and maintained a comparatively rapid speed. Although this is a research similar to a short-term prediction, it serves as a wake-up call for the surging amount of carbon dioxide emissions during this period of time.

Fan, et al. (2007) used China's input-output table in 1997 to estimate China's energy demand and carbon emissions in 2020. They designed their baseline scenario as this: in the following 20 years, China will maintain its current speed of development, people's livelihood will come to a comparatively well-off level, there will be a medium urbanization rate and the energy efficiency will achieve the goal of energy planning. In 2010 and 2020, China's energy demand will respectively reach 2. 39 billion tons and 3. 6 billion tons standard coal equivalent and the carbon dioxide emission, respectively 5. 21 billion tons and 7. 63 billion tons.

In 2007, the *World Energy Outlook* issued by the IEA made a special report on China's carbon dioxide emission scenario, spanning from 2005 to 2030. Based on the world energy model, the IEA designed three scenarios specifically about China: baseline scenario, alternative scenario and high growth scenario. In the baseline scenario assumption, from 2007 to 2030, China's average annual GDP increase rate is 6%, among which the percentage of the tertiary industry boasts the highest increase, increasing from 40% in 2005 to 47% in 2030. In population, the IEA predicted that China's population increased at an average annual rate of 4‰, with the total population reaching 1. 46 billion in 2030. IEA adopted the UN's prediction of China's urbanization. In 2015, China's urbanization rate will reach 49% and in 2030, 60%. The urban population increased with an average annual rate of 2%. In 2030, the rural population will be reduced to 570 million. The energy consumption per capita of the urban residents is far higher than that of the rural residents. Therefore, urbanization puts a higher demand on energy. In its high growth scenario model, with a consistent growth in exports and the investment stimulus to heavy industry, the increase rate in GDP reaches 7. 5% and by 2030, the GDP will be 42% higher than that of the baseline scenario.

Table 10 Setting of the IEA Baseline Scenario Parameters and the Estimated Value

	2005	2015	2030	2005 - 2015 Increase Rate (%)	2005 - 2030 Increase Rate (%)
Key assumption					
GDP increase rate					4.7% ①
Percentage of the service industry (%)	40	43	47		
Population (100 million)	13.1	13.9	14.6		
Urbanization rate (%)	40	49	60		
Energy demand (100 million tons' standard coal equivalent)					
Coal	15.6	26.7	34.3	5.5	3.2
Petroleum	4.7	7.8	11.5	5.2	3.7
Natural gas	0.6	1.6	2.8	10.0	6.4
Nuclear power	0.2	0.5	1.0	8.8	6.5
Hydropower	0.5	0.9	1.2	6.1	3.8
Biomass	3.2	3.2	3.2	-0.1	0
Total (excluding biomass)	21.6	37.5	51.3	5.7	3.5
Carbon dioxide emissions (100 million tons)					
Electricity generation	25.0	44.50	62.02		3.7
Industry	14.30	21.86	23.73		2.0
Transportation	3.37	6.64	12.55		5.4
Life and service industry②	4.68	6.22	7.15		1.7
Others③	3.65	7.09	9.03		3.7
Total	51.01	86.32	114.48		3.3
Emission per capita (ton)	3.9	6.2	7.9		

Note: ① 2002-2010: 5.7%, 2010-2030: 4.7%; ② including agriculture; ③ including other sources and non-energy emissions.

Data source: IEA, 2007, pp. 285, 286, 287, 314 and 313.

The technological advance and facility updating have improved China's energy utilization efficiency. In the IEA's baseline model, the energy consumption in electricity generation through thermal power in 2030 will be lower by 15% compared with 2005, that in iron and steel and cement will respectively decrease by 14% and 17%, and transportation lower by 32%. The average annual increase in China's primary energy demand is 3.5% (not including biomass) and until 2030 China's total energy demand will reach 5.13 billion tons' coal equivalent, with coal remaining the major energy source, accounting for 63% of the total energy. The demand on petroleum has doubled and the percentage of the petroleum used for transportation in the demand on petroleum will increase from 35% in 2005 to 55% in 2030; the percentage of natural gas in the energy demand will increase, from 3% in 2005 to 5% in 2030; nuclear power was lower than 2% and the percentage of other renewable energies was 0.9%.

From 1990 to 2005, the average annual increase rate in China's carbon dioxide emissions was 5.6%. In the baseline scenario, from 2005 to 2030, the increase rate will be 3.3% and in 2030 China's carbon dioxide emissions relevant to the energy will be 11.45 billion tons, 66% higher than that of the USA and taking up 27% of the global emissions. Although the total amount is high, China's carbon emissions per capita are still lower than that of developed countries. In 2005, China's carbon dioxide per capita relevant to the energy was 3.9 tons and by 2030 the emissions under the baseline scenario will be doubled, approaching 8 tons.

Economic growth is considered to be the most important factor influencing the greenhouse gas emissions, but this is only one aggregate indicator. Undeniably, the consumer's consumption model and lifestyle have influenced the industrial structure and the energy demand as well as the greenhouse gas emissions. Based on the social and economic baseline scenario in 2007 by the IEA, Guan, et al. (2008) introduced the consumption pattern and production structure into the IPAT model. In the consumption structure, the percentage of food and agricultural products in the urban and rural residents' consumption expenditure will decrease respectively from 39% and 21% in 2002 to 17% and 6% in 2030. The percentage of the transportation and service product consumption by the urban and rural residents will increase respectively from 33% and 27% in 2002 to 44% and 39% in 2030. The percentage of the manufactured goods remains basically the same. The consumption expenditures per capita of the urban and rural residents are respectively 15,600 yuan and 3,613 yuan (the constant price in 2002).

In the baseline scenario, Guan, et al. predicted that by 2030 China's carbon dioxide emissions will be 11.9 billion tons and emissions relevant to the production activities will increase from 4.8 billion tons in

2005 to 11 billion tons in 2030, the residents' direct emissions from 213 million tons to 900 million tons, mainly from the increase in the natural gas consumption from private transportation. Judging from the structure, from 2002 to 2030, the carbon emissions related to production will have increased by 222%, among which the consumption per capita will contribute a share of 362% (assuming that other factors are invariables), mainly attributable to the increase in the urban household's consumption. The contribution of the efficiency improvement will offset 193%, a half of the contribution made by the consumption increase. Changes in the consumption structure and industrial structure respectively will contribute a share of 5% and 42% to the carbon emission increase. The former made a smaller contribution in that the percentage of the carbon-emission-intensive manufacturing industry remains basically the same. It should be noted that the urban residents' final consumption, with a percentage of 49%, takes the place of the fixed asset investment, becoming the greatest contributor to the increase in carbon emissions, while the latter's contribution rate decreased to 33%.

Jiang Jinhe and Yao Yufang (2003), through empirical studies on the development experience of different countries, proposed that if the humanistic development potential is met, in other words if people's basic needs are satisfied, then the GDP per capita in 2050 will reach about 10,000 dollars, the energy consumption per capita, 3.7 tons' standard coal equivalent, the primary energy, 5.77 billion tons' standard coal equivalent and carbon dioxide emissions, 11.4 billion tons.

Vuuren, et al. (2003) adopted the IMAGE/TIMER simulation model[①] and based on the SRES issued by the IPCC, have set two baseline scenarios for China's energy and emissions from 1995 to 2100,

---

① The Integrated Model to Assess the Global Environment (IMAGE) was developed by the Dutch National Institute for Public Health and the Environment and has been in use for 12 years for studying the long-term dynamics of the global climate change, including the position of different types of greenhouse gases in the grain demand, land utilization changes, energy demand and supply, energy and industrial greenhouse gas emission, oceans and the air. IMAGE is also connected to the world economic model and world population model. TIMER (Targets IMage Energy Regional model) is a part of the IMAGE model, with the function to simulate the changes in the energy system by utilizing the annual investment information, including 17 regions and five energy demand sectors (industry, transportation, resident, business and others) and 6 to 8 types of energy carriers in the world.

with the policy selection centered on the period 1995-2050 and the historical data from 1971 to 1995. These models only consider the carbon dioxide emissions produced by energy consumption. Since these scenarios were set at the beginning of a new round of China's economic growth, it is expected that China's carbon emissions will approach that of the USA after 2030.

Table 11 China's Baseline Scenario based on SRES

	Globalization Background (A1b-C)	Regional Management Scenario (B2-C)
Social and economic background	Thanks to human capital, technical innovation and free trade, China and the world have maintained a rapid and successful economic growth. China will continue to implement its opening-up policy and maintain its fast technology progress. It will strive to increase the percentage of the service industry in GDP from 34% in 2000 to 60% in 2050. Its population is expected to reach 1.53 billion in 2030. This reflects a positive attitude towards globalization and technology transfer, assuming that globalization gives rise to rapid technology transfer and makes renewable energy sources and other clean technologies available on a large scale.	In the Regional Manager Scenario, China's development mainly depends on its domestic resources. The economic growth is comparatively slow and the trade and technology transfer are restricted. China will use domestic resources for its economic development to maintain the equality in the future and the balance between different regions and urban and rural areas, the environmental problems, such as food, water and air pollution receiving increasing attention.
Energy consumption	With a lifestyle of a fast tempo and featured by intensive material pursuits, the energy consumption in China will increase rapidly. By 2050, the energy consumption per capita in China will be on a par with the current level of OECD countries. In the final consumption, traditional biological energy resources will be replaced in the process of modernization while the coal consumption will shrink due to its environmental problems and inconvenience. These gaps will be filled by electric power and natural gas. Petroleum will maintain its growth for the expansion of the transportation department. Coal will also retain its dominant status with its cost advantages. Despite the increase in nuclear power and hydropower, their percentage will not surpass 10%. The oil and natural gas imported will reach 80% and 50% respectively.	A large part of the energy system depends on domestic resources. Limited international trade and technology transfer lead to a low technology efficiency in energy production and final consumption. Coal is the major energy and clean coal is used in the production technology.

(contd.)

	Globalization Background (A1b-C)	Regional Management Scenario (B2-C)
Carbon Emissions	In 2030, the carbon dioxide emission will be 9. 5 billion tons and in 2050, 13. 9 billion tons. The largest source is coal. In 2050, the carbon dioxide per capita will approach the global average level.	In 2030, the carbon dioxide emission will be 7. 3 billion tons and in 2050, 9. 9 billion tons. In 2030, the carbon dioxide per capita will approach the global average level.

Data souce: Detlef van Vuuren, et al. Energy and Emission Scenarios for China in the 21st Century-Exploration of Baseline Development and Mitigation Options, *Energy Policy*, 31, 2003, p. 372.

The baseline scenario proposed by Jiang Kejun, et al. (2008, 2009) depicted the basic trend of China's economic development in the future. The national economy maintains rapid growth, but with a gradually slowing-down; the percentage of the service industry and the urbanization rate will increase continually, reaching 44. 5% and 70% in 2030 respectively. As part of the global economy, China's economy will improve and expand its international trade. Therefore, China can depend on importing energy resources from international markets to satisfy some of its demand on energy supply. China's technological development is currently at the medium level, that is to say, by 2030 the energy efficiency in our major high energy-consuming industry will be close to the world's advanced level. According to their estimation, China's energy demand will come to 5. 66 billion tons of standard coal equivalent in 2030, 10% higher than that estimated by the IEA baseline scenario; the percentage of coal consumption will fall to 51. 8%, 13% lower than the IEA; the carbon dioxide emission will be 11. 66 billion tons, 200 million tons more than the IEA. Compared with the IEA's estimation, Jiang Kejun, et al. hold a positive attitude towards China's expected oil and nuclear power consumption. From 2005 to 2030, the increase rate of the two will be 5. 3% and 9. 2%, 1. 6% and 2. 7% higher than that estimated by the IEA.

Table 12 Parameter Setting and Estimated Value of Carbon Dioxide Emission Baseline Scenario by National Energy Research Institute

	2005	2010	2020	2030	2040	2050	2005 - 2030 Increase Rate (%)
Key Assumption							
GDP increase rate (%) e		9.67	8.38	7.11	4.98	3.60	
Percentage of the service industry (%)	39.8	40.8	44.5	50.2	56.3	61.2	
Population(100 million)	13.07	13.60	14.40	14.70	14.70	14.60	
Urbanization rate (%) Energy demand (100 million tons of standard coal equivalent)	43	49	63	70	74	79	
Coal	15.4	24.2	29.9	29.3	30.0	29.2	2.6
Oil	4.4	6.3	11.0	15.9	17.1	18.4	5.3
Natural gas	6.0	1.1	2.7	4.6	5.3	6.7	-1.1
Nuclear power	0.2	0.3	0.9	1.8	3.8	6.0	9.2
Hydropower	1.3	2.2	2.9	3.6	3.8	4.0	4.2
Biomass	0	0.2	0.3	0.4	0.7	0.9	—
Total	21.9	34.4	48.2	56.6	62.0	66.6	3.9
Carbon dioxide emissions (100 million tons)	51.7	78.2	101.9	116.6	129.3	127.1	3.3

Note: ① Range of increase rate.

Data Source: Jiang Kejun, Hu Xiulian, Zhuang Xing & Liu Qiang: China's low-carbon scenario and low-carbon development in 2050. *Sino-Global Energy*, 2009(6).

Jiang Kejun, Hu Xiulian, Zhuang Xing, Liu Qiang & Zhu Songli: China's energy demand and carbon dioxide emission scenario in 2050, *Advances in Climate Change Research*, 2008: 4(5).

The baseline scenario proposed by Wei Yiming, et al. (2008) assumed that from 2010 to 2030 China will maintain rapid economic growth, but with a slowing-down increase rate year by year, with population, urbanization rate and technology improvement at a medium speed, having reached the preset energy conservation targets. In 2030, the carbon dioxide emission will be 11.54 billion tons. This research is featured by the differentiated analysis of different regional development and emissions.

2. *Mitigation Scenario*

Mitigation scenario, also called stabilization scenario, intervention scenario. Compared with the baseline scenario, mitigation scenario research will preset the intensity target or aim at mitigating climate change and consider how to adopt appropriate measures to lower the greenhouse gas emission. These measures include not only technological possibilities, but also various institutional, cultural and legislative factors influencing the greenhouse gas emission. There can be various mitigation scenarios, such as different aims for emission reduction and those that favor a certain special type of technical means or energy (Jayant Sathaye & Stephen Meyers, 1995).

Based on the two baseline scenarios of SRES (2000), Vuuren, et al. (2003) designed corresponding mitigation policies, including stimulating the investment in improving energy efficiency, levying the energy tax and carbon tax, using clean energies to stimulate and increase the percentage of nuclear power, hydropower and renewable energies. Based on the A1b—C baseline scenario, if the energy efficiency is improved, the carbon emissions in 2050 will be reduced by 10.8%, the investment in energies will increase by 9% and the consumer's cost by 3%. If one ton's carbon is levied with a tax of 30 dollars, the carbon emissions will be reduced by 30.6%, the investment in energies will increase by 16% and the consumer's cost by 20%. Based on the B2—C baseline scenario, if the energy efficiency is improved, the carbon emissions in 2050 will be reduced by 14.4%, the investment in energies will increase by 12% and the consumer's cost by 1%. If one ton's carbon emission is levied with a tax of 30 dollars, the carbon emissions will be reduced by 29.8%, the investment in energies will increase by 16% and the consumer's cost by 15%. Generally speaking, the carbon tax is the most effective.

In the mitigation scenario of IEA (2007), the Chinese government adopted enforcing policy measures to ensure the increase in the energy efficiency and the effective protection of the environment. This can be called a sustainable development method, with a lower demand on energy and less carbon emissions. The government enhanced the implementation of current policies and adopted new ones to prohibit the increasing demand on energies, controlling the average annual increase rate at 2.5%. In 2030, the demand on fossil fuels will be 4.64 billion tons' coal equivalent, 14.7% lower than that estimated by the baseline scenario, among which the demand on coal and petroleum lowers by 23.2% and 19.2% respectively. As a compensation, the demand on nuclear power increases by 79%, and on solar power, wind power and other renewable resources increases by 57.4% . Compared with the baseline scenario, the energy demand decrease in a mitigation scenario results from various aspects. For example, the central government "closed down and renovated" small and inefficient industrial enterprises and power plants and replaced them with highly efficient modern enterprises. In the long run, such a change in the economic structure will play an increasingly important role in lowering energy consumption and contribute a share of 43% to the reduction in energy demand. The improvement in energy efficiency and the transformation of the energy structure will contribute the remaining 57% . Policy measures can mitigate the increase in energy imports and the increasingly aggravated partial pollution as well as curb the carbon emission increase. The relative decrease in the total energy consumption and the improvement of the energy structure will decrease the carbon emission in 2030 by 22.5% compared with the 11.45 billion tons in the baseline scenario, with an amount of about 2.6 billion tons.

Recently, "low carbon" has emerged as a popular concept. There can be different definitions of low-carbon emissions. One is the realization of the common aspiration cherished by the human community, namely to realize an emission level with a low temperature rise globally. At present, the most discussed is the emission level with a target of 450ppmv and 550ppmv intensity. Also discussed is the emission level with an even lower intensity target and the low-carbon emissions in the country or the region should be realized under such a global emission level. The other is to make the greatest efforts to decrease greenhouse gas emissions in the country or the region based on its natural resource conditions (Jiang, et al., 2009).

Jiang Kejun, et al. (2009) proposed a low-carbon scenario to consider the low-carbon emissions to be realized in China through national policy under the factors of national energy security, domestic environment and a low-carbon road. This scenario mainly considers domestic social, economic and environmental development demands and the energy and emission scenario to be realized with domestic efforts under the factors to enhance technological advances, change the economic development model, transform the consumption pattern and realize low energy consumption and low greenhouse gas emissions. In 2030, the primary energy demand will increase from 2.19 billion tons' coal equivalent in 2005 to 4.47 billion tons' coal equivalent, with the carbon dioxide emission being 8. 6 billion tons.

Furthermore, they proposed another enhanced low-carbon scenario, which was based on the following three aspects: first, under the global joint efforts, with further improved technological advances and rapid decrease in key technology costs, developed countries' policies will gradually expand to developing countries; second, after 2030, China's economy will be the world's largest and it can increase its input to a low-carbon economy to better use the opportunity provided by a low-carbon economy to promote its economic development; third, China's technology development has maintained a global leading position in some areas, such as the clean coal technology and the carbon dioxide capture and storage technology (CCS), which has been applied on a large scale in China. Against such a backdrop, in 2030 China's energy demand can be controlled to around 4. 27 billion tons' standard coal equivalent, with the carbon dioxide emission being 8. 17 billion tons.

Wang and Watson (2008) proposed China's future road towards low-carbon emissions. If adhering to the principle of an equivalence between emissions per capita and emissions per unit of GDP, with the target of 450 ppmv, China's emission potential in the 21st century will be 70 billion tons and 111 billion tons (in carbon) respectively, with an annual carbon dioxide emission of 2. 57 billion tons and 4. 03 billion tons. According to the two important topics, stimulating technical innovation and eliminating social inequalities, China's future development can be divided into four scenarios, which can be summarized as follows: in 2050, China's total economic volume will be 8 to 13 times higher than present, dominated by the service industry; the energy demand will increase by 15% to 100% compared with 2005, the energy intensity will decrease by 76%-87% while the carbon emission intensity will decline to 4%-7% of 2005 and carbon emissions by 15%-70% compared with 2005. In the four scenarios, S1 has realized a lowest emission of 70 billion tons, reaching the emission peak around 2020, which is featured by drastic technological advances and innovation, concern for social welfare and equality. The economic growth is the slowest, with that in 2050 being 8. 7 times higher than that in 2005, but the carbon emission intensity is the lowest. The way to realize this scenario includes improving energy utilization efficiency and replacing coal with renewable resources as the major energy; change the economic structure, reduce the percentage of the heavy chemical industry, develop high-tech industry, service industry and high value-added industry and decrease the percentage of the industry to 20% while the service industry reaches 75%; the residents are more aware of the environment and choose a green lifestyle, such as preferring the environment-friendly architecture and transportation and living in small towns and rural areas. Under the S2 and S4 scenario with a high globalization level and concerned more with efficiency and personal success, the economic growth is more rapid, but the energy demand is increasing, with an emission of 110 billion tons.

Wei Baoren (2008), based on the comparison between China's energy consumption per capita and that of Japan and Germany, proposed the two scenarios, environment-friendly and environment-improved scenario. The former refers to the fact that, since 2010, China has implemented energy conservation and emission reduction and maintained an average annual decrease rate of 4% based on the energy consumption per unit of GDP. Under the medium growth scenario in which GDP in 2050 is 12 times higher than that in 2005, by 2050 10,000-yuan GDP energy consumption will be 0.808 ton's standard coal equivalent, 16.8% of that in 2003, an equivalent of Japan's level in 1973 and 1.37 times higher than the level in 2003. By 2050, our energy demand will reach 4.31 billion tons' standard coal equivalent, with the energy consumption per capita being 3.1 tons' standard coal equivalent, 1.8 times higher than China's level in 2005 and 53% of Japan's level in 2003. The carbon dioxide emission will be 6.8 billion tons. This requires the whole society to save to its utmost. Under the latter scenario, by 2050 China's energy consumption per unit of GDP will reach Germany's level in 2003. From 2010 to 2050, the energy consumption per unit will decrease by 3.3% annually and, by 2050, the energy demand will reach 5.77 billion tons' standard coal equivalent, with the energy consumption per capita being 2/3 that of Germany and the carbon dioxide emission 10.08 billion tons.

After 2012, the decision is yet to be made. < < < Research in China has not posed definite and rigid targets for greenhouse gas alleviation. Just as Jiang Kejun, et al. proposed, "to make the greatest efforts to decrease greenhouse gas emissions in the country or the region based on its natural resource conditions". Wang and Watson, based on the principle of an equivalence between emissions per capita and emissions per unit of GDP, raised a quota for China's carbon emissions, which might as well be an attempt for the scenario research of China's obligations in emission reduction.

IV. Evaluation and Prospect of China's Greenhouse Gas Emission Scenarios

1. Evaluation

Overall, the existent greenhouse gas emission scenarios show optimism about China's future economic growth: although the economic growth rate may gradually slow down, there will be no turning point. Against such a social and economic backdrop, by 2030 the energy demand and carbon dioxide emissions will be two times higher. In the mitigation scenario, the energy consumption decreases, the low-carbon energy increases its percentage and the CCS technology and transformation of the lifestyle are the key to greenhouse gas emission reduction, a 20%-70% decrease compared with the baseline scenario. Specifically, the evaluation of the scenario research on China's greenhouse gas emissions is as follows:

(1) Whether baseline scenario is reliable

The baseline scenario is similar to the long-term prediction. It is very difficult or even borders on the impossible to draft an accurate blueprint for the future 50 years based on the past 30 years' experience. The earlier the baseline scenario, the larger the gap between it and the reality. For the index increase, a difference of 1% will make no difference in the short term, but the influence will be significant in the long run. Therefore, predicting the long future time series with a short time series will result in an expanded scope of possibilities because of a big variance, that is to say, the indefiniteness of the future result is increased.

Besides, the intervention of the business cycle makes the prediction unreliable. Prediction is generally made according to the historical time series while the nearer it is to the present, the more power it is endowed with. Therefore, if the prediction is made at the economic slump, then when the economy prospers we can find that the estimated economic growth rate in the following decades tends to be small and vice- versa. For example, before China's new round of a prosperous business cycle, Vuuren, et al. believed that China's carbon emissions will surpass that of the USA around 2030, which is also what most of the international institutions believe. However, from 2003 to 2006, China's energy consumption rate reached beyond many institutions' expectations. For example, EIA predicted the baseline scenario in 2005's *International Energy Outlook* that by 2025 China's carbon dioxide emission will exceed that of the USA, ranking it the 1st in the world. Even in the high growth scenario, China's total carbon emissions still remain lower than that of the USA in 2015. With the lapse in time, the EIA continued to adjust China's emissions upward while adjusting the USA's emissions downward because of its influence on the financial crises. In 2007, the Netherlands Environmental Assessment Agency was the first to announce that China's carbon dioxide emissions ranked 1st in 2006. If so, the baseline scenario made in China's economic prosperity period is very likely to be excessively high.

(2) Overconfidence in technological advances

Mitigation scenario research shows optimism in solving energy and carbon emission problems through technological advances, without even a wisper of pessimism. This is why many scenarios are confident of China's economic growth. Technological advances can either capture and store current greenhouse gases or develop "low-carbon" energy to replace "high carbon". In a word, all the difficulties in the future can be resolved through technological advances.

The fetish about technological advances partly comes from the Western world's breakthrough in the "increasing limit" brought about by the Rome Club. Technological advances are conceived to be the most important reason for the breakthrough in the limit. However, we should realize that the limit has been prolonged at least for the following reasons: firstly, the international biological and environmental movements in the 1970s promoted the implementation of environmental and energy conservation policies in developed countries and alleviated the environmental pollution to some extent; secondly, with the enforcement of domestic environmental management, the multinationals, to lower their costs, resorted to international direct investment and transferred the polluting industry to developing countries; finally, developed countries, making use of communication and internet technologies, completed their transfer towards low-energy-consuming industries. Although those high-polluting and high-energy-consuming industries are not located inside the developed countries, they have consumed the environmental capacity and resource space of developing countries. The process of developed countries' "limit breakthrough" is the process in which the global biological environment "turns better partially but degenerates as a whole" (Zheng & Qian, 1998). It can be seen that the role of technological advances in economic growth is exaggerated.

Even if we concede that technological advances are of some use to growth, technologies are not free lunches. In the enhanced low-carbon scenario by Jiang Kejun, et al. (2009), the hope lies in international cooperation and China's development and application of clean coal and CCS technology. Wang and Watson (2008) said that to realize the lowest emission scenario, we should improve energy efficiency and replace coal with renewable resources. New technologies are expensive and enterprises have to recover their costs. Besides, it is uncertain whether such technologies can be developed or not. Perhaps, we should also keep conservative expectations about technological advances. Over a long period of time, we still have to rely on non-renewable resources. After all, it is too risky for us to base our good life in the future merely on technological advances.

(3) Restrictions of resources and environment

All scenarios have such implications that other resources and the environmental capacity will remain unchanged all the time and will not stem growth. Establishing a scenario means making a series of consistent and coherent assumptions of the relationship among the research phenomena, the deciding factors and the expected development. The requirement of consistent and coherent assumptions distinguishes the scenario analysis from the variable analysis and sensitivity analysis. The latter shows the variable's influence on the future development merely by changing one or several parameters. Under the consistent assumption, we need to make a systematic and selective description of the current situation and identify the most important external factors which decide the future process. In the greenhouse gas emission scenario, the burning of fossil fuels is the biggest contributor to greenhouse gas emissions and also the most important external factor deciding the future process while whether other resources are sufficient is the premise. A mere consideration of energy supply while overlooking other resources will make the greenhouse gas emission scenario detached from reality. In setting the model, the energy supply and demand are the focus while various social and economic development indexes are predetermined variables. However, variables showing resources and the environmental capacity are not included in the model at all.

Unlike developed countries, China not only faces the problem of climate change and energy structure, but a series of bio-environmental problems cropping up with the economic growth, for example, water resources shortage, soil degradation, extinction of bio-diversity and even social problems, such as the uneven distribution between the rich and poor and twisted values. Many questions cannot be answered if we only depend on assumptions while giving up searching for solid evidence: whether China's future bio-environmental problems will disappear with the economic and social development or become irreversible by reaching the threshold, whether China can tide over the peak of the environmental Kuznets curve safely and soundly like developed countries. If they become "unrestraint" and "gratuitous", the scenario research into the greenhouse gas emissions will become much less reliable.

Take water resources as an example. Currently in China, the urban residents in the North have a limited supply of domestic water. Since the founding of New China, many cross-region and cross-river water transfer projects to ensure the water supply for cities in the north have been accomplished. From the Yellow River to the Yangtze River, the development of cross-river water transfer is growing. Even so, it is hard to say that the water demand in the north has been satisfied. When the population is increasing and the urbanization rate is growing, how can the residents' water supply be ensured?

Firstly, there is the change in domestic water demand. Drinking water is essential for people's survival. Its scale hinges on three factors: 1. The population change: In 2030, it is expected that our population will reach 1. 46 billion, an increase of 11% over the current population. If the population structure and average water usage remain the same, then the domestic water demand will increase by 11%. 2. The change in the population structure: On the one hand, urbanization brings more pressure on a concentrated water supply. The urban residents' domestic water is generally supplied from a concentrated source, while the rural residents have different accesses to water. The percentage of the villages with a concentrated water supply takes up only 14. 8% in the total

2.711 million national villages[①]. On the other hand, the urban residents have a higher water usage than the rural residents. In 2006, the daily domestic water usage for the urban residents was 189.8 liter/person while the residents in administrative villages with a concentrated water supply had a daily usage of 76.1 liter/person, less than a half of that of the rural residents. Therefore, urbanization means an increase in the domestic water usage of the concentrated water supply. Currently, our nominal urbanization rate[②] is about 45% and if, according to the scenario set by the IEA, the urbanization rate in 2030 reaches 60%, then there will be about an 880-million population in urban areas, an increase of 47% over the current 590 million permanent urban residents. If we assume that the urban residents' water demand per capita remains unchanged, then the total concentrated water supply for the urban residents grows by 47%. This is the lowest increase. As a matter of fact, the immigrant workers in the cities currently have a far lower demand on domestic water than the urban residents. When they settle down in the urban area, their lifestyle tends to follow the citizens and the demands on the concentrated water supply will be higher. Compared with the current 456-million population with urban registration households, it will increase by 93%. 3. The change in the domestic water usage per capita in urban households: During 2000-2005, the water usage per capita in urban households who have access to water usage[③] was maintained around 145 liters and it was assumed that such a percentage remains stable. Based on the above factors, if we assume that in 2030 the popularization rate[④] of our urban residents' water usage reaches 100%, then the total domestic water usage in the urban areas' concentrated water supply will double that of 2005. In the Energy Research Institute's scenario with an urbanization rate of 70%, the total

---

① 2006 *City, County and Village Construction Statistical Bulletin.*

② The percentage of the permanent urban population in the total population. It is called "nominal urbanization" in the sense that although alien residents, especially the immigrant workers working in the cities, they have no urban registration households and cannot enjoy what the urban residents enjoy.

③ Those who have access to concentrated water supply, including household water supply and public water supply sites.

④ Water usage popularization rate = population for water usage /the total population * 100%. In 2007, our urban water usage popularization rate was 93.8% and that of the county was 81.2%.

household water usage in the concentrated water supply will be 2.4 times higher than that in 2005.

Table 13 Daily Water Usage per Capita of China's Urban and Rural Residents in 2006

Type	City	County	Village and Town	Including: Town	Village County	Village
Daily water usage per capita (liter)	189.8	122.7	—	102.5	78	76.1

Data source: 2006 *City, County and Village Construction Statistical Bulletin.*

Secondly, to improve employment for the increasing urban population, we must develop industry and the service industry. In 2007, the total dependency ratio① of our population was 37.4% and if we assume this ratio remains unchanged, then in 2030 the labor population among the 876-million urban population will be 640 million. If we assume the age of the labor population in urban areas ranges from 20 to 60 and there is an even intensity in the population distribution, then the labor population is about 510 million. In 2007, our urban employment population was 290 million and by 2030 the urban area should add 210 million posts. So much employment can only be provided by the service industry if a lesser demand on water resources is to be maintained. In the social scenario of the IEA (2007), the percentage of the service industry in 2030 will be 47% and Jiang Kejun, et al. (2009) proposed that in 2030 the percentage of the service industry would be 50% and in 2050, 60%. Only Wang and Watson (2008) made the target to improve the percentage of the service industry to 75% by 2050. If the most optimistic view permits, such a target can be achieved. In 2050, the total industrial volume will be four times higher than at present and the service industry 14 times. Unless the efficiency of the industrial water usage decreases to 25% of the present level, the total industrial water usage will be higher than the current level.

---

① The coefficient of gross dependency ratio, which refers to the ratio between the non-working-age population and the working-age population in the total population. Generally it is represented with "%" to illustrate what the non-working-age population is to be provided for by every 100 working-age population. In China, it refers to the percentage of those below 15 and above 65 in the population ageing from 15 to 65.

(4) Development, equity and sustainability

The problem of climate change is a new problem facing human beings. Like other problems, the plan to cope with climate change must be related to the development, equity and sustainability of human society. A plan targeted at development will bring about a series of social problems since it may lead to unevenness between the rich and the poor without equity. This is not the aim of development and if without sustainability, development and equity are meaningless. Therefore, in the scenario, we must consider different dimensions of these problems. In the scenario of Von Vuuren, et al. (2003) which is based on the SRES baseline scenario and the scenario of Wang and Watson (2008), efficiency and equity is in a reversal relationship. The high efficiency scenario in which the economy grows rapidly means an increasing dependence on the global market and an aggravated domestic social inequity. In contrast, a scenario in which the economic growth slows down may be more grounded on the domestic market and allows for an even development between different regions. As for the scenario research of China's greenhouse gas emission, we need to be more concerned about the equity and sustainability of the scenario.

To conclude, some scenario researches only consider the energy supply required in reaching the social and economic development target and disregard the supply of other resources and relevant environmental capacity restrictions. Undeniably, energy is the core driving force behind the social development in modern times and it can be replaced by other resources. For example, energy can help man to dig deeper in the groundwater extraction or change the sea water into fresh water or to treat the sewage. However, the existent scenario researches fail to discuss the cost for energy to replace other resources. Therefore, even if the future energy demand and fossil fuel supply calculated from these scenarios can be ensured, nevertheless the supply of other resources and relevant environmental capacity are not "unrestraint" or "gratuitous". The greenhouse gas emission scenario should change the situation in which the research is single-handedly conducted by the energy or economic experts. Instead, integrated researches are needed to study more areas, such as water, land, population and forests which carry the resources and environment for social development. Only in this way can we make comprehensive and applicable scenario plans.

2. Prospect

The greenhouse gas produced by human activities comes from the following sources: the burning of fossil fuels, the industrial production process and the chemical process of agriculture and wastes. All these emissions are related to human's production activities. The larger the production scale is, the more energies are consumed and the more greenhouse gas emissions will be. However, the ultimate end of production is consumption. Therefore, the greenhouse gas emission, in the final analysis, should be attributed to human's consumption behavior. The more products human have consumed, the more energies are used and the more greenhouse gas emissions will be. There are several factors deciding the consumption and consumption structure of Chinese residents.

Firstly, population. The scale of the population is the basic factor deciding greenhouse gas emissions. Since the founding of New China, China's population has been soaring. Overall, our population grew from the 570 million at the beginning of the founding of New China to 1,320 million in 2007, becoming a country with the largest population in the world. To meet the residents' basic needs, a certain amount of energy has to be consumed.

Since China implemented the birth control policy, China's population has been under effective control. According to the research findings of the "Study on the Input and Efficiency of Birth Control" Group of the National Health and Family Planning Commission, during two decades, the childbirth decreased by 250 million. If calculated from 1970s, the population decreased at least 300 million up to now. The rapid population increase has been under effective control (Men & Zeng, 2004). In a dozen of years, our total population (not including Hong Kong Special Administrative Region, Macau Special Administrative Region and Taiwan) will still maintain a net increase of 8 million-10 million annually. To build a well-off society in an all-around way and achieve the goal of per capita GDP reaching around 3, 000 dollars, the total fertility rate must stable around 1. 8. This is also China's level in 1990s. According to such a prediction, the total population in 2010 and 2020 will reach 1. 36 billion and 1. 45 billion respectively; the peak of the total population will appear at 2030s, reaching around 1. 5 billion①.

Under the current policy arrangement, China's future population increase may be less than what the plan expected. The major reasons are: the change in the concept about birth, the increase of the diseases related to birth, the increase in the cost of bringing up children and the change in the attitude of providing for the aged. These factors will inhibit the growth of newly born population. Of course, the concern about the aging society and the population quality may make the government loosen its "the second child" policy in some regions on certain conditions②. However, the Chinese people's attitude towards pregnancy inclines more and more towards that of developed countries. China's total population is not likely to surpass the expected number.

Secondly, the material standard of living. Since 1970s, the population of some economically developed countries has stagnated and even shows signs of decreasing. However, their energy consumption sill maintains a high level because people's material standard of living is increasing while the material production is at the cost of energy consumption. A look at the household appliances can give some revelations. Much of what man was capable of is now done by various small household appliances, such as the induction cooker, microwave oven, cleaner, humidifier and water dispenser. From the television, washing machine and refrigerator to the air conditioner and computer, all these appliances are consumers of energy.

During the more than 30 years since the reform and opening up, China's GDP per capita increased 10 times, with its material living standard greatly improved. Household appliances are accessible and affordable to more and more consumers. In 2007, every one hundred households among the urban residents had 54 home computers, 137

---

① The "11th Five-Year" Plan for population development and 2020 Plan of the People's Republic of China.

② At present, according to *Population and Family Planning Law of the People's Republic of China*, China encourages later marriage and later pregnancy, advocates one child for one couple: those who satisfy conditions stipulated in the laws and regulations can have the second child. The details are subject to the stipulations of the people's congress or its standing committee of the province, autonomous region and the municipality. In most of the *Population and Family Planning Regulations*, it is stipulated that one couple could only have one child, with the exception that the couple come from one-child families, or are minorities or the first child in the rural household in the poor area is a girl. There are different policies in different regions.

color TVs and 95 air conditioners. There was also a rapid increase in the durable consumer goods possessed by the rural residents. In 1985, every one hundred rural households had 2 washing machines and every 10, 000 households had 6 refrigerators while in 2007, the number increased to 46 and 2, 612 respectively. The increasing trend to durable consumer goods and the emergence of new products put a higher demand on energy. The bicycle was the most important transportation means for urban and rural residents, the number of which reached a peak in the 1990s, with an average of 2 in every urban household and 3 in every two rural households. However, it was gradually replaced by the car and motorcycle. (At the end of 2008, China's private car ownership was 19. 47 million[①], with an average number of 15 for every 1, 000 persons.)

Table 14 Average Ownership of Durable Consumer Goods in Every 100 Households

Item	1978	1985	1990	1995	2000	2007
Urban area						
Washing machine	—	48. 29	78. 41	88. 97	90. 50	96. 77
Refrigerator	—	6. 58	42. 33	66. 22	80. 10	95. 03
Air conditioner	—	—	0. 34	8. 09	30. 80	95. 08
Home computer	—	—	—	—	9. 70	53. 77
Family car	—	—	—	—	0. 50	6. 06
Bicycle	—	152. 27	188. 59	194. 26	162. 72	—
Rural area						
Washing machine	0. 00	1. 90	9. 12	16. 90	40. 20	45. 94
Refrigerator	0. 00	0. 06	1. 22	5. 15	20. 10	26. 12
Bicycle	30. 73	80. 64	118. 33	147. 02	98. 37	97. 74
Motorcycle	0. 00	0. 00	0. 89	4. 91	40. 70	48. 52

Data source: *China Statistical Yearbook.*

Although in the past 30 years the material living standard of the Chinese people has been greatly improved, up to now there is no trend of saturated or slowing consumption. For example, the consumption of cars and large family housing is in the ascendant. In 2002 when the

① 2008 *National Economy and Social Development Statistical Bulletin.*

consumption of car was soaring, the sales of cars exceeded 1 million, while in 2008 China's car sales reached 5.0469 million①, with an increase of 400%② in five years.

Even if the population can be brought under control, the desire for improved material living standards is insatiable. Why do people pursue an improved living standard? To put it simply, for improved living qualities. According to Maslow's demand theory, man's basic need is to satisfy his physiological needs: food and heat. These factors can be quantified. For example, the daily quantity of heat intake for every normal person can be converted to the amount of food. When such needs are satisfied, people will have spiritual needs, such as social values, dignity and good taste. These needs change with the social trends. If society inclines to measure a person's social value through the products he or she has consumed and position his or her social status with famous-brand products and luxuries, then it may stimulate people's pursuit of income and fortune. Such a pursuit unleashes an insatiable greed for material and economic growth, which means the increasing consumption of energy and materials is inevitable. If people define life quality as the inner content and satisfaction and the harmonious co-existence with nature, maybe man doesn't need to rely on such an enormous material consumption for happiness.

Thirdly, technological advances: It is generally believed that technological advances can decrease energy consumption and furthermore, the emissions. However, the reality is that technological advances have stimulated people's consumption and increased the total emissions. Explanations are needed in two aspects: on the one hand, technical innovation developed new products, such as the refrigerator

---

① Zhu Yiping: Annual car sales exceeded 5 million in 2008 for the first time. *China Auto Market*, 2009(3).

② Up to now, the government has actively supported the use of family cars. In 2000, in the Fifth Plenary Session of the 15th Central Committee of CPC, "encouraging the household to buy cars" was first proposed. In 2001, the program outline approved in the Fourth Session of the 9th National People's Congress also explicitly encouraged the household's consumption of cars. At the beginning of 2009, *Plans to Adjust and Reinvigorate the Automobile Industry* promulgated to cope with the international financial crises was proposed to decrease by half the vehicle purchase tax on the passenger vehicles with a displacement of 1.6 liters or below, namely to decrease the tax rate from 10% to 5%. These policies have stimulated the consumption of private cars.

and air conditioner. Their emergence increased energy and material consumption; on the other hand, technological advances have improved efficiency and decreased energy consumption, but the total energy consumption does not necessarily decrease. For example, after the energy performance of the car has been improved, it may stimulate car sales and the mileage increases. This depends on the demand elasticity for cars.

The expectation of technologies is also evidenced in the development of renewable energy and low-carbon energy, the technological breakthrough of energy efficiency and the greenhouse gas capture and storage, etc. A mitigation scenario has great expectations for these technologies, in the hope that under the premise of maintaining economic growth and satisfying people's material desires, these technologies can replace non-renewable energies or store carbon dioxide under deserted land.

However, technological advances have both pros and cons. On the one hand, they can improve labor productivity and, on the other hand, they can also stimulate energy and resource consumption and have unpredictable influences on the environment. Currently, the evaluation of new technologies seems to only include economic feasibility, but it is unable to assess their long-term environmental influence. Coal, as the engine of the industrial revolution, has revealed its greenhouse effect after several centuries. We should be more rational in relying on technological advances for a solution to the greenhouse gas emission problem.

Will China's future scenario be today's America, Germany or Japan? In 2005, China's energy consumption per capita was 1.5 tons' standard coal equivalent. If one day this number reaches 9.8 tons' standard coal equivalent as that of America today, then China needs to consume 13 billion tons' standard coal equivalent, which is equivalent to the total global energy consumption in 2005. Even if it reaches the present level of Japan or Germany, China also needs to consume more than 6 billion tons' standard coal equivalent, 15 trillion kilowatts in total. It is risky to rely entirely on new energies or low-carbon energies brought about by technological advances.

Table 15 Comparisons between Countries in Energy Consumption per Capita and Car Ownership among Every Thousand People

Country	China	Japan	Korea	America	Germany	World
Energy consumption per capita① (tce)	1.5	4.9	4.7	9.8	5.0	2.1
Car ownership among every thousand people②	14.8	282.3	48.4	572.2	487	

Note: ① data in 2005. ② data of other countries are of 1990, with the exception of China which are of 2008.

Data source: *International Statistical Yearbook (2008)*.

China is in the midst of a strategic transformation. While enjoying material abundance, the Chinese people are facing a vacuum somewhere in their spiritual life. The standard of social values tends more towards materialism, with the increasing rate of GDP as a measurement of a region's competitiveness and income and fortune as a sign of a person's success. If the Chinese people continue in their pursuit of a highly material lifestyle, then China needs a high growth scenario at the cost of a possible unsustainable consumption of natural resources. Mitigating climate change will become a castle in the air. The government's intervention is a key factor in the mitigation scenario. However, the government consists of people and the policy decision-making itself is manipulated by the social values. If society regards material fortune as the yardstick, then the government will naturally bow to GDP growth. The government's decision-making in turn proves and enhances the social value by leading the people's choice and judgment and poses great pressure on the realization of the mitigation scenario. The greatest pressure on the mitigation scenario comes from man's insatiable desire for materials. China's greenhouse gas emission reduction is fundamentally dependent on the Chinese people abandoning the "greed for the larger and hankering for the foreign" mindset, establishing new values and seeking new lifestyles and development modes.

References:

[1] Gao Shuting, Zhang Huiqin, Yang Lirong & Wang Qiuling. A tentative study of China's greenhouse gas emission estimation, *Research of Environmental Sciences*, 1994(6). 高树婷、张慧琴、杨礼荣、王秋玲:《我国温室气体排放量估测初探》,《环境科学研究》1994 年第 6 期。

[2] Jiang Kejun. Brief introductionto the second new emission scenario symposium

of the IPCC Third Working Group. *Advances in Climate Change Research*, 2005(2).

姜克隽:《IPCC 第三工作组第二次新排放情景研讨会简介》,《气候变化研究进展》2005 年第 2 期。

[3] Jiang Kejun, Hu Xiulian& Zhuang Xing, et al. China's low-carbon scenario and low-carbon development in 2050. *Sino-Global Energy*, 2009(6).

姜克隽、胡秀莲、庄幸等:《中国 2050 年低碳情景和低碳发展之路》,《中外能源》2009 年第 6 期。

[4] Jiang Kejun, Hu Xiulian & Zhuang Xing, et al. China's energy demand and carbon dioxide emission scenario in 2050, *Advances in Climate Change Research*, 2008: 4(5).

姜克隽、胡秀莲、庄幸等:《中国 2050 年的能源需求与 CO2 排放情景》,《气候变化研究进展》2008 年第 4 卷第 5 期。

[5] Jiang Jinhe & Yao Yufang. Quantity analysis of the potential for humanist development and space for the carbon emission demand. *Journal of Quantitative & Technical Economics*, 2003(11).

蒋金荷、姚愉芳:《人文发展潜力与碳排放需求空间的定量分析》,《数量经济技术经济研究》2003 年第 11 期。

[6] Men Kepei & Zeng Wei. Research on the prediction of China's future population development in 50 years. *Journal of Quantitative & Technical Economics*, 2004(3).

门可佩、曾卫:《中国未来 50 年人口发展预测研究》,《数量经济技术经济研究》2004 年第 3 期。

[7] Qian Jie & Yu Lizhong. Research on the contribution of the fuel fossil to carbon dioxide emissions in Shanghai. *Shanghai Environmental Sciences*. 2003: 22 (11).

钱杰、俞立中:《上海市化石燃料排放二氧化碳贡献量的研究》,《上海环境科学》2003 年第 22 卷第 11 期。

[8] Wei Baoren. *China's Energy Demand and Scenario Analysis of Carbon Dioxide Emissions*. China Environmental Science Press, 2008.

韦保仁:《中国能源需求与二氧化碳排放的情景分析》,中国环境科学出版社 2008 年版。

[9] Wei Yiming, et al. *China's Energy Report (2008): Carbon Emissions Research*. Science Press, 2008.

魏一鸣等:《中国能源报告(2008):碳排放研究》,科学出版社 2008 年版。

[10] Wu Xuan. Calculation of carbon dioxide during the cement production and analysis of its utilization method. *Environmental Protection Science*, 2006(6). 吴萱:《水泥生产中 CO_2 产生量计算及利用途径分析》,《环境保护科学》2006 年第 6 期。

[11] Zhang Guobao ed.. *China's Energy Development Report (2009)*. Economic Science Press, 2009.

张国宝编:《中国能源发展报告(2009)》,经济科学出版社 2009 年版。

[12] Zhang Renjian, Wang Mingxing & Zheng Xunhua, et al. Analysis of the current situation of China's carbon dioxide emission sources. *Climatic and Environmental Research*, 2001(3).

张仁健、王明星、郑循华等:《中国二氧化碳排放源现状分析》,《气候与环境研究》2001 年第 3 期。

[13] Zheng Yisheng & Qian Yihong. *Profound Anxiety——Sustainable Development Problem in Contemporary China.* China Today Press, 1998.

郑易生、钱薏红:《深度忧患——当代中国的可持续发展问题》,今日中国出版社 1998 年版。

[14] Zhu Songli. A tentative analysis of greenhouse gas emissions and measures on emission reduction in the cement industry. *Energy of China*, 2000(7).

朱松丽:《水泥行业的温室气体排放及减排措施浅析》,《中国能源》2000 年第 7 期。

[15] Auffhammer, Maximilian and Richard T. Carson. Forecasting the Path of China's CO_2 Emissions Using Province-level Information, *Journal of Environmental Economics and Management*, Vol. 55, 229-247, 2008.

[16] Dabo Guan, Klaus Hubacek, Christopher L. Weber, et al. The Drivers of Chinese CO_2 Emissions from 1980 to 2030, *Global Environmental Change*, 2008, 626-634.

[17] F. R. Veeneklaas and L. M. van den Berg. Scenario Building: Art, Craft or Just a Fashionable Whim, in J. F. Th. Schoute et al. (eds.), *Scenario Studies for the Rural Environment*, 11-13.

[18] J. Schoonenboom, Overviewand State of the Art of Scenarios Studies for the Rural Environment, in J. F. Th. Schoute et al. (eds.), *Scenario Studies for the Rural Environment*, 15-24.

[19] Jayant Sathaye and Stephen Meyers. *Greenhouse Gas Mitigation Assessment: A Guidebook.* Kluwer Academic Publishers, 1995.

[20] Morita, Tsuneyuki and John Robinson. Greenhouse Gas Emission Mitigation Scenarios and Implications, in IPCC, *the Third Assessment Report on Climate Change*, 2001.

[21] Vuuren, van Detlef, Zhou Fengqi, Bert de Vries, et al. Energy and Emission Scenarios for China in the 21st Century-Exploration of Baseline Development and Mitigation Options, *Energy Policy*, 369-387, 2003.

[22] Wang, Tao and Jim Watson. China's Energy Transition: Pathways for Low Carbon Development, Sussex Energy Group, SPRU, University of Sussex, *UK and Tyndall Center for Climate Change Research*, 2008.

[23] Ying Fan, Qiao-Mei Liang, Yi-Ming Wei, et al. A Model for China's Energy Requirements and CO_2 Emissions Analysis, *Environmental Modeling & Software* 22, 378-393, 2007.

Appendix: abbreviations

CO_2: carbon dioxide

UNFCCC: United Nations Framework Convention on Climate Change

IPCC: Intergovernmental Panel on Climate Change

ORNL: Oak Ridge National Laboratory

CDIAC: Carbon Dioxide Information Analysis Center

PBL: Netherlands Environmental Assessment Agency

IEA: International Energy Agency

EIA: Energy Information Administration

Tce: ton's standard coal equivalent

Coping with Climate Change: Enlightenment Offered by Arid Prairie Areas[①]

By LI Wenjun

I. Introduction

Global climate change is one of the current heated topics in academic study and politics. If the IPCC makes the right prediction, then how to cope with climate change, namely to adjust the system to adapt to the ongoing and future possible climate change will become the key. Recently, a large amount of literature has discussed the "adaptation" to climate change, such as IPCC (2007), UNDP (2007), Heltberg, et al. (2009) and Smit and Wandel (2006). There is such a consensus that climate change is a natural process, but if human society takes wrong measures it will turn into a man-made disaster. For example, starvation, just as the Nobel Prize for Economics winner Sen (1981) pointed out, is a man-made disaster arising from climate risk because of a decrease in the grain output resulting from human society's failure to cope with natural disasters, which plunges man into starvation.

At present, the international community's research on climate change is biased on a macro-regional level and the national level and focuses on conceptual theoretical research, model prediction and scenario analysis in methodology, while ignoring the summary and analysis of the experience and lessons in coping with climate change from regional practices, local knowledge and unofficial institutional

① This research was funded by the National Science Foundation of China (40871252) and Ford Foundation. The basic data and material of the case study in the article have been published and for more details, please refer to Li Fangjun & Zhang Qian (2009).

arrangements. Undoubtedly, although climate change is a global issue, man's response will ultimately be evidenced locally. However, in the scientific research, policy making and the public forum concerning climate change, the local residents who are directly influenced by climate change are seldom taken into consideration. In the report of the IPCC (2007), except for the indigenous residents of the polar regions, indigenous residents and permanent residents in other regions are seldom mentioned; besides, the attention the indigenous residents in the polar region have received comes from the assumption that these groups may helplessly fall to victim to climate change rather than the realization of the possible contribution they may have made to coping with climate change (Salick and Ross, 2009).

As a matter of fact, through the combination of local knowledge and new technologies, the indigenous residents have many unique methods and ways to judge and cope with climate change, which may help the whole of society to cope with climate change on a broader scale. Byg and Salick (2009) believed that, unlike the macro and regional climate change involving much scientific research currently, the local knowledge will make an invaluable contribution to a better understanding of global climate change, such as providing information about local environments and focusing on key problems unnoticed by the macro scientific researches (Kloprogge and Van der Sluijs, 2006). Generally, the empirical research from foreign scientists tries to reveal the objective reality, so the researchers are required to be insulated from the system in order to keep an unbiased and objective perspective; unlike this, local residents' observations and conceptions are embedded in the local social cultural background and natural environment. Their conception can reflect what they have discerned as well as the actual influences climate change has had on their life (Danielsen et al., 2005). Besides, the local's observation is local, which is unattainable for most scientific research and models (Wilbanks and Kates, 1999; Berkes et al., 2001; Laidler, 2006; van Aalst et al., 2008). Also, local knowledge and the resident's conception have a direct bearing on people's decision-making, such as whether to take immediate action (Alessa et al., 2008) and what short-term and long-term countermeasures to take (Berkes and Jolly, 2001). The local process can influence the global process and vice versa (Wilbanks and Kates, 1999).

Also, the indigenous residents and other local residents are key components of many biological systems and they become the key to improving these systems' capacity for fighting disturbances from external variables. If the decision maker and the mainstream scientists of today's relevant areas can broaden their horizon and draw lessons from local knowledge and culture, they may provide new thinking for the international community to cope with climate change.

No matter what the present prediction of global climate change is, a certain fact is that the climate variability will become aggravated, the extreme severe weather will increase and the future will become more unpredictable. These features undoubtedly belong to the natural environment facing the arid prairie for thousands of years and the traditional production method of animal husbandry and the corresponding social relations and institutional arrangements, in essence, are incorporated into a system operating for over a thousand years in human society and which has adapted itself to the environment. I believe the research on this system will offer enlightenment to those making plans to cope with climate change at the national level. This article will take the arid prairie in Inner Mongolia as a case study and analyze the pasture areas' experience of coping with climate change from production methods, property relations and social relations, in the hope of providing a new perspective for China and other regions to cope with climate change based on such a case study.

II. Data and Methods

Besides the secondhand documentary material with noted sources in the article, most of the data and information about the production system and corresponding institutional arrangements of animal husbandry in the Inner Mongolia Steppe come from the field investigation of the research groups in the Steppe after 2006. From the west to the east, the investigation includes: the Ejin Banner, the Right Banner and the Left Banner of the Alxa League; the Etuoke Banner and the Uxin Banner of Erdos; the Sonid Left Banner, Xilinhot and East Ujimqin Banner of Xilin Gol League; the Hexigten Banner of Chifeng. The types of biological system covered include steppe desert, desert steppe, typical steppe and the transition zone between cropping area and nomadic area. In particular, the detailed data and information about the farm households who adopt the strategy of "Aote'er"[①] mainly come from the household tracking investigation into the B Gacha[②] in the Sonid Left Banner of Xilin Gol League in April, 2006, October, 2006, July to August, 2007, July 2008 and July 2009.

The B Gacha in the case study is situated in the Sonid Left Banner of Xilin Gol League, belonging to the desert steppe zone. According to the material from the Banner's weather bureau, from 1957 to 2006 the annual average precipitation of the whole banner was 189mm, with an average anomaly rate of about 20%. The total area of the B Gacha is 700 square kilometers, among which the natural grassland is 670 square kilometers. The main type of the vegetation is high-plain desert steppe, accounting for a percentage of 89% of the total area of the grassland.

The herdsmen in the B Gacha are mainly Mongol nationalities. In 2006, the total population was 372 in 105 households, among which 75 were engaged in animal husbandry production. Other farm households become migrant workers in the city without ownership of livestock and give up animal husbandry production, the main economic activity and income source of the B Gacha. The livestock includes the horse, cow, camel, sheep and goat. From 1961 to the present, the total livestock in the Gacha reached a peak in 1999, about 54, 525 sheep units; the increasing trend has been disrupted by the natural disasters since 1999 and until the 2006 annual animal husbandry census, the total livestock in the Gacha was 34, 153 sheep units.

The weather in the B Gacha is unstable because of its location in the desert steppe zone, with frequent occurrences of unfavorable weather. According to statistics, from 1967 to 2006, the occurrence rate of serious snow and drought disasters in the Sonid Left Banner was 24% and 20% respectively, namely, about once in every four to five years and most of the natural disasters took place in the north part of the Banner. Also, on a small scale, the unfavorable weather also cropped up frequently. "Aote'er" is the traditional strategy adopted by local herdsmen to cope with unfavorable climate. Therefore, B Gacha is a

---

① "Aote'er" strategy means the husbandry strategy used by traditional Mongolia herdsmen to cope with climate change, namely, when inclement weather occurs in the grassland (such as drought or blizzard), they will transfer the livestock temporarily to other grasslands uninfluenced or little influenced by the weather and when the weather turns better, they will transfer the livestock back.

② Gacha is the Mongolia language, meaning a village in the rural area.

good choice for the research on how herdsmen cope with unfavorable weather.

In-depth interviews, anthropological oral history and second-hand data collection are methods used in the research. Investigations into the household registration of the farm households in the B Gacha were conducted, interviews were made with local governmental sectors such as the Animal Husbandry Bureau of the Sonid Left Banner, the grassland operation and management station, the grassland station and the statistical bureau and second-hand data were collected from those governmental sectors and the library of Sonid Left Banner. 28 samples were selected randomly among the 75 animal husbandry households for the household registration investigation, with a sampling rate of 40%. The interview with the farm households includes: (1) the cost-return data of the animal husbandry production; (2) the cost-return data of the "Aote'er" strategy and the fixed drylot feeding; (3) relevant data and oral descriptions of the local dual grazing-grass contracting process and herdsmen's "Aote'er" strategy before and after the contracting. The interviews with the governmental sectors and the second-hand data collection are mainly centered on the statistical data on local vegetation, weather and animal husbandry production over the years and the government's attitude towards the herdsman's "Aote'er" strategy.

III. Features of the Climate in the Arid Steppe

1. Drastic Variation in Precipitation

To illustrate the variation in the precipitation of the Inner Mongolia Steppe, this article used the precipitation data during the 35 years from 1971 to 2005 in 13 weather stations in Xilin Gol League to calculate the precipitation change rate[①] in different regions and in Xilin Gol League, see Table 1. As is shown in Table 1, except for Xilinhot City, Naran-bulag and Erenhot, although the annual precipitation change rate in

① The change rate here adopts the coefficient of variation (CV) in statistics to measure the statistical data of the variation level of each observed data in the precipitation material.

most regions of Xilin Gol League was less than 33% ①, the regions with a change rate over 33% in the spring and summer precipitation, extremely important to the growth of vegetation, were in absolute predominance.

Table 1 Annual and Growing-Season Precipitation Change Rate in the 13 Regions of Xilin Gol League (1971-2005) (Unit: %)

Region	Annual	Spring (April-June)	Summer (July-August)
Xilin Gol League	18.0	29.4	30.6
Duolun	19.2	30.1	28.7
Zhenglan Banner	21.6	37.9	35.4
Taipusi Banner	17.6	38.1	29.7
West Ujimqin Banner	23.0	38.3	42.4
Zhengxiangbai Banner	19.9	38.8	32.7
Xianghuang Banner	23.5	41.0	37.6
Abaga Banner	25.5	44.1	44.3
Xilinhot City	30.5	45.1	52.2
Sonid Left Banner	25.6	45.2	43.4
Zhurihe	27.4	46.8	49.0
Naran-bulag	30.0	47.7	44.6
Sonid Right Banner	29.0	53.6	42.7
Erenhot	37.1	56.7	57.1

Data source: Inner Mongolia Weather Bureau.

2. *Frequent Occurrence of Extreme Weather*

According to the Chronicle of the Sonid Left Banner, the Banner is a region frequently plagued by natural disasters. Most commonly seen disasters are drought, snow disaster, black frost and wind damage. The Banner has small amounts of precipitation, with a quarter of its annual precipitation concentrated in the last ten-day period of July and first ten-

① To judge the influence of the variation level of precipitation on the grassland's first productivity, at present the widely accepted proposition is by Ellis and Swift (1988) that when the precipitation CV exceeds 33% this is regarded as an index for the precipitation variation level in arid areas. For those over 33%, it is deemed that the non-living factor like precipitation has made a greater contribution to vegetation than the grazing of the herbivores. The new grassland ecology defines such a system as an imbalanced system.

day period of August. From the last ten-day period of May to the first ten-day period of August, the grassland is at its key period for growth and the precipitation during this time and its timing will decide whether there will be a drought or not. In the Banner a severe drought will occur on average every four years. The "snow disaster" is a serious natural disaster in the winter pasturing area. The grassland is covered with heavy snow, making it hard for the livestock to search for food and the livestock are starved to death. This is why it is called the snow disaster and it occurs every 3 to 4 years on average. However, if the winter pasturing area is not covered with snow for a long time or if the accumulated snow is too thin to provide drinking water for the livestock, they will lose weight, suffer from abortions or even die. This disaster, which occurs for lack of snow, is called "black frost". "Wind disaster" includes the yellow wind and white wind. The first is called a sandstorm meteorologically, in which the strong wind blows the sand and makes the air rather turbid. It refers to the weather of sand and wind with a horizontal visibility of less than 1,000 meters. In the Banner it mainly occurs from April to May, with an average recorded frequency 2-3 times annually and in the most frequent year it was 8 times. The latter is called a blizzard meteorologically, in which a large amount of snow is blown with the strong wind and the horizontal visibility is less than 1,000 meters. The white wind is very commonly seen in the Sonid Left Banner, mainly occurring from November to March. The enforcing white wind influences transportation and grazing, bringing risks to both man and livestock. Men are easily lost and suffer from the cold and the livestock may be startled, lost and even die. It occurs 3.5 times annually on average, 19 times at most. Also, locust plagues, cold winds, cold rain, wet snow, hail and flood may occur occasionally.

Figure 1 shows the 9 droughts, 4 wind disasters, 11 snow disasters and 3 hail disasters during the 56 years from 1945 to 2000 and the fluctuations in the number of the livestock.

IV. Methods to Cope with Climate Change in the Pasturing Area of the Inner Mongolia Steppe: Experience and Lessons

1. Production Mode

Dominating the Inner Mongolia Steppe before the 1950s was the traditional nomadic operation method in which man was moving with the livestock. As the livestock moved with different seasons, man also inhabited the area of verdant water plants; in the ensuing era of the collective people's commune, the livestock still moved and the major labor force based on the division of labor also moved with them. However, the elderly, women and children, began to settle down in an area following the government's encouragement and advocacy, thus forming the "settling-down nomadic" method in which the livestock moved while man settled down. After the implementation of the dual grazing-grass contracting system since the 1980s, with the division of the grassland to certain households, the livestock couldn't move freely over a large area. After 30 years' settling down, most herdsmen gradually came out of the Mongolia yurts and moved into the brick-made houses and finally the situation of a "settled lifestyle and settled grazing" was formed. If the division standard is based on whether the livestock moves, the "traditional" animal husbandry in this article refers to the production method before the grassland contracting system in the 1980s.

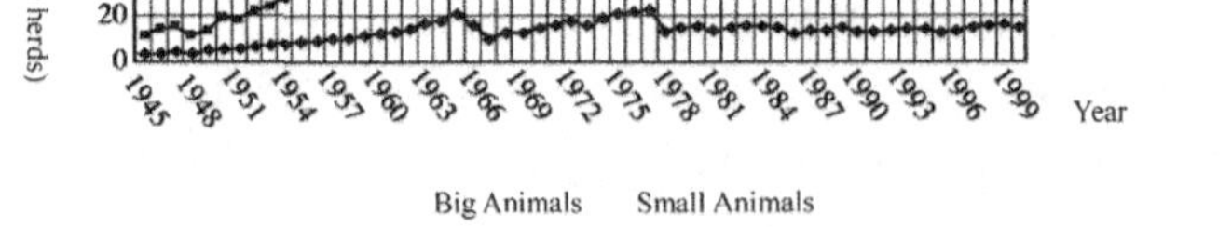

Figure 1 Annual Changes in the Livestock Number of the Animal Husbandry Industry in the Sonid Left Banner and the Occurrence of Natural Disasters (1945-2000)

Data source: based on the Animal Husbandry Chronicle of the Sonid Left Banner (1995) and interviews on the household registration (focusing on those after 1995).

Owing to the unpredictability in the temporal and spatial distribution of the grassland resource resulting from drastic climate change, to move about freely and flexibly is the key to the livestock's survival. Actually, the nomadic people and their livestock diminish or even eliminate the risk for survival brought about by unpredictable climate changes through migration. It is the migration around a large area following the resource distribution that decides the sustainability of their production of animal husbandry. Such immigration or seasonal movement generally takes place between the predetermined places based on a different wet season and dry season, such as the commute between the summer camp and the winter camp; it may also be random movement, which happens under extremely unfavorable weather conditions, making it unable to predict which grassland has the highest output. In the Mongolian language, it is called "Aote'er".

Among the banners, according to the historical record of the Sonid Left Banner (Chronicle of the Sonid Left Banner, 2004), "Aote'er" is a long existent grazing method used since time immemorial. Even after the collective era since the founding of the People's Republic of China and the semi-privatized system of the grassland after 1980s, such a method has been used by the herdsmen. Since 1951 there have been four cases of accepting "Aote'er"① between league and banner or even between countries, mainly concentrating on the husbandry cooperative and people's commune era. Among the four, two accepted "Aote'er": one was that the banner government arranged the "Aote'er" livestock from Dornogovi in the People's Republic of Mongolia to spend winter on the Hongge'ersumu border in the north in October, 1956; the other was the arrangement of 24, 500 "Aote'er" livestock to spend winter in the Siziwang Banner in the Ulanqab League in November, 1957. Two were going towards "Aote'er": one was that some livestock went to the East Ujimqin Banner in Xilin Gol League in October, 1963; the other was that the 160,000 livestock in ten communes of the whole banner went to other leagues in the winter of 1966. During the moving and accepting

① Accepting "Aote'er" is corresponding to going "Aote'er": the party which borrows the key resources for unfavorable weather conditions is called going "Aote'er"; correspondently, the party which is using the key resources is called accepting "Aote'er".

process, the banner government had been serving as the organizer, arranging the grassland for the "Aote'er' livestock in the banner and the movement between leagues and banners.

Besides the above mentioned going "Aote'er", going "Aote'er" also happened among the Gachas in animal husbandry. According to our investigations, in the collective era, there were two forms of going "Aote'er" in the B Gacha of the Sonid Left Banner: (1) the herdsmen immigrated to the Gacha when there was small-range unfavorable weather; (2) a collective was described as going "Aote'er" with a Gacha as a unit when unfavorable weather occurred over a large area. Herdsman Nuoribu recalled the going "Aote'er" scenario in the Gacha: "every Haote① divides a certain amount of grazing grasslands based on the stocking livestock group, but there are no clear boundaries among the grasslands in the Haote. Generally, they are fuzzily divided with a hilltop or a stump. When the weather changes the herdsman can use the grassland of the neighboring Haote as well. " There were four collective going "Aote'er" in the Gacha: (1) from the autumn of 1964 to the autumn of 1965, to Yihegaolesumu in the Abaga Banner; (2) from the summer of 1967 to the summer of 1968, to the juncture of the East Ujimqin Banner and the Jirem League and Hinggan League; (3) in the winter of 1977, to Saihan'gaobisumu in the Sonid Left Banner; (4) from the autumn of 1980 to the autumn of 1981, to Yihegaolesumu in the Abaga Banner. Also, there were some small-scale going "Aote'er". Owing to the group grazing in the collective era, going "Aote'er" sometimes occurred with the livestock group as its unit. For example, in 1982 and 1983, for a lack of grass in the winter, the horse group in the Gacha was transferred to the neighboring Hujiletu Pasture in the Sonid Right Banner and Baogeduowulasumu in the Abaga Banner.

Going "Aote'er" in essence is a process for the herdsman to have access to key resources② through transferring the livestock in unfavorable

---

① Haote is the Mongolian language, referring to the settlement of several neighboring households in the same Gacha.

② In an environment in which the precipitation and other weather conditions are highly changeable, in a certain space there will be areas with relative stable grass output and these areas are the key factors deciding the number of livestock under the most unfavorable weather conditions. Therefore, they are called key resources. See details in Scoones (1995, 1993) and Illius and O' Connor (1999). In the grazing husbandry system, "key resources" usually become places offering assistance in the time of droughts, namely places with high precipitation and grass output.

weather conditions, which symbolizes the herdsman's strategy to follow the differentiated temporal and spatial resource distribution during highly changeable weather. Such a migration method enables the herdsman to maintain a high stocking rate even in the drought years while avoiding sustained pressure on a certain grassland at a certain period of the year. In the following I will take the herdsman's going "Aote'er" in the B Gacha of the Sonid Left Banner of Xilin Gol League as a case study and explain how this strategy decreases or even eliminates the risk brought about by uncertain environmental changes from the perspective of the economy and ecology.

Economically, the herdsman's choice of going "Aote'er" can overcome the problem of the unavoidable temporary diminishing of the high opportunity cost brought about by the disaster and remove the economic and technological restrictions posed by the importing of fodder grass. Take the anti-drought strategy of the 26 husbandry households in the B Gacha in 2006 as a case study. Among the 26 investigated households, 25 chose to go "Aote'er" to obtain key resources and the remaining one failed to rent grassland for late contact and ended up in fighting the disaster at the fixed original place, replacing the natural key resources with artificial feed. This provides a sample for our comparative study. Considering there is only one sample not going "Aote'er" in the fixed group (Household 2 in Table 2), I have selected a sample (Household 1 in Table 2) among the 25 households in the moving group, the grazing management capability of which is equivalent to the sample mentioned above. Here the "grazing management capability" means the per capita livestock management scale and grassland area, the time period of going "Aote'er", drylot feeding in captivity and the educational background of the head of the household. At the same time, the average number of the 25 households is used as the reference. The checking project of the cost-return analysis is as follows. In the cost checking, those related to the moving livestock include: rent for the grassland receiving the livestock, the livestock transportation fee after renting the intermediary vendor's vans, the water rate for purchasing and transporting water for man and livestock and the livestock loss occurring during the movement (calculated at the livestock's current price); costs for fighting the disaster at the fixed original grassland include: cost for purchasing hay, corn and ensiling to feed the animal and the treatment fee for sickness in the livestock resulting from their inadaptability to captivity. In terms of the comparison of returns, the price of slaughtering in the autumn is double that in the summer. In consideration of the opportunity cost brought about by slaughtering in the summer, here I mainly compare the two groups' income differences incurred by different slaughtering rates in the autumn and summer.

Table 2 Cost-Return Analysis of Going "Aote'er" and Anti-Disaster at a Fixed Place

Item	Unit	Household 1: Going"Aote'er"		25 Households Average	Household 2: Fixed Drylot Feeding	
Basic Conditions	Sheep unit/person	Per capita sheep unit	81	—	Per capita sheep unit	83
	Mu/person	Per capita grassland area	2175	—	Per capita grassland area	2611
	Day	Period of migration	30	41	Period of drylot feeding	50
	Sheep unit	Number of livestock in migration	360	590	Number of livestock for drylot feeding	250
	—	Education background	Junior highschool	—	Education background	Junior high school
Cost Analysis	Yuan	Grassland rent	3600	8370	Hay	9375
	Yuan	Transportation fee	1000	4139	Corn	4000
	Yuan	Drinking water rate	0	596	Ensiling	625
	Yuan	Livestock loss	0	1498	Treatment for livestock's illness	1000
	Yuan/sheep unit/day	Total cost	0. 43	0. 62	Total cost	1. 20
Return Analysis	%	Slaughtering rate in spring and summer	0	17	Slaughtering rate in spring and summer	94
	%	Slaughtering rate in autumn	100	83	Slaughtering rate in autumn	6

Data source: interviews in July, 2007.

The result of the cost-return analysis (Table 2) shows that the daily cost of Household 1's going "Aote'er" is 0. 43 yuan/sheep unit, the average daily cost of the 25 households is 0. 62 yuan/sheep unit and both of them are far lower than the daily 1. 2 yuan/sheep unit feeding cost of Household 2 with fixed drylot feeding. As far as the return is concerned, Household 1 has guaranteed 100% livestock sales in the autumn; an average of 17% livestock are slaughtered in the summer among the 25 households and 83% in the autumn. Overall, the herdsman who fights the disaster through migration can basically ensure the slaughtering of a large number of livestock in the autumn at a high price. In contrast, Household 2 without going "Aote'er", to ease the economic pressure of feeding the livestock, has slaughtered 94% of the livestock in advance in the spring and summer, leaving a mere 6% for slaughtering in the autumn. If Household 2 catches up with the herdsman's going "Aote'er" and follows the average level of the said 25 households in slaughtering the livestock, its livestock sales return will increase by 51 yuan/sheep unit. Therefore, when unfavorable weather occurs, the going "Aote'er" strategy is more economically efficient than the fixed drylot feeding in the family pasture in fighting the disaster.

Ecologically, through going "Aote'er", the risk of an overuse of grasslands can be avoided. Changeability is the basic feature of the ecological system in the arid area. The unfavorable weather will damage the grazing environment and pose threats to grazing. However, this is only one of the natural states in the ecological system and the ecological system will alternate between different states with the varying of external temporal and spatial conditions to provide opportunities for the mitigation of the risk (Westoby, et al. 1989). Such opportunities are actually the occurrence of key resources. Key resources are induced by the temporal and spatial heterogeneity of climate change and grazing resources, so they also appear in different temporal and spatial dimensions. For specific spatial arid and semi-arid grasslands, the change in the vegetation incurred by unfavorable weather is irreversible. As the external weather pressure diminishes or disappears, such as the improvement in precipitation and the melting of snow, the grassland will have chances to recover to a good condition.

However, modern society, on account of the external world's improper understanding of the husbandry area's social and economic system, makes improper interventions, which renders it increasingly harder for the implementation of going "Aote'er", an effective method to diminish risks. In the ideal treatment, the long-term policy implemented in the husbandry area is, in essence, based on the concept of facing the changes with unchanged attitudes and countering all the uncertainty with stability, a concept which is concretely reflected in the measure of replacing nomadism with "settled lifestyle and settled grazing"; by digging wells in the arid area and artificial grass planting to resist the unstable grass output incurred by changeable climate and to change the thousand-year-long traditional and backward production method that is dependent on heaven for grazing; when disasters crop up, they *fight* them by constructing covered sties and increasing external system input rather than by *avoiding* them through migration. After the 1980s, when the grasslands in the husbandry area were contracted to households, the herdsman's ability to choose migration was impaired and their ability to depend on the system itself for addressing risks was gone.

(2) Property System

The grassland contracting policy beginning in the 1980s was the greatest reform of land ownership in the history of the Inner Mongolian husbandry area. By bestowing a semi-private land ownership of the grassland on the farm household, this policy defined the boundary of certain grasslands for their users and changed the correct relationship of the grassland between the households. As a matter of fact, in the last two decades, the land rights reform distributed a patch of land to the ownership of every person, with the original hope of pursuing efficiency and fairness, namely, to establish a land rights plan based on the market and on the premise that everyone has their own land so that the land can be effectively utilized (Ybarra, 2008) . The grassland contracting policy implemented by China in the Inner Mongolian husbandry area and later promoted in the whole of the north husbandry area coincided with the move to establish a nationwide ownership society.

The land rights system which contracts grasslands to households weakens the herdsman's ability to seek benefits[①] based on information,

---

① For users whose livelihood depends heavily on natural resources, the ability to seek benefits in resources is equally important to the rights. Sometimes, the former is even more important than the latter. For example, the land rights can endow on a person the right to make benefits from a patch of land, but if the owner has no labor capacity, no capital, it means he has no capacity to maintain his livelihood with returns from the land. Therefore, an overemphasis on the land rights may sometimes make the resource users' capacity for benefit seeking invisible. See details in Li Wenjun and Zhang Qian (2009), pp. 51-55.

cooperation of labor forces, capital and market knowledge, thus impairing their ability to lower risks through migration.

To begin with, before the grassland contracting system, when a disaster year broke out, information could be circulated in time between different tiers of the collective society for the searching of key resources to transfer the livestock and it could be ensured that the livestock could be transferred to places with key resources in time. However, since the creation of the grassland contracting system, every household has to inquire about and judge the direction of key resources all by itself, competing against nature single-handedly. Because of the limitations in communication and knowledge, the decision-making in animal husbandry will be delayed, which will result in losses in animal husbandry. The herdsman's reminiscence of the going "Aote'er" organized by the Gacha reflects the in-time migration to avoid disaster, which greatly diminished the losses incurred by procrastination. After the contracting, for a single farm household, owing to the difficulty in obtaining the information about key resources in time, losses will be incurred in their husbandry operation. For example, as Household Bate'er described how he contacted grasslands in 2006, "I went out to search for grasslands at the beginning of June and I've heard which places have the best grasslands. However, much of the information is false and we had better have a look in person. Last year, I heard that grasslands in a specific place offered the lowest price and went there by motorcycle, only to find the price was rather high." This is how the risk of delaying the herdsman in the disaster-stricken grassland has increased.

In finding grasslands, most of the herdsmen depend on relatives and friends for possible areas. If they have no connections, the rent for the grassland is even higher. In the drought in 2006, almost all the farm households in the B Gacha went to rent grasslands. With a high demand, it was hard for them to find grasslands. Some households finally found grasslands at a price of 8 yuan per sheep, per unit/month, but the opportunity was lost because of others with a higher price offer. They had no choice but to seek other opportunities. Some herdsmen spent more than ten days in order to find grasslands. Herdsman Batu who crossed leagues and went to Ulanqab recalled that back then he needed to find somewhere to keep his sheep safe no matter how far he had to go. The grassland he found offered a rent of 5 yuan per sheep per unit/month, cheaper when compared with the 8 yuan per sheep per unit/month. However, the transportation fee he had to pay was four times higher than others. Besides, the long wait during this period of time was excruciating to both the herdsmen and the livestock because during the 45 days' grazing prohibition①. They could not feed on green grass and their constitution was weakened. Some households had more than ten sheep dead before migration. Some of them sold the livestock at a low price, 100 yuan for one sheep, 280 yuan for a couple of ewes and 1,000 yuan for a horse. These prices were less than a half of the normal market price after the autumn.

Judging from the migration method, since the livestock can only feed on a minimal amount of forage grass for survival during the grazing prohibition period and because of the drought, they have no access to green grasses even in June. Their weak constitution renders them unable to reach the migration site without transportation. Therefore, the herdsman has to look hard for possible transportation to convey the livestock. These vehicles are largely owned by merchants and the transportation price is mainly set according to the distance. Inside the banner, the price is generally 400 yuan per vehicle and is higher crossing banners or leagues. For example, the price of herdman Batu to Ulanqab was 1,500 yuan per vehicle. Besides, during the process there will be certain livestock losses. On the bumpy journey, the livestock, with too weak a constitution may be squashed or squeezed to death. Many herdsmen recalled that there were many dead livestock dumped by the road. Among the 25 households, 6 had their livestock die during the transportation, 2 at least and 10 at most. Experienced herdsmen adopted two ways to decrease their losses: one was to request the driver to drive at a steady rate and the other was to arrange one person to stand among the sheep and support the sheep whenever it fell so that it would not be crushed to death. When they returned, since the livestock had recovered their health and the herdsmen were unable to stand more

① The grazing prohibition policy in the spring is added after the grassland contracting policy to treat the grassland degradation. According to the government's requirement, the B Gacha has begun the implementation of the grazing rest policy in the spring since 2002. From 2002 to 2005, the grazing rest period spanned 60 days, from April 1 to June 1; from 2006 to present, it shrank to 45 days, from April 1 to May 15. The herdsman's livestock must be fed in captivity during the grazing rest period and cannot go out for grazing.

transportation fees, most of them walked their livestock back their own grasslands. The returning route was basically by the high road to avoid hedges and for fear of incurring costs by trespassing on others' grasslands. Since the 500 meters on the two sides of the road belong to the grazing prohibition area, the herdsmen had to hurry their livestock for fear of being fined. Before the contracting system, going "Aote'er" could choose the shortest straightline distance because there were no hedges.

In terms of the labor force, the grassland rights boundary formed between the farm households makes them independent in their husbandry production. The method to improve their capability of seeking benefits through labor cooperation no longer exists. In tradition, corresponding to the diversity of the livestock is the temporal and spatial differentiation in the resource distribution in the arid and semi-arid grasslands. The traditional five-animal raising (camel, horse, cow, sheep and goat) in the Inner Mongolian Plateau shows the consistency between the production method and the natural ecology. However, such a production method needs labor division and cooperation. Following the grassland contracting system, we see the disappearance of such labor division and cooperation, leading to incompetence in using the resources with high efficiency. Similarly, after the dual grazing-grass contracting system, the farm households which are independent of each other are subject to more capital, technology and market restrictions and the household's capability to seek benefits from the resources are influenced. For example, it is hard to develop a sound processing industry for the diary and meat products and there is no competitiveness if the household faces the market all by itself (whether to purchase grass fodder or to sell the animals).

And the findings from the grassland management system research prior to the privatization of the grassland (Mwangi and Dohrn, 2008; Fernandez-Gimenez, 2002; 1999; Verdery, 1999; Toulmin, 1995; Scoones, 1994) show that in using the grassland, the herdsman succeeds in managing the grazing resources flexibly by maintaining changeable physical boundaries and the users' boundaries. Contrary to the "clear definition", such a grassland property rights arrangement shows the features of "incomplete definition" and "fuzzy" boundaries. The herdsman's requirement for such flexible boundaries is related to the grazing environment's variability. When there is a lack of grazing resources because of changes in weather, the herdsman will adjust the grassland boundary and the user's scale. The maintenance of the boundary is to ensure the herdsman can obtain key resources in emergencies. The research finds that in the herdsman's practices, "fuzzy" doesn't necessarily mean "ambiguity". The herdsmen manage the use of their grasslands by defining "who has what right of what things at what time", but such definitions are not fixed and can be adjusted flexibly according to realities (Mwangi and Dohrn, 2008). In this sense, Verdery (1999) pointed out that "fuzzy" is actually a sarcasm about the private property rights which advocate the fixed demarcation of the grassland relationship by men: "the property rights concept of the new liberalism invariably considers the undertakers of rights and obligations as individuals and endows the individual with the right to exclude others physically and legally. Apart from that, all the property rights arrangements are considered to be fuzzy. ...but usually the reality is that there are overlapping ownerships of a certain item among different people. Therefore, the "self" in the 'self' and 'non-self' relationship defined by such a system doesn't necessarily refer to an individual, but usually a group."

Furthermore, what are the major reasons for the herdsman to maintain a fuzzy property rights boundary? From the perspective of cost-return, in the region with a high risk of unforeseen climatic changes, the cost of excluding others may be very high (owing to the losses incurred by the immobility of the livestock and the cost of excluding aliens) because in such regions such costs usually will exceed the returns. Traditionally, the altruism among the herdsmen in using the grassland can facilitate the migration of the livestock and help the herdsmen to scatter the livestock based on the precipitation conditions so as to decrease the risk brought about by the environmental uncertainty and increase the total grazing income (Goodhue, et al. 2000). Our tracking research on the going "Aote'er" strategy of the B Gacha in the Sonid Left Banner in Inner Mongolia also proves the necessity of such flexible boundaries. Going "Aote'er" is a grazing strategy embedded in the traditional nomadic system, which, in essence, is the process by which the herdsman gains key resources in unfavorable weather by migrating the livestock. The herdsman's going "Aote'er" practice is actually a process adjusting the boundary for the grassland users based on the distribution of key resources. Although, at a certain moment, the spatial distribution for the users in the grazing system is relatively fixed, owing to weather changes some people need to move to key resources and the user group for key resources is thus changed. Actually, going "Aote'er" represents the herdsman's requirement to make flexible adjustments of the grassland's physical boundaries and the users' boundaries so as to obtain key resources. Contrarily, the "one land for one household" property rights model established by the grassland contracting policy asks for an explicit definition of the grassland's physical boundaries and the users' boundaries, namely to define the physical boundary of "one land" and concentrate the contracting and operating rights for this land on one household. In this way, in utilizing the grassland, there occurs a contradiction between the policy's requirement of a fixed boundary and the herdsman's need for a flexible boundary, which has influenced the herdsman's livelihood and the resource utilization and management and hence "the tragedy of the private land" (Li & Zhang, 2009).

3. Social Relations

The above-mentioned reform of the property rights institutional arrangement has changed the social relations fundamentally and influenced the herdsman's capability to cope with risks as an individual.

Just as McCay and Jentoft (1998) pointed out, "the inefficacy of the resource management and the loss of the social benefits result from an unimproved property right and at the same time may also cause a series of social relation factors which cause 'community failure', such as the conflicts between competing groups, the privileged elites' opportunism, the differences in the member's ability to establish and implement management systems and the actual dilution of the mutual understanding and trust among people." We observed in the B Gacha case the same "community failure" process after the dual grazing-grass contracting, which was mainly evidenced in the severing of the reciprocal community bond that impaired the herdsman's capability to cope with unfavorable climate conditions.

In the arid grassland with drastic climate changes, every herdsman, as an individual, has an expectation: when other herdsmen need to go "Aote'er" and enter my grassland, I am willing to provide assistance to them because when the weather reverses[1], they will return my help. In such an expectation based on reciprocity, the present exchange among the members is regarded as the core "friendly" relationship. For example, in daily grazing life, if a person uses another person's horse or camel, the host will get a silk kerchief or wine as a present. The friendliness between the herdsmen facilitates their ability to adjust the resource users' boundaries. In entering key resources, the departing party will "leave some livestock as a token of gratitude for using others' grassland" (Herdsman Nuoribu, interview in 2007). It can be seen that based on the shared reciprocity, the herdsmen show their friendliness with presents, which effectively contributes to a consensus between the party entering key resources and the party using key resources. In the process of sharing key resources, the users consolidate their friendship through shared labor. According to the herdsman's memory, before the grassland contracting system, the two parties (going "Aote'er" and accepting "Aote'er") would discuss the number of livestock and the grazing place for "Aote'er". The time restriction was relatively loose, depending on the weather and the utilization condition of the accepting party's grassland resources. If the staying time was long, the two parties would share their labor and cooperate in grazing even until the completion of a production cycle of the animal husbandry.

After the grassland contracting, with the grassland further divided into a single household, the grassland rights boundary between the herdsmen made them independent in husbandry production. As the labor cooperation decreases, with the weakening of internal information communication in the community, the reciprocal bond sustained with friendliness, trust and communication also begins to break up. In the exchange of key resources, since the right arrangement itself will lead to an advantageous control of the key resources' contractor over the

---

① In arid regions, owing to obvious spatial and temporal differentiations in precipitation, it happens frequently. In our research, we find that even in the neighboring two households' grasslands, one may face the threat from drought in a certain year while the neighbor enjoys verdant grasses because in the key season (for example, spring), it gets timely rain. In the investigation in the summer of 2008, a household suffering from drought described that they could see the dark clouds scudding over the sky of the neighboring grassland and the rain fell over the grassland, but there was not a raindrop on his grassland at all.

borrowers, if social distrust grows in people's minds, so does the possibility to reach consensus and realize reciprocity. First of all, owing to insufficient information communication between the herdsmen and the weakening of the social and moral bond, the engaging party will default on the contract or even deny the contract in the transaction, which makes the transaction even more difficult. For example, Herdsman A'le told what he had encountered: "we had agreed on the rent of 8 yuan per sheep per unit/month for the grassland. Later, when someone offered 10 yuan per sheep per unit/month, the host broke his promise and I had to look for other grasslands. It took 10 days for me to contact a grassland." The result is: among the 25 going "Aote'er" samples, 3 households were delayed due to the accepting party's breaking of their promise and had to look for further distant grasslands; also, 8 households procrastinated for five days in contacting grasslands and they had to sustain their production with high-cost feeding. In addition, the weakening of the social mutual help and friendliness concept greatly increases the difficulty in reaching a consensus between two parties. The accepting party begins to impose a cash charge on the requesting party and in most circumstances it asks the other party to pay in advance. However, not every household has the paying ability① at that time and to enter key resources they have to resort to usury, which further aggravates their production burden in fighting the disaster. Other households will charge tolls and even charge fees for drinking water if the livestock drink water bulbs in their grasslands at a price from 0. 50 yuan per sheep to 1 yuan per sheep. If there is no money, they will first confiscate a dozen sheep of the requesting party until cash is paid. In contrast, when the society was constructed based on reciprocity and mutual trust, a present was offered before the departure and the herdsmen would not be repudiated for their inability to offer presents. Finally, since the two parties are unequal in using key resources, even if a transaction is agreed upon, they cannot develop a constructive cooperation relationship and deepen their friendship. As a result, the requesting party will wish to end such a relationship earlier and may rush their livestock back when its own

① For the feature of the production cycle of the animal husbandry, usually only after the slaughtering of livestock in the autumn can the herdsman have sufficient cash income.

family grassland is not yet fully recovered. And this is unfavorable to the recovery of the disaster-stricken grassland.

More seriously, the betrayal of the party controlling key resources in the reciprocal relationship will change the social rules as a whole and, as time goes by, the social relationship will be plunged into a vicious cycle. Because if the party needing key resources and the provider cannot cooperate well in the first transaction, when the weather condition reverses, the needy party will be unwilling to conduct reciprocal cooperation and may impose more rigid conditions for the transaction with their controlling status. Ultimately, both of the parties will end up as complete losers; contrarily, if in the first cooperation the provider of key resources is willing to initiate a reciprocal relationship, then, as the condition reverses, it will be offered with the same help. As a matter of fact, as the herdsmen use the reciprocal bond, they are also investing in it, which will ultimately enhance overall social trust, friendliness and mutual help.

Therefore, in a highly fickle environment, the expansive friendliness, mutual help and cooperation based on reciprocity among the herdsmen can promote the flexible adjustments of the key resources boundary and the users' boundary and generally guarantee that the herdsman can obtain key resources. However, the change in the grassland property rights has changed the social relationship, making the herdsmen independent of each other. As the expected reciprocity corresponding to the environment's uncertainty weakens, the possibility for the herdsman to gain key resources increases and his overall capacity to cope with risks decreases.

V. Revelations of Global Climate Change

For a system, disturbances and risks are not always bad, but the capability to cope with the change decides whether the system can be sustained. To tackle the shortage of environmental resources for survival and the variability, for thousands of years man, grass and livestock in the arid grasslands developed an effective system to cope with climate change. The production and living style, the social relations and the corresponding institutional arrangements are the best strategies to face uncertain natural changes. However, in recent decades, because of improper outside intervention, the system's innate capability to cope with extreme climate is being weakened and is even disappearing[①].

Here I am not objecting to outside intervention to a certain system, but such intervention should be consistent with the features of the system rather than going against it. Whether the domestic government or an international organization, mainstream development intervention is all based on such a premise that the future is predictable, but such an assumption is predicated on the already existing model in an agricultural area with a stable climate. The plan and development project is based on this premise. However, in an uncertain and changeable environment, this is doomed to be wrong. The arid and semi-arid husbandry area is typically highly unpredictable and changeable. From this season to the next season, no one knows what will happen. For uncertain events, taking countermeasures as the changes occur is the feature of the grazing strategy, including timely avoidance of disasters and grasping the opportunity to propagate the livestock. However, the past lessons show that the more uncertain a place is, the more attractive it is for the decision makers who wish to "bring welfare to the world" to implement their rules through general development ideals. A large amount of investment is devoted to predicting the unpredictable environment and constructing irrigation projects to decrease the influence of the variability in the precipitation. These projects for the husbandry area's development are made irrespective of the changeability and uncertainty of the environment and are inclined to achieve inapplicable and generalized solutions by simplifying complicated problems. Consequently, the ensuing " tragedy of the public land" is the only solution for grassland privatization, the so-called " intensification " which brings the development concept of replacing grazing husbandry with a fixed pasture model. Here what I oppose is not modern science and technology itself, but the way to use it. In a highly uncertain system, modern science and

---

① Research shows that the global climate change will make the arid husbandry area more arid, but more probably it will offer opportunities for the rejuvenation of the traditional animal husbandry. Because for a long time the living environment has decided that the herdsman is the "canary in the mine", who is most sensitive to future risks and can offer directions. And their production and living style has been proven by history over thousands of years that they are strategies most adaptable to uncertain natural changes. Therefore, climate change will provide a platform for the herdsmen to show their relatively advantageous living style and their territory will be expanded (Nori, et al. 2008).

technology should be targeted at how to improve the efficiency of traditional grazing husbandry, such as how to adapt it to the changeable environment and improve migration efficiency rather than trying to resist the natural uncertainty with highly scientific technologies.

Drawing from the experience and lessons in the husbandry area's methods to cope with a highly changeable climate, the decision maker and the academic may get some revelations about how to tackle global climate change:

Firstly, climate change is global, but the ultimate way to cope with it should be concretely implemented in the local area. The outside intervention of the international community and the government to the local system should be consistent with the local features rather than going against them. We should be cautious about improper outside intervention which may ultimately result in the collapse of the system. Secondly, we should fully realize the restrictions of modern science and technology. While applying them, we should respect and learn local knowledge and regional non-official institutional arrangements. This may be human society's ultimate outlet to cope with climate change. In the end, in an unpredictable environment, consistency may cost much less than resistance. If the IPCC made the right prediction, climate change will cause even greater environmental uncertainty. Instead of struggling in an uncertain environment for certainty, we had better accept the hard reality and reconsider and position our countermeasures.

For human society, climate change is an external variable, but it also can become the last straw, either crushing the camel or being the spark lighting up man's new era.

References:

[1] Li Wenjun & Zhang Qian. *Interpreting the Grassland's Predicament: on the Problems of Utilizing and Managing the Arid and Semi-Arid Grassland.* Economic Science Press, 2009.

李文军、张倩:《解读草原困境:对于干旱半干旱草原利用和管理若干问题的认识》,经济科学出版社 2009 年版。

[2] Local Chronicle Compiling Commission of the Sonid Left Banner. *Chronicle of the Sonid Left Banner.* Inner Mongolia Culture Press, 2004.

苏尼特左旗地方志编纂委员会:《苏尼特左旗志》,内蒙古文化出版社 2004 年版。

[3] Alessa, L. , A. Kliskey, P. Williams and M. Barton. Perception of Change in Freshwater in Remote Resource-dependent Arctic Communities. *Global Environmental*

Change. 2008. 18, 153-164.

[4] Berkes, F. and D. Jolly. Adapting to Climate Change: Social-ecological Resilience in a Canadian Western Arctic Community. *Conservation Ecology.* 2001. 5 (2), 18.

[5] Berkes, F., J. Mathias, M. Kislalioglu and H. Fast. The Canadian Arctic and the Oceans Act: The Development of Participatory Environmental Research and Management. *Ocean and Coastal Management.* 2001. 44, 451-469.

[6] Byg, A. and J. Salick. Local Perspectives on a Global Phenomenon-Climate Change in Eastern Tibetan Villages. *Global Environmental Change.* 2009. 19, 156-166.

[7] Danielsen, F., N. D. Burgess, A. Balmford. Monitoring Matters: Examining the Potential of Locally-Based Approaches. *Biodiversity and Conservation.* 2005. 14, 2507-2542.

[8] Ellis, J. E. and D. M. Swift. Stability of African Pastoral Ecosystems - Alternate Paradigms and Implications for Development. *Journal of Range Management.* 1988. 41 (6), 450-459.

[9] Fernandez-Gimenez, M. E. Reconsidering the Role of Absentee Herd Owners: A View from Mongolia. *Human Ecology* 1999. 27 (1), 1-27.

[10] Fernandez-Gimenez, M. E. Spatial and Social Boundaries and the Paradox of Pastoral Land Tenure: A Case Study from Post-Socialist Mongolia. *Human Ecology.* 2002. 30 (1): 49-78.

[11] Goodhue, R. E. and N. McCarthy. Fuzzy Access Modeling Grazing Rights in Sub-Saharan Africa. In: N. MaCarthy, B Swallow, M Kirl, and P. Hazell, editors. *Property Rights, Risk and Livestock Development in Africa, Nairobi, Kenya.* International Livestock Research Institute, 2000, 191-210.

[12] Heltberg, R., P. B. Siegel and S. L. Jorgensen. Addressing Human Vulnerabilityto Climate Change: Toward a "No-Regrets" Approach. *Global Environmental Change.* 2009. 19, 89-99.

[13] Illius, A. W. and T. G. O' Connor. On the Relevance of Nonequilibrium Concepts to Arid and Semiarid Grazing Systems. *Ecological Applications.* 1999. 9 (3), 798-812.

[14] IPCC. ClimateChange 2007. http://www. ipcc. ch/.

[15] Kloprogge, P. and J. Van der Sluijs. The Inclusion of Stakeholder Knowledge and Perspectives in Integrated Assessment of Climate Change. *Climatic Change.* 2006. 75, 359-389.

[16] Laidler, G. J. Inuit and Scientific Perspectives on the Relationship between Sea Ice and Climate Change: the Ideal Complement. *Climatic Change.* 2006. 78, 407-444.

[17] McCay, B. J. and S. Jentoft. Market or Community Failure Critical Perspective on Common Property Research. *Human Organization.* 1998. 57 (1), 21-29.

[18] Mwangi, E. and S. Dohrn. Securing Access to Drylands Resources for Multiple Users in Africa: A Review of Recent Research. *Land Use Policy*, 2008. 25, 240-248.

[19] Mori, M., M. Taylor and A. Sensi. Browsing on Fences: Pastoral Land

Rights, Livelihoods and Adaptation to Climate Change, IIED issue paper no. 148. Nottingham: RussellPress. 2008.

[20] Salick, J. and N. Ross. Traditional Peoples and Climate Change. *Global Environmental Change*. 2009. 19, 137-139.

[21] Scoones, I. Exploiting Heterogeneity: Habit at Use by Cattle in Dryland Zimbabwe. *Journal of Arid Environments*. 1995. 29, 221-237.

[22] Scoones, I. *Living with Uncertainty: New Directions in Pastoral Development in Africa*. London: Intermediate Technology Publications Ltd. 1994.

[23] Scoones, I. Whyare there so many Animals Cattle Population Dynamics in the Communal Areas of Zimbabwe. In: Behnke, R. H., Scoones, I., Kerven, C. (eds.), *Range Ecology at Disequilibrium: New Models of Natural Variability and Pastoral Adaptation in African Savannas*. Overseas Development Institute, London (248pp). 1993.

[24] Sen, A. *Poverty and Famines: An Essay on Entitlement and Deprivation*. Oxford University Press. 1981.

[25] Smit, B. and J. Wandel. Adaptation, Adaptive Capacity, and Vulnerability. *Global Environmental Change*. 2006. 16, 282-292.

[26] Toulmin, C. Combating Desertification: Setting the Agenda for a Global Convention. *Drylands Issues Paper*, IIED, London. 1995.

[27] United Nations Development Programme (UNDP). *Human Development Report* 2007/2008: Fighting Climate Change: Human Solidarity in a Divided World. New York. 2007.

[28] Van Aalast, M. K., T. Cannon and I. Burton. Community Level Adaptation to Climate Change: The Potential Role of Participatory Community Risk Assessment. *Global Environmental Change*. 2008. 18, 165-179.

[29] Verdery, K. Fuzzy Property: Rights, Power and Identity in Transylvania's Decollectivization. In Burawoy, M and Verdery, K. (eds.) *Uncertain Transition: Ethnographies of Change in the Postsocial World*. Rowman & Littlefield Publishers, Lanham and Oxford. 1999. 53-82.

[30] Westoby. M., Walker, B. H. and Noy-Meir, I. Opportunistic Management for Rangelands not at Equilibrium. *Journal of Range Management*, 1989. 42: 266-274.

[31] Wilbanks, T. J. and R. K. Kates. Global Changein Local Places: How Scale Matters. *Climatic Change*. 1999. 43, 601-628.

[32] Ybarra, M. Violent Visionsof an Ownership Society: The Land Administration Project in Peten, Guatemala. *Land Use Policy* 2008. 26: 44-54.

Coping with Challenges Posed by Climate Change: Safeguarding and Cherishing China's Rights to Development①

*Research Group of the Environment and Development Research Center, Chinese Academy of Social Sciences**

At present, in respect to the climate change problem, China is not only the "maker of the greatest problem" in the Western country's public opinion, with its carbon dioxide emissions increasing at a rate constantly beyond the international energy organizations' expectations and rising more rapidly as the world's largest emission country,② but also the "largest cooperator" competed for by the Western countries in their strategy for China's enormous market capacity which attracts the international capital; at the same time, as a developing country, China is among the major forces to counter and appeal to change the unfair

---

① This article was published with the title "China Is Confident to Cope with Challenges Posed by the Climate Change Problem" in the *China Economic Times* (8th edition) on January 6, 2010. While collected in this book, the title and content are slightly adjusted.

* Group members: Zheng Yisheng, Li Yuhong, Zhang Youguo and Zhang Xiao. During the research process, researcher Zheng Yuxin and Xu Songling of the Environment and Development Research Center, Chinese Academy of Social Sciences participated in the discussion of some problems. Researcher Zhou Dadi of the Energy Research Institute, National Development and Reform Commission and researcher Wang Yi of the Sustainable Development Strategy Research Group, Chinese Academy of Sciences offered valuable suggestions to the first draft. Here I would like to extend my gratitude to all of them.

② Netherlands Environmental Assessment Agency (PBL) believed that China's carbon dioxide emissions (burning of fossil fuels and cement production) ranked the world's 1st in 2006. According to our estimation, in 2006, China's carbon dioxide emissions actually didn't surpass that of America. It may surpass that of America after 2008.

deeds by developed countries on the climate problem.

Although China is at the stage of post-industrialization, it still lacks the resources and environmental conditions enjoyed by developed countries in their rise. It is indubitably an unprecedented enormous challenge for China to face the international pressure from greenhouse gas emissions without the completion of its modernization objective. This is a dual challenge: it has to develop, but it cannot develop through a long-term consumption of the resources and environmental capacity disproportionate to the population, as the Western developed countries did.

For this, we must not only safeguard our rights to development, but also cherish our rights to development. Neither of these two can be ignored. The former concerns the advocacy of an equal right to development in the international community; the latter relates to China's more fundamental strategy, namely, no matter how the global financial crises will influence China's economic and social development or how uncertain the future international cooperation on alleviating climate change is, China needs to further combine the tackling of climate change challenge with the transitioning into an independent and sustainable development model rather than limit our focus on energy strategies.

In this article, we will first make a basic judgment of the relationship between China's economic development and the climate change problem. Based on this, we have proposed a long-term strategy to cope with the climate change challenge.

I. Basic Judgment on the Relationship between the Climate Change Problem and Our Economic Development

1. Developed countries are very likely to capitalize on climate change and energy technology reform to restrict China's development, which further broadens the economic development gap between them and newly emerging developing countries. China's imitation of developed countries' development mode will constitute an enormous obstacle for our technical innovation.

In the most recent twelve years, in stark contrast with developed countries' vacillation on the implementation of greenhouse gas "emission reduction", there are the military-competition-like studies on their energy technologies. The scientific arguments over the cause and consequence of global warming will not necessarily hinder the emergence of a real energy technology reform. For example, in the face of the prospective exhaustion of the global petroleum and gas resources, the cross-national petroleum companies are stepping their evolution into comprehensive energy companies, actively developing renewable energies, developing new energy technologies and participating in greenhouse gas emission reduction. ① Some European countries have made considerable new technological achievements.

In America, a pattern "passively" formed in the financial crises but corresponding to the world's trend in the understanding of climate change has been initiated, a situation focusing on the promotion of economic growth in the new energy era and maintainence of their advantageous position. Once the "stage of a shortage in low-carbon energies or carbon emission space" approaches, America is very likely to rely on the combination of its special political clout, financial status and new energy technological advantages, having formed a new world hegemony and an international economic transaction mechanism of long-term benefits. Just as with other historical changes, under the new situation brought about by the climate change problem, some countries will lag behind the trend or even be exploited and controlled by other countries. Those countries with too little ability to make their choice and too little free methods in the international cooperation, especially those vacillating on their self-development strategies are most likely to lose development opportunities. In the resource "reshuffling" process resulting from coping with climate change, they will lose their original advantages or development momentum.

Take a look at our technological advances and industrial upgrading and we will find the factors which hinder the breakthrough of the locked development mode: for example, the central and local economic relationship problem epitomized in the finance and taxation system and the government's function positioning problem have encouraged the role of extensive growth; take another example, an economic pattern overly dependent on the export restrictions for upgrading the economic structure

① Qian Bozhang. Cross-national petroleum companies accelerating the promotion of new energy strategies. *Sinopec Monthly*, 2006 (12).

and the improvement of the innovation ability, etc. Since China has not reformed these factors in good faith and even enhanced them consciously or unconsciously, it is still bogged down in the Western world's high energy-consumption and high material-consumption development track after proposing their ecological civilization. This has greatly impaired our self-innovation ability and coordination ability, but in coping with the certain or uncertain challenges in the future, such abilities are what we can always rely on.

2. *Even if there is no climate change problem, no pressure from the commitment to emission reduction, it is hard for China to sustain itself with its current development mode.*

China's environmental problem is not restricted to climate change, but many other environmental problems haven't received as much international attention as climate change does, problems which are closely related to the livelihood of more than a billion of Chinese people.

Take water pollution as an example. In recent years, China's drinking water sources have been polluted by increasingly severe water pollution. The frequent occurrence of pollution events in the water sources seriously impacts the residents' drinking water safety. According to the *Water Quality Monthly of the 113 Concentrated Drinking Water Sources in Priority Cities for Environmental Protection* issued by China's National Environmental Monitoring Center in June, 2006, the water quality in 16 cities and 74 drinking water sources failed to live up to the standard, the former taking up 14% in the priority cities and the latter, 20. 1% in the drinking water sources of the priority cities; there was 527 million tons' of water failing to reach the standard, taking up 32. 3% of the total water amount in the priority cities. According to our group's research, with the increase of the urbanization rate, the domestic water demand for China's urban residents in 2030 is at least 2 to 3 times higher than present. ① If at the current water pollution scale and speed, it will be very difficult to ensure our drinking water safety for a rather long period of time.

Some scientists have already alerted that the environmental

① Refer to Li Yuhong's "China's Greenhouse Gas Emissions and Evaluation of Scenario Research" in this book for details.

pollution problems accumulated during over two hundred years' of industrialization in the Western world have caused serious environmental consequences, the consequences of which may erupt in China in a concentrated period of time and may become untreatable. ①

The overall environmental exacerbation escalates social contradictions and the energy and resource shortage poses unprecedented serious threats to sustainable economic development. Will China's future situation be the same as today's America, Germany or Japan? In 2005, China's energy consumption per capita was 1.5 tons' standard coal equivalent. If one day the number reaches America's 9.8 tons' standard coal equivalent, then China needs to consume 13 billion tons' standard coal equivalent, a number equivalent to the world's total energy consumption in 2005 and 57 times higher than China's new energy (hydropower, nuclear power and wind power) scale in 2008. Even if it reaches the level of today's Japan and Germany, China will need to consume more than 6 billion tons' standard coal equivalent. ② In the future, China can never be today's America or any other developed country and must proceed from its own national conditions to explore new development ideals and strategies.

3. "Surgery-type carbon dioxide emission reduction scenario" under the traditional development mode may lead to even more bad results.

In China, some people regard the climate change problem as a pure "external disturbances", believing that as long as China is not bound by the international commitment to emission reduction at an early stage, we can successfully sustain the current development momentum and realize modernization. And when it reaches the turning point of the environmental Kuznetsk curve, all the problems will be resolved automatically. However, contrary to such a view, is that it is not necessary for us to worry about making earlier commitments to emission reduction because this can force us to directly adopt the latest technologies and make use of later low-cost advantages and realize leapfrog emission reductions.

---

① www.ccwe.org.cn/ccwe/upfile/file/xiegaodi.pdf.

② Based on relevant data from *China Statistical Yearbook* (2009) and *International Statistical Yearbook* (2008).

Our studies show that these two views have their own theoretical support, but are not oriented to our special development mode. Although contrary to each other, they may collide and integrate into a situation with "two sides": on the one hand, the economy develops according to the current mode; on the other hand, generally adopting foreign energy technology equipment. The "low-carbon" scenario similar to "partial surgery" is likely to yield fewer results with many efforts, making China overly dependent on and locked into foreign technologies. In accentuating "low-carbon", it has overlooked the problem of social balance and the environmental problems other than greenhouse gas.

To sum up, an important problem facing our climate strategies comes not from whether China needs energy conservation and emission reduction in the future, but from whether to choose "environmental improvement under a new development mode" or "energy conservation and emission reduction under the current development mode." If we choose the former, no matter how uncertain climate change is, China can pursue a sustainable and coordinated development on its own initiative, which is an insightful "regretless choice", if we choose the latter, China will be plunged into a passive situation under such circumstances.

To cope with climate change, China has already put forward systematic policies with energy strategies at the core. To smoothly implement these concepts, it is particularly necessary to further combine the tackling of the climate change problems with the overall long-term objectives of transforming China's development model.

Those who don't look into the future cannot well prepare themselves for the current moment. To actually transform the development model, we cannot expect to solve the problems specific to such a large developing country as China by simply imitating and following developed countries, which is, in fact, "using the mindset which causes the problem to solve problems." While learning experiences from developed countries, we should consider it our long-term development strategy to seek opportunities to get rid of traditional development methods which have long locked our development. These are dual wisdoms required to cope with the climate change problem. This doesn't mean we should repudiate industrialization and its material input, but rather call for a brave spirit to make innovations based on national conditions and the fact-seeking attitude to identify the pros and cons. Without these, it is hard for China to avoid the trap of extensive growth to focus on the real demand of the Chinese people and the improvement of the national strengths. It is also hard for China to have development freedom in a future world filled with uncertainties and make its deserved contributions to the ecological civilization as a great rising country.

II. Long-term Strategy to Cope with the Climate Change Challenge

1. China should show to the international community its ideals and methods in coping with the climate change problem and conceptually make its corresponding historical contributions.

China, as a great developing country, can and also should make contributions to the world's harmony and progress:

First, it is China's ultimate aim to have all the Chinese people, 20% of the total world population live a comparatively well-off life. The emergence of a "two-type" harmonious society in itself is China's most meaningful contribution to the world's sustainable development.

Second, China stands firmly in line with the third world countries and also those who have concerns for the world's destiny, to resist and criticize the selfish and unfair actions of some developed countries in the climate change problems and promote a more fairer international order. America, with a population of 5% of the world's total, is consuming 22% of the world's energy,[①] but its performance in world affairs, especially the climate change problem, is rather disappointing. Historical experiences show that it is not possible to change the long-term trend of the global environmental problem "turning better partially but degenerating overall", construct a generally clean world and solve the global climate change problem peacefully in a stable and sustainable way without the global in-depth fairness of resource utilization and development freedom. If those countries which take long-term possession and consumption of the resources disproportionately to their population continue to overlook this problem, they will lose their morality stand. We should keep enhancing international cooperation, with which to

① The population data was of 2007 and the energy consumption data of 2005, which were based on relevant data from *International Statistical Yearbook* (2008).

promote a positive interaction between fairness and the environmental problem.

Third, we should advocate and realize sustainable consumption and production methods and firmly oppose luxurious consumption. First, there is a considerable proportion of the population in China with a comparatively low living standard. The energy consumption will increase in the future and we have to reserve for them the carbon emission space; second, we should take explicate measures to restrict the users' luxurious energy consumption, including China's own new luxurious groups; third, guide consumerism reasonably, establish lifestyles countering the imitation of America's lifestyle worldwide and advocate sustainable consumption. As a large oriental country with a five-thousand-year history, China should present to the world its ecological civilization principle "let others also live a happy life."[①]

2. *Well prepared for the transition period and making active adjustments; making efforts to transition into a voluntary and sustainable development mode*

In the Copenhagen Summit, China showed the world its determination to reduce greenhouse gas emissions. However, China's energy supply structure, highlighted by coal, and its national condition at its current industrialization stage, help to decide that we should make an utmost effort to realize our emission reduction objective. The future decade will witness China's transition to a period with a higher emission reduction target. We should lose no time to make policy adjustments and develop systems in relevant areas and enhance the actual ability for the whole society to adapt to these risks. We should not only focus on the completion of indexes and lose opportunities for innovation and transition. In development, China has a large room for various choices, from equipment updates, technological improvements, urban and rural development plans for lifestyle and institutional arrangement. We should be careful not to ignore and sacrifice these choices for the pursuit of short-term benefits. Or else, we will inevitably continue to be locked in the existent international division of labor system. Cherishing our rights

---

① [American] Ervin Laszlo. *Radical Changes*. trans. Du Mo. China CITIC Press, 2002.

to development will not only create conditions for the autonomous transition into low-carbonization and avoid being plunged into the "passive" mitigation scenario mentioned above after 2020, but also lay a foundation for China's transition onto an autonomous and sustainable development road. Following are some insightful adjustments:

(1) Adjust our export-oriented economy to a more reasonable level in the structure adjustment

At present, China's overdependence on exports and foreign investments for economic growth and employment is rather passive for a large country and should be reformed in the long run. The transition to a "domestic demand satisfying" economy needs to be completed step by step, but with a firm stand, making it more consistent with the requirements of China's overall sustainable development rather than only relying upon the short-term benefits of a specific department and invested group. This requires an adjustment and sorting out of a series of domestic relationships, including the industrial structure, finance and taxation policy, import-export policy and a package of financial reforms, etc.

(2) Improve the technological progress pattern

Through 30 years' of economic development, China should be capable to be self-reliant in its development of key technologies. Therefore, on the one hand, we should emphasize international technology transfer and on the other hand, we should develop and give recognition to our self-innovation ability. In technological choices, we should not only develop and master the "high, sophisticated and cutting-edge" technologies, but also select some environment-friendly technologies attracting the labor force employment in the production field of common consumer goods. China's basic national condition predetermines that the objective of technological advances cannot be too unified and should appeal to the participation of the large, medium and small-sized enterprises to contribute to diversified, multi-tier and multi-form technological progresses. We should guard against three unfavorable conditions: first, the predisposition toward "worshipping foreign investment and foreign things," which is unfavorable to the healthy competition and development of domestic enterprises; second, the greed for a "large" pattern of "one-leg development" in technologies. We should prevent ourselves from generalizing our focus on the large while discarding the small; third, the preference of the "top-down" singularity and concentrated decision-making and the restrictions on local technical innovation, technological diversity and discarding of traditional wisdom.

(3) Establish economic, cultural and social mechanisms to guide sustainable consumption methods

Sustainable consumption refers to "providing services and relevant products to meet man's basic needs, improving life quality while consuming the minimal natural resources and poisonous materials, minimizing the waste and pollutants produced from the life circle of services and products so that the needs of our posterity will not be jeopardized."[①] China's consumption model should be consistent with China's national condition of few resources and a large population and rather than more with the national condition of a large "waiting to be rich" group. China's further energy conservation and emission reduction should penetrate into the guidance of consumption. This includes: levying high taxes on high energy consumption, for example, on luxuries such as living in large houses and using cars with large emissions; raising rigid low-energy-consumption requirements on urban planning, such as depending more on public transportation. The Chinese people should promote their traditional virtue of diligence and thriftiness, enhance socialist cultural and ethical development, advocate those who are rich first to live an abundant but not luxurious life and lead others on their road of prosperity rather than following suit with the Western consumerism and high-consumption model in their value and lifestyle. Under current circumstances, we need to transform the generalized "expand domestic demand" into one guided by categorization. To establish the economic, cultural and social mechanisms guided by the sustainable consumption method, we need to proceed from the public's long-term interests, not disturbed by the few interest groups. We should place the few people's partial and short-term benefits under the principle of long-term targets and principles through general social consensus.

The above three adjustments are both the key and the difficulty. It will shake the accustomed thinking pattern and the invested interest of some groups and even increase the obstacles and pressures facing us. It is by no means possible for a few experts and management departments

---

① United Nations Environment Program (UNEP): *Policy Factors of Sustainable Consumption*, 1994.

to handle this. The historical and national mission to promote a new development mode will inevitably involve more than one generation. The active participation of the whole society and the transparent and open decision-making process have invaluable influences on improving the decision-making, innovation level and the whole nation's awareness of a sustainable development.

III. Promote China's Long-Term Strategy Consensus with the Climate Change Problem

All was settled in the Copenhagen Conference. People are more aware of the following facts: first, the human society has made many efforts towards the possible disasters caused by the climate change problem, but until now, it hasn't worked hand in hand as an interested community. We still need to make continued efforts to promote global cooperation; second, it is not that the energies in the world fail to support the human's existence, but that they cannot sustain the current lifestyle mankind is pursuing. Compared with developing countries, developed countries almost have everything under their privilege, but their grudge for developing countries' "free ride" in the climate cooperation has exceeded their fear of human's common disasters. Their desire for benefits surpasses their determination to shoulder responsibilities. They are unwilling to implement the "shared but differentiated principle" in the emission reduction action they are completely capable of handling. It is not they can't, but rather they won't; third, the environmental influence caused by China's rapidly expanding economic scale has become a global topic. China's energy consumption per capita is only 15% [①] of that of America, but some Western opinions have ignored the fact that China is a developing country and imposed tremendous international pressure on China. Those who spread such opinions obviously lack the courage to face fairness rather than analytical abilities. The Western countries' dual attitude towards China that on the one hand, they exaggerate and accuse the influence of China's total environmental capacity and on the other hand, they compliment and compete for China's open and enormous market

① Data of 2005, based on relevant data from *International Statistical Yearbook (2008)*.

volume, which shows what they are really concerned with is their own interests and what they have ignored is the Chinese people's wellbeing. The pressure from such selfishness, arrogance and prejudice can only serve to make us more determined to seek a self-reliant and sustainable development road. We hope the Copenhagen Conference can offer an opportunity for us to secure further strategic consensus and to understand in depth and implement the scientific development outlook.

The Copenhagen Summit caused unprecedented national attention, which instills into us an intense feeling about how closely intertwined China is with the world. In confrontation of the complicated external challenges, only through insight and self-improvement can the Chinese people realize their aspiration to live a happy and esteemed life and make their special historical contributions to the co-existence and common prosperity of the whole world.

Part III

Globalization and China's Environment and Development

Thoughts on China's Energy Conservation and Emission Reductions

By ZHENG Yuxin

In recent years, the most eye-catching measure adopted by China in coping with the resource and environment challenges is the binding energy conservation and emission reduction objective in the "11th Five-Year" Plan. The Plan stipulated that by the end of 2010, China should realize the objective of decreasing its energy consumption per unit of GDP by 20% and its major pollutant emissions by 10%. Owing to the central government's rigorous regulations and implementations, the energy conservation and emission reduction work has obtained remarkable achievements. In implementing their energy conservation and emission reduction objectives, governments of different levels have made brilliant progresses in the construction of the surveillance systems and the material methods for surveillance and the objectives of energy conservation and emission reduction that they are expected to achieve.

Undoubtedly, the "energy conservation and emission reduction" objectives set in the "11th Five-Year" Plan and its active implementation is a step forward for China to change their traditional unbinding growth. While fully affirming the achievements, we should also note that the realization of these objectives hinges, to a certain degree, on the global economic crises, the realization of the indexes other than the binding indexes is not optimistic and there exist uneven regional developments. To effectively alleviate the resources and environmental pressures facing China, China's "energy conservation and emission reduction" long-acting mechanisms and overall long-term strategies have to be strengthened. Considering the background in which the world is facing a great energy structure transformation and the practice to implement a scientific development outlook, it is necessary to adjust our "energy conservation and emission reduction" objectives and more solid measures of energy conservation and emission reduction should be taken in broader areas in constructing a resource-saving and environment-friendly society and more active explorations should be made in more in-depth development models and institutional construction.

I. About China's Energy Conservation and Emission Reduction Objectives

1. Replacing the Energy Intensity Index with a Carbon Emission Intensity Index

(1) Smart move

In September, 2009, the Chinese government made a remarkable commitment in carbon emission reduction and used the carbon emission intensity——carbon dioxide emission index based on per unit of GDP rather than the absolute index of carbon emission used by developed countries. India also followed China and used the carbon emission intensity index. China promised to decrease its carbon emission intensity by 40% to 45% by 2020 compared with 2005 while India promised a decrease of 20% to 25%.

For developing countries at the high-carbon development stage, to develop a low-carbon economy is undoubtedly an enormous challenge. However, the Chinese government has taken active measures after analyzing the current situation. It has implemented emission reduction steps on its own initiative, which is not only a wise move but also of profound significance.

Internationally, China's voluntary promise not only shows its attitude towards the responsibility of global warming but also encourages developed countries to make more commitments to carbon emission reduction.

In today's world, developed countries occupy a dominating position in the global political and economic pattern, but China's status has changed significantly. China's voluntary commitment will help China to play a more active role in making international economic and political new rules. China's active intervention is undoubtedly beneficial for the maintenance of the benefits of developing countries.

It can be predicted that carbon emissions will become a new rule for international economic and politics and become a hot topic[①] for their international political diplomacy in the future. From the perspective of foreign trade, if China's efforts in energy conservation and emission reduction can be recognized by the international community, it will foster a favorable environment for their exportation. For China, this means it can obtain economic benefits while discharging its international obligations.

In China's commitment, the carbon emission intensity index is used. It is a relative index, with its binding force embodied in the requirement that the increasing rate of carbon emissions should be lower than that of the economic growth. It allows the continued growth of absolute emissions and leaves room for China's economic development.

The mitigation of the carbon emission intensity is, fundamentally, a problem about accelerating the industrial structure upgrading and technological advances and is, to a large extent, consistent with development. Economic growth, on the one hand, facilitates energy consumption and the increase of carbon emissions while on the other hand, also promotes the structure upgrading and technological advances and further mitigates the carbon emission intensity. The rapid economic growth is helpful to accelerate the structure upgrading and technological advances. It will enhance the effects of the latter and is favorable for the carbon emission intensity to decrease at a comparatively fast speed. Obviously, the mitigation of the carbon emission intensity is, to a large degree, a matter of development.

Although the fulfillment of China's commitment is hard, it can be realized through ongoing efforts. According to the "11th Five-Year" Plan, China can decrease its energy consumption per unit of GDP by 20% by 2010 compared with 2005. If the energy structure remains unchanged, to reach the objective to decrease the carbon emissions by 40%-45% by 2020 compared with 2005, it means during the decade from 2011 to 2020, the energy intensity should decrease by another

---

① Some signs have proved this. The US Environmental Protection Agency (EPA) officially listed the carbon dioxide and other five greenhouse gases as noxious gases in December, 2009 and enlarged the application scope of America's "Clean Air Act." It has been publicly discussed in America as to how to impose energy conservation and emission reduction pressure on countries and manufacturers providing goods to America by levying a "carbon tariff" and the congress has scores of proposals in this regard. Zhu Liwen, Secretary of the United States Department of Energy, also made it explicitly clear to levy carbon emission taxes on developing countries including China and India.

20% - 25% compared with 2005. If considering the contribution of the increased percentage of the renewable resources in energy (from 10% in 2010 to 15% in 2020①) and other contributions (for example, the lowering of agricultural carbon emissions and the increase of the forestry area), the fossil energy intensity can be further lowered. If so, the space for development can be enlarged.

Invariably accompanying the changes of the industrial structure is the economic growth, with the former as an important source of the latter. Since China's economy is still expected to maintain a rapid growth rate during 2011 to 2020, this means ensuring great improvements of China's technological level and industrial structure. With various measures, we have good reasons to believe that during this decade, the decrease of the energy intensity brought about by this will not be lower than 20% to 25%. At the same time, even until 2020, when China realizes its 40% - 45% objective in decreasing the carbon emission intensity, there is still a huge gap between China's energy intensity or carbon emission intensity and that of developed countries. In Table 1, it can be seen that China's carbon emission intensity in 2006 was 11 times higher than that of Japan and even it realizes its emission reduction target by 2020, its carbon emission intensity is also at least 5 times higher than that of Japan. This means that China still boasts tremendous potential in decreasing carbon emission intensity. In contrast, developed countries, with a slower speed in the changes of their industrial structure and technological advances than developing countries, see their potential for decreasing carbon emission intensity lagging far behind that of developing countries.

Table 1 Major Carbon Emission Indexes in China, Japan and America (2006)

	China	America	Japan
Carbon dioxide/first - time energy supply (t CO_2/toe)	2.98	2.45	2.30
Carbon dioxide emission per capita (t CO_2/capita)	4.27	19.00	9.49
Carbon dioxide emission per unit of GDP (kg CO_2/2000 US $)	2.68	0.51	0.24
Carbon dioxide emission per unit of GDP (PPP) (kg CO_2/2000 US $ PPP)	0.65	0.51	0.34

Note: PPP-Purchasing Power Parity, toe-ton oil equivalent

Data source: International Energy Agency website http://www.iea.org/stats/index.asp.

① According to our renewable energy development target.

(2) Significant strategic decisions

In making a long-term target to decrease carbon emissions, China should not only develop policies, but more importantly, think in terms of strategies. Currently, the world is on the verge of a science and technology revolution and the "petroleum peak" and the global warming are calling for an industrial revolution toward green and sustainable energy. China's active development of a low-carbon economy and participation in international cooperation, in the final analysis, are to grasp the opportunities brought about by the international economic transition and to solve its own long-term development problems. The key problem in China's energy policies is an over percentage of coal in the energy structure (about 70%) and its dependence on imported petroleum (over 50% and showing signs of increasing). The former is an important reason for China's severe pollution and the latter concerns China's energy security problems. A rigid carbon emission restriction is an important condition for the development of a low-carbon economy, which will effectively promote the decrease of fossil energy consumption, the application of green technologies and the development and utilization of renewable energies and other alternative energies. This will help to allay China's dependence on imported petroleum and push China toward its strategic goal of implementing a green energy supply.

Many people are scrupulous of developing a low-carbon economy in China. A popular view is to assume that the attribution of global warming to human action in itself is a scheme fabricated by developed countries, with which to curb developing countries' growth. With limited global resources, they maintain their high consumption by limiting developing countries' energy consumption; or even if it's not a scheme, it illustrates developed countries' attempts to make use of its advantages in new energy technologies and the rule restricting carbon emissions to gradually crush developing countries in order to maintain their global dominance.

Scientifically speaking, until now there are still different voices expressing their reasons for global warming. It has been the focus of discussions about how much human action has influenced the climate change. With insufficient evidence to deny our influence, it will never be wrong for us to prepare for the worst. The uncertainty between human action and global warming is one of the reasons why America refused to sign the *Kyoto Protocol* and until now it still claims that it won't sign any agreements like the *Kyoto Protocol.* And compared with other developed countries, America shows a rather negative attitude, but it has changed greatly its attitude in discharging the obligation of emission reduction and developing low-carbon technologies. The change in America's attitude, to a certain degree, proves greater consensus on the authenticity and scientificness of human action to global warming.

It is undeniable that developed countries have their own strategic intentions which is unfavorable to the growth of developing countries. However, whether this can be realized does not depend on their subjective will. We would probably not forget how arrogant America was to require China to open its market by raising high the banner of free trade, although China enjoyed the rights to protect its national industries. However, more than ten years later, the situation has reversed. It is China that is promoting free trade and requires America to open its markets while America adheres to its protectionism. So, how the problem evolves depends on who can better grasp the opportunity and improve its own competitiveness more effectively.

Currently, although the new energy is green, basically it charges a higher cost and provides little employment, thus lacking competitive advantages against traditional fossil energy in the market. Therefore, it is hard to substitute the traditional fossil energy with it. To solve such a problem, we must first settle the problem of value judgment. For example, besides a cheap price of coal and its abundance in China, the lavish coal consumption, to a large degree, results from an underestimation of the negative effect produced by coal consumption, owing to the dysfunctioning of the market and a similar underestimation of the environmental effect of clean energies. If no one is willing to pay for the environmental cost or the environmental effect or keeps underestimating the environmental influence, then green energies are hard to develop.

If we are clear in our value orientation and attach enough importance to the alleviation of our reliance on imported petroleum and the decrease of the percentage of coal being used, then we will make our utmost efforts to promote the development and utilization of clean alternative energies by making effective policies and institutional arrangements. As long as we take proper measures, according to China's national conditions, remain unwavering in our adherence to the self-reliance spirit and committed to improving our self-innovation ability,

China is very likely to maximize the decrease of its reliance on foreign technologies and important foreign strategic resources, thus successfully avoiding various risks and maintaining long-term, stable and sustainable development.

China enjoys enormous potential, which will be unleashed through pressure. Certainly, this doesn't mean China has to subjugate itself to the pressure from other countries. Instead, it means China should never waver in its stand to guarantee the national interests, its rights to development and its sovereignty and territorial integrity. In confrontation of power, it makes no difference to stir or appease it and backing down usually leads to more sufferings. With China's increased strength, China should be tougher in its foreign policy. China's putting itself under more pressure shows its confidence and courage, which is also an effective measure to overcome sloth, surmount obstacles, unleash potential and accelerate development.

In its transitioning into a new energy system, China's late-mover advantage also cannot be ignored. For so many years, the slow spread of clean energy technology is closely related to developed countries' "technology lock-in." From production to living, developed countries have bogged down in the current existing technological and economic system of petroleum energy, which includes a series of package management systems from the company to the governmental organization. China, as a developing country, is far from westernized in its consumption methods and its urbanization is yet to be completed. China still has 800 million farmers in the rural areas. Although China's total energy consumption is increasing rapidly, its increase of energy consumption per capita still lags far behind that of developed countries. Compared with the consumption level of developed countries, China's current energy consumption is in the ascendant stage. Overall, China's current consumption method is less energy-consuming and much greener than that of developed countries. ① China not only enjoys larger room in choosing its technology and consumption methods, but also in its policy and institutional arrangements.

---

① In 2008, America's National Geographic Society and the international research company ClobeScan observed the consumers' consumption behavior from 14 countries in "Greendex™ 2008: Consumption Choice and Environment——Global Tracking Investigation". The result showed that Brazil and India were the greenest, followed by China and America was the least.

After China's official commitment of decreasing its carbon emission intensity to the international community, carbon emissions will undoubtedly become another binding index for China's energy conservation and emission reductions. The proposal of lowering carbon emission intensity as an important strategic decision means China's development of its low-carbon economy comes to an official start. It can be predicted that China will try hard to promote the "low-carbon" economy in its "12th Five-Year" Plan, making low-carbon economy as the "tong" to facilitate the coordinated development between China's ecological resource environment and economy and pushing China toward a green and sustainable development.

It should be noted that the energy conservation and emission reduction objective set in the "11th Five-Year" Plan failed to make subdivisions of energies. In this way, the decrease of energy consumption means the decrease of all types of energies. As a matter of fact, the orientation of our energy policy is not targeted at a generalized decrease of the total energy consumption or a leveling decrease of various energies, but increasing the supply of renewable energies and other clean energies while decreasing fossil energy consumption; or in other words, not a simple increase of energy efficiency, but also an optimization of the overall energy structure. Obviously, it is hard to reflect the orientation of our energy policy by decreasing 20% of the energy consumption per 10,000-yuan GDP. Nevertheless, compared with the decrease of energy intensity, the decrease of carbon emission intensity can show China's energy policy orientation more comprehensively and accurately.

Considering all possibilities, the substitution of energy intensity with carbon emission intensity is of great significance.

2. *Understanding Energy Intensity and Carbon Emission Intensity*

There is a large gap between the energy intensity or carbon emission intensity in developing countries and that in developed countries. For example, China's energy intensity in 2006 was 4.3 times higher than that of America, and 9 times higher than that of Japan; its carbon emission intensity, 5.25 times higher than that of America and 11.17 times higher than that of Japan. Understanding this phenomenon and the variability of energy intensity and carbon emission intensity contributes to a better comprehension of energy conservation and emission reduction.

(1) Energy intensity and carbon emission intensity is a major reflection of the development stage

The large gap between the energy consumption per unit of GDP in developed countries and developing countries primarily results from the differences in the industrial structure and the different energy intensity in different industries. In particular, there is a huge gap between the energy intensity in the second industries and the tertiary industries, with the former 3 times higher than the latter. Of course, the gap between the technological levels also exerts relatively little influence. It is no doubt that when China's industrial structure is upgraded to the developed country's level, China's energy consumption per unit of GDP will also decrease significantly. However, it is unrealistic to demand that China's industrial structure be on a par with that of developed countries in a short span of time. There are many factors influencing an economy's industrial structure, such as resource abundance, developmental stage and the development strategy implemented. However, among these influencing factors, the economic and social developmental level or stage is decisive. As China is at the stage of accelerating industrialization and urbanization, it is inevitable that it will develop an industrial structure highlighted by high energy-consuming and high-polluting industries. Such a developmental stage is insurmountable and will still be sustained for a long time to come. Although the industrial policies and development strategies also have certain influences on the industrial structure, the basic factor deciding an economy's industrial structure is still the structure of market demand while the latter in turn is subject to the economic developmental level and the income level within the economy. This is the fundamental reason why it is hard for the industrial structure upgrading to surpass the economic development stage.

We have to be aware that energy intensity or carbon emission intensity is not part of the energy efficiency index. In China, some people habitually regard the energy consumption per unit of GDP as the measurement of energy economy efficiency and based on the fact that there is a large gap between developed countries and China in the energy consumption per unit of GDP, they come to the conclusion that there is the same large gap between their energy efficiency. Obviously, this has exaggerated the energy efficiency gap. It is even more irrational for some people to overestimate China's potential for emission reduction. As a matter of fact, if we compare the same industries, we can find that the gap between the energy efficiency in developing countries and developed countries is not that large in their energy consumption per unit of GDP. For example, the standard coal consumption of per ton's steel in China was 741 (2005), in Japan, 646 (2003), with the former 15% higher than the latter. China's energy consumption per unit of GDP (converted with the official exchange rate) was 9 times higher than that of Japan (2006), and 3 times higher than the global average. Therefore, if based on this, it is an obvious exaggeration for us to assume that China's energy efficiency is only 1/9 of that of Japan. Therefore, in comparing energy efficiency, it is more reasonable to use the index in kind. This can avoid the incomparability brought about by the conversion of the exchange rate and the differentiation in the industrial structure.

(2) In the same developmental stage, the later emergent countries have more technological advantages than the earlier developed countries

In the finding[①] of research conducted on the energy consumption per unit of GDP in Britain, America, Germany, French and Japan, we can find that the changes in the developed countries' energy consumption per unit of GDP result in the following rules: first, chronologically, the peak of all the countries' energy consumption per unit of GDP is basically consistent with their acceleration of industrialization: the peak in Britain occurred the earliest, around 1880; that in America and the Federal Republic of Germany was relatively later, around 1920; that in France even later and in Japan the latest. Second, experience from developed countries shows that technological advances have obvious influences on the decrease of energy consumption. The later a country completes its industrialization, the lower its peak in the energy consumption per unit of GDP will be, from Britain's 1.0 toe/thousand US $, America's 0.9 toe/thousand US $ to Japan's about 0.3 toe/thousand US $. Such a phenomenon shows that different countries have similar developmental stages and the same process of industrial structure upgrading during

① Bai Quan. The evolution of foreign countries' energy consumption per unit of GDP and its revelations. *Energy of China*, 2006(12).

their development. In such a process, when they are at the same developmental stage, the later comers have more technological advantages compared with the earlier developed countries. This means technological advances can transcend the developmental stage.

Although it is hard for China's industrial structure to surpass the different stages experienced by developed countries in its industrialization, China's current technological level is much higher than that of the industrialized country at the same developmental stage. Take the energy conservation and environmental protection technology as an example. At the time when developed countries' technology was at the forefront in the world, the development of their technologies were situated against the backdrop of global energy and environmental capacity, with far less energy and environmental pressure and less ensuing pressure for energy conservation and emission reduction. Therefore, they were much less motivated to develop energy conservation and environmental protection technologies. With increasing global energy and environmental pressure, developed countries have made great progress in developing energy conservation and environmental protection technologies. China has imported many advanced energy-conserving and clean technologies from developed countries and applied them in its economic environment. It can be predicted that the peak of both China's energy intensity and pollution intensity can and should be lower than what developed countries experienced back then.

Judging from a practical situation, since China still has a very large economic growth space, it has enormous potential to realize energy conservation and emission reductions through industrial structure upgrading. Although such potential is restricted by the developmental stage and will gradually unleash itself with economic growth, there will be considerable changes accompanying China's highly rapid economic growth, whose influence on the industrial structure evolution, upgrading and energy conservation and emission reduction should not be ignored. Whether in the short term or in the long run, technological advances are effective means and fundamental methods for China to realize energy conservation and emission reductions. However, since technological advances are not manipulated by the developmental stage, China, although at a comparatively low developmental stage, can still use comparatively high technological crafts and products as well as high energy conservation and environmental protection technologies. This enables China to have a smaller gap in its technologies compared with developed countries than in the industrial structure. This may be the reason[①] why China's potential to realize energy conservation and emission reductions through technological improvements is smaller than that through industrial structure upgrading.

(3) Differentiate carbon emissions and carbon consumption

We should realize that the large gap between the carbon emission intensity or energy intensity in China and other developed countries comes from other factors besides the gap in the industrial structure and technological level. It is a well documented fact that China is renowned as "the global factory." Multinationals from all over the world transfer their manufacturing industries to China because of China's good investment environment, abundant cheap labor force with good qualities, cheap land, improved infrastructure and an enormous consumption market. The formation of the "global factory" is, to a large degree, a result of the multinationals' optimized resource distribution system worldwide. The products from China's enterprises, multinational operations or joint ventures not only supply the Chinese market, but also serve the demand of the world. Up until now, China has already produced a quarter of the industrial products of the world and its dependence on foreign trade has reached over 60%. It is worth mentioning that it is the foreign countries' transfer of their high energy-consuming industries into China that has formed the trend of the international market's soaring demand on China's steel and iron and other high energy-consuming products. The export of China's major energy-consuming products are burgeoning. In 2007, the exports of the cement, plate glass, steel, copper and aluminum products, paper and paperboard were respectively 5.46, 5.53, 10.09, 3.46, 14.25 and

---

① A recent study from the Institute of Quantitative & Technical Economics, Chinese Academy of Social Sciences shows that among the major sources which have contributed to the 20% target of energy consumption per 10,000-yuan GDP set in the "11th Five-Year" Plan, the decrease of the energy consumption from the industrial structure adjustment was about 9%-10%, from technological advances, about 6% and from the internal industrial structure adjustment, about 4%. These findings show that the contribution from the structural adjustment is about 60%-70%, which is obviously larger than the influence of technological advances. Shen Lisheng. Work essay: Research on Energy Conservation and Emission Reduction from the Perspective of Input-Output. August, 2008.

6. 49 times higher than that in 2000. China continues to be the world's largest choke producer, consumer and exporter, with the share of the choke trade volume from Shanxi in the global choke market being as high as 50%. [1] As a result, in order to serve the global needs, China retains more energy consumption and carbon emissions domestically. As a matter of fact, China only symbolizes a production area concept here, which means it is not the Chinese consumer who has consumed so much energy and discharged so much carbon.

At present, it is obviously unreasonable for the international discussion on the emission reduction obligation to focus on what the energy consumption and carbon emission is in the production area during its production, which excludes the consideration on who is the end consumer of these energies and emissions. For now, carbon emissions are a highly moralized problem, therefore, those countries with more exports of energy-intensive products and more carbon emissions should shoulder greater responsibility for global warming. In fact, the export-oriented economy has similar problems, especially those economies with exports of energy-intensive products. They are actually exporting energies while decreasing emissions for others. Now it is those who are consuming and enjoying the products from energy consumption who are accusing and punishing (levying carbon taxes) those energy users for their consumption of energy and discharge of carbon in their production. This is absolutely ridiculous.

Carbon emission intensity is the ratio between carbon emissions and GDP. For the numerator, energy consumption or carbon emission faces problems in their calculation as mentioned above. As the denominator, GDP also faces the same problem. If we adopt the GDP calculated from purchase power parity (PPP) for comparison, the gap between China and developed countries in energy intensity or carbon emission intensity will be greatly distorted. In Table 2, we can find that if calculated in this way, China's energy intensity is 0. 22 while that of America is 0. 21, a rather slight difference. Therefore, more studies are needed on how to evaluate who has the responsibility for carbon emission reduction.

---

① See Yang Minying. Report on China's energy strategy development. *Development Collections by Institute of Quantitative & Technical Economics, Chinese Academy of Social Sciences (2008)*. Social Sciences Academic Press, 2008.

Table 2 Major Energy Indexes in China, Japan and America (2006)

	China	America	Japan
First-time per capita energy supply (toe/capita)	1.43	7.43	4.13
First-time energy supply per unit of GDP (toe/thousand 2000 US $)	0.90	0.21	0.10
First-time energy supply per unit of GDP (PPP) (toe/thousand 2000 US $ PPP)	0.22	0.21	0.15

Note: PPP-Purchase Power Parity, toe-ton oil equivalent

Data source: International Energy Agency website http://www.iea.org/stats/index.asp.

3. Improving the Effectiveness of the Emission Reduction Targets

Although the energy conservation and emission reduction work during the "11th Five-Year" Plan has scored remarkable achievements, it should be noted that there is still room for improvement from goal setting to implementation.

(4) The setting of binding indexes is unfavorable to the completion of other indexes

At present, any mention of "energy conservation and emission reduction" in China seems to be directed at the efforts to fulfill the energy conservation and emission reduction goal proposed in the "11th Five-Year" Plan. Since the energy conservation and emission reduction index is divided and delegated to different provinces and municipalities, the National Development and Reform Commission and the Ministry of Environmental Protection have established the checking system for energy conservation and emission reduction to impose greater administrative pressure on the local governments. Therefore at present, the governments at different levels have narrowed their focus on completing these indexes.

Obviously, it is not our intention to see them overlook other indexes closely related to the ecological environment and human health for their excessive concentration on completing these two binding indexes for energy conservation and emission reduction. However, practices show that the completion of other indexes, except these binding indexes, is not satisfactory in many regions.

It can be expected that more rigorous measures will be implemented since the target to lower carbon emission intensity will become the new binding index and its China's commitment to the international community. It is hoped that there will be no bypassing of other indexes and problems for an excessive concern over this index.

We can see that owing to different developmental stages, China's environmental problems and the problems concerning its emission reduction are very different from those of developed countries. At present, China's environmental pollution problems are still centered on the discharge of traditional pollutants and its priority emission reduction lies in the discharge of industrial pollution and domestic sewage. For example, air pollutants such as smoke dust, industrial dust stive and sulfur dioxide, wastewater pollutants such as chemical oxygen demand, petroleum, cyanide prussiate, arsenic, mercury, lead, cadmium and hexavalent chromium as well as industrial solid wastes, hazardous wastes in particular rather than the greenhouse gases. When it is not obligatory to shoulder the responsibility of reducing the greenhouse gas emission, than China made its commitments to reducing carbon emission intensity on its own initiative, which doesn't mean that it should attach more importance to greenhouse gases than traditional pollutants.

China's decrease of their carbon emission intensity is primarily out of strategic consideration. China wants to realize its strategic objectives of green energy and energy security through its commitment to decreasing the carbon emission intensity, which is a long-term strategy. From the perspective of fairness, global warming is the developed countries' historical responsibilities. In addition, differentiation should also be made in the real emission based on its different nature. The emission of China and other developing countries is from development while that of developed countries is from luxury enjoyment. The actual energy consumption per capita and carbon dioxide emission of developed countries are much larger than those of China, with the number in America being respectively 5. 19 and 4. 45 times higher than that in China in 2006, and in Japan, 2. 89 and 2. 22 times higher. It is absolutely reasonable if China and other developing countries refuse to shoulder their emission reduction obligation.

However, to treat the pollution brought about by traditional pollutants is of real urgency, which is a far cry from the greenhouse gas emission reduction problem in obligation and interests. With China's continued and rapid economic growth, its industrialization is featured by a high temporal compression and China's environmental resource situation is rather grim since China is at the critical developmental stage of its pollution-intensive heavy chemical industries. The discharge of pollutants are encroaching every corner of our homeland and jeopardizing our health, which requires an immediate solution and the government is responsible for providing more effective protection and treatment to the environment.

Among many indexes of one type, only a few are binding ones, which actually lowers the demand of non-binding indexes. A distinguishment between binding and non-binding indexes is unfavorable for the environment as a whole to become better. We should proceed from the reality, then make and fully implement proper standards based on specific carrying capabilitis or risks.

(5) Emission reduction should serve the demand of environmental quality

Judging from China's current environmental situation, the weak link in China's environmental protection lies in its surveillance. An important reason for China's extremely grim environmental situation is the failure to abide by the law, loose enforcement of the law and weak environmental surveillance. The department of environmental protection should step up its surveillance work. The control over environmental risks should also start from the improvement in the management ability within the department of environmental protection. This is closely related to the deficient environmental management system. We must make it a top priority to construct the environmental management system. It is obvious that the enforcement of the energy conservation and emission reduction target established in the "11th Five-Year" Plan has greatly promoted the construction of China's environmental management system.

The main function of the government's environmental protection department is to make feasible environmental and emission standards and conduct effective surveillance. Its work aim should focus on improving the environmental quality. The emission standards should serve the needs of environmental quality. Therefore, if we stray away from the specific environmental quality targets, the significance of the emission reduction target will be discounted.

There exists an obvious disconnect between the energy conservation and emission reduction target set in the "11th Five-Year" Plan and its role in improving the environmental quality. For example, at present, the frequent occurrence of hazy weather in China's large cities shows that air pollutants, especially the intensity of the inhalable particles has already been rather high and the air quality is more and more dependent on and sensitive to the meteorological conditions. The adsorption capacity of the inhalable particles is very strong, which poses a great threat to human health. This obviously cannot be solved by decreasing sulfur dioxide and COD by 10%.

The cardinal number causes some problems for the relative quantity index of energy conservation and emission reduction. Because the cardinal number is very different, on the one hand, it makes the index decomposition extremely difficult and leads to many unreasonable decompositions, making some newly-established enterprises constantly complain about their responsibility for decreasing energy consumption and emission; on the other hand, the completion of the emission reduction index doesn't necessarily mean that the environmental problem has been significantly improved. Different regions have different conditions. For some highly polluted regions, even if they have completed the two indexes, they may still face serious pollution. However, for some economically developed regions, even if they complete the two indexes and the enterprise reaches the emission standard, if the total emissions surpass the environmental carrying capacity, the regional environmental quality can still not be improved. In comparison, it is more effective to implement total pollutant emission control based on actual regional conditions.

It is essential to require the emission reduction effect to be embodied in the improvement of the environmental quality. This involves the problem of cost-benefit analysis. We should try to obtain more benefits with a minimal cost and put our limited efforts to those yielding the best results. In environmental protection, we should make it a priority to treat pollution which poses serious threats to human health and avoid the ecological environmental disasters which are hard to recover or which take a lot of money to recover.

II. To Transform the Development Model Is the Key to Energy Conservation and Emission Reduction

One of the fundamental reasons for China to face the grim environmental and resources challenge is that it is following in the footsteps of developed countries. On the one hand, it is trying hard to catch up with developed countries and follow their old road and on the other hand, it cannot enjoy the resources and environmental capacities enjoyed once by developed countries. Therefore, the ultimate outlet to cope with the resources and environmental challenges is to transform the development model and its corresponding production method and consumption pattern. Practices show that the efforts made by us in "energy conservation and emission reduction" are still following the direction of developed countries and thus are restricted by the scope of developed countries' traditional development model.

1. It will lead us to nowhere if we follow developed countries' old roads

As long as we made some analyses of the efforts being made by China to achieve its "energy conservation and emission reduction" goal, we can find that basically it is still following the road once taken by developed countries. At present, our "energy conservation and emission reduction" work is mainly focused on the production area, the sifting out of the "inferior and small" and the outdated capacity. Basically, the improvement of the requirements for market access is oriented by technology updating. To improve energy technology efficiency, the relevant departments in China have made enormous efforts in price, management and other incentive policies. The efficiency of developed countries, including energy efficiency, is indeed higher than that of our country and it is not wrong to follow developed countries. According to the calculation of the quantity of goods produced, our energy efficiency is about 20% lower than that of developed countries on average. [①] To bridge such a gap, it should take at least one or two decades.

It can be seen that the current "energy conservation and emission reduction" target can only ensure our energy intensity to reach the level of developed countries. However, by keeping up with developed countries, we still cannot avoid relapsing into the old energy predicament experienced by America and other developed countries. America's prosperity is secured on the basis of high resource consumption. America, with its less than 5% population in the world, is consuming 20% of the global energy. The resource efficiency of America and other developed countries is high, but so is their energy consumption per capita. America's energy consumption per capita is 5

---

① See Yan Lin. *The Last Half Barrel of Oil——Global Economic Strategic Reorganization*. Chemical Industry Press. 2007.

times higher than that of China. The gap between China and developed countries in energy consumption levels is much larger than that in energy efficiency.

Another group of figures[①] can illustrate that developed countries' economic growth pattern is energy-intensive. For the 12 years from 1990 to 2002, China's total energy consumption rose from 879.92 million toe to 1,228.57 million toe, an increase of 39.6%; the total energy consumption of high-income countries rose from 4,299.13 million toe to 5,201.12 million toe, an increase of 21.0%; among those countries, Japan, renowned for its thrift, also had its total energy consumption increase from 445.92 million toe to 516.93 million toe, an increase of 15.9%. China's high increase rate is attributable to its low cardinal number. During those 12 years, China's energy consumption per capita only increased by 185 kgoe and that of high-income countries, 536 kgoe, among which Japan increased by 448 kgoe. That is to say, the increase of energy consumption per capita in high-income countries was 2.90 times higher than that in China during those 12 years, among which Japan was 2.42 times higher. However, during those 12 years, China's rapid economic growth was at an extensive stage while America's economy was increasing at a slower speed and Japan's economy was basically stagnant.

For developed countries' such an energy-intensive economic growth pattern is decided by the capitalist production method. The capitalist economy regards the increase of capital and the profit growth as its primary aim. The capital's expansive and greedy nature determines its unceasing pursuit of unrestricted economic expansion, with endless expansion of reproduction and continued expansion of capital. As a result, on the one hand, it leads to a rapid energy and material consumption and on the other hand, there is an increasing number of wastes dumped into the environment and the limit of the planet's environmental and resources carrying capacity is overlooked, which leads to rapid environmental degradation and such a soaring increase is secured on the basis of high consumption. The consumption level of developed countries is far ahead of the planet's environmental and resources share which every one of us deserves. There is much

① Data source: *International Economic Statistical Yearbook (2005)*. China Statistics Press, 2005.

luxurious, wasteful, ostentatious and bandwagon consumption, which leads man to the unsustainable development track characterized by resource shortages and environmental damage.

Since the 1970s, the environmental problem has received attention in developed countries. In the past, when pollution discharge was out of control, they would inhibit pollution discharge and enhance terminal treatment through such economic methods as gradually levying taxes on or charging fees for the discharge of wastes. With the increase of the pollution discharge standard and the promotion of clean production, the environmental cost of the enterprises' production was also increased significantly. For this reason, developed countries have made corresponding industrial structure adjustments, among which an important measure was to transfer industries with high energy consumption, and large pollution discharge but low added value to developing countries. On the surface, developed countries have solved their domestic pollution emission reduction problem through the transformation of its production model and structure adjustments. However, since there is no fundamental change in their production and consumption method, to a large degree, their emission reduction is dependent on pollution transfer and the "emission increase" in developing countries.

With the global economic integration, the production and consumption methods of developed countries are expanded rapidly to the rest of the world. Based on the estimation of the World Wildlife Fund, man's action scale has exceeded the planet's biological carrying capability by 20%. If with man's current resource consumption rate, by 2050, human beings on the planet will have consumed the natural resources equivalent to that of two plants in total. [①] Obviously, under the traditional energy system, the world's resource and environmental capacity are not able to support developing countries to follow developed countries. This is the central problem why the current global resource and environmental problem is escalating day by day and where the major interest conflict lies between developed countries and developing countries.

The pursuit of capital accumulation renders capitalism a money-worshiping society. The development road with the pursuit of fortune as

---

① World Wildlife Fund, 2006 *Living Planet Report*, 2006.

the ultimate aim not only incurs high resources and environmental costs, but also turns people into greedy money grubbers, causing them to suffer from the vicious result of losing their humanist spirit. Since the 1960s, developed countries have begun to reflect on this detour road and have made constant adjustments to this road, instilling humanistic content and reversing it toward the direction of humanistic development. New social development thoughts and movements such as environmentalism, post-modernism, anti-globalization movement and sustainable development have emerged, serving as reflections on and providing criticisms for the existent development model.

However, under capitalism, the rectification of the traditional development road is undoubtedly beneficial, but it cannot shake the capitalist market economic system based on privatization and the production and consumption method resulting from such a basic system. Facts show that although developed countries' energy production efficiency is higher than that of China and they have taken many measures to save consumption resources, the traditional production and consumption method makes it hard for them to change such a growth pattern irrespective of resource restriction and lack of temperance.

At present, China is basically following the old industrialization road once taken by developed countries and until now, it cannot find ways to excel on his road. It merges better and better into the global economic system dominated by developed countries. Although China has become more aware of the fact that the road taken by developed countries is not suitable for China's national conditions and China must embark on a new road through reform. However, with the progress of opening up, especially China's accession into the WTO, with a large amount of international capital flooding in, China's production and consumption method is more and more geared toward that of developed countries. China's room for choice in its development model is narrowing. The rule of the WTO is known to be the global economy legislation, which is forcefully binding to every country. Therefore, during its transformation of the development model, China will be inevitably restricted by the WTO as well as by the traditional production and consumption method. Undoubtedly, China is facing enormous challenges in how to transform its development model, explore new development methods and construct a new production and living style ...

2. Demand side management is in urgent need to step up

Obviously, China's "energy conservation and emission reduction" should not be one increasing energy efficiency and saving energy consumption in the production area on the one hand, while pursuing luxurious, wasting and high energy-consuming lifestyle in the consumption area on the other hand. Such a dual attitude should be changed as soon as possible. We should regard energy conservation and saving in the consumption area as a more important aspect in "energy conservation and emission reduction" and adopt more enforcing measures of demand side management.

It should be noted that China's era of mass consumption is approaching. During recent years, the consumption measured by the total retail sale of the social products have been on the rise, with its increase rate in 2003 being 9.1%, in 2004, 13.3%, in 2005, 12.9% and in 2006, 13.7%, and in 2007, surpassing 15% and 2008, approaching 22%, far higher than the GDP increase rate. "The consumption group with the greatest consuming capability is indiscriminately imitating developed countries' lifestyle. Many people conceded that the developed countries' consumption and living style is not suitable for China, but they still follow such a trend. Under economic globalization, how to weaken the unending and continuous guiding influence[①] of developed countries' consumption method on the consumption habit of China's medium and high-income groups" constitutes the greatest challenge for us to cope with the grim energy environmental situation and to construct a conservation-minded society.

For China, although there exists reasonable space for the increase of energy consumption, it is unfeasible to simply put consumption into a right of one's own and leave it as it is. It is absolutely necessary to enhance demand side management and guide and control consumption properly. We should encourage proper consumption and inhibit irrational consumption and combat waste. Especially we should make great efforts to stem the government's ostentatious habit in keeping up appearances

---

① Zheng Yisheng. Uncertainty, Lock-in and "Prioritizing Energy Conservation" Strategy——Discussion on Methodology. Work essay of the Environment and Development Research Center, Chinese Academy of Social Sciences, 2007.

and effectively monitor the public power's utilization of public resources; we should encourage a simple material life and a fulfilled spiritual life and make policies to guide consumption, avoiding plunging the consumers into consumerism.

China is facing a task to transform its growth driven by investment and export into "consumption growth", an aim which is not completely contrary to our saving concept, but more or less strays from our concept. Such an approaching transformation will put the problem of the demand side management of the energy environment on the agenda. It should be said that at present, China is at a critical historical crossroad. Lifestyle is the final decisive factor for the demand and supply structure. Once it is formed and saturated, for the method dependence, it cannot be reversed. We can never be led down the road by the dream of a Western lifestyle.

Although it is hard to resist the temptation of developed countries' exemplary consumption behavior, it cannot be denied that there is large room for the demand side management, which is receiving more and more attention in China and is being strengthened. For example, China has already imposed restrictions on the consumption of private cars and promulgated some restrictive measures on the housing area, energy conservation for architectural buildings, over-packaging and one-time consumption. However, this is far from enough. There is no clear consumption policy in China's economic development planning and there are not enough studies on how to encourage thrifty habits, while avoiding insufficient consumption.

China should make use of its institutional advantages in its demand side management and consumption guidance. China is a socialist country, which means it is evident that China will follow the "people-oriented" scientific development road. To realize the sustainable development, man must control their material desires, especially after the realization of what exists in a comparatively well-off society. It should make more efforts in constructing its spiritual homeland, which is particularly important for a country with such a large population. Therefore, the key to the transformation of the traditional development model lies in forming a simple material lifestyle but with a rich spiritual and cultural lifestyle with Chinese characteristics.

III. Take Solid Measures to Promote the Construction of a Conservation-Minded Society

All the products consumed by human beings are not possible without energies, emissions, and whatever we are saving, such as saving energies and reducing emissions. As a matter of fact, the potential for saving is enormous. As long as you're willing, you can start from every little action around you. Therefore, the promotion of constructing a saving and environment-friendly society is an unavoidable road to widely spread energy conservation and emission reduction and to cope with energy environment challenges.

1. Discarding Economism and Consumerism

China is facing tremendous population, resource and environmental pressures. However, in reality, wasting resources is a very common phenomenon and this runs contrary to our promotion of energy conservation and emission reduction.

Owing to the reflection on the "poor socialism" and the desire of "getting rich," China relapsed into the developed countries' traditional development road centered on the accumulation of wealth during a period of time and the humanist pursuit of socialism was marginalized. Many people think what "focusing on economic development" and "development is of overriding importance" conveys is that the economy is supreme and the total economic growth should be the top priority while other objectives should be subject to it. Even spiritual civilization and moral construction are considered to serve economic development and all problems are "restored to" an economic problem. These are typical concepts of economism.

In practice, economism is represented in the blind and one-sided pursuit of the short-term increase of GDP, extensive utilization of natural resources, human resources, extensive environmental pollution and an overlooking of man's spiritual fulfillment, humanistic pursuit and man's own development. If such a developmental concept is introduced by putting an emphasis on materialism and overlooking the impact on humanity, then the construction of a conservation-minded society will only be empty rhetoric.

An important contemporary manifestation of economism is consumerism. Since the latter half of the 20th century, as economic growth is increasingly restricted by a lack of effective demand and consumption is unprecedentedly encouraged, consumerism emerged at the right moment, rising as the concept of dominating man's lifestyle and became the core of Western social values. At present, it assumes a dominant role globally. It is absolutely no blessing for developing countries as consumerism accompanies globalization in its expansion worldwide. Consumerism is but the logic of capital expanding globally, which serves the benefits of cross-country capital.

The lifestyle of consumerism is different from the consumption behavior in the general sense, because its main content is the worship of material enjoyment. Consumerism not only attaches importance to the use value of consumer goods, but more to their symbolic meaning, which regards consumption as the fundamental method for "spiritual fulfillment and self-gratification." In the market, there seems no other meaning but to grip more and more material wealth and become a consumption machine. Globally speaking, consumerism is the important reason for luxurious consumption, excessive consumption and wasting of resources, which brings resources and environmental risks to humanity. Here, economists directly or indirectly legitimized ostentatious and luxurious consumption. In contemporary society, stimulating consumption is the government's most significant guiding principle.

Although such consumerism also exists in the West, with moral restraints at the religious and spiritual level and strong criticism from the intellectual circle, therefore, consumerism is not that rampant in the face of public opinion. However, in China, commercialism and consumerism are usually encouraged and become more rampant and are difficult to rein in. The market-oriented reform in China, while instilling vigorous power in China's economy, also activates the Chinese people's material desire and greed at an unprecedented scale. Many consumers and adolescents are guided by a twisted consumption concept and their humanistic pursuit quickly slips to a back seat, as a result of the powerful media's daily publicity of economism and consumerism. In China's "face" tradition, consumerism, combined with the mindset of the upstart and the public money consumption, renders luxurious consumption more and more prevailing in China. China's per capita

GDP is only about 3, 000 dollars, ranking 104th in the world. ① However, China is the world's second largest market for luxuries. Since luxurious consumption can create market demands, it is applauded by economists. If we leave these bad habits uncriticized, the conservation movement will find it hard to secure substantial advances.

Consumerism not only leads to the degradation of resources and environmental conditions, but brings serious negative influences on man's spiritual and social development. The consumption fever or greed activated by consumerism creates serious social psychological imbalances. With the income gap expanding, consumerism causes anxiety, agitation and perplexity for those who are eager to live a fashionable life and leads to a tense, inharmonious and unstable social interpersonal relationship.

As China is more and more integrated into the global economic system, it is now hard for China to abandon consumerism. However, we have to face a series of problems such as "how much consumption is enough," "what is the consumption level that the planet is able to support" and "how to realize man's sustainable development." Undoubtedly, there are many perplexities and many problems asking for value judgments, which need our indefatigable exploration. However, for a sustainable development and a better future, we should foster an environment against luxurious consumption and promote the public awareness which regards it shamefully to waste and gloriously to save; at the same time, we should lead people out of the bandwagon and ostentatious mindset and to develop proper and rational consumption habits. We should encourage them to help others and develop a consumption and living style that is featured by a simple material life but a rich spiritual life.

2. Valuing humanistic development and improving wealth effectiveness

The underdevelopment of China's humanism has a direct bearing on the effectiveness of the wealth structure, which is also a kind of waste since it means a decrease in resource efficiency. The pursuit of happiness to the end of our life and fortune is one means to realize it. "Happiness in our life is related to wealth, but is not decided by how

---

① According to IMF2008 ranking.

much we own. Instead, it hinges on our life value, lifestyle and our feelings under certain living conditions through comparing with others". When our basic need is generally satisfied, whether our life is happy or not depends more on fair wealth distribution, the sound mindset of the citizen as an individual and the harmony and profundity of interpersonal communications. "With economic development and the improvement of our cultural level, more and more people will no long equate happiness with the satisfaction from material desire and sensual desire. " An investigation shows that from 1945 to 1990, the per capita income in America increased about 3 times, but their average sense of happiness, instead of increasing, declined slightly. ① This reflects the ineffectiveness of the wealth structure.

The low efficiency of a planned economy during a long period and the disturbances of the "Cultural Revolution" had reduced the Chinese people to extreme poverty. At the beginning of the reform and opening up, economic growth improved people's general living standard and wealth increase became an effective means to realize a happy life. With the continued increase of China's total economic volume and the underdevelopment of humanism, especially the broadening of the income distribution gap, China's social disharmony has escalated, which shows wealth accumulation is not that effective as a means to realize the objective. Wealth increase can no longer contribute a great deal to the realization of the social target, which is evidenced in the wasting of resources consumed during growth. The acceleration of humanistic development will improve the social effect of wealth accumulation and objectively is an act to save resources.

Therefore, the underdevelopment of humanism influences the efficiency of turning wealth into development targets. We usually only pay attention to the efficiency of turning resources into wealth, but overlook the efficiency of turning wealth into development targets. An emphasis on the efficiency of the latter should be the feature of a socialist country. The Party Central Committee proposed to construct a harmonious society and develop a socialist core value system, which showed the efforts already made by the committee to improve the latter efficiency. The transformation of the development model is the most

---

① Lu Feng. Criticism of economism. *China Environment and Development Review (Vol. 2)*, Social Sciences Academic Press, 2004.

important way for conservation. The traditional industrial road is constructed on the basis of a large amount of consumption resources and is not suitable for China. Constructing a conservation-minded society means that China must embark on a new road through reform, a new road featured by humanistic development. The road of humanistic development has two meanings.

The first is that the construction of a conservation-minded society should have a good humanistic environment.

China is a socialist country. In fact, socialism reflects a kind of culture, a kind of humanistic spirit or pursuit. It is evident that we should walk on the road of humanistic development. The cruel reality shows that nature can satisfy a few people's greed, but is unable to feed the unrestrained desire of billions of people. The production and consumption method oriented by economism and consumerism is unsustainable. Therefore, the key to transforming the traditional development model lies in forming a lifestyle, with Chinese characteristics, which features a simple material life, with a rich spiritual life.

Thrift has been a traditional Chinese virtue for several thousand years. The whole generation of the New China was brought up under the traditional political encouragement of practicing thrift, living a hardworking and plain life, being self-reliant and striving to be strong. We should inherit these good traditions, educate the next generations with this thrifty concept, regulate social energy consumption behavior and try hard to avoid wasting consumption. All these are basic in constructing a "resource-saving society."

As for whether we should inhibit our desires is another question on which people have different opinions. Some believe that if we realize an absolute resource consumption decrease by "inhibiting desire" and achieve the goal of saving resources, then this will lead to insufficient consumption demand, economic shrinking, an increasing unemployment rate and social depression. Obviously, this is not true. To begin with, it is impossible for an individual's desire to be free of any restrictions in society. Whether it's public or the production sector's resource consumption behavior, they all need the restrictions from society. The public's energy consumption behavior should be guided and their inappropriate behavior should be rectified. To teenagers and adolescents, we should conduct education and educate them that scientific, reasonable and restrained consumption behaviors are important contents for the construction of a conservation-minded society. In addition, when people's income reaches a certain caliber, generally speaking, their "inhibiting desire" will not be included in the basic needs, but in the luxuries. This is what they should really inhibit.

The second is that humanistic development is an effective means to realize conservation.

Humanistic development emphasizes "putting people first." The development with "fortune as the basis" and humanistic development differ in two ways. The first is that they have different ultimate goals; and the other is that the effectiveness of their different means is different. The humanistic development means is an overall epitome of Aristotle's thinking over 2,000 years ago, namely, "money is obviously not what we are pursuing, but a useful instrument to realize other things."

According to Marxism, the development goal we are pursuing is our overall development. Amartya Sen (the Nobel Economic Prize winner in 1998) is renowned for his concern about the nationals' welfare increase and his advocacy of humanistic development. He and others defined humanistic development as "expanding man's choice scope" and "the development goal is to provide opportunities for all the people to live a fulfilled life," which criticizes the action of emphasizing material while overlooking humanity.

The development goal of "putting people first," comprehensive, coordinated and sustainable scientific development outlook and the construction of a harmonious society is a rectification of the traditional development view with fortune as the basis. Socialism means to realize social harmony and equity through reasonable institutional arrangements. Institutional arrangements and wealth accumulation are only means and social harmony, equity and justice is our aim and pursuit. Obviously, this is a road of humanistic development.

The development which puts people first is not only a guarantee for the realization of a harmonious society, but also a fundamental means to construct a conservation-minded society. Wealth, as a means to the end, has its effectiveness embodied in the realization of goals. When resources are limited, we should first satisfy people's basic needs. The humanistic development which puts people first is aimed at a harmonious society. It places emphasis on developing man's self-development through the creation of equal opportunities and the satisfaction of man's basic needs, the improvement of people's welfare and poverty alleviation, more expansive and quality education, medical services and social security for all the social members. Under such aims or such a development model, the same volume of wealth will bring people more welfare. In other words, the same welfare only asks for less wealth and less resources, which, obviously, has positive influences on resource conservation and environmental protection. Needless to say, with the same amount of wealth, compared with a polarized society, people enjoy more welfare in an average rich society and the effectiveness of wealth is higher. From the perspective of the effectiveness of wealth, the expanding income gap currently in China runs contrary to the construction of a conservation-minded society.

To sum up, we should not blindly follow the steps of developed countries in our energy conservation and emission reduction. For China, the old road taken by developed countries cannot sustain us anymore because the world's resources and environmental capacity cannot allow China and other developing countries to look ahead to developed countries. We should not simply restrict our energy conservation and emission reduction in the production area but make energy conservation and savings in the consumption area a more important part in "energy conservation and emission reduction." We should also adopt more powerful measures in demand side management. Against the backdrop of globalization, China should make active explorations in how to transform its development model, seek new development methods, and construct a new production method and lifestyle. And China should focus on changing the unrestrained and unbinding growth pattern in its conservation-minded society and environment-friendly society construction, restraining its growth under the resources and environmental conditions; at the same time, we should not only stress the improvement of the efficiency which turns resources into wealth, but also the efficiency which turns wealth into social development targets.

Comparisons between the G20 Countries' Eco-efficiency: Analysis Based on the DEA Model

By LI Jing

I. Introduction

The G20 consists of America, Britain, Japan, France, Germany, Canada, Italy, Russia, Australia, China, Brazil, Argentina, Mexico, Korea, Indonesia, India, Saudi Arabia, South Africa, Turkey and the European Union. The GNP of these countries accounts for 85% in the world and two thirds in the population.

At the same time, the G20 also represents the major countries causing environmental pollution or greenhouse gas emissions in the world. Its total carbon dioxide emissions accounts for around 80% of the world's total emissions, in which developing countries like China and India have shown rapid increases in their total carbon emissions and are called by developed countries as "major carbon emission countries," and for developed countries, their carbon emissions per capita still remain at a very high level. This becomes the "rationale" for developed countries and developing countries to point fingers at each other in global climate negotiations. For example, in the 4th Ministerial Meeting of the Gleneagles Dialogue on Climate Change, Clean Energy and Sustainable Development held in Chiba on March 15, 2008, the former British Prime Minister Blair pointed out that America's annual greenhouse gas emissions per capita exceeded 20 tons and that of Europe and Japan exceeded 10 tons respectively. Developed countries have realized industrialization, the process which brought about climate risks, while developing countries are constructing an industrialized society. No country would give up economic growth and neither should developed countries place such expectations on developing countries. It should be remembered that many products produced by developing countries will be exported to developed countries for consumption. ①

Obviously, the G20 not only represents major global economies, but also major core countries which decide the direction of global climate and make climate conventions. Therefore, it is necessary to initiate studies on the coordination level between these countries' economic development and environmental emissions, namely, the eco-efficiency based on making clear G20 countries' economic development level, energy consumption conditions and environmental emissions. Based on this, we should also examine the changes in the eco-efficiency resulting from policy preferences and the differences in the environmental regulation levels.

II. Literature Review

1. Eco-efficiency Concept and Theory Studies

(1) Studies on the concept of eco-efficiency

The studies of the concept of eco-efficiency. In 1990, Schaltegger and Sturm first proposed the concept of eco-efficiency or ecological efficiency, namely, the ratio between the increased value and the increased environmental influence. The concept of eco-efficiency was widely recognized and accepted through the book *Changing Course: A Global Business Perspective on Development and the Environment* published in 1992 by the World Business Council for Sustainable Development (WBCSD). This book pointed out that the enterprise circle should change their entrenched image as the polluter and strive to become an important promoter for global sustainable development. To achieve this aim, a new concept—eco-efficiency which combines environmental and economic development should be developed to cope with the challenges of sustainable development. The WBCSD further defined eco-efficiency② in the Rio Earth Summit, in 1992 as eco-efficiency = product or service value/environmental

---

① See http://news.cctv.com/special/C17274/01/20080316/102319.shtml.

② There are disagreements on the translation of eco-efficiency into Chinese, especially on the understanding of the prefix eco. Some translated it into "ecological efficiency" or "environmental efficiency", assuming eco should be ecological; while some believed that eco itself not only means ecological, but also economical. For example, Eiichiro Adachi (2002) clearly defined that "Eco-efficiency" "means combining economical and environmental efficiency" (see http://www.asria.org/events/taiwan/may02/lib/EiichiroA.pdf). We think that translating it into "ecological efficiency" or "environmental efficiency" has obviously not grasped the profundity of the concept and therefore, we agree with Eiichiro Adachi's (2002) definition of the connotation which is a complete understanding and translation, including the economical and environmental aspect. Therefore, we think the Chinese translation of "经济环境效率(eco-efficiency) " is more accurate.

influence to evaluate how much value can be created with one unit of environmental influence. The less environmental influence the enterprise's activity has caused, the greater the economic value it has created, the larger the figure will be and the higher the eco-efficiency. The definition of the WBCSD has been widely accepted, namely "while satisfying man's needs for high-quality life, to decrease the influence of the whole life cycle on the environment at least by the same level of the planet's estimated carrying capacity by providing services and products with price advantages. To put it simply, to minimize the influence and maximize the value." The basic concept of eco-efficiency means to maintain or continue to expand total economic activities on the premise of not increasing environmental influence in order to improve human society's welfare and realize human society's sustainable development. ①

According to the eco-efficiency concept of the WBCSD, it can be defined as: eco-efficiency must provide products or services which have price competitiveness, satisfy man's needs and ensure life quality and at the same time it can gradually decrease the biological influence and resource consumption intensity in the life cycle of the products or services by the same level of the estimated planet carrying capacity. In fact, the WBCSD defines eco-efficiency as a part of the large concept of Sustainable Production and Consumption (SPC). Generally speaking, WBCSD's definition of eco-efficiency primarily stressed the following seven aspects:

(1) Decreasing the raw material intensity of the products or services (saving natural resources); (2) decreasing the energy intensity of the products or services (saving energies); (3) decreasing the discharge of noxious and hazardous substances; (4) improving the recycling rate of resources; (5) trying to utilize renewable resources as efficiently as possible; (6) improving the products' service life; (7) increasing the products and services' intensity.

Fussler (1996) proposed within sustainable consumption, that eco-efficiency actually includes three aspects: (1) developing a sustainable consumption method to coordinate the relationship between

---

① As for the numerate "product or service value" of eco-efficiency as defined by the WBCSD, our understanding should not be limited to the market value. If we expand the scope of eco-efficiency to the macro area, then value here should include more non-market value: not only the value obtained through the market, but also the value embodied in the non-market utilization or welfare benefits, such as higher education level, clean air and comfortable environment, longer life expectancy, higher forest coverage rate, greater bio-diversity and etc.

environmental anxiety and man's life quality; (2) bringing more attention to the environment through clean production and the distribution of products and services; (3) creating value through products and services representing man's life quality.

The Organization for Economic Cooperation and Development (OECD) believed that the WBCSD's definition about eco-efficiency is flexible and emphasizes practicality, which can be converted into the actual action of the government, industry and other organizations and households. However, it is not enough to adopt eco-efficiency itself as the basis for policy making. We should further understand the relationship between the driving forces behind economic activities and environmental damage and changes and the motivation from the producer and consumer's behavior, psychology and ethics. Therefore, OECD defined eco-efficiency as: the ecological resource efficiency satisfying human's needs (OECD, 1998), which can be seen as the ratio between output and input ("output" refers to the products and services value provided by an enterprise, industry or the whole economy while "input" refers to the environmental pressure caused by the enterprise, industry or economies).

The earlier international definition of the eco-efficiency concept was limited to the range of the micro players, such as focusing on how the enterprise is able to manage clean production, to produce as many products or services with minimal resources or environmental pressure, and how they go about obtaining market value. With deepening studies, the connotation and range of the eco-efficiency concept is expanding, not only focusing on micro players such as how the enterprise, individual and household adhere to and practice eco-efficiency concepts, but also beginning to emphasize how macro players such as the region or the country implements eco-efficiency concepts; the expansion also enlarges the connotation of the concept itself, from a mere focus on how micro players create more products or services with less environmental pressure to the emphasis on how to minimize the environmental influence while creating more utilization or welfare, with more non-market value included.

(2) Establishment of the eco-efficiency theory

The enterprise, as the major player of the micro economy, is the basic unit influencing regional, national and global sustainable development and also the major implementer of sustainable development actions. At present, most enterprise managers agree that the enterprise's sustainable development is the prerequisite for the enterprise's operation (IFOK, 1997; Hedstrom et al., 1998; Holliday, 2001). The WBCSD is an association consisting of more than 150 international enterprise leaders, which is favorable to find solutions to sustainable development problems through dialogues. Many enterprises appointed officials for sustainable development and periodically published sustainable development reports. The sustainable development strategy actively adopted by the enterprises shows they have discharged their environmental and social responsibilities, which, undoubtedly, provides important supports for the sustainable development at other levels. Therefore, it is called the "business link to sustainable development," And then eco-efficiency becomes the guiding principle for many enterprises.

Since the WBCSD is an association organized by international enterprises' leaders, undoubtedly, they will pay more attention to micro players, especially about the enterprise's eco-efficiency. However, eco-efficiency is also the most important measurement index for the macro players' sustainable development. From the perspective of the environmental economy, as it directly connects environmental influences and economic development, it becomes the most popular concept and philosophical thinking since the 1990s. Some regions or countries also begin to treat regional economic development and environmental pollution behavior by applying the eco-efficiency concept. While trying to create better products and services, they also try to minimize the use of natural resources and its influence on the environment. In addition, apart from the above mentioned reasons, there are other reasons for the international acceptance of eco-efficiency: first, although some indexes similar to the concept of eco-efficiency can also partly reflect the economy's environmental economy and sustainable development, such as the economic output of per unit pollution (discharge), yet its narrow connotation has limited its utilization scope; second, other so-called index systems reflecting the relationship between the environment and the economy, although avoiding the deficiency of a single index measurement, they have overlooked the alternativeness among the indexes and are unable to provide more accurate guidance for the measurement of the economy; third, various indexes should be summarized into a widely acknowledged standard to provide convenience for policy-making. Eco-efficiency can compensate the deficiency of the above mentioned concepts and can be used for easy comparisons.

From 1992, when the concept of eco-efficiency was initiated to the present, not only is it widely accepted by multinationals, but also its ideals and practices are maturing with the active promotion of the WBCSD, which became the core business concept developed and practiced by enterprises. Its influences are expanding among the government, the financial industry and other private sectors. The financial industry, enterprise leaders, government and other stakeholders have gradually realized that besides responsibilities and obligations, they must quantify the enterprise's environmental performance from the perspective of risks, commercial opportunities, profits and surplus.

With eco-efficiency, sustainable development is no longer rhetoric or the coat of image promotion. It has become a thinking pattern, a management philosophy and a movement. For enterprises, it is a tool, firmly planting them at an advantageous position in international competition; it is also a social responsibility and mission, making enterprises exert influences on the society while aiding in the maintenance of a peaceful, stable and healthy global village. For the public, it raises and deepens their awareness of sustainable production or consumption concepts in production, consumption and other links. For countries or regions, their pursuit of higher eco-efficiency means the creation of more market value and non-market value while minimizing the environmental impact so as to maximize people's welfare and the utility level.

(3) Domestic eco-efficiency concept and theoretical research

Concerning ongoing research related to the eco-efficiency concept. China's studies on eco-efficiency started comparatively late, most of which still focused on the exploration on how to combine the eco-efficiency concept with China's actual conditions. As for the definition of eco-efficiency, most Chinese scholars have enriched or expanded the definition based on the WBCSD's definition. Wang Jinnan (2002) believed that eco-efficiency was a concept of technology and management, which focused on maximizing the improvement of productivity of the energy and material input and aimed at decreasing the resource consumption of the per unit product and the pollutant discharge. Zhou Guomei (2003) defined eco-efficiency as the efficiency of how ecological resources satisfy man's needs, which can be measured by the ratio between output and input. However, Liao Hong, Zhu Tan (2002) and Xia Kaixuan, et al. (2007) directly defined the WBCSD's eco-efficiency as "ecological economic efficiency" and some literature called it "economic environmental efficiency" (Zhang & Xun, 2007). Obviously, the concept of eco-efficiency in China basically follows the definition of the WBCSD or other foreign research institutions or scholars and there is no unified definition of eco-efficiency.

The studies on the theory and application of eco-efficiency. Yue Yuanyuan and Su Jingqin (2004), based on sorting out foreign eco-efficiency concepts and practices, proposed policies for China to implement a eco-efficiency strategy and based this idea on a macro perspective that a government should implement eco-efficiency in the policy, finance and index assessment system and the enterprise in product development, design, craft, functions, services and treatment. Zhu Dajian and Qiu Shoufeng (2006) combined eco-efficiency with the circular economy and assumed that eco-efficiency is the most proper measurement for the circular economy and inhibiting the consumption of natural resources (DMI), decreasing environmental influence (DPO) and GDP eco-efficiency indexes are proper indexes of the circular economy. Gao Qianshan (2007) thought that eco-efficiency was an important index of the enterprise's environmental auditing evaluation. Bu Danlu (2007) pointed out that eco-efficiency was closely related to the enterprise's environmental cost management and proposed measures to control the enterprise's environmental cost. Li Bing, et al. (2007) studied the relationship between eco-efficiency and the ecological footprint and pointed out that eco-efficiency should be defined as the ratio between the enterprise's output and its ecological footprint. Zhu Dajian, et al. (2005) pointed out that eco-efficiency was the crystallization of a country's green competitiveness, which included four situations and proposed the C (China) model of the development from the material increase to material decrease. These should be realized with technologies.

While introducing foreign theories on eco-efficiency, domestic studies should focus on the combination of eco-efficiency and the circular economy and sustainable development. Eco-efficiency is a proper measurement of the circular economy and technological advances are a guarantee for all this; you should start from the level of enterprises, having explored the relationship between eco-efficiency and the enterprise's environmental cost and its sustainable development.

However, the studies on eco-efficiency in China still only stay at the introduction period. There is no unified Chinese translation of this term and they cannot grasp the right connotation of eco-efficiency. Especially they cannot recognize its non-market value, but overemphasize the comparison between market value and environmental pressure; in the range of applying the eco-efficiency concept, there are also inconsistencies and confusions. Many studies fail to note or realize how to apply this concept and theory at the micro and macro level, what the differences in its connotation and there are no further explorations offered; from the research content, there are no systematic theoretical frameworks of China's eco-efficiency theory and we should conduct more in-depth studies.

2. Assessment Methods and Empirical Studies of Eco-Efficiency

Until now, in terms of eco-efficiency, there are only definitions and theoretical developments. However, if we are to look into the eco-efficiency research subject in depth, we need to use proper methods to conduct empirical studies, in which Life Cycle Assessment (LCA) and Data Envelopment Analysis (DEA) are two commonly used methods.

(1) "Life Cycle Assessment (LCA)" method and the empirical study of eco-efficiency

The most used method is called "Life Cycle Assessment" (LCA), namely, to obtain the enterprise's eco-efficiency by assessing a specific product's life cycle, including the extracting, processing, transporting and circulating, use, reuse, maintenance, recycling and ultimate disposal of the raw material and the potential influence of the resource, energy consumption and waste discharge on the environment, and quantifying these influences. Researchers in China and other countries conducted many studies on the methodology of LCA, including studies on inventory analysis, distribution method and environmental influence categorization, locating environmental factors and logistic analysis. The selection method and quality of the LCA data have a direct bearing on the accuracy of the evaluation result (ISO14000); Xi Deli, et al. (1997) did studies on the steps and methods to obtain product data through an industrial pollution coefficient and the flow chart of the enterprise's production; Mo Hua, et al. (2003) adopted five independent indexes reflecting data quality. The research graded each index from 1-5 based on the nature of each unit and data in the system and formed the vector element of the data's quality index; then converted the quality index into the corresponding composite data quality index based on the percentage of the arithmetic average of the vector element of the data quality in the total index range, obtained each data's random distribution and performed uncertainty analysis of the inventory data. Lu Zhongwu, et al. (2000) analyzed the influence of the logistics during iron and steel production on energy consumption; Wang Shoubing, et al. (2001) studied the resource exhaustion potential. Based on a comprehensive consideration of the resource consumption rate, storage and other specific conditions, they proposed a method to calculate the resource exhaustion potential and the equivalent coefficient; Liu Jianglong, et al. (1996) proposed the concept of metal's environmental impact factor and made comprehensive considerations of the factors such as the abundance, energy consumption and pollutant discharge volume of the metal resource and the threats posed to organisms using a weighted average approach; Su Xiangdong, et al. (2002) proposed the quantitative evaluation method of the composite proportionality coefficient and established the quantitative calculation principle for the environmental influence of the simple metal and the quantitative assessment model for the environmental influence of the nonferrous material according to such factors as the environmental features of the metal element, the actual extracting and metallurgical process and biological effect.

Researchers have done a large amount of practical work on the application of LCA, Kou Xinli (1999), Hao Weichang (2000) and Li Guiqi (2002), et al. studied the environmental influence of polyethylene, ABS resin, metallic aluminum and steel and iron material; Liu Jianglong, et al. (2000) evaluated the environmental influence of different techniques in the process of strengthening the metal material surface; especially that of a successful application of the LCA method to guide the environmental coordination design and of the secondary resource to develop wearproof spherulitic graphite and cast iron materials is of guiding significance to the development and design of materials. The "material's environmental coordination evaluation study" supported by the "863" Plan evaluated and studied seven representative materials in China such as the iron and steel, cement, aluminum, engineering plastic, architectural coating and ceramics, obtained the basic environmental data of the above mentioned materials and developed database management and evaluation software.

During the past twenty years, the LCA method has developed rapidly and been put into wide usage. However, it still has room for improvement in the application range, assessment range and method and data collection, for example, the demarcation of system boundaries, data selection, types of environmental hazards, weight factors, computing methods and selection of the evaluating process. These all include subjective man-made factors including assumption, selection and value judgment, which have influenced the objectivity of the LCA's assessment results. Besides, it is more obvious that the LCA method is more suitable for the eco-efficiency evaluation at the micro or industrial level but not the macro level. Therefore, further studies should be conducted in the many aspects of LCA.

(2) "Data Envelopment Analysis (DEA)" method and the empirical study of eco-efficiency

Foreign studies on the DEA method of eco-efficiency. Another method to evaluate eco-efficiency is DEA. Nevertheless, the basic assumption of the original DEA model is that the relative efficiency assessment should minimize input and maximize output, namely to yield the most output with the least input (Charnes et al., 1978). But the real production process is not so. Some production processes create obvious by-products, among which many are products we don't wish to produce, called "undesirable output," such as pollution. We must minimize the undesirable output to realize the optimal economic efficiencies which the original DEA model can only increase, thus betraying the original intention of the efficiency evaluation. It is obvious that the original DEA model is no longer suitable to treat undesirable output and should be improved.

Some scholars have tried at attempts to measure the economic efficiency (including undesirable output) with the DEA assessment technology. Earlier studies treated undesirable output like pollution as a shadow price (Pittman, 1983). Fare et al. (1989) was the first one to employ the input-output weak disposability to treat the pollution variable, with the basic thought that to reduce undesirable output like pollution, we must sacrifice good output; he proposed a nonlinear programming method in the form of a hyperbola (the hyperbolic method) to treat, for example, the situation of papermaking production. However, because of the complicacy in solution-seeking, the application is greatly restricted. Hailu and Veeman (2001) treated the undesirable output variable as input (as the input variable method). Zhu (2003) and Scheel (2001), et al. also proposed a reciprocal transformation method to treat the undesirable output variable (reciprocal transformation method), namely to transform the undesirable output Y^b into $1/Y^b$ and treat it as desirable output, which can be resolved in the classic DEA model. Seiford and Zhu (2002) proposed a solution that they first multiply the undesirable output with -1, then seek a proper conversion vector to make all the negative undesirable output into positive (conversion vector method). On this basis, they constructed a DEA method to treat undesirable output under the VRS (Variable Return to Scale) condition. Fare et al. (2003) proposed a directional distance function from the perspective of weak disposability and output, which was widely used (directional distance function method). Tone (2003) proposed a DEA model based on a slack-based measure to treat undesirable output (SBM method) and tried his best to take the input and output slackness problem caused by angles and radial directions into consideration.

Domestic studies on the DEA method of eco-efficiency. There are a few studies in China on the evaluation of the enterprise or regional eco-efficiency with the DEA method and show that the research method is repetitive. Sun Guangsheng, et al. (2003), based on the analysis of the disposability of the output, applied the DEA model in the analysis of the eco-efficiency of the industrial production and based on this result, they made an empirical assessment of the eco-efficiency of the industrial production in different regions in 1997. Ke Jian & Li Chao (2005) applied the original model CCR① of DEA in the evaluation of the coordination between the resources, environment and economic development in different parts of China with the resource and environment as the input variable and the economic growth as the output variable. Ma Yujun, et al. (2007) selected the service value of the ecological system, the ecological green equivalent, the per capita

① The DEA model CCR is one of the original models, which is an efficiency assessment method on the premise of an unchanged return to scale and was named after the combination of the initials of Charnes, Cooper and Rhodes.

ecological footprint deficit and the composite index of the environmental quality as the output variables (without the treatment of the pollution variable) and evaluated Suzhou's environmental construction with the CCR model. Zhang Bing, et al. (2008), based on the current eco-efficiency evaluation method, constructed the index system for the enterprise's eco-efficiency evaluation and introduced pollutant discharge into the DEA model as a kind of undesirable input. They evaluated the eco-efficiency of the enterprises in Hangzhou Bay Fine Chemistry Industrial Park. These studies treated pollution or environmental variables as the input of DEA to study the eco-efficiency of the region and enterprise. However, this runs contrary to the essence of the production process and the measured eco-efficiency is also inaccurate.

Study on China's economic or regional productivity or efficiency in consideration of environmental pollution. With China's economic development, its economic growth efficiency has also improved correspondingly. A large amount of research literature uses the enterprise's micro-level data, industrial data and the urban and inter-provincial data to prove that China's productivity and efficiency have improved significantly after the reform and opening up. At the same time, the research results also show that the economic efficiency in the eastern area is much higher than that in the central and western areas (Jefferson, Rawski and Zheng, 1996; Jefferson et al., 2003; Sun, Hone and Doucouliagos, 1999; Wu, 2000; Zheng, Liu and Bigsten, 1998 and 2003). However, one major deficiency in these empirical studies is that they indiscriminately overlooked the influence of the costs of the environmental pollution to economic efficiency. In recent years, some studies began to follow the influence of the environmental pollution on the macro economic efficiency. Hu Angang, et al. (2008) considered the environmental pollution factor and used the DEA's directional distance function method to re-rank China's provincial technical efficiency. Tu Zhengge (2008) also used the directional distance function to study the coordination between China's provincial industry and environment. Wang Bing & Wu Yanrui (2008) used the Malmquist-Luenberger productivity index (with a directional distance function for calculation) to study the influence of the APEC region and country's environment management on the total factor productivity. These studies have applied eco-efficiency in the macroeconomic area to study the coordination between the economic efficiency and environment, which has enriched China's practical studies on regional eco-efficiency. However, such limited studies all use the directional distance function and fail to mention other methods, and also there are no other methods for comparison.

Overall, there is an increasing trend in China to use the DEA method to do studies on regional eco-efficiency. However, there are such problems as limited studies, repetitive research methods, incomparability between the research findings for different methods or data and lack of in-depth studies. Especially in the research methods, there is no literature which makes a systematic summarization of these methods and compares the application occasions of these methods and the differences in the findings.

III. Measurement Method of the Eco-Efficiency

1. General Introductionto the Eco-Efficiency Measurement

Eco-efficiency is actually a composite index measuring the economy's coordinate development between its economic benefit and environmental protection. For example, as is defined by the WBCSD, eco-efficiency = product or service value/environmental influence; its essence is to create better products and services with less consumption of natural resources and environmental influences. It is based on this that eco-efficiency, as a composite index, has covered contents in many aspects and became a proper choice to measure an economy (nation, region and enterprise) . Since the measurement of eco-efficiency will unavoidably involve the product or service value and the value or price of the pollutant discharge and the market price of the pollution is generally unavailable, such evaluations are usually full of man-made or subjective factors; a nonparametric method called data envelopment analysis (DEA), for its inconsideration of the price of the pollutant discharge, cracks such a hard nut.

It has been proved that the DEA method is a very effective instrument to measure the efficiency and productivity of similar decision-making units. Therefore, it is widely applied in the evaluation of the productivity and efficiency in industries, cities, regions and the world. The original DEA model is called the CCR model (Formula 1), namely, the efficiency model under constant returns to scale (CRS); if the restriction $\sum_{\lambda} = 1$ is added, it is called the BCC model,[①] namely, the efficiency model under variable returns to scale (VRS) (in which X, Y represent input and output vectors, x_0, y_0 represent the input and output of the specific evaluated units, ϕ, scalar and λ, weight vector).

$$\begin{aligned} &\max \phi \\ &st \\ &X\lambda + s^{-} = x_0 \\ &Y\lambda - s^{+} = \phi y_0 \\ &\lambda \geqslant 0 \end{aligned} \tag{1}$$

As evaluated by Charnes, et al. (1978), the basic assumption of the original DEA model believes that the relative efficiency evaluation of DEA requires that the input must be minimized while the output must be maximized, namely, to produce the most output with the least input. However, the real production process is not so. Some production processes will bring obvious by-products, among which many are products we don't want, called "undesirable output or bad output." For example, with paper-making, there are a large number of by-products, such as sewage, exhaust gas, and waste residues. The undesirable output must be minimized to realize optimal economic efficiencies while the traditional DEA model can only increase it, betraying the original intention of the efficiency evaluation. It is obvious that the original DEA model is no longer suitable for the treatment of undesirable output. Some scholars make many attempts to measure the economic efficiency (including undesirable output) with the DEA assessment technology. In summary, there are 6 basic treatment methods: the hyperbolic method, reciprocal transformation method, conversion vector method, directional distance function method and SBM method and etc. (see above literature review on the methods).

2. The Strong or Weak Disposability of Undesirable Output

If undesirable output is considered in the production process, then how to choose the efficiency evaluation of the decision-making unit between the two disposal technologies (the strong disposability technology and the weak disposability technology of undesirable output) for improving efficiency is critical. As for the strong disposability, if

① Similar to how the CCR model is named, BCC model was named after the initials of Banker, Charnes and Cooper.

during the production process, the undesirable output (such as pollutant discharge) can be disposed (increased or decreased) free from any restrictions or limitations, it can be said that this production process shows the strong disposability of undesirable output. As for the weak disposability, it means that to decrease undesirable output, part of the desirable output must be sacrificed. In other words, to meet the restricted standard (or regulation) of a certain kind of pollutant discharge, we have to consider paying some price (regulation cost) (Zofio and Prieto, 2001)①.

If we assume there are n independent decision-making units (DUM), represented as $DMU_j(j = 1, 2, \ldots, n)$. Each decision-making costs m input $x_{ij}(i = 1, 2, \ldots, m)$ and produces s desirable output y^g and k undesirable output y^b. When undesirable output shows strong disposability, the production possibility set can be represented as:

$$T^S = \{(x, y^g, y^b) \mid \sum_{j=1}^{n} \lambda_j x_j \leq x, \sum_{j=1}^{n} \lambda_j y_j^g \geq y, \sum_{j=1}^{n} \lambda_j y_j^b \geq y^b, \lambda_j \geq 0, j = 1, \cdots, n\} \tag{2}$$

When undesirable output shows weak disposability, the production possibility set can be represented as:

$$T^W = \{(x, y^g, y^b) \mid \sum_{j=1}^{n} \lambda_j x_j \leq x, \sum_{j=1}^{n} \lambda_j y_j^g \geq y, \sum_{j=1}^{n} \lambda_j y_j^b \geq y^b, \lambda_j \geq 0, j = 1, \cdots, n\} \tag{3}$$

3. Directional Distance Function Method

Fare et al. (2003) proposed a directional distance function from the perspective of output and they first defined an output set P (x):

$$P(x) = \{(y^g, y^b): x \text{ can produce } (y^g, y^b)\} \tag{4}$$

The above set satisfies three qualities:

(1) Weak casual disposability of undesirable output. $(y^g, y^b) \in P$

---

① For example, for a paper-making factory, paper is its desirable output and the sewage discharged is its undesirable output. Weak disposability implies that if the input remains unchanged, a decrease of 10% sewage discharge requires a correspondent decrease of 10% paper production.

(x), for example, $0 \leqslant \delta \leqslant 1$ meaning $(\delta y^g, \delta y^b) \in P(x)$. (2) Casual disposability of desirable output. $(y^g, y^b) \in P(x)$, $y^{g'} \leqslant y^g$, shows that $(y^g, y^g) \in P(x)$. (3) Zero correlation between undesirable output and desirable output. $(y^g, y^b) \in P(x)$, if $y^b = 0$, then $y^g = 0$.

Quality (1) shows that under a given input level, the feasible method to decrease undesirable output is to decrease desirable output; quality (2) shows that desirable output can be disposed casually; quality (3) shows that unless the production is ceased, desirable output must bring about undesirable output and the correlation of the two only occurs at the zero point. Based on the above qualities, they defined the directional distance function as:

$$\vec{D}_0(x, y^g, y^b; g) = \sup\{\beta: (y^g, y^b + \beta g) \in p(x)\} \tag{5}$$

In which g is the "direct" vector proportionate to the output and when $y = (y^g, -y^b)$, it shows an increased desirable output and decreased undesirable output. Fare et al. (2003) also provided an explanatory figure (see Figure 1).

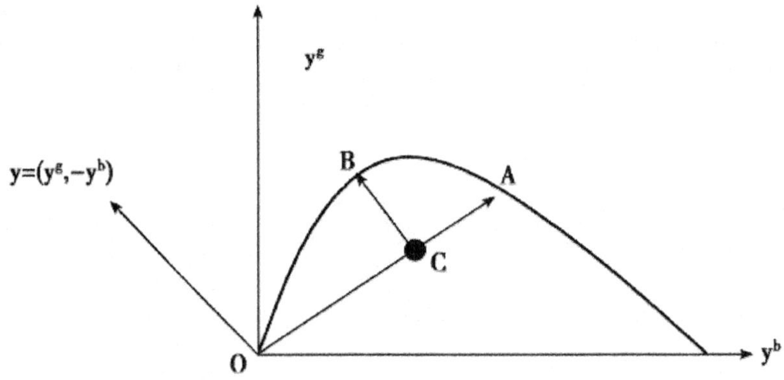

Figure 1 Directional Distance Function Figure

In Figure 1, as for the output measurement point C, if the output efficiency point obtained from the traditional distance function and efficiency measurement principle is A, the output efficiency is OC/OA. If the undesirable output and desirable output increase at the same rate of OA/OC, then the evaluated unit is considered as efficient. However, the efficiency point of the directional distance function is B rather than A. The reason is that if the evaluated unit production is restricted by the undesirable output, then we should not improve the efficiency by increasing the desirable output and undesirable output concurrently. Instead, we should seek the direction g which increases desirable output while decreasing undesirable output to improve the efficiency. In the figure, if the evaluated unit changes from C to B (namely having decreased undesirable output and increased desirable output), then it will be judged as efficient on the basis of the directional distance function. On this basis, they have constructed the linear programming method of the directional distance function for a solution:

$$\begin{aligned} &\vec{D}_0(x, y^g, y^b; y^g, -y^b) = \max\beta \\ &s.t. \\ &Y^g\lambda + s^{g+} = (1+\beta)y_0^g \\ &Y^b\lambda = (1-\beta)y_0^b \\ &X\lambda - s^- = x_0 \\ &\lambda \geq 0 \end{aligned} \quad (6)$$

Modeling on the measurement which adopts the standard distance function technology efficiency, the efficiency measurement of the directional distance function can also be defined as an index between 0 to 1.

$$\text{Directional technology efficiency index} = \frac{1}{1+\vec{D}_0(x, y^g, y^b; y^g, -y^b)}$$

It is worth noting that under this definition, when the measurement point is at the production forefront, the value of the directional distance function is 0 and the corresponding technology efficiency is 1.

Since the directional distance function has properly solved the efficiency evaluation problem of undesirable output, therefore it is widely applied in empirical testing. Fare et al. (2003) used the directional distance function to measure the eco-efficiency of 92 power plants' pollutant discharge. Magnus Lindmark and Peter Vikstrom (2003) used directional distance function method to examine the productivity increase and restraint in the world's 59 countries after the undesirable output (carbon dioxide and sulfur dioxide) had been introduced. They made an interesting conclusion: from 1965 to 1990, when the "undesirable output" variable was not used, the productivity of developed countries and some newly emergent industrial countries (like

Korea) enjoyed comparatively high increases and the restraining trends were obvious while that of those underdeveloped countries almost had no increase and there was no obvious restraining trend; when the two output variables (carbon dioxide and sulfur dioxide) were added, the overall productivity increases were lower than that without "undesirable output." Compared with the first condition, the productivity increases of America and other developed countries enjoyed comparatively small changes while that of those underdeveloped countries showed obvious increasing and restraining trends. The productivity increase rate of some newly emergent countries or regions declined greatly. This shows that the rapid productivity increases of some newly emergent industrial countries or regions are obtained at the cost of people's other welfares.

4. Data Selection and Processing

The sample selects the G20's 19 countries and the European Union, but since the European Union is an economy rather than an independent country and the above mentioned 19 countries also include Britain, France, Germany and Italy which are major members of the European Union, if we continue to use the overall data of the European Union, then it will lead to the problem of repetitive calculations. Based on this, we excluded the aforesaid four countries from the European Union and added another 10 members of the European Union. They are: Belgium, Denmark, Greece, Spain, Switzerland, Finland, Portuguese, Austria, Hungary and Ireland①. In general, the sample country includes 30 nations and the time spans are from 1980 to 2005, 26 years in total.

The data in this article came from the World Bank Development Index (WDI) database, the International Energy Agency (IEA) and the Penn World Table and etc. The explanation of major indexes and variables is as follows:

Economic activities and labor force indexes: primarily refer to the economic output (represented with the GDP at dollars calculated at the constant price in 2000), material capital input (capital stock) and the

① At present, the European Union consists of 27 countries. Except for the 15 selected member countries, there are another 12 member countries. However, since their data were unavailable, they are not included.

quantitative labor force. Among them, the capital stock is processed according to the method in most literature as follows: form the measurement index of Investment I with the capital at the constant price; first, we must evaluate the original year's (1980) capital stock K_0. When it is stable, the capital output ratio (K/Y) is constant which means that the increase rate of the capital and output is equal, therefore, $dK_t = I_t - \delta K_t \Rightarrow (dK_t/K_t)\ (K_t/Y_t) = (I_t/Y_t) - (\delta K_t/Y_t)$. Since when it is stable, the output increase rate is equal to the capital increase rate, $(dY_t/Y_t)\ (K_t/Y_t) = (I_t/Y_t) - (\delta K_t/Y_t) \Rightarrow (g_t + \delta)\ (K_t/) = (I_t/Y_t)$, then $(K_t/Y_t)* = (I_t/Y_t)*/(g_t^* + \delta)$, in which * stands for stable value, δ for rate of depreciation, setting at 7%. The output increase rate g_t^* at the stable condition is not the actual output increase rate $g_{t.}$ Based on the assumption of King and Levin (1994), it has the following equation: $g* = \lambda g + (1 - \lambda)\ g_w$, in which g_w is the world's economic average increase rate during the sample period, about 4%, g, the average output increase rate and λ, weight, set at 25%. In this way, using the average investment I and GDP in the first five years of the sample period, it is easy to get a stable capital output ratio and if multiplying the average annual output GDP in the said five years, we can get the original year's capital stock K_0. The annual capital stock can be obtained from the perpetual inventory method $K_t = I_t + (1 - \delta)$. In this way, we can estimate the capital stock in dollars, calculated at the constant price of 30 countries in 2000.

Energy use and environmental index: energy use, especially the fossil energy use, is the major reason causing global warming and here it is represented as the total energy consumption; the environmental index is measured with different countries' carbon dioxide emissions.

The descriptive statistics of the major variables are shown in Table 1.

Table 1 Simple Descriptive Statistics of the Variables in Representative Years

Year	Index	Carbon Dioxide Emissions	Energy Consumption Volume	GDP	Capital Forms	Labor Force	Capital stock
		K_t (1,000 tons)	K_t (1,000 tons' petroleum equivalent)	100 million dollars (constant price at 2000)	100 million dollars (constant price at 2000)	10,000 persons	100 million dollars (constant price at 2000)
1980	Average	501059. 7	189590. 2	5156. 7	1112. 0	4660. 0	10317. 9
1980	Maximum	4624761. 0	1811648. 0	51280. 0	8206. 2	50312. 8	77160. 1
1980	Minimum	26054. 9	8485. 0	338. 6	81. 3	125. 3	729. 2
1980	Standard Deviation	906916. 5	346952. 6	10261. 1	1991. 0	10139. 6	18994. 7
1981	Average	488688. 8	187395. 9	5266. 9	1114. 1	4759. 3	38118. 8
1981	Maximum	4455721. 0	1761646. 0	52574. 0	8427. 8	51674. 5	72168. 8
1981	Minimum	25586. 1	8505. 0	349. 8	79. 7	126. 9	20028. 8
1981	Standard Deviation	876591. 1	338825. 2	10516. 6	2069. 9	10406. 7	14401. 9
1985	Average	518934. 1	200130. 6	5902. 1	1232. 7	5150. 0	17145. 5
1985	Maximum	4424461. 0	1781406. 0	60110. 0	10070. 0	57872. 4	23380. 8
1985	Minimum	26413. 9	8862. 0	348. 0	67. 1	131. 7	13025. 6
1985	Standard Deviation	910506. 5	348233. 7	11974. 5	2367. 8	11540. 2	2673. 4
1990	Average	566437. 9	224703. 0	7072. 0	1603. 0	5674. 5	22485. 5
1990	Maximum	4816160. 0	1927628. 0	70550. 0	13591. 5	65013. 7	29996. 3
1990	Minimum	30611. 7	10409. 0	432. 2	70. 5	133. 2	16715. 1
1990	Standard Deviation	990826. 9	382489. 7	14274. 8	3025. 6	12883. 3	3577. 8
1995	Average	599890. 7	244754. 5	7920. 9	1733. 2	6074. 9	24047. 1
1995	Maximum	5181892. 0	2088484. 0	79728. 0	13415. 0	70015. 5	31747. 8
1995	Minimum	33179. 5	11002. 0	383. 5	76. 0	146. 8	18928. 4
1995	Standard Deviation	1067037. 0	413474. 7	15937. 5	3276. 0	13887. 0	3663. 6
2000	Average	628313. 5	266083. 1	9136. 9	2087. 2	6486. 7	28572. 5
2000	Maximum	5792339. 0	2304191. 0	97648. 0	20007. 0	73892. 9	40890. 2
2000	Minimum	41520. 1	14285. 0	470. 3	140. 6	175. 9	21426. 8
2000	Standard Deviation	1127291. 0	450734. 9	18912. 8	4049. 8	14773. 2	4523. 5
2005	Average	720568. 1	289235. 2	10602. 6	2312. 3	6895. 2	32620. 1
2005	Maximum	5897151. 0	2384601. 0	110464. 3	21190. 5	77604. 7	44373. 3
2005	Minimum	42945. 0	16326. 8	577. 0	138. 6	208. 2	23760. 4
2005	Standard Deviation	1299005. 0	483722. 5	21202. 5	4220. 1	15666. 7	5127. 5

Data source: the World Bank Development Index (WDI) database, IEA, Penn World Trade.

5. Data Analysis

1. Eco-efficiency Comparison

Based on the linear programming of formula (6), we can obtain the eco-efficiency of 30 countries during 1980 to 2005, with which to examine the coordination levels between these countries' economic development and environmental regulation. Before we obtain the result, it is essential to explain that formula (6) is based on the weak disposability of DEA and is from the perspective of output, namely, to control the sample country's carbon dioxide emissions, we must consider sacrificing certain output losses. The linear programming of formula (6) equates the weight of the input and output variable, namely, input: desirable output: undesirable output = 1: 1: 1. And the eco-efficiency for the representative years is based on the programming calculation shown in Table 2.

Table 2 The Eco-Efficiency of G20 Countries in Representative Years

Nation	Abbreviation	1981	1985	1990	1995	2000	2005
Argentina	ARG	0.811	0.767	0.710	0.757	0.732	0.820
Australia	AUT	0.658	0.652	0.631	0.638	0.642	0.656
Austria	AUS	0.836	0.835	0.836	0.860	0.891	0.842
Belgium	BEL	0.758	0.745	0.743	0.745	0.786	0.818
Brazil	BRA	0.854	0.835	0.792	0.767	0.732	0.761
Canada	CAN	0.666	0.666	0.666	0.663	0.677	0.663
China	CHN	0.521	0.522	0.524	0.531	0.555	0.551
Denmark	DNK	0.800	0.765	0.823	0.822	0.948	1.000
Finland	FIN	0.737	0.750	0.750	0.712	0.767	0.726
France	FRA	0.808	0.844	0.889	0.918	0.967	0.956
Germany	GER	0.688	0.679	0.705	0.765	0.804	0.800
Greece	GRE	0.759	0.698	0.661	0.654	0.644	0.666
Hungary	HUN	0.576	0.572	0.589	0.575	0.583	0.609
India	IND	0.569	0.557	0.551	0.547	0.548	0.558
Indonesia	INA	0.601	0.590	0.591	0.583	0.560	0.567
Irish	IRL	0.712	0.703	0.702	0.730	0.799	0.862

(contd.)

Nation	Abbreviation	1981	1985	1990	1995	2000	2005
Italy	ITA	0. 820	0. 814	0. 812	0. 809	0. 822	0. 808
Japan	JPN	1. 000	1. 000	1. 000	1. 000	1. 000	1. 000
Korea	KOR	0. 658	0. 648	0. 649	0. 634	0. 639	0. 656
Mexico	MEX	0. 688	0. 681	0. 641	0. 648	0. 673	0. 680
Poland	POL	0. 524	0. 526	0. 542	0. 543	0. 555	0. 574
Portuguese	POR	0. 884	0. 794	0. 756	0. 724	0. 711	0. 725
Russia	RUS	0. 520	0. 520	0. 522	0. 519	0. 520	0. 528
Saudi Arabia	SAU	1. 000	0. 602	0. 592	0. 579	0. 571	0. 577
South Africa	ZAF	0. 568	0. 551	0. 548	0. 540	0. 539	0. 546
Spain	SPN	0. 758	0. 761	0. 767	0. 752	0. 748	0. 751
Switzerland	SWE	0. 868	0. 908	1. 000	1. 000	1. 000	1. 000
Turkey	TUR	0. 672	0. 632	0. 620	0. 613	0. 597	0. 628
Britain	GBR	0. 743	0. 743	0. 758	0. 788	0. 831	0. 854
America	USA	1. 000	1. 000	1. 000	1. 000	1. 000	1. 000
Average		0. 735	0. 712	0. 712	0. 714	0. 728	0. 739

Data source: calculation by the author.

Figure 2 shows the basic variation of the eco-efficiency in the 30 countries from 1980 to 2005, which can be roughly captured by a "V" shape, meaning that these countries at least have experienced the stage from a high eco-efficiency to vacillation and rebound. The variation during this period can be attributed to developed countries' efforts to control carbon emissions and developing countries' increasing carbon emissions for their efforts to vigorously develop the industrialization, but the overall fluctuations are small. In Table 2, the "best practitioners" are developed countries represented by America and Japan. While realizing industrialization, they made certain achievements in environmental regulation and showed a good coordination between economic development and environmental regulation.

Take 2005 as an example, we can subjectively categorize eco-efficiency or the coordination between economic development and environmental regulation into the following types:

First, if the eco-efficiency is during (0. 9-1. 0], it represents high-

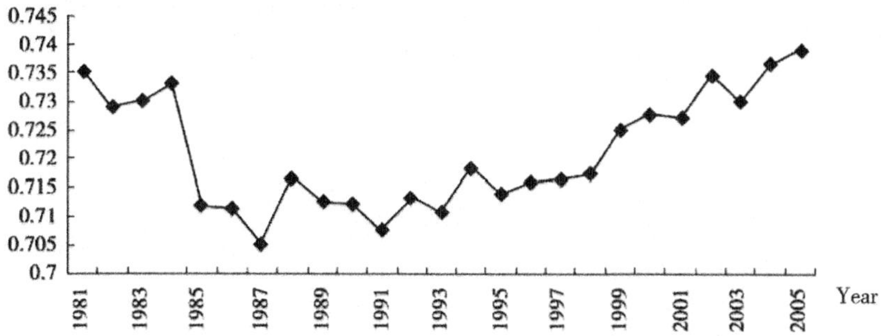

Figure 2 Variation Trend of the Eco-Efficiency in G20 Countries

coordination nations, represented by America, Japan, Denmark, France and Switzerland;

Second, if the eco-efficiency is during (0. 7- 0. 9], it represents comparatively high-coordination nations, represented by Argentina, Austria, Belgium, Brazil, Finland, Germany, Irish, Italy, Portuguese, Spain and Britain;

Third, if the eco-efficiency is during (0. 6- 0. 7], it represents nations of average coordination level, represented by Australia, Canada, Hungary, Greece, Korea, Mexico and Turkey.

Fourth, if the eco-efficiency is below 0. 6, it represents low-coordination nations, represented by China, India, Indonesia, Poland, Russia, Saudi Arabia and South Africa.

From the above categorization, we can identify an obvious rule, namely, the eco-efficiency is in a positive correlation to a nation's national income per capita, with the correlation coefficient reaching 0. 7116 (see Figure 3). Further studies show that the two have obvious linear correlation, rather than an "inverted U shape" or a polynomial relationship. This is different from the variation trend of the Environmental Kuznets Curve (EKC).

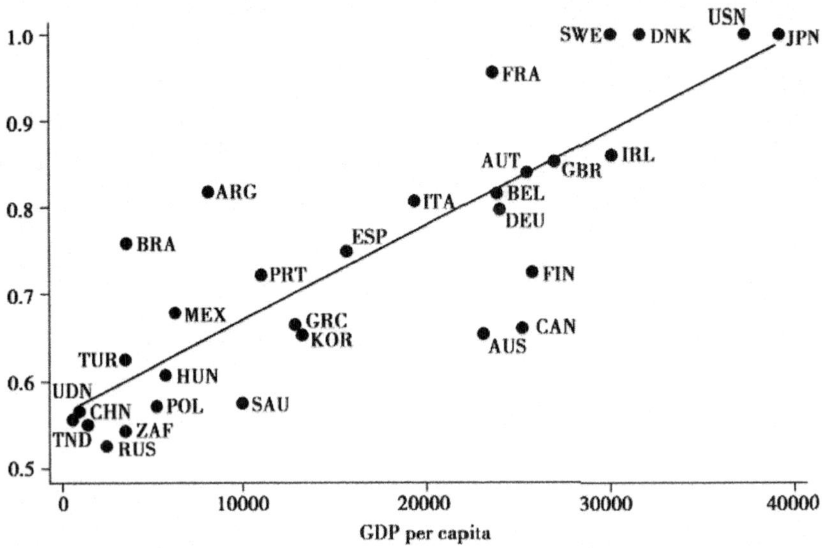

Figure 3 Relationship between the Eco-Efficiency Index (EEI) and per Capita GDP of G20 Countries in 2005

2. Comparison between the Eco-Efficiency under Different Weight Settings

The above mentioned analysis used the same input and output weight, which considered the economic growth and environmental protection (regulation) as being equally important. It is generally felt that environmental protection and economic development are uncoordinated and contradictory: the advocacy of environmental protection will inevitably slow down the economic development; the pursuit of the economic development index is at the sacrifice of the environment. If the nation's policy is biased, it may be biased toward economic growth, but it may also be biased toward environmental protection (regulation). The biased policy will surely influence the coordination between economy and environment and also symbolizes a differentiated attitude toward environment and economic development. An interesting question is if the government fails to treat economic development and environmental protections equally, then how will the eco-efficiency change?

To answer this question, we might as well divide the government's attitude toward the relationship between the two into three types: first, treat the two equally; second, make economic development as the priority, namely, endow more weight to the economic output GDP than environmental protection; thirdly, make environmental protection as the priority, namely, endow more weight to environmental protection than economic development. As for the first condition, we have already made estimation analysis of it in the first section. As for the second and the third conditions, we first assumed that the corresponding weights between the desirable output GDP and the undesirable output carbon dioxide was 2: 1 and 1: 2. Similarly, with formula (6) linear programming, we changed the weight setting and the average eco-efficiency variation as shown in Figure 4.

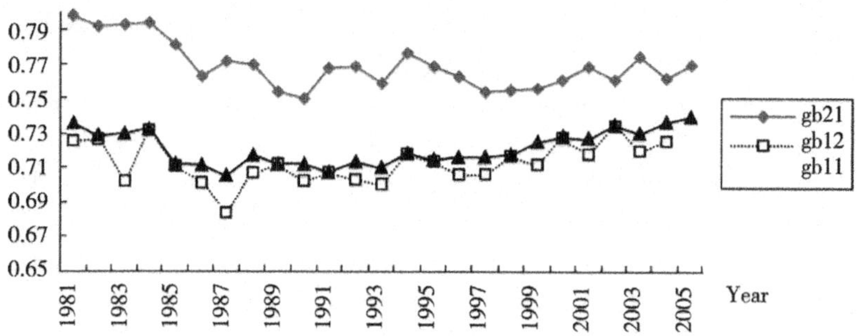

Figure 4 Comparisons between the Average Eco-Efficiency of Different Weights

Note: gb21, gb12 and gb11 respectively stand for the weight ratio 2: 1, 1: 2 and 1: 1 between the desirable output GDP and carbon dioxide emission.

Figure 4 shows the comparisons between the eco-efficiencies under different weight settings. It proves that the government's different policy bias will change the country's eco-efficiency and influence the coordination level between economic development and environmental protection. When the government's policy is biased toward economic development (weight 2: 1), the eco-efficiency is obviously higher than that when the two are equally treated, an average of about 6% higher; when the policy is biased toward environmental protection (weight 1:2), the eco-efficiency is around 1% lower than that when the two are equally treated. It can be seen that the change of the eco-efficiency is more sensitive to the policy's bias toward economic development than environmental protection. The policy implication shows that the bias toward economic development rather than environmental protection in a short term has more room for efficiency improvement. Therefore, different countries have a stronger "impulse"① to develop their economy, improve their national income and accumulate more wealth in a short span of time.

3. Comparisons between the Eco-Efficiency under Different Environmental Regulations

This article primarily considered three scenarios:

- Scenario 1: the direction vector is g = (y, 0), and in designing the production technology, the undesirable output is not considered.
- Scenario 2: the direction vector is g = (y, -b), and the undesirable output has weak disposability in technologies.
- Scenario 3: the direction vector is g = (y, -b), and the undesirable output has strong disposability in technologies.

In Scenario 1, there are no environmental regulations. In Scenario 2, there are rigid environmental regulations under which the desirable output increases and the undesirable output decreases and should be realized at the same rate. In Scenario 3, there are even more rigid environmental regulations under which the undesirable output can be processed freely and the desirable output should be increased.

Corresponding to formula (6) is Scenario 2. With slight adjustments, formula (6) can respectively correspond to Scenario 2 and Scenario 3. Refer to formula (7) and (8) for detailed linear programming.

$$\overset{1}{D}_0(x, y^g, 0; y^g, 0) = max\beta$$

$$s.t.$$

$$Y^g\lambda + s^{g+} = (1+\beta)y^g_0$$

$$X\lambda - s^- = x_0$$

$$\lambda \geqslant 0 \qquad (7)$$

① But the above conclusion and policy implication cannot be understood as the mere economic development without any attention to environmental protection is favorable to improve the national eco-efficiency, since the above mentioned is year-by-year evaluations irrespective of the long-term impact and the risk brought to economic development when the threshold value is exceeded.

$$\vec{D}_0(x, y^g, y^b; y^g, -y^b) = max\beta$$

s. t.

$$Y^g\lambda + s^{g+} = (1+\beta)y_0^g$$

$$Y^b\lambda - s^{g-} = (1-\beta)y_0^b$$

$$X\lambda - s^- = x_0$$

$$\lambda \geq 0 \qquad (8)$$

In Scenario 1, it is irrespective of the environmental pollution problem, but only considers the efficiency of the economic development; or it can be said that there are no scenarios for environmental regulations. Scenario 2 occurs when the pollution has weak disposability, which means that to protect the environment, and to decrease carbon dioxide emissions, we must consider the impact on or cost of the economic output while making environmental regulations. Scenario 3 assumes that the pollution can be disposed freely (decreased or increased) and more rigid regulations can be enforced. From the DEA programming model under these three regulation scenarios, three eco-efficiencies under different conditions can be obtained.

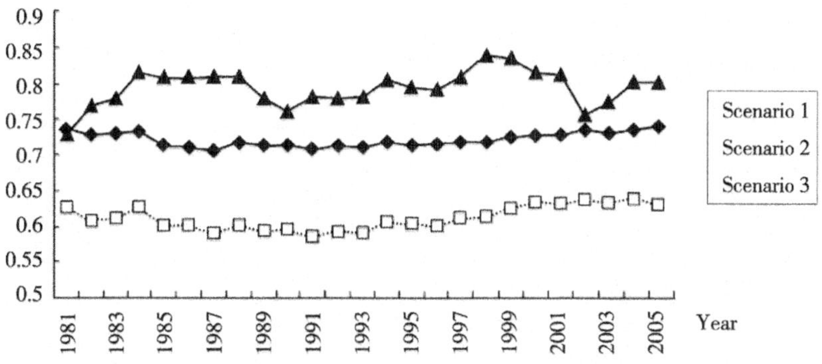

Figure 5 The Eco-Efficiency under Different Regulation Scenarios

Figure 5 shows the comparisons between the average eco-efficiency of G20 countries under the three different regulation scenarios. Obviously, when there are no environmental regulations or when carbon dioxide emission remains untreated, the average eco-efficiency is higher than the efficiency of the other two scenarios; when the environmental regulation policies grow from weak to strong, the eco-efficiency is decreasing, which shows that the eco-efficiency varies with the rigidity level of the environmental regulation policies. Rigid environmental regulation policies will, to a certain degree, jeopardize a nation's economic development abilities and income levels. The more rigid the policies are, the higher the regulation costs will be.

Table 3 The Eco-Efficiency of G20 Countries under Different Regulation Scenarios in 2005

Nation	Scenario 1	Scenario 2	Scenario 3
Argentina	0. 964	0. 820	0. 804
Australia	0. 669	0. 656	0. 641
Austria	0. 894	0. 842	0. 828
Belgium	0. 861	0. 818	0. 816
Brazil	0. 898	0. 761	0. 695
Canada	0. 826	0. 663	0. 649
China	0. 545	0. 551	0. 375
Denmark	1. 000	1. 000	0. 903
Finland	0. 899	0. 726	0. 718
France	0. 919	0. 956	0. 954
Germany	1. 000	0. 800	0. 765
Greece	0. 734	0. 666	0. 607
Hungary	0. 714	0. 609	0. 400
India	0. 552	0. 558	0. 247
Indonesia	0. 749	0. 567	0. 258
Irish	0. 862	0. 862	0. 509
Italy	0. 881	0. 808	0. 576
Japan	1. 000	1. 000	0. 370
Korea	0. 642	0. 656	0. 659
Mexico	0. 810	0. 680	0. 146
Poland	0. 844	0. 574	0. 497
Portuguese	0. 760	0. 725	0. 860
Russia	1. 000	0. 528	0. 783
Saudi Arabia	1. 000	0. 577	1. 000

(contd.)

Nation	Scenario 1	Scenario 2	Scenario 3
South Africa	1.000	0.546	0.235
Spain	0.742	0.751	0.685
Switzerland	1.000	1.000	1.000
Turkey	0.656	0.628	0.471
Britain	1.000	0.854	0.840
America	1.000	1.000	1.000

Data source: calculation by the author.

6. Research Conclusion and Discussion

1. Research Conclusion

This article first fully summarized the concept and theoretical development of eco-efficiency and its empirical application in China, pointed out the unanimous contradiction or inconsistency on the definition of the eco-efficiency concept in studies both in China and foreign countries; in China, there are still confusion about its translation and connotation; there are also conflicts between the micro and macro aspect in the application range or area of the eco-efficiency research. We have sorted out these problems and redefined their concepts, and pointed out that it is not only applicable to the micro area but also the macro area. Next, we made a systematic summary of the methodology on eco-efficiency, which can generally be divided into two basic methods: one is LCA (Life Cycle Analysis) and the other is the nonparametric DEA method. The first requires the research subject to be the extracting, processing, manufacturing, transporting and circulating, use, reuse, maintenance, recycling and ultimate disposal of the micro economic players' raw materials. It evaluates and quantifies the potential influence of the resources, energy consumption and waste discharges on the environment and obtains its eco-efficiency, which is not suitable for mid-scale and macro level analysis. The second, since it is nonparametric, it can exclude the market price of the pollutant from its consideration, which is more suitable for the efficiency evaluation of the major economic players involved in market behaviors and when you are unable to estimate the market price of the pollutant discharge. It can not only be used in the evaluation of the micro players, but also be used in the evaluation at the mid-scale and macro level. This article summarized six different methods to evaluate the DEA's eco-efficiency and pointed out the deficiencies of the current studies, particularly in China, which are unable to distinguish different methods and point out their connections.

Based on the literature review above, this article used the directional distance function of the nonparametric DEA method as the basic method of this research. Because of its good applicability, it is commonly used in foreign literature. This article analyzed the characteristics and merits of the directional distance function method in processing undesirable output and compared the eco-efficiencies of the 30 nations in G20 from 1980 to 2005. The main conclusions are as follows:

First, under weak disposability, when economic development and carbon dioxide emission are treated equally (same weight), the sample countries can be divided into four types based on the coordination level between their economy and environment: high-coordination countries, comparatively high-coordination countries, countries of average coordination level and low-coordination countries. From this division, we found that the eco-efficiency level is in obvious positive correlation or linear correlation with the nation's income level, with the correlation coefficient reaching 0.71.

Second, the article simulated the influence of the government's policy bias on eco-efficiency. When the policy is biased toward economic development, the average eco-efficiency during the sample period is 6% higher than that when the two are equally treated; when the policy is biased toward environmental protection, the average eco-efficiency during the sample period is only 1% higher than that when the two are equally treated. It shows that the government's policy bias can indeed change eco-efficiency which is more sensitive to the bias toward an economic target than environmental protection.

Third, the article simulated how the presence or absence of the government's environmental regulation policy and its enforcement level influence the national eco-efficiency. The research finds that when the pollutant discharge is not considered or there is no environmental regulation policy, the eco-efficiency is maintained at a high level; when the environmental regulation becomes rigid, the average eco-efficiency is decreasing. It shows that more rigid environmental regulation policies at least harm the national economic output in a short span.

2. Discussions on the Result

The conclusion that developed countries or high-income countries have higher eco-efficiency are only relative evaluations and objective descriptions with the DEA method under the condition that the economic development and carbon emissions in the G20 countries cannot be changed. This research didn't take the historical responsibilities and obligations of the two groups into consideration, which means the results cannot be used to show that developing countries and developed countries share the same emission reduction obligations and the conclusion cannot be used to guide the international climate negotiations.

Although the international community has already tried its best to allow for the fairness and justice principle, in reality, the two major interests groups, developed countries and developing countries, still have great conflicts in the environmental problem, on which there still exists various unfair phenomena. Internationally, it can be said that a large number of contemporary environmental policies create unequal benefits and burden distributions and almost all developed countries tend to maximize environmental burden for developing countries and maximize their enjoyment of environmental benefits. Such a phenomenon is called environmental unfairness. The above mentioned evaluation result is only one manifestation of the environmental unfairness.

Because of the large gap between the development level of developed countries and developing countries, first, there is obvious unfairness in the two interest groups' possession and utilization of international resources; second, there is unfairness in the distribution of environmental benefits and responsibilities. Through several centuries' industrialization and resource appropriation, developed countries have transferred their pollution to developing countries and have left the good environment all to themselves, while at the same time, refusing to shoulder their pollution responsibilities. Finally, developed countries set green trade barriers in international trade to maximize their environmental benefits and limit developing countries' development. The green trade barrier actually refers to a country setting specific and discriminatory trade barriers to the importation of foreign goods or trade barriers, unnecessary to normal environmental protection under the pretext of protecting their ecological environment and with the aim to limit importation and protect of its own supplies.

To improve developing countries' eco-efficiency and promote a coordinated development between economy and environment, the fundamental way is to maximize economic growth and improve income while minimizing environmental pressure; unite developing countries to change the current "game rule" in the environment and trade dominated by developed countries and establish fair environmental protection and climate convention rules or laws based on the principle of "shared but differentiated principle," at last, a fair environmental and climate system which can coordinate the interests of developed countries and developing countries is not possible without international dialogues and cooperation on environmental issues.

References:

[1] Charnes A., W. W. Cooper, E. Rhodes. 1978. Measuring the Efficiency of Decision Making Units. *European Journal of Operational Research*, 2 (6): 429-444.

[2] Charnes, A., Cooper, W. W., 1962. Programming with Linear Fractional Functions. *Naval Research Logistics Quarterly*, 15: 333-334.

[3] Fare, Rolf, Grosskopf, Shawna and Pasurka, Carl A. 2003. Environmental Production Functions and Environmental Directional Distance Functions: A Joint Production Comparison (February 19, 2003). *Available at SSRN*, http://ssrn.com/abstract = 506222.

[4] Fare, Rolf, Shawna Grosskopf, C. A. K. Lovell, and Carl Pasurka. 1989. Multilateral Productivity Comparisons When Some Outputs are Undesirable: A Nonparametric Approach. *Review of Economics and Statistics*, 71 (1): 90-98.

[5] Fussler, Claude. 1996. *Driving Eco Innovation*. Pitman Publishing.

[6] Hailu, Atakelty, and Terrence S. Veeman. 2001. Non-Parametric Productivity Analysis with Undesirable Outputs: An Application to the Canadian Pulp and Paper Industry. *American Journal of Agricultural Economics*, 83 (3): 805-816.

[7] Hedstrom G, Poltorzycki S, Stroh P. 1998. Sustainable Development: The Next Generation. *Prism-Sustainable Development: How Real, How Soon, And Who's Doing What?* No. 4 (1998), Cambridge MA: Arthur D. Little: 5-19.

[8] Holiday C. 2001. Sustainable Growth, the Dupont Way, *Harvard Business Review*, September 2001: 129-134.

[9] IFOK. 1997. Bausteine fur ein zukunftsfahiges Deutschland, Diskursprojekt im Auftrag von VCI und IG Chemie-Papier-Keramik, Wiesbaden: Gabler.

[10] Jefferson, Gary H., Albert G. Z. Hu, Xiaojing Guan and Xiaoyun Yu. 2003. Ownership, Performance, and Innovation in China's Large and Medium Size Industrial Enterprise Sector. *China Economic Review*, 14: 89-113.

[11] Jefferson, Gary H., Thomas G. Rawski and Yuxin Zheng. 1996. Chinese Industrial Productivity: Trends, Measurement Issues and Recent Developments. *Journal*

of Comparative Economics, 23: 146-180.

[12] King, Robert G. and Levine, Ross. 1994. Capital Fundamentalism, Economic Development, and Economic Growth, *Carnegie-Rochester Conference Series* on Public Policy, 40: 259-92.

[13] Magnus Lindmark and Peter Vikstrom. 2003. Global Convergence in Productivity—A Distance Function Approach to Technical Change and Efficiency Improvements. Paper for the conference "Catching-up growth and technology transfers in Asia and Western Europe", Groningen 17-18 October, 2003.

[14] OECD. 1998. Eco-Efficiency, Pre-Publication copy.

[15] Pittman, Russell W. 1983. Multilateral Productivity Comparisons with Undesirable Outputs. *Economic Journal*, 93: 883-891.

[16] Schaltegger, Sturm. 1990. Okologische Rationalitat: Ansatzpunkte Zur Ausgestaltung Von Okologieorienttierten Management Instrumenten. *Die Unternehmung*, 4: 273-290.

[17] Scheel, H., 2001. Undesirable Outputs in Efficiency Valuations. *European Journal of Operational Research*, 132: 400-410.

[18] Seiford, L. M., Zhu, J., 2002. Modeling Undesirable Factors in Efficiency Evaluation. *European Journal of Operational Research*, 142: 16-20.

[19] Sun, Haishun, Phillip Hone and Hristos Do ucouliagos. 1999. Economic Openness and Technical Efficiency. *Economics of Transition*, 7 (3): 615-636.

[20] Tone, K. 2003. Dealing with Undesirable Outputs in DEA: A Slacks-based Measure (SBM) Approach. *GRIPS Research Report Series* I-2003-0005.

[21] Wu Yanrui. 2000. Is China's Economic Growth Sustainable? A Productivity Analysis. *China Economic Review*, 11: 278-296.

[22] Zheng Jinghai, Xaoxuan Liu and Arne Bigsten. 1998. Ownership Structure and Determinants of Technical Efficiency: An Application of Data Envelopment Analysis to Chinese Enterprises (1986-1990). *Journal of Comparative Economics*, 26: 465-484.

[23] Zheng Jinghai, Xiaoxuan Liu and Arne Bigsten. 2003. Efficiency, Technical Progress, and the Best Practice in Chinese State Enterprises (1980-1994). *Journal of Comparative Economics*, 31: 134-152.

[24] Zhu, J., 2003. Quantitative Models for Performance Evaluation and Benchmarking: Data Envelopment Analysis with Spreadsheets and DEA Excel Solver. Kluwer Academic Publishers.

[25] Zofio, J. L., A. M. Prieto. 2001. Environmental Efficiency and Regulatory Standards: the Case of CO_2 Emissions from OECD Industries. *Resource and Energy Economics* 23: 63-83.

[26] Bu Ludan. Ecological efficiency and environmental cost management. *Finance and Accounting Monthly (Synthetic)*, 2007(10).

步丹璐:《生态效率与环境成本管理》,《财会月刊》(综合)2007 年第 10 期。

[27] Gao Qianshan. Ecological efficiency——an important index of enterprise environmental performance auditing evaluation. *Economic Forum*, 2006(7).

高前善:《生态效率——企业环境绩效审计评价的一个重要指标》,《经济论坛》2006 年第 7 期。

[28] Hao Weichang. *Evaluation of the environmental load of metal materials and*

the development of their LCA database. Lanzhou University, 2000.

郝维昌:《金属材料的环境负荷评价及其 LCA 数据库的开发》,兰州大学,2000年。

[29] Hu Angang, et al.. Provincial technical efficiency ranking in consideration of the environmental factors (1999-2005). *China Economic Quarterly*, 2008(7).

胡鞍钢等:《考虑环境因素的省级技术效率排名(1990-2005)》,《经济学(季刊)》2008 年第 7 期。

[30] Ke Jian & Li Chao. Research on the coordinated development between China's regional resources, environment and economy based on DEA clustering analysis. *China Soft Science*, 2005(2).

柯健、李超:《基于 DEA 聚类分析的中国各地区资源、环境与经济协调发展研究》,《中国软科学》2005 年第 2 期。

[31] Kou Xinli. *Evaluation of the environmental load of high polymer materials.* Lanzhou University, 1999.

寇昕莉:《高分子材料的环境负荷评价》,兰州大学,1999 年。

[32] Li Bing, et al.. Research on the enterprise's ecological footprint and ecological efficiency. *Environmental Engineering*, 2007(25).

李兵等:《企业生态足迹与生态效率研究》,《环境工程》2007 年第 25 期。

[33] Li Guiqi. Nie Zuoren & Zhou Hemin, et al.. Evaluation of the environmental coordination in iron and steel production. *Journal of Central South University of Technology*, 2002 (33).

李贵奇、聂祚仁、周和敏等:《钢铁生产的环境协调性评价》,《中南工业大学学报》2002 年第 33 期。

[34] Liao Hong & Zhu Tan. Exploration of the relationshipbetween ecological economy efficiency and environmental management development. *Shanghai Environmental Sciences*, 2002(21).

廖红、朱坦:《生态经济效率环境管理发展的关系探讨》,《上海环境科学》2002 年第 21 期。

[35] Liu Jianglong, Ding Peidao & Qian Xiaorong. Environmental impact factor of metal materials and their evaluation. *Progress in Environmental Science*, 1996(4).

刘江龙、丁培道、钱小蓉:《金属材料的环境影响因子及其评价》,《环境科学进展》1996 年第 4 期。

[36] Liu Jianglong, Ding Peidao & Zhang Jing. Quantitative evaluation of metal materials' surface strengthening process influence on the environment. *China Surface Engineering*, 2000(1).

刘江龙、丁培道、张静:《金属材料表面强化过程对环境影响的定量评价》,《中国表面工程》2000 年第 1 期。

[37] Lu Zhongwu & Cai Jiuju. The influence of the logistics of iron and steel production process on energy consumption. *Acta Metallurgica Sinica*, 2000(36).

陆钟武、蔡九菊:《钢铁生产流程的物流对能耗的影响》,《金属学报》2000 年第 36 期。

[38] Ma Yujun, Huang Xianjin, Xiao Sisi & Wang Shu. Evaluation of regional ecological environmental construction performance based on the DEA model——take Suzhou in Jiangsu Province as an example. *Resources and Environment in the Yangtze*

Basin, 2007(6).

马育军、黄贤金、肖思思、王舒:《基于 DEA 模型的区域生态环境建设绩效评价——以江苏省苏州市为例》,《长江流域资源与环境》2007 年第 6 期。

[39] Su Xiangdong, Wang Tianmin & He Li, et al.. Environmental load evaluation model of nonferrous materials. *Acta Scientiae Circumstantiae*, 2002(22).

苏向东、王天民、何力等:《有色金属材料的环境负荷定量评价模型》,《环境科学学报》2002 年第 22 期。

[40] Sun Guangsheng, et al.. Application of DEA in evaluating industrial production environmental efficiency. *Journal of Anhui Normal University (Natural Science)*, 2003(2).

孙广生等:《DEA 在评价工业生产环境效率上的应用》,《安徽师范大学学报(自然科学版)》2003 年第 2 期。

[41] Tu Zhengge. Coordination between environment, resources and industrial growth——analysis of the industry above the designated scale based on directional environment distance function. *Economic Research*, 2008(2).

涂正革:《环境、资源与工业增长的协调性——基于方向性环境距离函数对规模以上工业的分析》,《经济研究》2008 年第 2 期。

[42] Wang Bing & Wu Yanrui. Environmental regulation and total factor productivity increase: empirical study of APEC. *Economic Research*, 2008(5).

王兵、吴延瑞:《环境管制与全要素生产率增长:APEC 的实证研究》,《经济研究》2008 年第 5 期。

[43] Wang Jinnan. Developing circular economy is the strategic choice of the environmental protection in the 21st century. *Research of Environmental Sciences*, 2002(15).

王金南:《发展循环经济是 21 世纪环境保护的战略选择》,《环境科学研究》2002 年第 15 期。

[44] Wang Shoubing, Wang Rusong & Wu Qianhong. A method to calculate theresource depletion potential and equivalent coefficient in the life cycle evaluation. *Journal of Fudan University (Natural Science)*, 2001(40).

王寿兵、王如松、吴千红:《生命周期评价中资源的耗竭潜力及当量系数的一种算法》,《复旦学报》(自然科学版)2001 年第 40 期。

[45] Xi Deli & Peng Xiaoyan. Obtaining of the inventory analysis data in LCA. *Environmental Science*, 1997(18).

席德立、彭小燕:《LCA 中清单分析数据的获得》,《环境科学》1997 年第 18 期。

[46] Xia Kaixuan, et al.. Research on car sharing service based on economic biological efficiency theory. *Management World*, 2007(11).

夏凯旋等:《基于经济生态效率理论的汽车共享服务研究》,《管理世界》2007 年第 11 期。

[47] Yue Yuanyuan & Su Jingqin. Ecological efficiency: foreign practices and China's policies. *Studies in Science of Science*, 2004(22).

岳媛媛、苏敬勤:《生态效率:国外的实践与我国的对策》,《科学学研究》2004 年第 22 期。

[48] Zhang Bing, et al.. The enterprise ecological efficiency evaluation based on

DEA: take enterprises in the Hangzhou Bay Fine Chemistry Industrial Park as an example. *System Engineering Theory and Practice*, 2008(4).

张炳等:《基于 DEA 的企业生态效率评价:以杭州湾精细化工园区企业为例》,《系统工程理论与实践》2008 年第 4 期。

[49] Zhang Qun & Xun Zhiyuan. Project environmental efficiency evaluation based on DEA. *Science & Technology Progress and Policy*, 2007(24).

张群、荀志远:《基于数据包络分析方法的项目环境效率评价》《科学进步与对策》2007 年第 24 期。

[50] Zhou Guomei, Peng Hao & Cao Fengzhong. Index system of circular economy and industrial ecological efficiency. *Urban Environment & Urban Ecology*, 2003(16).

周国梅、彭昊、曹凤中:《循环经济和工业生态效率指示体系》,《城市环境与城市生态》2003 年第 16 期。

[51] Zhu Dajian & Qiu Shoufeng. Ecological efficiency is the proper measure of circular economy. *China Population Resources and Environment*, 2006(16).

诸大建、邱寿丰:《生态效率是循环经济的合适测试》,《中国人口 · 资源与环境》2006 年第 16 期。

Part IV
Trade and Sustainability

Influences of International Trade on China's Energy Demands and Environmental Quality

By ZHANG Youguo

I. Introduction

Since the Second World War, a prominent feature of the evolution of global political and economic relations has been the ongoing deepening and expansion of globalization. Since 1978, against such a worldwide backdrop, China has begun to implement the basic national policy of overall opening up and gradually integrating itself into the global economic system. Up to now, China's opening up policy has been in place for 30 years. During this process, China's foreign trade has made great progress and contributed enormously to China's economic development. However, at the same time, there are many problems with China's trade development strategy. The trade growth has also brought many negative influences on China's economic and social development. Many scholars have reflected upon China's trade development strategy. The influence of trade on China's energy demand and ecological environment has been a problem of wide concern during recent years.

With the increase of foreign trade, China has long been acknowledged as a "global factory." With China's accession to the WTO, its trade has increased rapidly. However, concomitantly, China's resource consumption and environmental pollution have been aggravated. It is exactly owing to this that people naturally relate the rapid trade increase with China's energy consumption and environmental pollution during recent years, assuming that trade expansion is one major reason for the difficulties in improving China's energy conservation and environmental pollution.

How much does trade really contribute to China's energy consumption and pollutant discharge? Since the reform and opening up, what are the changes in the influence of trade on China's energy consumption and relative environmental influences? Are these changes mainly caused by the trade expansion or the technical changes of the trade department or by the structural changes of the trade products? How should we view and cope with the influences of trade on China's energy consumption and environment? Answers to these questions can provide important references for relevant policy makers and researchers to have an objective understanding of the trade influence on China's energy consumption and environment and make appropriate polices and introduce appropriate measures.

This article consists of the following parts: the second part is a literature review; the third part introduces the methodology; the fourth part is an explanation of relative data processing; the fifth part is the result; the sixth part is a review on the environmental influence of China's trade; the seventh part is the conclusion.

II. Literature Review

Internationally, studies on the measure of environmental influence caused by trade began in the 1990s. Lee and Roland-Holst (1993) proposed the "Embodied Effluent Trade, EET" concept to describe a country's resource consumption in producing exports. This concept was widely applied in relative studies, such as Wyckoff and Roop (1994), Antweiler (1996), Lee and Roland-Holst (2000), Ahmed and Wyckoff (2003), Peters and Hertwich (2005), Peters and Hertwich (2006), etc.

Since the global warming problem is assuming prominence, the influence of trade on energy consumption and relative pollutant discharge has caused great concern among researchers. Therefore, most studies on EET are targeted at studies on the influence of trade on energy consumption and carbon dioxide. In these studies, EET mainly refers to Energy Embodied in Trade and Carbon Embodied in Trade. In the measurement about Energy Embodied in Trade, most cases are about developed countries. Wyckoff and Roop (1994) discovered that at the middle 1980s, in the six largest OECD countries, the carbon content in the imported industrial manufacturing products accounted for 13% of the total carbon emissions, with France reaching as high as 40%. Peters and Hertwich (2005) found through calculations, that in Norway, 72% of its carbon dioxide emission was induced through exportation while exportation only contributed a 38% share to Norway's GDP. Therefore, the carbon dioxide intensity of Norway's export department is much higher than that of other departments. However, there are also studies focusing on developing countries. For example, Machado (2001) estimated that in 1995, the energy and carbon dioxide in each dollar's exports in Brazil was respectively 40% and 50% higher than that of imports. In addition, Mukhopadhyay (2006) also found that in Thailand's trade with OECD countries, the embodied effluent in its exports was obviously higher than that in its imports and he believed that the environmental trade condition in Thailand was not optimistic.

In recent years, literature on the influence of trade on China's energy consumption and environment has increased rapidly. A part of it was to examine or simulate the correlation between trade liberalization and environmental pollution (such as Zhang, et al., 2003; Zheng, 2005). However, in recent years, more and more literature has focused on the trade-caused ecological or environmental pressure through quantitative measurement. Methodologically speaking, except for a few articles (Chen, et al., 2005; Li, 2005; Peng, 2006; Liu, et al., 2008), the analysis in most literature was based on the input-output model.

Ma Tao, et al. (2005) calculated the pollution footprint of the industrial products in the international trade. Shen Lisheng (2007) measured the influence of export and import on energy consumption from 2002 to 2005 based on the input-output table. The results showed that the energy conserved from imports was higher than the energy consumed in exports. Still using the input-output model, Shen Lisheng, et al. (2008) found that after 2003, the total SO_2 emissions in exports was higher than the total emission reduction from imports and its influence on environmental resources was a "deficit." Similarly, Qi Ye, et al. (2008), based on the estimation of the input-output model, found that according to the conservative estimation on the imports and exports with China's energy consumption efficiency, China's energy import and export basically leveled off from 1997 to 2006; nevertheless, according to the optimistic estimation after the adjustments made to imports with Japan's energy consumption efficiency, China is a net energy exporter, with the annual net energy exportation ranging from 50 million to 100 million tce. The estimation of Chen Ying, et al. (2008) shows that in 2002, the total embodied energy in China's exports was about 410 million tce, accounting for 27.6% of our countries total primary energy consumption. The total embodied energy from imports and exports offsets with each other. In 2002, the embodied energy in China's net export was 240 million tce, taking up 16% of the primary energy consumption in that year. Yao Yufang, et al. (2008), based on the results from the estimation of China's non-competitive input-output table in 2005, found that the energy consumption in the export trade was 656 million tce, accounting for 29% of the total energy. The import trade saved 359-million-tce energy, accounting for 16% of the total energy. If we analyze based on foreign trade, the energy consumption from the export trade in 2005 was higher than the energy saved from the import trade, with the gap being 297 million tce. Therefore, the conclusion is that the trade policy is biased toward the export trade structure, which needs adjustments.

It should be noted that many researchers have estimated the influence of trade on China's carbon emission. Whether we assume the imports are produced with the same technology that produces our national products or we use estimation data on different countries' carbon emission intensities, the estimations of Ahmed and Wyckoff (2003) show that in 1997, the carbon content in China's exports was obviously higher than that in its imports. Wang and Watson (2007) found that in 2004, China's carbon dioxide, in net exports, was 1,109 million tons (MT). According to the estimation of Pan et al.. (2008), in 2002, China's carbon dioxide in net export was 623 MT. However, both the conservative and optimistic estimations made by Qi Ye, et al. (2008) show that China was a net carbon exporter from 1997 to 2006. The estimations of Yao Yufang, et al. (2008) show that in 2005, China's exports led to 1,460 million tons' of carbon dioxide emission transfer, accounting for 29% of the total carbon dioxide emission from energy consumption. The imports decreased by 796 million tons' of carbon dioxide emission, accounting for 16% of the total carbon dioxide emission from energy consumption. China's carbon dioxide emissions in net exports were 664 million tons, accounting for 13% of the total carbon dioxide emission from energy consumption. Weber, et al. (2008) found that in 2005, the carbon dioxide emissions from the production of China's exports was 1.7 billion tons, 1/3rd of China's total carbon emissions. However, this percentage was only 12% (230 million tons) and 23% (760 million tons) respectively in 1987 and 2002.

In the bilateral trade with major trade partners, China is also a net carbon exporter. Shui and Harriss (2006) adopted the economic input-output—lifecycle analysis software developed by Carnegie Mellon University and analyzed the carbon emissions in Sino-America trade. The result shows that the carbon dioxide from China's exports to America increased from 213 MT in 1997 to 497 MT in 2003 while the carbon dioxide from America's exports to China were even less. They thought that America's exports to China for its clean production and energy efficiency technologies were a "win-win" strategy because this was helpful for America to decrease its trade deficit and carbon emissions to China. Li and Hewitt (2008) found that in 2004, in Sino-Britain trade, the carbon content in China's exports was 186 million tons' carbon dioxide ($MTCO_2$), while that in Britain's exports was only 2. 3 $MTCO_2$. Wang Wenzhong and Cheng Yongming (2006) found that in 2004, in Sino-Japan trade, the carbon content in China's exports was much higher than that in Japan.

However, many questions need to be addressed in the existent literature. For example, a large part of literature (Ahmed and Wyckoff, 2003; Wang and Cheng, 2006; Pan, et al., 2008; Qi, et al., 2008) hasn't considered the influence of import on the intermediate input. Yao Yufang, et al. (2008) didn't analyze the variation trends of China's carbon embodied in trade. Wang and Watson (2007) didn't consider the indirect carbon emission influences of exports. Liu Qiang, et al. (2008) only estimated the carbon content of China's major exports, without considering the influences of the trade of goods and services. The estimations of China's export carbon content made by Shui and Harriss (2006) and Li and Hewitt (2008) were not based on China's input-output model, but on that of America and Britain. In addition, these studies failed to make empirical analyses of the driving factors behind the changes in China's carbon embodied in trade.

III. Methodology

1. Model

Inevitably accompanying the economic activities is the energy consumption and pollutant discharge in industrial production. We can simply divide the economic activities into demand and supply. To some degree, it can be assumed that demand gives rise to supply and triggers a series of supplying economic activities such as production and circulation. Therefore, although a large amount of pollutant discharges occur in the link of production and circulation, it is the end demand which causes the production of these pollutants (Munksgaard and Pedersen, 2001) . Generally, we can divide the end demand into consumption, capital formation and exportation. Just as we can regard consumption, investment and exportation as the " troika " for the economic growth, we can also consider them as the "engine" for energy consumption and relevant pollutant discharge.

To measure the influence of trade on resources and the environment, Lee and Roland-Holst (1993) proposed the concept of " Embodied Effluent Trade, EET, " a simple and clear concept. However, in calculating the EET, they regard the pollutant discharge coefficient from direct production in different industries as the basis and have overlooked the mutual influence between trade activities and national economic activities without considering the indirect environmental influence of trade. Therefore, there is no comprehensive measurement of the EET. Since different economic activities share expansive, direct or indirect relations, the production of a certain trade product will not only directly consume resources and produce relevant pollutant discharge, and also bring the production of other relevant intermediate products for the production of this product. Therefore, the production of this trade product will cause indirect resource consumption and pollutant discharges as well.

Therefore, to add the indirect pollution caused by trade into the consideration for the comprehensive measurement of the embodied effluent export, we must combine the influential mechanism of trade on economic activities with the production of pollution. This needs a systematic economic analysis method or model and the input-output model, the basis for the checking of national economy, is undoubtedly a proper choice.

It is for these reasons that since the 1970s and 1980s, in relevant studies on economic and environmental problems, the environmental and economic input-output model has been improved and developed (such as Leontief & Ford, 1970; Miller and Blair, 1985 et al.). At present, this model has been widely applied in the studies on the environmental influences of resident's consumption (such as Munksgaard, et al. ,

2000), the environmental influence of trade (such as Peters and Hertwich, 2006), the mutual influences of industries in environmental pollution and resources consumption and the ownership problem of the ecological footprint. Some literature provides details on the relevant theories and technologies for the studies on EET with the input-output analysis method (such as Lenzen, et al., 2004; Peters and Hertwich, 2005). This article also constructed the measurement model of trade influence on the environment based on the input-output model.

The core of the input-output model is the input-output coefficient matrix A, each line of which stands for the input-output "technology" of an economic sector. The coefficient matrix A of the non-competitive input-output table can be divided into two parts A^d and A^{im}, respectively representing the national product technology coefficient and imports technology coefficient in the departmental product input requirement, namely $A = A^d + A^{im}$ (United Nations, 1999). Make r kinds of resources or pollutant discharges in the production sector into the $r*1$ vector Q, among which Q_i represents the total resource consumption or total pollutant discharge of the ith type; the total output of the national economy sectors constitutes $m*1$ total output vector X, among which X_i represents the total output of the sector i; the end use of domestic products or services in different sectors constitutes the end use vector F.

In investigating relevant problems concerning the environment and economy, generally we can assume there is a certain proportion between pollutant discharge and input (Beghin, et al., 1996), or between pollutant discharge and output (Copeland, et al., 2004). This article takes the latter assumption that the resource consumption or pollutant discharge in different departments is in proportion to their output. Make the resource consumption or pollutant discharge produced by per unit monetary value in different departments, namely the direct resource consumption or pollutant discharge coefficient into the $r*m$ matrix Ω, among which the element w_{ij} represents the direct resource consumption or pollutant discharge of per unit output in department i. Then based on the basic principle of the input-output model, we can obtain:

$$Q = \Omega X = \Omega(I - A^d)^{-1} F \tag{1}$$

Among which, $(I - A^d)^{-1}$ is the Leontief inverse matrix, which reflects the complete consumption of the end use of different departments to other departments. And $\Omega(I - A^d)$ can be calculated as the complete (including both direct and indirect) resource consumption or pollution coefficient vector of the end products in different departments. Make its ith element as ε_{ij}, which represents the jth resource completely consumed or the jth pollutant discharge produced by the end product of per unit monetary value in the ith department.

Make $L = (I - A^d)^{-1}$, S^e is the *m* order export structure vector constructed by the percentage of the national products or services in the exports. We assume the total exports as *ex* and define the resource consumption or pollutant discharge caused by exports as the embodied effluent export, then:

$$Q^e = \Omega L S^e \times ex \quad (2)$$

Q_e is the r column vector, and its Q_i^e represents the total i^{th} type pollutant discharge produced by the total export of domestic products or services.

Assume that the imports are produced with the exporter's technology[①]. Make S^m into *m* order imports structure vector constructed by the percentage of the national products or services in the exports. If we assume the total imports as *im*, then we can obtain the amount of saved effluent imports (namely the energy consumption or pollutant discharge saved in importation) by:

$$Q^m = \Omega L S^m * im \quad (3)$$

Q^m is the r order column vector, which reflects the environmental cost saved by China through its import of other countries' products. Its Q_i^m represents the total discharge of the ith pollutant caused by total imports.

If we define the gap between the embodied effluent export and the saved effluent import as the net embodied effluent trade Q^n, namely:

$$Q^n = \Omega L S^e * ex - \Omega L S^m * im \quad (4)$$

Obviously, Q^n is also r order column vector and its Q_i^n represents the gap between the embodied effluent export and the saved effluent import of the ith type pollutant.

In the research on trade, people usually use the trade condition to measure a country's comparative advantage in trade. Antweiler (1996) proposed the Pollution Terms of Trade (PTT) by referring to the above mentioned concept. According to his definition, PTT is the ratio between the embodied effluent in per unit monetary value exports and

① Obviously this is different from the actual situation, which may cause some deviations of the calculated result.

that in the per unit monetary value imports. From the definition of Antweiler (1996), we can obtain the trade condition of the ith type resource or pollutant:

$$PTT_i = [Q_i^e / ex] / [Q_i^m / im] \quad (5)$$

Among which PTT_i is the trade condition of the ith type resource or pollutant. Obviously, if the trade condition of a certain resource or pollutant in a country is higher than 1, then this country is at a disadvantageous trade position in terms of resources or pollutants because this means this country has consumed more resources or discharged more pollutants in exporting per unit value products or services than in importing the same value products or services in foreign trade.

2. *Decomposition of the Changes in Resource Consumption or Pollutant Discharge Caused by Trade*

Formula (2) and (3) show that the changes of the embodied effluent export (import) at different times are caused by the changes in four factors: the direct resource consumption or pollutant discharge coefficient matrix Ω of different industries, input technology coefficient L, the export (import) product structure S^e(S^m) and the trade scale ex (im). The environmental influences produced by the changes of Ω can be thought to be caused by the changes of the resource consumption or pollutant discharge efficiency in the enterprise's production and we might as well call it the efficiency effect. The environmental influence produced by the change of L can be thought to be brought about by the changes of the enterprise's input combination and we might as well call it the input effect. Since both the two factors Ω and L are decided by the enterprise's micro production behavior model or technology selection and we can call the changes of the resource consumption or pollutant discharge brought about by their changes as technology effect. The resource consumption or pollutant discharge changes caused by the changes of the later two factors can be correspondingly comprehended as the trade's structure effect and scale effect①.

① Grossman and Kruger (1993) decomposed the environmental effect of the trade liberalization into the scale effect, structure effect and technology effect. Obviously, this is not the same with the decomposition of the factors in China's embodied effluent trade in this article.

To distinguish the above mentioned three environmental effects of the trade changes, this article adopts Structural Decomposition Analysis (SDA) to make incremental decomposition of formula (2) and (3) and obtain:

$$\Delta Q^{e} = Q^{e}(t) - Q^{e}(t-1) = \Delta Q_{int}{}^{e} + \Delta Q_{inp}{}^{e} + \Delta Q_{str}{}^{e} + \Delta Q_{act}{}^{e} \quad (6)$$

$$\Delta Q^{m} = Q^{m}(t) - Q^{m}(t-1) = \Delta Q_{int}{}^{m} + \Delta Q_{inp}{}^{m} + \Delta Q_{str}{}^{m} + \Delta Q_{act}{}^{m} \quad (7)$$

Among which Δ represents the changes of the corresponding factors. The adoption of formula (6) and (7) can distinguish the influence of the variation of various factors on the change of carbon emissions and carbon intensity. However, it should be pointed out that the form of formula (6) and (7) is not unique. This is the "non-uniqueness problem" in the structural decomposition stressed by Dietzenbacher and Los (1998).

The commonly used method to define the specific decomposition form of formula (6) and (7) is to assume that a certain factor changes while other factors stay at their base period level value (namely the Laspeyres index method) or report period level value (namely the Paasche index method). For example, for a certain factor (like M), the influence of its variation (ΔM) corresponding variable depends on other (n - 1) factors' value (namely t period or t - 1 period value). However, there may be large gap between the level value of different factors in the base period and report period, therefore, these two processing methods are not only too random, but also may easily lead to large deviations, namely, the decomposition residual. To overcome the deficiency of the above structural decomposition method, there are two commonly seen methods formed in the empirical analysis. One is the polar decomposition① proposed by Fujimagari (1989) and Betts (1989), for example, Munksgaard, et al. (2002) adopted this method to decompose the structure of the carbon emission influence from Denmark's

① Polar decomposition means making the average value between the influence values of the corresponding variable of the changes of the various factors by decomposing from the first factor and the influence value of the various factors by decomposing from the last factor as the influence value of the corresponding variable of various factors. For example, for $y = x_1 x_2 x_3$, from 0 to t period, the influence of factor x_2 on y can be represented as $0.5 * x_{1t}(x_{2t} - x_{20}) x_{30} + 0.5 * x_{10}(x_{2t} - x_{20}) x_{3t}$. The subscript 0, t respectively represents the value of the variable at 0 period and t period.

consumption; the other is the mid-point weight decomposition①.

However, Dietzenbacher and Los (1998) pointed out that these two methods are theoretically deficient. Because if the change of a variable is decided by n factors, then the decomposition beginning from different factors will result in different decomposition equations, which means that the variable has n! various decomposition forms. They think that it is reasonable to measure the influence of the factor's varying corresponding variable with the average value of the varying corresponding variable's influence of each factor in the n! decomposition equations. However, although we can get a simple and approximate average solution of the average value through polar decomposition and mid-point weight decomposition, these two methods are theoretically deficient.

Nevertheless, Seibel (2003) further proves that if other $(n-1)$ factors have k $(0 \leqslant k \leqslant n-1)$ factors with the value of the $t-1$ period and another $(n-1-k)$ factors with the value of the t period, then the expression of the influences produced by the factor's varying corresponding variables are $(n-1)!/[(n-1-k)! * k!]$ in total and the decomposition equations of a single expression are $(n-1-k)! * k!$ in total. In this way, when k has ranged from 0 to $(n-1)$, the expressions of the influence of the varying corresponding variables of each factor are 2^{n-1} in total, with the occurrence of each expression decided by the corresponding k. This means that the variation of each factor has 2^{n-1} variable influence values and the 2^{n-1} value may vary greatly.

Specifically, for formula (6) and (7), their decomposition equations are $4! = 24$ in total and each factor's expressions to the consumption of each resource or pollutant discharge are $2^{4-1} = 8$. Take the expression of (ΔQ_{str}^{e}), the influence of the variation in the export structures on energy consumption or pollutant discharge, Table 1 shows its 8 expressions and the occurrences of each expression. If so, the variation of each factor will produce 8 values for the influence of each

① Mid-point weight decomposition is again divided into two. Since one is not rigorously founded mathematically (Li, 2004), I will not introduce it here. The other is rigorously founded mathematically. For example, from 0 to t period, the influence of factor x_2 on y can be represented as $0.5 * x_{10}(x_{2t} - x_{20}) x_{30} + 0.5 * x_{1t}(x_{2t} - x_{20}) x_{3t}$. The subscript 0, t respectively represents the value of the variable at 0 period and t period.

resource consumption or pollutant discharge and these 8 values may vary greatly. This article uses their average value to measure the influence of the factor variation on each resource consumption or pollutant discharge.

Table 1 Expressions of ΔQ_{str}^{e}

k	Form of Expression	Expression	Occurrence Times
0	1	$\Delta Q_{sr}^{e}=\Omega(t-1)L(t-1)[S^{e}(t)-S^{e}(t-1)]ex(t-1)$	6
1	3	$\Delta Q_{sr}^{e}=\Omega(t)L(t-1)[S^{e}(t)-S^{e}(t-1)]ex(t-1)$	2
		$\Delta Q_{sr}^{e}=\Omega(t-1)L(t)[S^{e}(t)-S^{e}(t-1)]ex(t-1)$	2
		$\Delta Q_{sr}^{e}=\Omega(t-1)L(t-1)[S^{e}(t)-S^{e}(t-1)]ex(t)$	2
2	3	$\Delta Q_{sr}^{e}=\Omega(t)L(t)[S^{e}(t)-S^{e}(t-1)]ex(t-1)$	2
		$\Delta Q_{sr}^{e}=\Omega(t-1)L(t)[S^{e}(t)-S^{e}(t-1)]ex(t)$	2
		$\Delta Q_{sr}^{e}=\Omega(t)L(t-1)[S^{e}(t)-S^{e}(t-1)]ex(t)$	2
3	1	$\Delta Q_{sr}^{e}=\Omega(t)L(t)[S^{e}(t)-S^{e}(t-1)]ex(t)$	6

Note: n = 4 means that the factors deciding the embodied effluent trade are 4. In the table, k refers to the other three factors' level values when they range from the t − 1 period except for structural variation. Dietzenbacher and Los (2000) pointed out that there may be interdependence between the factors and on a temporary basis, this problem has not been considered in this article.

IV. Data Processing

1. Drafting of the Comparable Price Input-Output Table and Its Extended Table

The input-output analysis needs to be supported by a large amount of data, among which the primary one is the officially published input-output table. Mainly due to data restrictions, the empirical analysis concerning the embodied effluent trade is mostly predicated on a country's input-output table (Peters & Hertwich, 2006). My analysis is also based on China's input-output table. In consideration of the limitations of energy and pollution data, this article divides the economic system into 26 departments (see the Appendix) . To analyze the environmental influences of the trade increase, we need to compare the trade volume and embodied effluent trade in different years. Therefore, predicated on the basic input-output tables in 1987, 1992, 2002 and 2007 issued by the National Bureau of Statistics, I obtained the input-output basic table of the 26 departments through integration and division. In consideration of the incomparability of the price of different years, I transformed the input-output tables in 1987, 1992 and 2007 into an input-output table of comparable prices with the price in 2002 as the evaluation base with various price indexes published officially.

In order to make a reliable quantitative analysis of the trade environmental influence in recent years, based on the basic input-output table of the 26 departments in 2002 mentioned above and applying the RAS method, I obtained the input-output extended tables in 2003, 2004 and 2006. In compiling the extended table, the added value data of different departments and other end use data (except those on export) all coming from the *China Statistical Yearbook* and *Annual Statistic Report on Industry in China* over the years; the total output data is converted from the total output value of different departments according to certain coefficients, because the total output in the input-output analysis not only includes the total output value but also the value-added tax. The import and export data of the agricultural and industrial departments are converted from Article 98, Chapter 22 imports and exports quota, issued by the General Administration of Customs of the People's Republic of China, based on a certain ratio① and the import and export data of the service industry came from the *Balance of International Payments*. Of course, to obtain the input-output extended table of comparable prices calculated at the price in 2002, the above basic data are deflated according to various official price indexes②.

2. *Drafting of Non-Competitive Input-Output Table*

In China, the commonly used input-output table generally refers to

① The National Bureau of Statistics of the People's Republic of China and some scholars (for example, Shen Lisheng, 2007) also adopted similar methods to convert the data on imports and exports into departmental data.

② Primarily refers to the producer price index of industrial products, the GDP deflator of major industries in the *China Statistical Yearbook* over the years and all the volumes of *China's Foreign Trade Index* compiled by the General Administration of Customs of the People's Republic of China.

competitive ones, for example, the input-output tables issued by China's National Bureau of Statistics over the years. Among such tables, the intermediate use and end use actually are the synthetic products of domestic products and imports. The total imports of all departments form a single group, representing the imports for intermediate use and end use and are considered as negative output. To avoid exaggerating the environmental influences of various end uses, this article needs to distinguish the input-output table for domestic products and the one for importing products, namely the non-competitive input-output table.

To get such input-output tables, we need to divide imports among different intermediate input and end demands (including exports). The method adopted in this article is as follows: first, define the imported products included in the exportation. According to different methods of trade, the product trade data issued by China's customs can be divided into general trade, import processing trade, customs warehousing trade, bonded warehousing intermediary trade and other 15 categories. Among these, the goods under bonded management are mainly used for temporary storage or processing exported products after they enter the border. In principle, they will not be put into the domestic economic cycle before exportation and basically will not have any impact on the domestic economy. Therefore, the products exported through customs warehousing trade and bonded warehousing intermediary trade are mainly imported products without going through the domestic economic cycle. This part of the export values should be offset and deducted in the total exports to avoid exaggerating the exportation's economic and environmental influence.

In analyzing the trade's contribution to economic growth, Yin Jingdong (2007) believed that the imported products for processing materials supplied by clients, assembling according to client-supplied samples and processing with imported materials primarily served for exportation and should be deducted from it. At the same time, most of the customs warehousing trade and bonded warehousing intermediary trade, which belongs to intermediary trade and their imported products, should also be deducted from exportation. The author believes that the products imported through the trade method mentioned above, which are processed domestically and then exported, should be regarded as intermediate imported products that have participated in the production process. From the perspective of input-output analysis, they should not be deducted from exportation. Since the imports from customs warehousing trade and bonded warehousing intermediary trade are not wholly exported through intermediary trade, they cannot be wholly deducted from exportation and only those exports should be deducted from the total exports. In principle, those imports do not participate in domestic economic activities and in evaluating the environmental influences of imports, hence they should be excluded from consideration.

In addition, these products, imported through the customs warehousing trade and bonded warehousing intermediary trade, will not enter the domestic economic system until they pass the customs' final examination. Therefore, in considering the environmental influence of imports, these parts of imported products should be excluded from consideration to avoid exaggerating the influence of importation on the domestic economic environment influence. Their value should be offset and deducted from importation.

We should offset and deduct from the gross fixed capital formation the imported equipment of the processing trade and the foreign-invested enterprises as the value of the invested imported equipment, objects and the imported equipment in the export processing zones represent products imported through the above mentioned method which are primarily investments, and are not in the usual consumption choices of residents and governments.

Finally, we should divide the rest of the imports value with the deduction of the above mentioned bonded imports value and the equipment imports value among the intermediate use and end use (not including exportation) through the method of percentage split[①] for deductions.

3. Energy Consumption and Major Pollutant Discharge Data

The energy consumption data of different departments in this research come from the *China Statistical Yearbook* and *China Energy Statistical Yearbook* over the years and the pollutant discharge data, from the *China Statistical Yearbook on Environment* over the years. There are

① Other scholars also adopt such a method to divide imports, for example, Chen Xikang (2002).

two points that need further elaboration. One is that in the energy consumption data tables in 1987 and 1992, issued by the statistical department, the industries were roughly categorized and the industrial energy consumption data in the yearbook needs to be divided to obtain the industrial energy consumption data for this research. This research is primarily based on the industrial fixed price GDP and divides the totaling of the industrial energy consumption data based on certain ratios.

The other is that China's official SO_2 and COD emission data primarily consists of two parts: industrial pollutant discharge and domestic pollutant discharge. However, the published industrial pollutant discharge data are not the complete enterprise pollutant discharge data. The accumulative value of industrial data only accounts for around 85% of the total industrial pollutant discharge. The sources of the remaining 15% industrial pollution are hard to identify. For the sources of this part, my research divides them into the fossil energy consumption of different industries by weight.

The domestic pollutant discharge actually includes the pollutant discharged from the service industry. For the sources of these pollutants, this research will also divide them based on the energy consumption of domestic sectors and different service industries. Because the COD emission of the agricultural sector has no official statistical data, this research excludes it from consideration. Since the earliest official sub-sector pollutant discharge data is from the year 1993, we evaluate the SO_2 and COD emission in 1987 and 1992 based on the data in 1993. The specific method is to assume the ratio between the pollutant discharge and energy consumption of different industries in 1987 and 1992 is the same as 1993.

We have no choice but to evaluate the carbon dioxide emission data of different industries since there are no official data available. According to relevant studies domestically and abroad, both the carbon dioxide emission evaluation framework and the carbon dioxide emission intensity coefficient of relevant energies proposed by IPCC are authoritative. However, since the energy consumption data provided by China's official statistical departments or energy departments cannot wholly satisfy the requirements of IPCC's evaluation method, therefore, we need to modify the method based on data availability. While evaluating the carbon dioxide emission over the years, the data on average heat value of different fuels adopted in this research come from the *China Energy Statistical Yearbook* 2005; the carbon emission coefficient comes from the IPCC emission inventory guideline ("Revised 1996 IPCC Guidelines for National Greenhouse Gas Inventories: Workbook (Volume 2), http://www.ipccnggip.iges.or.jp/public/gl/invs5a.html", Table 1-2 of Chapter I). To avoid repetitive calculations, my research evaluates carbon dioxide emission based on the end energy consumption of different departments. The carbon dioxide emission produced from the production of power and heat is distributed among the departments based on the ratio between the power and heat at the end consumption of different departments.

V. Empirical Analysis

This part of the research calculates China's total Embodied Effluent Trade (EET) from 1987 to 2006 and analyzes China's environmental trade condition based on this; and divides the scale effect, structure effect and technology effect of the changes in China's EET.

1. Energy Environmental Influence of Trade and Its Changes

(1) The energy environmental influences of exportation and its changes

Since the late 1980s, trade has had increasing larger impacts on China's energy consumption and major pollutant discharges (as shown in Table 2). Among these, the embodied effluent export of the energy, namely, the energy consumption from exportation increased rapidly, from 96.36 Mtce in 1987 to 688.33 Mtce in 2006, an increase of more than 6 times. Since China's accession to the WTO (2002-2007), it increased particularly rapidly: a total 388.38 Mtce in four years, with an annual increase of 18.07%; exceeding the total increase rate (203.59 Mtce) and the annual increase rate (7.86%) of the previous 15 years (1987-2002).

From 1987 to 2007, the embodied effluent export of different pollutants increased to different levels. The embodied effluent export of CO_2 increased from 66.31 Mt-c to 477.58 Mt-c, an increase of more than 6 times. That of SO_2 increased from 1.2867 million tons to 7.6365 million tons, an increase of nearly 5 times. That of COD increased slightly slowly, from 1.1652 million tons to 2.4345 million tons, also more than doubled. Since China's accession to WTO, the increasing rate of the embodied effluent export of CO_2, SO_2 and COD has reached 18.32%, 16.80% and 6.70% respectively, also obviously higher than that before China's accession to the WTO (7.85%, 6.92% and 2.79%).

With the year-on-year increases of the embodied effluent export of energies and pollutants, their corresponding percentages in the total energy consumption and pollutant discharge in national production sectors has also been on the rise (hereinafter referred to as "percentage of the embodied effluent export"). Among them, the percentage of the embodied effluent export of energies, CO_2, SO_2 and COD rose from 14.11%, 13.99%, 12.28% and 18.37% in 1987 to 31.88%, 32.04%, 29.40% and 26.92% in 2007.

The continued increase of the percentages of the embodied effluent export of energies and various pollutants impacts the ongoing enhancement of the exportation's environmental influences on China. At present, the percentages of the various embodied effluent exports have exceeded or approached one third, which has exerted an unneglectable influence on China's energy consumption and pollutant discharges. To some extent, this proves people's intuition and judgment of how trade influences the resources and environment.

(2) The energy environmental influences of importation and its changes

According to the above mentioned analysis, to some extent, we can comprehend the environmental influences of importation as positive, namely, it "has saved" the energy consumption of corresponding products or services and decreased the relevant pollutant discharges. Since the late 1980s, while the exportation has exerted an increasing influence on the environment, the influences of importation on the environment were also increasing (as shown in Table 2).

The saved effluent import of energies increased from 149.18 Mtce in 1987 to 402.91 Mtce in 2007, an increase of about 2 times. Overall, the annual increase rate of the saved effluent import of energies since China's accession to the WTO has exceeded that from before the accession. And after the accession, the annual increase rate of the saved effluent import of energies increased from 4.84% to 5.86%.

Table 2 **Embodied Effluent Trade: 1987-2007**

	Year	Embodied Effluent Trade			Percentage of the total energy consumption or pollutant discharge in the production sector (%)		
		Export	Import	Net Trade	Export	Import	Net Trade
Energy Consumption (Mtce)	1987	96.36	149.18	-52.82	14.11	21.85	-7.74
	1992	169.06	211.68	-42.62	20.30	25.42	-5.12
	2002	299.95	303.08	-3.13	25.00	25.26	-0.26
	2003	373.92	373.25	0.67	26.77	26.72	0.05
	2004	494.24	428.00	66.24	30.22	26.17	4.05
	2005	608.69	493.60	115.09	33.40	27.08	6.32
	2006	669.74	433.12	236.62	33.48	21.65	11.83
	2007	688.33	402.91	285.42	31.88	18.66	13.22
Carbon Dioxide Emission (Mt - c)	1987	66.31	104.12	-37.81	13.99	21.97	-7.98
	1992	118.58	148.85	-30.27	20.31	25.50	-5.19
	2002	205.99	207.73	-1.73	25.07	25.28	-0.21
	2003	257.85	257.14	0.71	26.84	26.76	0.07
	2004	341.77	295.86	45.90	30.36	26.28	4.08
	2005	422.01	339.57	82.44	33.59	27.03	6.56
	2006	464.43	300.12	164.31	33.64	21.74	11.90
	2007	477.58	278.07	199.50	32.04	18.65	13.38
SO_2 Emission (104 t)	1987	128.67	194.26	-65.60	12.28	18.53	-6.26
	1992	247.51	294.29	-46.78	17.88	21.26	-3.38
	2002	351.25	334.05	17.20	24.07	22.89	1.18
	2003	470.85	443.50	27.35	24.10	22.70	1.40
	2004	580.54	485.60	94.94	28.12	23.52	4.60
	2005	733.22	578.35	154.87	31.30	24.69	6.61
	2006	743.27	482.93	260.35	30.98	20.13	10.85
	2007	763.65	467.27	296.38	29.40	17.99	11.41
COD Emission (104 t)	1987	116.52	109.98	6.54	18.37	17.33	1.03
	1992	187.45	146.88	40.57	22.52	17.65	4.87
	2002	176.00	124.53	51.48	25.78	18.24	7.54
	2003	181.60	126.15	55.45	27.26	18.93	8.32
	2004	199.70	125.37	74.33	30.17	18.94	11.23
	2005	219.54	136.40	83.13	31.63	19.65	11.98
	2006	229.98	111.60	118.38	33.94	16.47	17.47
	2007	243.45	115.77	127.68	26.92	12.80	14.12

Data source: calculated by the author.

Similarly, from 1987 to 2007, the saved effluent import of different pollutants increased to different degrees, however from 2005 to 2007, they showed a downward trend. Among them, the saved effluent import of CO_2 increased from 104. 12 Mt-c in 1987 to 339. 57 Mt-c in 2005 and then decreased gradually to 278. 07 Mt-c in 2007. The saved effluent import of SO_2 also increased from 1. 9426 million tons in 1987 to 5. 7835 million tons in 2005 and then decreased to 4. 6727 million tons in 2007. Although the increase rate of the saved effluent import of COD was lower, its variation trend resembled that of CO_2 and SO_2. The percentages of the various saved effluent imports in the total energy consumption and corresponding pollutant discharge from national production sectors also showed the trend of rising and then declining.

The continued increase of the saved effluent import shows that China's adherence to opening up and its active use of the "two markets (international and domestic)," "two resources" strategy have made great contributions to China's energy conservation and environmental protection. However, in terms of China's current energy environmental situation, the percentages of the energy saved from imports and the pollutant discharge reductions seems still not high enough. From the perspective of energy alleviation and environmental restriction, it seems that we should further tap the potential of importation.

(3) China's environmental trade situation: the embodied effluent in net trade and environmental trade condition

If the exportation is said to have increased China's energy consumption and pollutant discharge, which has exerted a negative influence while the importation, saved energy consumption and decreased pollutant discharge, which has exerted a positive influence, then the embodied effluent in net trade obtained from the offset between the exportation's negative influence and the importation's positive influence is the overall influence of the trade on China's energy consumption and pollutant discharge. And such an overall influence has reflected the environmental trade situation China is facing. Since the late 1980s, how has China's environmental trade situation changed?

1. The embodied effluent in net trade and its changes

As shown in Table 2, the embodied effluent exports of energies, CO_2 and SO_2 was lower than their corresponding saved effluent imports. Their embodied effluent in net trade was respectively -52. 82 Mtce, -37. 81 Mt-c and -656. 0 thousand tons; equivalent to 7. 74%, 7. 98%

and 6.26% in the total energy consumption, CO_2 and SO_2 emissions from the national production sectors in the same year. Overall, the trade in 1987 effectively saved China's energy consumption and CO_2 and SO_2 emissions.

From 1987 to 2002, the increase rate of the embodied effluent exports of energies, CO_2 and SO_2 approached that of the saved effluent imports. However, the former was slightly higher than the latter, with the gap of the two increasingly bridging, namely, although the corresponding embodied effluent in the net trade was negative, and the absolute value was gradually decreasing. Until 2002, the energy and carbon embodied in export and the energy and carbon saved from import had been very close; but the sulphur embodied in exports exceeded that saved from imports.

Beginning from 2003, since the embodied effluent export of energies, CO_2 and SO_2 still grew faster than the saved effluent imports; therefore, the corresponding embodied effluent in net trade was rapidly increasing. In 2007, the percentage of the embodied effluent in net trade of the three substances in total energy consumption or corresponding pollutant discharge from the national production sectors has exceeded one tenth.

Since 1987, the embodied effluent exports of COD have been obviously higher than the saved effluent imports. Therefore, its embodied effluent in net trade also has been maintained at a comparatively higher level. Since 2004, its embodied effluent in net trade also has seen an upward trend. In 2007, its percentage in the total energy consumption or corresponding pollutant discharge from the national production sectors was 14.12%.

Since 2003, the embodied effluent exports of the above four substances have been obviously higher than their saved effluent imports. Whether the absolute value for its embodied effluents in net trade or the percentage in the total energy consumption or corresponding pollutant discharge from national production sectors, both of them were rapidly increasing. This means that in the most recent two years, the overall influence of trade on the environment has been unfavorable.

2. The embodied effluent in net trade of CO_2 and the accounting principle of carbon emissions

At present, the negotiation on greenhouse gas emission rights are becoming the heated topic of international concern. Many developed countries accuse developing countries, including China, of discharging an excessive amount of carbon dioxide in recent years. However, as a matter of fact, just as Gao Guangsheng (2006) pointed out, "under the current international trade order, a large part of the carbon dioxide emission from developing countries has served the consumption of developed countries through international trade." Therefore, trade has become an important factor in negotiations on the distribution of carbon emission rights.

In consideration of this problem, Munksgaard and Pedersen (2001) proposed the "production accounting principle" and "consumption accounting principle" for greenhouse gas emission accounting. The former refers to the accounting of the carbon dioxide emission from the production processes which have actually produced the carbon dioxide while the latter refers to the accounting of the carbon dioxide emission from various products and services for end use (including imports).

Peters and Hertwich (2006) pointed out that according to the production accounting principle, a country's pollutant discharge volume is equivalent to the pollutant discharge produced from the consumption of domestic products or services for end use. However, if according to the consumption accounting principle, a country's pollutant discharge volume is equivalent to the pollutant discharge produced not only from the domestic products for end use, but also from the imports and services consumed. Therefore, the gap of the carbon dioxide emission under the production and consumption accounting principle is actually the embodied effluent in net trade of CO_2.

Peters and Hertwich (2006) further pointed out that although under the consumption accounting principle, we also faced the difficulty in data unavailability and technologies, the adherence to this principle was more favorable for the control over global carbon dioxide emissions. Because if the pollutant discharge produced from the imports is distributed to the importer rather than the exporter, then to effectively control its carbon dioxide emission, the importer will choose the same type of products with low carbon intensity for importation. To some degree, this can effectively curb the endless transfer of the polluting industries to developing countries because the products produced by these countries generally have a higher carbon intensity. Therefore, if developed countries import products from these developing countries, it will obviously increase their carbon dioxide emissions, which is unfavorable to the alleviation of the pressure from greenhouse gas emission reduction. Therefore, the consumption accounting principle is helpful to make the environmental factor as an important comparable advantage factor for all countries to consider and stimulate them to improve the global environmental quality in weighing the cost and pressure of emission reduction.

Since 2003, China's embodied effluent in net trade of CO_2 has been positive and on the rise, reaching 199.50 Mt-c in 2007. This means that a considerable part of China's carbon dioxide emission is consumed by other countries through trade. That is to say, if under the consumption accounting principle, China's carbon dioxide emission will be 199.50 Mt-c lower than that under the production accounting principle.

3. Environmental trade condition and its changes

This is further seen from the perspective of China's environmental trade condition (shown in Table 3), in 1987, except that the COD trade condition was higher than 1, that of energies, SO_2 and CO_2 hung around 0.70. This means that the energy consumption and SO_2 and CO_2 emission produced with the exportation value of one yuan is equal to about 70% of the energy saved and pollutant discharge reduced with the importation value of one yuan. Obviously, at that time, China's overall environmental trade conditions occupied an obviously advantageous position.

Table 3 Environmental Trade Condition: 1987-2007

Year	Energies	SO_2	CO_2	COD
1987	0.69	0.68	0.73	1.17
1992	0.81	0.80	0.85	1.29
2002	0.82	0.82	0.87	1.17
2003	0.84	0.84	0.89	1.20
2004	0.88	0.88	0.91	1.21
2005	0.87	0.88	0.90	1.14
2006	0.96	0.96	0.95	1.27
2007	0.94	0.95	0.90	1.16

Data source: calculated by the author.

Until 1992, the trade condition value of energies, CO_2, SO_2 and COD increased significantly, respectively reaching 0.81, 0.80, 0.85 and 1.29. This means that from 1987 to 1992, China's environmental trade condition has obviously aggravated. From 1992 to 2002, the trade condition value of energies, CO_2 and SO_2 increased; that of COD slightly declined. Therefore, China's overall environmental trade condition during this period was still degrading.

From 2002 to 2007, the trade condition value of energies, CO_2 and SO_2 was constantly on the rise; until 2007, all exceeded 0.90. This means the energies, SO_2 and CO_2 emissions embodied in China's per unit value of products and services in exportation has almost approached that in importation. In 2007, the trade condition value of COD also increased to 1.16, namely, the COD embodied in per unit monetary value of exported products and services was still obviously higher than that of imported products and services. Therefore, it can be said that since 1987, China's overall environmental trade condition has been aggravating and at a faster speed after its accession to WTO.

Then, since the late 1980s, what has caused the obvious degradation of China's environmental trade condition? Or what does it mean? Since this research assumes that the embodied effluent of imports and exports with the same value from the same department is the same, therefore, the change of China's environmental trade condition can only be attributable to the structural change in the imported and exported products or services. So the degradation of the environmental trade condition means that in terms of imported products or services, the overall percentage of the energy and pollution intensive products or services in China's exported products or services is on the rise.

To conclude, since 2004, China's embodied effluent in net trade has been expanding, and therefore the overall influence of trade on China's environment is negative. This means that currently, China belongs to the net energy and environment exporters with a strong momentum for development. At the same time, since 1987, China's environmental trade condition has been degrading, with the obvious advantage of most material trade conditions gradually disappearing. China's current environmental trade situation and its development trend deserve our attention.

2. Decomposition of the Environmental Influence Change Brought about by Trade Growth——Scale, Structure and Technology Effect

The aforementioned analysis shows that since the late 1980s, trade is expanding, so is its influence on China's environment. Then, what are the roles played by the expansion of trade scale, the change of trade product structure and of trade products' energy or pollution intensity in changing the trade environmental influence? To clarify this question, this research uses the method and data introduced in the second part to decompose the embodied effluent trade since 1987 (as shown in Table 4). Since the input-output tables in 2003, 2004 and 2006 were obtained based on the basic input-output table in 2002 and through the RAS method, it is not that suitable to apply them in the structural decomposition, so this research has only reported the decomposition result of the four periods: 1987-1992, 1992-2002, 2002-2005 and 2005-2007.

The results show that the increase of energies, CO_2, SO_2 and COD embodied in the exportation from 1987 to 1992 was primarily incurred by the expansion of the export scale. The changes in the export structure have comparatively lesser influences on these indexes, but they have led to a slight increase in the energy consumption and various pollutants discharge. This means that the overall percentage of the energy-intensive products in exported products has increased slightly. The influence of the input structure is also smaller than that of the scale effect, but obviously greater than that of the export structure. The intensity effect is the only one which helps to reduce energy consumption and pollutant discharge, with its influence exceeding the input structure effect. Therefore, overall, the technology effect (the totaling of input structure effect and intensity effect), to some degree, prohibited the scale effect. However, the technology effect is only 6%-30% of the scale effect, so its prohibition is too weak to reverse the upward trend of the embodied effluent exports.

From 1992 to 2002, the way in which exportation influences energy consumption and CO_2 and SO_2 emissions was similar to that in the previous period: the scale effect led to a significant increase of energy consumption and pollutant discharge. Nevertheless, the input structure effect and intensity effect in this period have both been enhanced, particularly the intensity effect which obviously increases. The input structure effect is also favorable to reduce energy consumption and the emission of the two pollutants. Therefore, the technology effect plays a greater role in prohibiting the scale effect; the former is equivalent to 60%-80% of the latter, obviously higher than that in the previous period. However, as small as the structure effect is, it is also favorable to reduce energy consumption and the above mentioned two pollutants' emissions. Being different from the changes in the embodied effluent export of the three pollutants, the COD embodied in export decreased slightly in this period. This is largely due to the fact that for COD emission, the technology effect is as high as 86.19% of the export scale effect and the structure effect is also very obvious (equivalent to 17.18% of scale effect) which is favorable to COD emission reduction. Therefore, their total influence has exceeded the scale effect. Generally speaking, the technological change during this period, especially the decrease of the direct energy and pollution intensity of different sectors has effectively offset the influence of the export scale on energy consumption and various pollutants discharge.

From 2002 to 2005, enormous changes occurred in the embodied energies, CO_2 and SO_2 in exports, which were even higher than the aggregate-value of the changes during the previous two periods. The COD embodied in export in this period increased slightly, instead of decreasing as in the previous period. Such a change in the embodied effluent export was primarily incurred by the scale effect. Following right behind China's accession to the WTO, this period witnesses a rapid development for China's trade. Although during these several years, the scale effect hasn't surpassed that of the previous period (1992-2002), the intensity effect declined significantly during this period. In addition, since the input structure change also led to a significant increase of the embodied effluent exports, the prohibition of the technology effect to scale effect has obviously weakened and hence has resulted in a significant increase in the embodied effluent exports. The structure effect during this period is still small and except for COD, the trend of the export structure change is unfavorable to reduce energy consumption and CO_2 and SO_2 emissions.

From 2005 to 2007, the energies, CO_2 and SO_2 embodied in exports continued to increase, but with an obvious smaller increase rate than that during the period from 2002 to 2005. On the one hand, this is because the scale effect produced by exports is far smaller than that of the previous period and on the other hand, the technology effect is obviously greater than that of the previous period. Particularly when compared with the scale effect, the technology effect has exerted an increasingly greater influence. One important reason is that since 2006, the energy conservation and emission reduction policy measures implemented in China have taken great effect, thus enhancing tremendously the technology effect. However, the structure effect has still increased energies, CO_2 and SO_2 embodied in exports and such an influence is strengthening. The COD embodied in exports during this period is still increasing, but with a declining increase rate. The various effects produced by exporting COD are similar to those during the previous period.

The decomposition of changes in the saved effluent import is similar to the embodied effluent export (as shown in Table 4). This is primarily manifested in the fact that various changes of the saved effluent imports are decided by the changes of the import scale. The difference lies in that technological changes have a larger influence on the saved effluent imports than the scale effect. In the changes of the saved effluent imports, although the structure effect is small, it is negative in each stage. This means that since the reform and opening up, the percentage of the energy, CO_2, SO_2 and COD intensive products in China's imported products has been on the decline while that in the exported products has only declined during the period from 1992 to 2002, not during the other three stages. It is the difference between the changes in the saved effluent imports and the embodied effluent exports that has led to the continued degradation of China's environmental trade condition. It is worth mentioning that since the technology effect exceeded the scale effect of imports from 2005 to 2007, the saved effluent imports were on the decline during this period.

Table 4 Decomposition of Changesin the Embodied Effluent Trade Brought about by Trade Growth

Year		Decomposition of the changesin embodied effluent export						Decomposition of the changesin saved effluent import					
		Scale effect	Structure effect	Technology effect			Total effect	Scale effect	Structure effect	Technology effect			Total effect
				Input structure effect	Intensity effect	Total				Input structure effect	Intensity effect	Total	
Energy consumption (Mtce)	1987 - 1992	84.64	14.50	21.47	-28.40	-6.94	92.21	97.64	-9.31	18.58	-42.21	-23.64	64.70
	1992 - 2002	413.53	-15.74	-50.38	-208.38	-258.76	139.03	382.67	-4.39	-55.75	-224.33	-280.08	98.20
	2002 - 2005	364.56	3.65	6.60	-37.77	-31.17	337.04	259.59	-42.70	18.94	-27.22	-8.28	208.61
	2005 - 2007	206.46	31.16	-5.19	-208.74	-213.93	23.69	24.29	-11.77	-3.34	-147.51	-150.84	-138.33
CO_2 emission (Mt - c)	1987 - 1992	53. 90	10.76	17.07	-35.54	-18.48	46.18	63.72	-6.08	16.05	-47.34	-31.29	26.36
	1992 - 2002	247.88	-2.99	-45.03	-112.48	-157.51	87.38	232.45	-7.01	-53.67	-117.89	-171.56	53.88
	2002 - 2005	230.15	3.00	72.36	-84.01	-11.65	221.50	161.84	-27.33	74.69	-66.18	8.51	143.02
	2005 - 2007	135.69	21.01	-6.95	-93.54	-100.49	56.20	15.95	-4.04	-1.32	-73.41	-74.73	-62.82
SO_2 emission (10^4 t)	1987 - 1992	107.91	18.15	34.32	-41.53	-7.21	118.85	121.93	4.82	34.42	-61.14	-26.72	100.03
	1992 - 2002	502.80	-8.59	-70.89	-319.56	-390.45	103.76	444.90	-16.52	-87.12	-301.50	-388.62	39.76
	2002 - 2005	401.25	1.59	139.54	-160.41	-20.87	381.96	271.47	-49.62	140.69	-118.24	22.45	244.30
	2005 - 2007	227.94	26.91	-6.52	-217.90	-224.42	30.43	26.80	-3.16	7.31	-142.02	-134.71	-111.08
COD emission (10^4 t)	1987 - 1992	88.99	6.52	10.89	-35.47	-24.58	70.93	64.99	-6.32	11.58	-33.35	-21.77	36.90
	1992 - 2002	339.59	-58.33	2.41	-295.11	-292.70	-11.44	211.01	-7.58	-8.79	-217.00	-225.79	-22.36
	2002 - 2005	157.76	-15.31	-3.42	-95.50	-98.92	43.53	81.60	-9.63	1.04	-61.13	-60.09	11.88
	2005 - 2007	70.16	-10.06	10.13	-46.32	-36.19	23.91	6.47	-7.37	3.62	-23.36	-19.73	-20.63

Data source: calculated by the author.

Generally speaking, the improvement of energy efficiency and the decrease of pollution intensity have effectively stemmed the influence of the rapid expansion of China's export scale on the environment. Relatively speaking, the small structure effect means that since the late 1980s, China's trade structure hasn't changed much. Nevertheless, it should be noted that despite the small structure effect, in recent years, it has increased energy consumption and CO_2 and SO_2 emissions.

VI. Discussion: How to View the Influence of Trade on China's Environment

Since 1987, trade has exerted a greater influence on China's environment. With such unneglectable influences and the degrading environmental trade conditions, how should we view and cope with the influence of trade on China's environment and its changes?

To begin with, the strengthening influence of trade on China's environment is primarily owed to the increasing influence of trade in the national economy. The deepening of economic globalization is a proven fact in current global economic development. In conformance with such a global economic development trend, we should adhere to the opening up as our basic national policy and "making full use of the international and domestic markets and resources" is the right strategic choice for China to realize a sound economic development. As a matter of fact, with China's increasing integration into the world economy, the percentage of exports in China's end demand (calculated at the price in 2002) has risen from 13.34% in 1987 to 30.92% in 2007 (as shown in Table 5). Trade has become an important factor which influences China's economic development. However, the increasing influence of trade on China's environment is accompanied by the rapid growth of China's trade. Because there has been an enormous transformation in the economic development model, it is inevitable.

Table 5 Comparison between the Embodied Effluent Export and Export Value (Unit: %)

Year	Percentage of theembodied effluent export in the total energy consumption or pollutant discharge in the national production sector				Percentage of export in the end demand
	Energy	CO_2	SO_2	COD	
1987	14.07	13.07	12.28	18.37	13.34
1992	20.30	20.31	17.88	22.52	14.70
2002	25.00	25.07	24.07	25.78	21.77
2003	26.77	26.84	24.10	27.26	24.43
2004	30.22	30.36	28.12	30.17	28.15
2005	33.40	33.59	31.30	31.63	30.19
2006	33.48	33.64	30.98	33.94	31.95
2007	31.88	32.04	29.40	26.92	30.92

Data source: calculated by the author.

In addition, the increasing influence of exports on China's environment is not because the energy or pollution intensity of the exported products or services is higher than that of the domestic demand. Export doesn't necessarily lead to an extensive economic growth in China. We can make a simple analysis and comparison of this. As shown in Table 5, the percentage of the embodied effluent export of various substances in the total energy consumption or pollutant discharge of the national production sector is very close to that of its exports in end demand. This means that although the percentage of the embodied effluent export in the total energy consumption or pollutant discharge of the national production sector is increasing, there is no marked difference[①] between the energy and pollution intensity of export and overall domestic demand. Therefore, the increasing influence of trade on China's environment is primarily owed to the increasing percentage of export in end demand rather than a higher energy or pollution intensity of the exported products or services than domestic demand.

① Although as a whole, the energy or pollution intensity of domestic demand is close to that of exports, if we compare the energy or pollution intensity of export and of consumption and fixed capital formation, we will find that the former is much higher than that of consumption, but lower than that of fixed capital formation.

The degradation of the environmental trade condition is not a result of the exertion of China's comparative advantages, but a weak enforcement of China's environmental regulations and a poor awareness to promote environmental protection through trade. We must be clearly aware of such a fact that China doesn't boast comparative advantages in energies and environmental capacity, especially when we consider China's huge population and we can even say that China is greatly deprived in energies and environmental capacity. Superficially, the degradation of China's environmental trade condition results from an increase of the percentage of the energy and pollution intensity products in the exported product structure compared with the imported products, but a more profound reason lies in the deficient enforcement of China's environmental regulations and the failure of the market external cost concerning environmental influence to be effectively binding to the producers' decision making.

Specifically speaking, for various objective and subjective reasons, the economic decision making in the past was characterized by the "emphasis on economic growth and the negligence on environmental protection," which means during the decision making process, the environmental factor was not fully valued. Therefore, it results in the poor enhancement of relevant environmental regulations and cheap and even free environmental factors. This affords a price competitive edge to China's energy and pollution intensity products in the international market. As a result, the percentage of energy and pollution intensity products in export is continually increasing compared with that in import, which ultimately leads to the degradation of China's environmental trade condition. The decision making department hasn't a strong awareness to improve the nation's environmental quality through trade. A relevant market mechanism and policy system are yet to be established and improved to fully tap the potential of trade in protecting the environment. This also reflects the deficient enforcement of the environmental regulations from another perspective.

Finally, against the backdrop of an increasing global environmental awareness and more and more rigorous resources and environmental restrictions, we may still tap China's potential to realize energy conservation and emission reduction through import, but what we face are enormous challenges and pressure. At present, major industrialized countries have already been equipped with complete sets of infrastructures and have accumulated large amounts of capital. During this process, the global cheap mineral resources and environmental factors have been consumed in large quantities and have now become resources in great shortage. Developing countries can no longer have easy access to the resources and environmental capacity needed for their development as those industrialized countries did. These industrialized countries which have developed first have imposed pressure on developing countries (including China) under the pretext of environmental protection at every turn. Therefore, although China has great potential to promote its environmental protection through trade and by "making full use of two resources," we have to admit that we still face tremendous challenges and pressure.

VII. Conclusion

In this article, I have drafted the complementary input-output table of comparable prices from 1987 to 2006, on the basis of which I have estimated the influence of trade on China's energy consumption and SO_2 emissions. I have also decomposed the changes of environmental influence brought by trade. The result of the estimation shows that since 1987, China's embodied effluent trade has grown rapidly. At the same time, the percentage of various embodied effluent exports in the total energy consumption and corresponding pollutant discharge in the national production sector also rose continually, currently reaching around one third. This means that the environmental influences caused by export cannot be overlooked and also provides evidence for people's intuition.

As the embodied effluent exports are increasing rapidly, so are the embodied effluent imports in China. This has, to a large degree, saved China's energy consumption and reduced its pollutant discharge. However, in recent years, the increase rate of the latter has lagged far behind that of the former. Therefore, China's embodied effluent exports have always been higher than the saved effluent imports and China's embodied effluent in net trade is on the rise. This means that at present, China belongs to the energy and environment net exporter or pollution net importer. Since 1987, China's environmental trade conditions have degraded significantly.

The increasing influence of trade on energy consumption and

environmental influence is closely tied to the growth of trade. The influence of the growth of trade on the embodied effluent trade is mainly manifested in the scale effect and technology effect. If there is no technology effect, the scale effect will cause a much higher level of embodied effluent exports than the current level. The technology effect brought about by the improvement of the energy efficiency and the decrease of pollution intensity has effectively prohibited the environmental influence caused by China's rapidly expanding export scale. Relatively speaking, the small structure effect means that since the late 1980s, China's trade structure has had little influence on energy consumption and pollutant discharge.

It should be pointed out in particular that there are some objective reasons which have caused the current environmental trade situation facing China. Trade doesn't necessarily cause China's extensive economic development model. To improve the influence of trade on China's environment, in the long run, we should enhance environmental regulations and in the short term, we should take integrative measures to coordinate the relationship between trade, the environment and economic development.

Due to limited space, I have not fully analyzed the profound reason for the influence of trade on the environment; have not analyzed the trade flow between China and other countries; and have not discussed how to transform the trade growth pattern, how to make policies to improve the relationship between trade and the environment. All these questions should be further addressed in the future.

Appendix

Basic Department Division of Input-Output Table

Agriculture	Paper-Making, Printing and Stationery Manufacturing	Communication Device, Computer and Other Electronic Equipment Manufacturing
Coal Mining and Dressing	Petroleum Refining, Coking, Nuclear Fuel and Gas Processing Industry	Instrument and Machinery Manufacturing for Culture and Office
Petroleum and Natural Gas Extraction	Chemical Industry	Other Industries
Metal Minerals Mining and Dressing	Nonmetal Mineral Products	Power, Heat Production and Supply

(contd.)

Nonmetal Minerals Mining and Dressing	Metal Smelting and Calender Processing Industry	Construction Industry
Food Manufacturing and Tobacco Processing Industry	Metal Products	Transportation Storage and Post and Telecommunication Industry
Textile Industry	Manufacturing of General and Special Purpose Machinery	Wholesale and Retail Trade/ Accommodation and Catering
Clothing, Leather, Down and Their Products	Transport and Communication Facilities Manufacturing	Non-Productive Departments
Timber Processing and Furniture Manufacturing	Electric Equipment and Machinery Manufacturing	

References:

[1] Chen Liping & Yang Zhongzhi. Ecological footprint in China's import and export trade. *World Economy Study*, 2005(5).

陈丽萍、杨忠直:《中国进出口贸易中的生态足迹》,《世界经济研究》2005 年第 5 期。

[2] Chen Xikang. China's foreign trade input-output table in 1995 and its application. In: Xu Xianchun & Liu Qiyun ed. 2001 *China's Input-Output Theory and Practice. China Statistics Press*, 2002.

陈锡康:《中国 1995 年对外贸易投入产出表及其应用》,见许宪春、刘起运编:《2001 年中国投入产出理论与实践》,中国统计出版社 2002 年版。

[3] Chen Ying, Pan Jiahua & Xie Laihui. Embodied energy in the imports and exports of China's foreign trade and its policy implication. *Economic Research Journal*, 2008(7).

陈迎、潘家华、谢来辉:《中国外贸进出口商品中的内涵能源及其政策含义》,《经济研究》2008 年第 7 期。

[4] Li Gang. Analysis of the material flow of China's foreign trade ecological environmental cost. *Statistical Research*, 2005(9).

李刚:《中国对外贸易生态环境代价的物质流分析》,《统计研究》2005 年第 9 期。

[5] Li Jinghua. Weighted average decomposition method of the SDA model and its application in China's tertiary industrial economic development. *Systems Engineering*, 2004(9).

李景华:《SDA 模型的加权平均分解法及在中国第三产业经济发展分析中的应用》,《系统工程》2004 年第 9 期。

[6] Ma Tao & Chen Jiakuan. Pollution footprint analysis of China's industrial products in international trade. *China Environmental Science*, 2005(4).

马涛、陈家宽:《中国工业产品国际贸易的污染足迹分析》,《中国环境科学》

2005 年第 4 期。

[7] Peng Haizhen. Analysis of trade liberalization's influence on China's environment. *Finance and Trade Research*, 2006(4).

彭海珍:《关于贸易自由化对中国环境影响的分析》,《财贸研究》2006 年第 4 期。

[8] Qi Ye, Li Huimin & Xu Ming. Estimation of the embodied energy in China's import and export trade. *China Population, Resources and Environment*, 2008(3).

齐晔、李惠民、徐明:《中国进出口贸易中的隐含能估算》,《中国人口 · 资源与环境》2008 年第 3 期。

[9] Shen Lisheng. Changes in China's foreign trade structure unfavorable to energy conservation and emission reduction. *Management World*, 2007(10).

沈利生:《我国对外贸易结构变化不利于节能降耗》,《管理世界》2007 年第 10 期。

[10] Shen Lisheng. Influence of foreign trade on China's pollutant discharge. *Management World*, 2008(6).

沈利生:《对外贸易对我国污染排放的影响》,《管理世界》2008 年第 6 期。

[11] Yin Jingdong. Contribution of foreign trade to economic growth: requirements analysis of China's economic growth miracle. *Quantitative & Technical Economics*, 2007(10).

尹敬东:《外贸对经济增长的贡献:中国经济增长奇迹的需求解析》,《数量经济技术经济研究》2007 年第 10 期。

[12] Zhang Lianzhong, Zhu Tan, Li Muhan & Zhang Bowei. Empirical analysis of the influence of trade liberalization on China's environment. *Nankai Business Review*, 2003(3).

张连众、朱坦、李慕涵、张伯伟:《贸易自由化对我国环境影响的实证分析》,《南开经济评论》2003 年第 3 期。

[13] Zheng Yuxin, Fan Mingtai & Zhang Youguo. *Coordinated Development between China's Trade and Environment under WTO Framework——Overall Analysis Based on the CGE Model.* Research report, 2005.

郑玉歆、樊明太、张友国:《WTO 条件下中国贸易与环境的协调发展——基于 CGE 模型的总体分析》,研究报告,2005 年。

[14] Ahmed N. and A. Wyckoff. *Carbon Dioxide Emissions Embodied in International Trade*, DSTI/DOC (2003) 15, Organization for Economic Cooperation and Development (OECD), 2003.

[15] Antweiler, W. The Pollution Terms of Trade, *Economic Systems Research*, Vol. 8, No. 4, 1996, 361-365.

[16] Beghin Jhon, Sebastien Dessus, David Ronald-Holst and Dominique van der Mensbrugghe. *General Equilibrium Modeling of Trade and the Environment*, Technical Papers, No. 116, OECD Development Center, Paris, September, 1996.

[17] Copeland, Brian R., M. S. Taylor. Trade, Growth, and the Environment, *Journal of Economic Literature*, Vol. XLII, 2004, 7-71.

[18] Dietzenbacher Eric, Bart Los. Structural Decomposition Techniques: Sense and Sensitivity, *Economic Systems Research*, Vol. 10, No. 4, 1998, 307-323.

[19] Dietzenbacher, E. & Los, B. Structural Decomposition Analyses with

Dependent Determinants, *Economic Systems Research*, Vol. 12, No. 4, 2000, 497-514.

[20] Fujimagari, D. The Sources of Change in the Canadian Industry Output, *Economic Systems Research*, Vol. 1, 1989, 187-202.

[21] Grossman Gene, Alan Kruger, Environmental Impacts of a North American Free Trade Agreement, In Garber, Peter M. (ed.), *The Mexico – U. S. Free Trade Agreement*. Cambridge and London, MIT Press, 1993, 13-56.

[22] IPCC. Revised 1996 IPCC *Guidelines for National Greenhouse Gas Inventories: Workbook* (Vol. 2), 1996, http://www.ipcc-nggip.iges.or.jp/public/gl/inva5a.html.

[23] Lee Hiro, David Roland-Holst. International Trade and the Transfer of Environmental Costs and Benefits, OECD Development Centre, Technical Paper No. 91, 1993.

[24] Lee Hiro, David Roland-Holst. Trade-induced Pollution Transfers and Implications for Japan's Investment and Assistant, *Asia Economic Journal*, Vol. 14, No. 2, 2000, 123-146.

[25] Lenzen M., L.-L. Pade, and J. Munksgaard. CO_2 Multipliers in Multi-Region Input-Output Models, *Economic Systems Research*, Vol. 16, No. 4, 2004, 391-412.

[26] Li You, C. N. Hewitt. The Effect of Trade between China and the UK on National and Global Carbon Dioxide Emissions, *Energy Policy*, Vol. 36, 2008, 1907-1914.

[27] Machado, Giovani, Roberto Schaeffer, and Ernst Worrel. Energy and Carbon EmbodiedIn the International Trade of Brazil: An Input-Output Approach, *Ecological Economics*, Vol. 39, No. 3, 2001, 409-424.

[28] Mukhopadhyay Kakali. Impact onthe Environment of Thailand's Trade with OECD Counties, *Asia-Pacific Trade and Investment Review*, Vol. 2, No. 1, 2006, 25-46.

[29] Munksgaard Jesper, Klaus Alsted Pedersen, Mette Wier, Impact of Household Consumption on CO_2 Emissions, *Energy Economics*, Vol. 22, 2000, 423-440.

[30] Munksgaard J. and K. A. Pedersen. CO_2 Accounts for Open Economies: Producer or Consumer Responsibility?, *Energy Policy*, Vol. 29, 2001, 327-334.

[31] Pan J. Phillips J., Chen Y. China's Balance of Emissions Embodied in Trade: Approaches to Measurement and Allocating International Responsibility, *Oxford Review of Economic Policy*, Vol. 24, No. 2, 2008, 354-376.

[32] Peters Glen P., Hertwich E. G. *Energy and Pollution Embodied in Trade: The Case of Norway*, Technical Report, Industrial Ecology Programme, Norwegian University of Science And Technology (NTNU), Trondheim, Norway, 2005.

[33] Peters Glen P., Hertwich E. G. Pollution Embodied in Trade: the Norwegian Case, *Global Environmental Change*, Vol. 16, No. 4, 2006, 379-387.

[34] Rhee, H.-C., Chung, H.-S. Change in CO_2 Emission and its Transmissions between Korea and Japan Using International Input-Output Analysis, *Ecological Economics*, Vol. 58, 2006, 788-800.

[35] Runge, C. F. Trade Pollution and Environmental Protection, In Bromley, D. W. (ed.), *The Handbook of Environmental Economics*, Blackwell, Oxford, 1995.

[36] Seibel, Steffen. Decomposition Analysis of Carbon Dioxide Emission Changes in Germany - Conceptual Framework and Empirical Results, *European Commission Working Papers and Studies*, 2003.

[37] Shui, B., Harriss, R. C. The Role of CO_2 Embodiment in US - China Trade, *Energy Policy*, Vol. 34, 2006, 4063-4068.

[38] Wang T. and Watson J, Who Owns China's Carbon Emissions. Tyndall Briefing Note No. 23, October, 2007.

[39] United Nations. Handbook of Input-Output Table Compilation and Analysis, Studies in Methods Series F, No. 74, *Handbook of National Accounting*, United Nations, 1999.

[40] Weber, C. L., Peters, G. P., Guan, D., Hubacek, K. The Contribution of Chinese Exports to Climate Change, *Energy Policy*, Vol. 36, 2008, 3572-3577.

[41] Wyckoff A. W. and J. M. Roop. The Embodiment of Carbon in Imports of Manufactured Products: Implications for International Agreements on Greenhouse Gas Emissions, *Energy Policy*, Vol. 22, 1994, 187-194.

Influences of Free Trade on China's Sustainable Development[1]

——Case Study of the Dynamic General Equilibrium Analysis of China's Commitments in the Post-WTO Transition Period

By FAN Mingtai & ZHENG Yuxin

I. Introduction

In the late 20th century, while accelerating economic system reform and promoting economic transformation, China also stepped up its opening up and vigorously promoted its trade liberalization. It acceded to the World Trade Organization (WTO) in December, 2001 and became an important member of the world trade system. Since its accession to the WTO, an open China has been facing dual challenges from world trade liberalization and internationalization of environmental protection, not only committed to its promises of promoting trade liberalization, but also required to actively participate in the international coordination mechanism of environmental protection under the WTO framework. Therefore, it should coordinate trade liberalization and environmental protection policies under the framework of sustainable development. On the one hand, with China's rapid economic growth, its ecology and environment bears more and more pressure. China is in urgent need to incorporate the environmental factor into its trade strategy under the WTO framework and make full use of the trade mechanism to promote its environmental protection and sustainable development; on the other hand, since developed countries and developing countries are at different stages in terms of their environmental problems, while

[1] This report is revised based on the 2nd report of the national social science fund project "China's Trade and Environment Policy under the WTO Framework" completed in 2005. Thanks for the revision suggestions from Zhao Xiao et al.

transferring polluting industries to developing countries like China through trade mechanisms, developed countries also prevent China and other developing countries from participating effectively in the international competition and cooperation through green barriers in international trade such as product quality standards and technology restrictions. Therefore, China has to learn from the experience and management mechanism in environmental protection of developed countries and promote the process of trade liberalization. From China's reality and the international practices, after China's accession to the WTO, the interaction mechanism and arrangement between trade and environment has constituted an important component in promoting the coordination of sustainable development policies.

The interaction between trade and environment is a topic of international concern. In trade liberalization, the relationship between environmental problems and trade is introduced step by step and gradually assumes prominence. The General Agreement on Tariffs and Trade (GATT) in 1947 only indirectly mentioned that to protect the life and health of human and creatures as well as the endangering natural resources, relevant countries were allowed to deviate from normal trade rules provided that this would not create import discrimination and trade restrictions. In 1972, the relationship between the environment and trade was put on the agenda for the first time in the United Nations Conference on the Human Environment held in Stockholm, Sweden. It was suggested to establish environmental measures and the international trade group, which would deal with any trade policies concerning pollution and human environmental protection according to their request. It was not until 1994 that this group reported to the 49th Session of GATT. In 1995 when the WTO was officially established, the environmental problem was truly incorporated into the trade system and the Committee on Trade and Environment (CTE) was established officially and began to conduct its work. The establishment of WTO is a result of eight years' of negotiations between the members of GATT and its rules are called "global economic constitution" for its transcendence of national sovereignty. The core of the WTO rules is trade liberalization, among which rules concerning the environment are *Agreement on Technical Barriers to Trade* (TBT), *Agreement on the Application of Sanitary and Phytosanitary Measures* (SPS) and *Agreement on Trade-Related Aspects of Intellectual Property Rights*

(TRIPs) and etc; however, these rules are not always consistent with the environmental targets. From the perspective of legislation, the WTO rules have restricted the space for Multilateral Environmental Agreements (MEAs) to exert its influence; the WTO rules also provide the legal basis for the international community to challenge the national environmental policies, mutually reinforcing then with the trade rights. From the perspective of politics, the environmental standards will influence a nation's competitiveness in the international market and this is why in promoting trade liberalization, an emphasis on environmental problems may not secure the necessary national political support. In consideration of legislative and political aspects, the interaction between trade and the environment has always been a sensitive topic. From the economic aspect, the research on the relationship between trade and the environment enters the economists' perspective with the focus on environmental protection and sustainable development. Dean (1992), Cropper and Oates (1992), Beghin, Roland-Holst, and Mensbrugghe (1994) et al. commented on relevant studies. The general conclusion is: ① trade liberalization has double-sided influences on the environment (Dean, 2002). One is to promote the economic development by improving trade conditions and the environmental degradation caused by the economic development through traditional models. Here, the so-called traditional model refers to the model without the inception of environmental regulations; the other is that while promoting economic development and increasing income, trade liberalization will also upgrade the environmental standard and enhance the willingness to pay so as to indirectly appease the environmental degradation. This implies that trade liberalization will strengthen the effect of the environmental regulations. ② compared with environmental policies, trade policies are not an effective means to realize environmental targets (Anderson and Blackhurst, 1992), because generally speaking, environmental degradation is mainly due to the dysfunctional external market rather than trade. Of course, the trade and other economic policy failures are also partly responsible for the environmental degradation; even if in a suboptimum framework, the optimal policy to reduce pollutant discharge is also to levy environmental taxes, through which you should be able to directly inhibit the pollutant discharge.

However, the two basic questions are disturbing, namely: first, will the comparative advantages accompanying the promotion of trade liberalization lead to the professionalization of polluting industries and bring harm to the environment? Second, will the levying of domestic environmental taxes influence a nation's international competitiveness and harm its trade growth? Since there is no influential theoretical support, in recent years, foreign scholars have turned to making empirical analyses of the interactions between trade and the environment; owing to the theoretical features and technological development of the Computable General Equilibrium (CGE) model, generally, it is selected as the typical analysis tool to be applied in the quantitative analysis of the influence of trade liberalization on the environment or the influence of environmental policies on trade. Perroni and Wigle (1994) used the CGE model and obtained a standard conclusion from simulation and analysis, namely: if the environmental externality remains unsolved and the pollutant discharge tax is not introduced, trade liberalization will degrade environmental qualities; since the environmental quality is not endowed with a value in the welfare function, and trade liberalization is good for improving the welfare. However, if the pollutant discharge tax is introduced to solve the environmental externality, trade liberalization will not only improve the environment, but also increase welfare and ultimately promote sustainable development.

In recent years, with China's expansion of opening up, especially its accession to the WTO and the acceleration of the regional trade liberalization process, studies on the interaction between China's trade and environment have begun to emerge. For example, OECD (1994) developed the CGE model for the trade and environment project and applied it in China. The World Bank (1994) conducted studies on China's future (2020) greenhouse gas emissions. In China, overall, most studies are biased toward qualitative analysis or case studies; although the application of the CGE model in the quantitative simulation and comparison analysis of trade or environment policies has started in recent years, basically it is at the initial stages, with most of the studies strategically deficient in theory and with the data being comparatively rough in technology. It lacks the quantification mechanism of non-trade barriers and has introduced the CGE model, which fails to update the model and data in time and track, and conducts empirical studies on new trade and the environmental mechanism. Exceptions are studies made by Zheng Yuxin, Fan Mingtai, Zhang Youguo (2002), Li Shantong, Zhuo Fan (2002), et al.

This article will focus on the influence of China's trade liberalization on sustainable development. Here we take China's commitment at the transitory period (2006-2010) after its accession to the WTO as an example for trade liberalization; the sustainable development in discussion here is mainly in terms of the economy and environment, despite that China, as a developing country, should also take other priority areas (like trade and poverty elimination) into consideration while concerning the relationship between trade and the environment. To conduct quantitative studies on the influence of China's trade liberalization on the sustainable development, we have first examined China's commitment to trade liberalization at the transitory period after its accession to the WTO. Then, based on expanding the mechanisms of the general equilibrium relationship between trade and the environment and the influence of trade liberalization on the environment in People's Republic Computable General Equilibrium Model (PRCGEM) and according to the design of the baseline scenario and China's trade liberalization scenario from 2006 to 2010, we simulated and analyzed the influence and effect of China's commitment to trade liberalization at the transitory period after its accession to the WTO on the sustainable development and explored the mechanism of action about how trade liberalization influences the sustainable development of the economy and environment. Finally, we provide a conclusion and discuss the policy implications.

II. China's Commitment to Trade Liberalization after Its Accession to the WTO

Since 1994, when the WTO was founded, China has begun to apply for its establishment as a founding member of the WTO, but it did officially acceded to the WTO until the end of 2001. The most fundamental task of the WTO is to promote trade liberalization, so taking its accession to the WTO as the opportunity, China vigorously adjusted trade and other policies and promoted the trade liberalization process. The trade liberalization process involves cutting taxation on goods trade, reducing the non-tariff barrier on goods and service trade and promoting the processes of investment facilitation. Tariff and non-tariff measures are two major instruments of trade policies. The tariff adjustments influence the bilateral trade adjustments on consumption, production, trade and employment by influencing the change in the import price of goods and services against the domestic price. Non-tariff barriers include import quotas, import licenses and voluntary export restraints. Only a small part of non-tariff barriers can be quantified as tariff equivalents. For example, Anderson, Martin and Van der Mensbrugghe (2006) pointed out that although China didn't accede to the WTO until 2001, what China has done in trade liberalization to accede to the WTO actually began since 1995. According to the calculation of Ianchovichina and Martin (2004), from 1995 to 2001, the simple average level of China's statutory tariffs were cut from 36.3% in 1994 to 16.6% in 2001 and the trade-weighted average level, from 35.5% in 1994 to 12.0% in 2001; according to the protocol of China's accession to the WTO, by 2010, China's committed statutory tariff level after its accession to the WTO would be further cut to 9.8% in a simple average and 6.8% in a weighted average.

1. Tariff of Goods Trade andTariff-rate Quota Barrier

China has implemented three types of import rates: general rate, most-favored-nation (MFN) rate and preferential rate. The preferential rate applies to the imported goods from those countries and regions concluding a reciprocal tariff treaty with China, the MFN rate is for WTO members and the general rate is for imported goods from other regions. In 2005, in coordinating the Harmonized System (HS) 8-digit level, except for 46 types of goods with specific duty rates (including 8 types of agricultural products) and 7 types of goods with compound tariff, others are with ad valorem duties.

Since China's accession to the WTO in 2001, the Chinese government has gradually lowered its tariff rates according to its commitments. Before acceding to the WTO, China's simple average tariff rate was 15.3% in 2001; after its accession to the WTO, as was committed, it cut the rate to 12.4% in 2002, 11.3% in 2003, 10.4% in 2004 and 9.9% in 2005. According to the distribution of China's tariff rates on the HS 8-digit level in 2005: among the 7,750 types of goods with the HS 8-digit level, the import tariff rate for 68.8% goods ranged from 0-10%, including most of resource products such as petroleum and metal and manufactured goods such as chemical and photographic apparatus, non-motor products and motor products; the import tariff rate of 6.4% goods was higher than 20% including parts of the agricultural products, transportation equipment, manufactured goods and motor products. We divided the 7,750 types of goods with HS 8-digit tariff codes into 13 categories and calculated their average tariff rates and tax exemption rates.

Figure 1 shows: those with a simple average tariff higher than the average tariff of the whole goods (9.9%) including agriculture (15.3%), transportation equipment (13.3%), leather and etc. (13.1%), manufactured goods (11.8%), textile (11.4%) and fishery (10.5%). Those with a high tax exemption rate include wood, pulp and motor products.

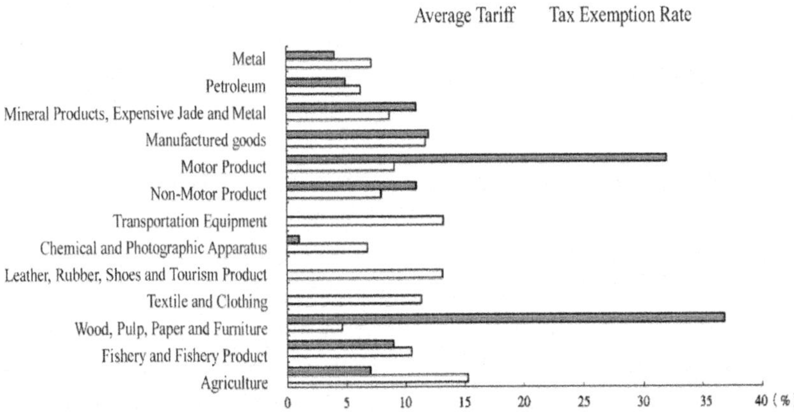

Figure 1 Average Tariff and Tax Exemption Rates of 13 Types of Goods in 2005

Tariffon Agricultural Products and Animal Husbandry Products

Since 2002, China has been fulfilling its commitment after acceding to the WTO to keep lowering the tariff on agricultural products and animal husbandry products. In 2005, the arithmetical average tax rate (MFN) of agricultural products was reduced to 15.3%, much lower than that of other WTO members; the average tariff of fishery and forestry products was respectively 10.5% and 4.6%. On the HS 8-digit level, among the 1,611 types of agricultural products imported by China, 1,554 were with an ad valorem rate of duty, 8 with a specific duty and the other 49 with a tariff-rate quota. Among all tax items of agricultural products, 81 enjoyed tax exemption, with the highest tax rate being 65%. The tax rate of 73% of the imported agricultural products ranged from 5% to 20%. The average tax rate of three major agricultural products, namely live animals and animal products (Chapter 1 to 5, except fish and fish products), peltry and leather (Chapter 41 to 43, except leather products and leather) and vegetable products (Chapter 6 to 14) was respectively 13.6%, 11.5% and 14.4%.

After its accession to the WTO, China promised to remove restrictions on the imported products of nine agricultural products through tariff-rate quota (TRQ) means, including wheat, grain, rice, soybean oil, palm oil, rapeseed oil, sugar, wool and cotton and has set a maximum annual quota. According to the report on China's import implementation rate of the agricultural tariff-rate quota (TRQ) products in 2004 issued by the WTO on April 6, 2005, only the actual quota implementation rate of cotton exceeded 100% and that of the other eight types of agricultural products (wheat, corn, rice, soybean oil, palm oil, rapeseed oil, sugar and wood) was lower than the maximum quota promised by China when it acceded to the WTO, especially the import of corn, which was below 5,000 tons. Some countries have shown concern for China's low quota implementation rate. However, a detailed analysis of China's low quota implementation rate and small number of imported TRQ products can reveal that this is subject to the low domestic market demand; besides, a dynamic observation shows that China's imported TRQ products is increasing each year, with an increase of 26.83% in 2004 compared to 2002. In particular, the implementation rate of cotton, palm oil and soybean oil exceeded 80% which shows that China has been fulfilling its commitment to improving the quota in good faith since it acceded to the WTO.

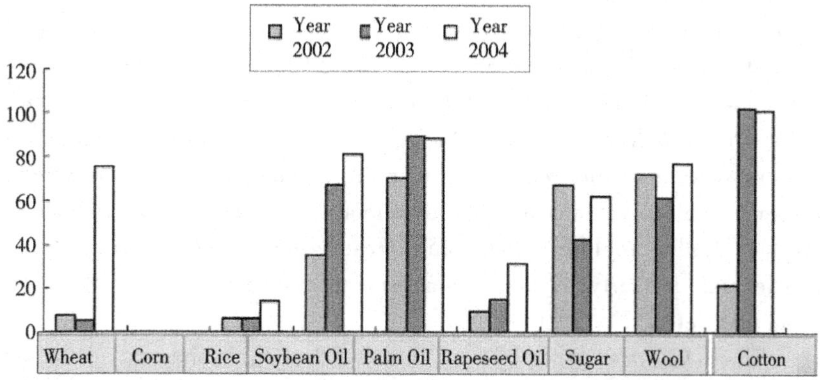

Figure 2 Import TRQ Implementation Rate of Agricultural Products in China (2002-2004)

Tariff on Industrial Products In 2001, the average tariff level of industrial products was 14.8%, in 2003, 10.3%, in 2004, 9.5% and in 2005, down to 9.0%. In 2005, China imposed a 3% to 6% import tariff on coke and other types of coal; as the net importer of iron ore and petroleum, China has exempted taxes on iron ore, crude oil and natural gas and imposed a 8% tariff on aluminum; the tax rate of most machinery products decreased to 5% and part of them enjoyed tax exemption. In 2005, the applicable average import tax rate of non-agricultural products in China was 9.3%. On June 1, 2006, the tax rate of vehicles and auto parts was cut to 25% and 10% respectively (average level). By the end of 2008, China has discharged its WTO obligation to cut the tariff on chemical products.

2. Non-Tariff Barrier on Trade and Investment

Goods Trade Non-tariff measures on goods trade include: animal and plant health inspection and quarantine measures, product specification and standards, customs management, price evaluation and port customs clearance, intellectual property rights, management transparency and appeal, conflict settlement, import permit registration procedures, provincial-level administrative management arrangement and national trade, etc.

Service Trade Service trade is realized through four models, namely cross-border supply (model 1), consumption abroad (model 2), commercial presence (model 3) and movement of natural persons (model 4). Upon acceding to the WTO, China made substantial commitments to ten departments, including 97 sub-departments in the service sector division table (W/120); relevant stipulations in *China's WTO Protocol* have provided basic principles for the legislation of China's service sector, which includes the detailed rules for commercial presence and movement of natural persons. The non-tariff barriers in service trade include ownership restriction, permit restriction, intellectual property rights, management transparency and national treatment, etc.

Since China's accession to the WTO, China has taken many measures in the liberalization of service trade and has hastened the fulfillment of its commitments. It has managed to promote the liberalization of service trade step by step with effective management. In recent years, China's service trade has grown stably at an annual rate of 15%. According to the WTO statistical data in 2003, China's total service trade reached 102 billion dollars, among which export was 46.7 billion dollars and import, 55.3 billion dollars.

The liberalization of service trade will improve productivity, decrease service cost through modernized cross-border transactions and payments so as to promote a commercial presence, movement of natural persons and consumption abroad and cause a spillover effect for manufacturing.

Investment Facilitation There are many non-tariff barriers on the bilateral investment in goods and service areas, including merger restrictions, implementation of intellectual property rights protection and protection of other property rights, stock equity and other joint-venture requirements, profit reports and relevant tax and foreign exchange management rules, transparency in the procedure of examination and approval, system and standard certainty, responsibilities and accountabilities of the governments of different levels in the procedure of examination and approval for investment and their consistency with the central government, movement of businessmen and domestic procedures to obtain in-time deliberation and remediation of the government's administrative behaviors. By eliminating some concrete regulations on foreign investment and streamlining the examining and approving procedure of foreign investments, better mechanisms are established for protection, transparency and dispute settlement, which provide better protection for bilateral investment. Since accompanying the investment is the import tariff decrease of a large number of capital goods, it will improve the capital return rate.

3. Quantitative Analysis Tool for the Influence of Trade Liberalization on Sustainable Development: Basic Structure of People's Republic Dynamic CGE Model (PRCGEM) and Some Expansion

The quantitative analysis tool for how trade liberalization influences sustainable development is the PRCGEM, China's economic dynamic CGE model of the general equilibrium relationship between trade and the environment and the mechanism of the influence of trade liberalization on the environment. The basic structure of the People's Republic Computable General Equilibrium Model (PRCGEM) used by us comes from the cooperation between the Policy Research Center of the Monash University in Australia and us, see Adams, et al. (1998), Zheng Yuxin, Fan Mingtai et al. (1999). However, this model has been expanded in the aspect of dynamics and the environment.

1. Basic Structure

This model consists of two parts: the first is static, including the behavior equation setting of various economies and governments during a certain period; the second is dynamic, including the intertemporal decision equation setting of various economies and governments, mainly for the investment and capital accumulation equation.

Like most applied computable general equilibrium models, the PRCGEM model is basically designed for comparative static analysis. The static model is in itself non-temporal, primarily used to simulate the immediate effect of one or more policy shocks rather than the corresponding adjustment of the time path. However, the current environmental edition can switch on the dynamic part to become a recursive dynamic model through the realization of the capital accumulation mechanism with a correlation between intensive investments with prospective earnings which can predict the time path effect of all the exogenous variables. The static part consists of the following eight parts.

The first is the production decision-making module, which can be divided into input decision-making and output decision-making. Figure 1 shows the corresponding decision-making.

The second is the domestic end demand module. The model distinguishes four domestic end demands, namely, investment demand, household consumption, government expenditures and inventory demand and makes respective assumptions on their demand behavior. The model assumes that the investor produces composite capital goods with import and domestic investment goods and with the investor as the price taker; this should minimize the cost under the restriction of production technology of the Wassily Leontief/CES 2-level nestling with no changes in returns to scale. The model assumes that the total household consumption demand is decided according to its fixed percentage in GDP; the composite commodity composition of the household consumption demand is decided by budget constraints and the principle of utility maximization. Since the utility function of the rural and non-rural residents respectively uses the STONE-GEARY utility function, it allows imperfect substitutability between different composite commodities and as a result, the household's end demand is the linear expenditure function of the composite commodity. The government expenditure demand can not only be processed as the exogenous variable, but also the endogenous variable. Most CGE models process the government purchases as the exogenous variable. However, this environmental CGE model processes the government demand as the endogenous variable, assuming that the government demand varies with the household's total demand.

The third is the international trade module, divided into import supply and export demand. This environmental CGE model accepts the ARMINGTON assumption, admitting the difference and imperfect partiality between domestic products and imported products. At the same time, the model assumes: China is a price taker in the external setting of the imports' global average price. Under such a price, the import supply has unlimited flexibility and is wholly decided by domestic demand and trade balance. In other words, for import supply, this environmental CGE model adopts small-country assumptions and assumes that the export demand is described by the downward sloping curve of the fixed price flexibility.

The fourth is the price module. The price system of this environmental CGE model is based on the following two assumptions: one is the perfect competition in the market, therefore, the commodity production and sales activities are at zero net profit; the other is a sole producer's price of each commodity, which doesn't vary with different production sectors, consumers or importers of the commodity. Here, the producer's price refers to the price accepted by the producer of domestic goods or the domestic supply price which adds the CIF accepted by the importer, the tariff and other costs. In this way, the model's assumption of the zero-net-profit production activities and the invariable returns to scale means that the producer's price is only the function of the input price; the model's assumption of the zero-net-profit sales activities means that the purchaser's price is the totaling of the commodity's producer's price, sales tax and commission.

The fifth is the market clearance module. Under general equilibrium conditions, the optimal supply and demand of the commodity and factor must be balanced. In other words, general equilibrium requires the commodity's market clearance and the factor's market clearance. It is worth pointing out that the labor market clearance doesn't mean that this model must be the full employment model and the capital market clearance also doesn't mean that there exists no dormant capital. The factor supply behavior assumption relies on the simulation to be conducted. Therefore, it is a closed part of the model and is related to the dynamic part.

The sixth is the necessary total definition. In terms of expenditures, it includes: total trade volume and its balance, domestic absorption, total GDP and definition of corresponding price index, etc.. According to the amount and price of the investment, consumption, export and import at the departmental or the commodity level and through totaling, we can get the respective total volume and price index of the investment, consumption, export and import and further, the domestic absorption, GDP and their corresponding price indexes. The resident's nominal income consists of the salary, capital gain and the government's transfer payment and subsidies. The model assumes that the laborer's nominal salary is exponentiated with the consumer's price index. It assumes that the government revenue primarily comes from the capital income tax and the direct or indirect tax of the domestic product and trade goods. According to China's new tax system implemented after 1994, the government revenue comes from the capital income tax of the resident and enterprise, the enterprise's value-added tax, consumption tax and business tax and import tariff and export rebates. Subsidies and export rebates are regarded as the government expenditure or the government's negative income. According to different simulation targets, in the closed model, the basic tax rate can be selected as the parameter of exogenous supply and the government's budget can be balanced by government savings or deficit; or the endogeny of the basic tax rate can be selected to balance government budget under the exogenous setting of government savings or deficit.

The seventh is the factor supply. The factor supply behavior is set according to the simulation to be conducted. Therefore, it is a part of the closed model.

The eighth is the environment module. This output of the module involves the intermediary products and services relating to the environment. The input of this module involves the environmental capital. The tax revenue system and subsidy system in this module are

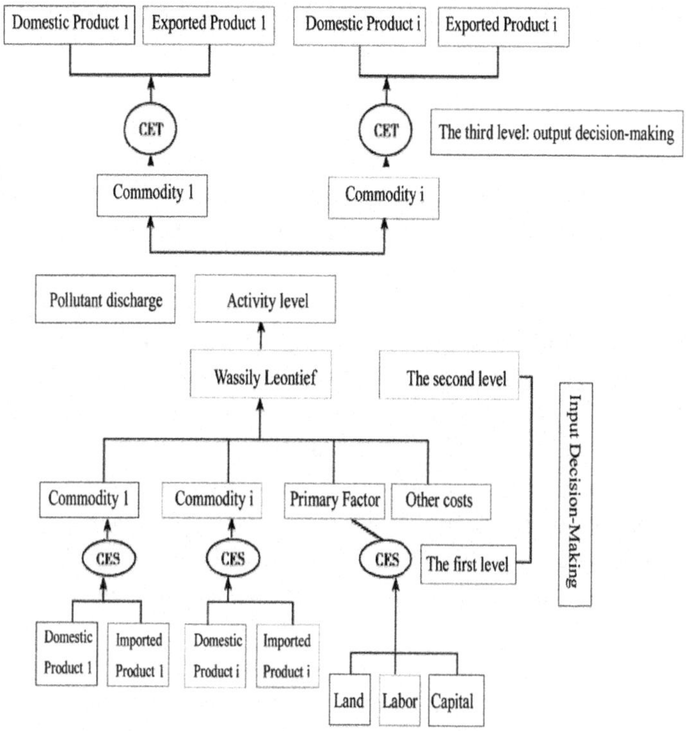

Figure 3 Production Structure Framework

related to the environment, and the price mechanism in this module also applies to the products and services about the environment.

2. Key Expansion

To make a quantitative analysis of the influence of trade liberalization on China's sustainable development, we make some key expansions of the current PRCGEM, including introducing the dynamic mechanism, the general equilibrium relationship between trade and the environment and the mechanism of the influence of trade liberalization on the environment.

(1) Dynamic mechanism

Model assumption: ① the relationship between interdepartmental labor mobility and the relative departmental wage rate and its corresponding employment situation. ② capital supply is realized through the opposite logic function in which the capital increase rate is regarded as the prospective earnings rate of the capital. Here, the prospective earnings rate is decided by the static expectations, which means that the investor only considers the period rent and asset price in forming their expected rate of return. The material capital is accumulated through the deduction of depreciation from investment to ensure capital supply. ③ the measure of total factor productivity is increased to reflect the technological and preference variation in the closed history. Through historical simulation and decomposition simulation of the increase headsprings, we first estimate the corresponding technological or preference coefficient; then use these technological or preference coefficients for scene reconstruction and extrapolate the model reference period from 1997 to 2005, and make further baseline forecasts of the period 2006-2010. The baseline forecast provides the implicit assumption about the baseline scenario.

(2) General equilibrium relationship between trade and the environment and the mechanism of the influence of trade liberalization on the environment

The model assumes that the pollutant discharge is related to economic activities through the pollutant discharge coefficient. It applies the CGE model for the estimation of the influence of trade policies on the environment, which involves the endogenesis problem of the environment pollution effect in the production function or effect function. There are three ways to include the environmental factor into the CGE framework (Xie and Saltzman, 1995). The first method is to expand the typical CGE model. While retaining its core structure, we add the pollutant discharge equation estimated according to the fixed coefficient of the departmental unit output or departmental unit intermediate input or the equation varying with the relevant price regulated by the environment or the tax exogenesis. The second method is to introduce the environmental feedback into the economic system. This environmental CGE model has set the pollution control cost in the production function or the environmental effect in the effect function. The third method is to set the production function of the pollution treatment activity or pollution treatment technology in the CGE model. We have adopted the first method. The environmental pollution intensity coefficient is generally measured by the corresponding pollutant discharge volume of unit output (or GDP). This environmental pollution intensity coefficient based on output (or GDP) means that under given technology conditions, the only way to reduce the environmental pollution is to reduce the output (or GDP); the pollutant discharge estimated through the environmental pollution coefficient usually has overlooked the pollution source outside the production process, for example, living consumption. Dessus, et al. (1994) proved that in the estimation through econometric regression, the pollutant discharge level can be explained with the input of a few industries in the input-output table. The technology based on the intermediate input allows the producer's pollution input substitution and uses the same pollution coefficient in the end consumption.

About the pollutant and pollutant discharge coefficient. Dessus, et al. (1994) designed the departmental pollutant discharge coefficient required in the trade and environment project of the OECD development based on the database of America's pollution coefficient in the World Bank (Martin, et al. 1991) and the pollutant discharge was represented with the vector with 14 types of pollution indexes. The 14 types of pollution are: the toxic substances discharged into water, air and soil (1-TOXAIR, 2-TOXWAT, 3-TOXSOL); the toxic metal substances of biological accumulation discharged into water, air and soil (4-BIOAIR, 5-BIOWAT, 6-BIOSOL); air pollutants (7-SO_2, 8-NO_2, 9-CO, 10-CO_2, 11-VOC volatile organic compound); Total Suspended Particulate (12-TSP); water pollution (13-BOD biochemical oxygen demand); total suspended particulate (14-TSS). The subdepartment pollutant discharge coefficient proposed by Dessus, et al. (1994) has provided a choice.

However, since the department pollution coefficient by Dessus, et al. (1994) differs in the industrial classification and lacks the support of empirical data, according to the current situation of China's environment statistics, we select waste water, waste air and solid wastes as the pollutants for analysis. For data limitations, during the current stage, we only use the pollution intensity coefficient based on output (or GDP).

With China's rapid economic development and improving living standards, people have a higher demand on the environmental quality and are more willing to make payments to support improvements. However, with China's accelerating industrialization and urbanization and for the traditional economic growth model to use resources and treat the environment, market mechanisms and institutional arrangements,

China is facing more and more resource restrictions and increasingly greater pressure in the carrying capacity of the ecological environment. In terms of the water environment, China is in a severe shortage of water resources which are unevenly distributed temporally and spatially. The water consumption for production, living and the ecological environment is increasing rapidly and the pollutant discharges relevant to water resources such as waste water, COD and ammonia nitrogen are also rapidly on the rise. This study shows that the agricultural non-point source pollution featured by a large consumption of ammonia fertilizer and pesticides and the animal manure is fast spreading and has become the major source of COD and ammonia nitrogen discharge in the water. The industrial water pollution mainly comes from the chemical industry, paper-making and printing industry, metal smelting and the calendering processing industry, electric power industry and the agricultural products processing and food industry at the urban-rural fringe areas. Since 1999, the domestic wastewater discharge has exceeded the industrial wastewater discharge. In terms of air environment, China's air pollution is rather severe. The industrial waste gas emission primarily comes from the burning of fossil energy, with the percentage of the fuel burning basically stabilizing at around 59% . The fossil energy is featured by coal and petroleum and since coal takes up around 68% in the total primary energy consumption, China's air pollution is coal-smoke pollution. Similar to water consumption, energy demand is increasing along with the rapid economic development and people's improving living standards. With the increase of energy consumption, the pollutants discharged into the air are also increasing. Since 1997, the SO_2 emissions in the waste air have far exceeded the environmental capacity (12 million tons/year) stipulated in the national second-level standard and the percentage of industries is constantly on the rise in the most recent four years. Owing to large emissions of sulfur dioxide, a large area in China suffers from acid rain. Acid rain and sulfur dioxide pollution have caused economic losses in crops, forests and human health. To a large degree, the future discharge level of air pollution hinges on the future trend of energy consumption. Evidence shows that with automobiles rising as the new consumer good, motor vehicles have become an important pollution source in major cities and this obviously has exacerbated the urban air pollution. In terms of the terrestrial environment, the solid wastes volume has been increasing stably since

1999. Solid wastes can be divided into production solid wastes and household refuse. Evidence shows that solid wastes discharge primarily comes from industrial and urban life.

Since relevant data on agriculture, service industry and living are unavailable, we only calculated the pollution coefficient in China's industrial sector. The industrial pollution coefficient in 2002 was calculated according to the pollutant discharge produced from the unit-full-aperture industrial added value (the fixed price in 1990) while that in 2003 was calculated according to the pollutant discharge produced from the unit-investigation-aperture total industrial output value (current year's price). It can be found that for different periods, the industrial pollution coefficients of the two apertures are different; however, they reflect basically the same relative pollution intensity distribution. For example, in industrial wastewater discharge, both the two coefficients show that the production and supply industry of the tap water is a high-discharging industry; in industrial waste gas emission, the hot water production and supply industry with electric steam is a high-discharging industry; in solid wastes discharge, metal mining and dressing industry is a high-discharging industry.

Table 1 China's Industrial Pollution Coefficient in 2002 and 2003
(Unit: 10,000 tons/100 million yuan, 100 million normal cubic meter/100 million yuan)

	Industrial Pollution Coefficient in 2002 (Fixed Price in 1990)			InvestigatedIndustrial Enterprise Pollution Coefficient in 2003(Current Year's Price)		
	Wastewater	Waste Gas	Solid Wastes	Wastewater	Waste Gas	Solid Wastes
02 # Coal Mining and Processing	117.92	3.03	31.71	20.53	0.64	5.79
03 Petroleum and Natural Gas Extraction	23.00	1.83	0.38	3.08	0.22	0.04
04 Metal Mining and Dressing	120.57	3.74	62.78	40.76	1.51	24.52
05 Non - Metal Mining and Dressing	28.43	1.17	3.25	47.92	1.94	6.08
06 Food, Beverage and Tobacco Industry	13.87	0.29	0.18	17.55	0.41	0.24
07 Textile Industry	98.72	1.34	0.36	25.88	0.41	0.11
08 Clothing	8.34	0.13	0.06	10.85	0.21	0.05

(contd.)

	Industrial Pollution Coefficient in 2002 (Fixed Price in 1990)			InvestigatedIndustrial Enterprise Pollution Coefficient in 2003(Current Year's Price)		
	Wastewater	Waste Gas	Solid Wastes	Wastewater	Waste Gas	Solid Wastes
09 Wood Furniture	7.37	0.90	0.20	10.18	0.60	0.23
10 Paper - Making and Printing	121.27	1.16	0.39	67.52	1.49	0.25
11 Petroleum Processing and Coking	138.52	10.66	3.13	6.41	0.01	0.20
12 Chemical Industry	22.62	0.77	0.34	19.96	1.30	0.43
13 Nonmetal Mineral Products	40.55	29.23	1.71	10.09	0.04	0.57
14 Metal Smelting and Calendering Processing Industry	67.20	10.18	5.09	14.08	4.35	1.38
15 Metal Products	19.77	0.98	0.14	7.84	4.54	0.05
16 Common Special - Purpose Equipment Manufacturing	7.84	0.26	0.11	4.08	0.13	0.07
17 Transport and Communication Facilities Manufacturing	11.98	0.80	0.16	3.78	0.04	0.04
18 Electric Equipment and Machinery Manufacturing	7.02	0.39	0.06	3.16	0.50	0.02
19 Electronic and Communication Device Manufacturing	5.23	0.22	0.02	2.32	0.10	0.01
20 Measuring Instruments and Culture & Office Machinery	8.23	0.23	0.03	3.74	0.25	0.03
21 Other Manufacturing Industries	90.33	3.44	1.15	5.79	1.79	0.03
22 Hot Water Production and Supply Industry with Electric Steam	200.22	49.51	15.47	37.99	9.64	3.17
23 Coal Gas Production and Supply Industry	133.86	13.37	4.23	13.47	1.70	0.50
24 Tap Water Production and Supply Industry	183.63	0.46	0.19	211.83	0.19	0.07

Note: the industrial pollution coefficient in 2002 was calculated according to the pollutant discharge of unit industrial added value (the fixed price in 1990) while that in 2003 was calculated according to the pollutant discharge of the unit added value of the investigated industrial enterprise (current year's price).

Data source: calculated according to *Statistic Outline on Environment in China* (2004) and *China Statistical Yearbook* (2004).

There are serious problems in the statistics on China's economy and environment, for example, excessively greater fluctuations of COD and SO_2 emissions at the absolute level. However, we still used the industrial pollution coefficient in Table 1 in the model. This also implies that we only consider industrial pollution problems. Unquestionably, this doesn't mean that we can ignore agricultural pollution problems, domestic pollution problems and ecological pollution problems. As a matter of fact, owing to the wide use of fertilizers, pesticides and other chemicals in modern agriculture, agricultural products and the environment have suffered severe pollution. While developed countries are enhancing their sanitary and phytosanitary measures (SPS measures), improving technical standards and increasing their testing projects and standards of agricultural products, the pesticide and veterinary drugs in the product surpassing the standard have become an important reason hindering the export of China's agricultural products. However, according to the investigation on the peasant households, in the most recent five years, the usage of fertilizers, pesticides and other chemicals in unit areas of crops have remained basically the same. In agricultural production, the price flexibility of the input of these chemicals is not obvious.

(3) Measuring trade distortions according to tariff equivalents

The purpose of replacing tariff with tariff equivalent to measure trade distortions is to reflect the mechanisms of action of parts of the quantifiable non-tariff barriers.

4. China's Trade Liberalization Process: Scenario Design and Simulation Outcome

China's trade liberalization process and the dynamic trajectory of China's environment pollution have provided important references for the design of the baseline scenario and trade liberalization simulation plan. Our simulation selected 2005 as the base year and estimated the influence of trade liberalization during 2006-2010. Here are the baseline scenario and trade liberalization scenario designed for our research.

Baseline Scenario It generally represents the business-as-usual scenario without policy changes. In the baseline scenario, we reconstructed the technology and preference variation determined through a simulation based on the historical period from 1998 to 2004.

First, we implicitly made a base year prediction for 2005[①] and then made a baseline prediction for macroeconomic indexes such as GDP, GNP, investment, consumption, export, import, labor force and capital. Figure 4 shows the macroeconomic dynamic trajectory of the baseline scenario from 2006 to 2010.

The setting of the baseline scenario should be based on the historical simulation reconstructed to the historical period from 1998 to 2004 and the technology and preference variation decided by the increase headspring decomposition simulation. As described before, we made a historical simulation and increased the headspring decomposition simulation according to the historical data from 1998 to 2004 and through the actual macroeconomic variation rate and the exogenous/endogenous transformation of the corresponding technology or preference variation rate. A typical example of the exogenous/endogenous transformation is the transformation between the GDP increase rate and the increase of the total factor productivity under the CD production function. In the historical simulation, we first assumed that the GDP was exogenous and the total factor productivity wa endogenous and worked out the increase rate of the total factor productivity according to the historical data on the increase rate of GDP; in the decomposition simulation of the increase headspring, we assumed that the total factor productivity was endogenous and the GDP increase rate was exogenous and worked out the GDP increase rate according to the increase rate of the total factor productivity which was already worked out. By these two steps, the history can be reconstructed. Of course, in the simulation process of historical reconstruction, because of different function settings and the role of general equilibrium rather than the partial equilibrium mechanism, the decomposition of the GDP increase headspring involves more than the changes in the total factor productivity. Through the historical simulation and the decomposition simulation of the increase headspring from 1998 to 2004, we have first estimated the corresponding technology or preference coefficient and then used them to simulate the historical reconstruction from 1998 to 2004.

---

① In other words, based on the compiling of the baseline equilibrium data in 1997 and according to the input and output in 2002 and the macro data from 1998 to 2004, we extrapolated the baseline equilibrium data to 2005. Although such extrapolation cannot ensure the authenticity of the input and output accounting in 2005, it has ensured the coordination of the baseline data by making the fullest use of the known information.

The baseline scenario regards 2005 as the base year and therefore, we first predicted the scenario of the base year 2005 according to the technology and preference variation decided by the simulation of the historical reconstruction from 1998 to 2004. Since we need to estimate the dynamic influence of trade liberalization from 2006 to 2010, therefore we should make a further baseline prediction of the period from 2006 to 2010.

Table 3 toTable 6 have provided the simulation outcome of the historical reconstruction of the macro economy, the subsector added value and the annual average increase rate of export and import from 1998 to 2005, and the baseline prediction of the macro economy, subsector added value and the annual average increase rate of export and import from 2006 to 2010. Among these, the average annual increase rate of GDP was 7. 8% from 1998 to 2005, 7. 3% from 2006 to 2010; the average annual increase rate of residents' consumption was respectively 7. 5% and 7. 0% from 1998 to 2005 and 2006 to 2010; the average annual increase rate of investment was respectively 8. 77% and 7. 77% from 1998 to 2005 and 2006 to 2010; the average annual increase rate of export was respectively 11. 3% and 10. 6% from 1998 to 2005 and 2006 to 2010 while that of import, 10% and 9. 3%; the average annual increase rate of the labor force was respectively 0. 90% and 0. 87% from 1998 to 2005 and 2006 to 2010. The average annual increase rate of capital was respectively 8. 29% and 8. 12% from 1998 to 2005 and 2006 to 2010. Overall, from 2006 to 2010, namely the "11th Five-Year" Plan period, China's economy still grew rapidly, with the IT-related electric and electronic industry and modern clothing industry as the high-growth industry of China's economy.

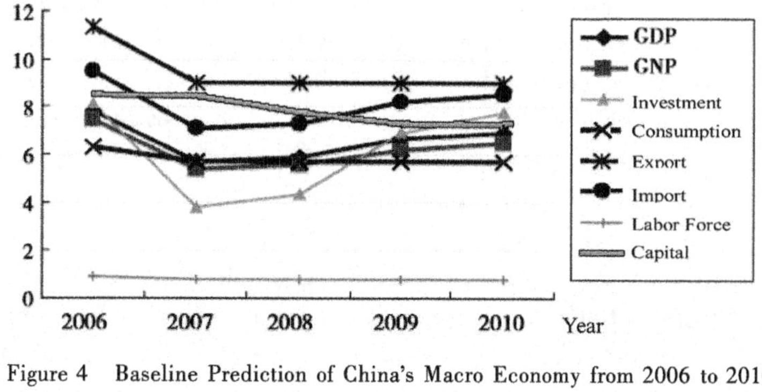

Figure 4 Baseline Prediction of China's Macro Economy from 2006 to 2010

Trade Liberalization Scenario According to China's commitment to the WTO and possible bilateral free trade arrangements, we have considered three trade liberalization scenarios, namely, goods trade liberalization (S1), service trade liberalization (S2) and investment facilitation (S3) scenarios.

Goods trade liberalization scenario (S1). The goods trade barrier is measured with a tariff equivalent, which reflects the comprehensive protection level of tariffs and quantifiable non-tariff barriers. The average tariff level of China's 2005 subsector goods trade was calculated based on the customs tariff in 2005; the quantifiable non-tariff barrier primarily considers the tariff quota promised in *China's WTO Protocol*, which primarily involves agricultural products, wool and fertilizers. Table 2 shows China's estimated tariff equivalent in 2005 in the ongoing feasibility research on the China-Australia free trade agreement.

Table 2 shows: according to the tariff equivalent measure, the goods with a high-level protection in trade in 2005 include wheat, beverage, sugar, clothing, automobiles and its components, etc.. Considering the promise made by China to the WTO for its accession and possible bilateral free trade arrangements and under the goods trade liberalization scenario, we assume that by 2010, the tariff equivalent would be basically cut off according to China's WTO commitment, with an average annual reduction rate of 1.31% overall.

Service trade liberalization scenario (S2). The service trade barrier primarily refers to the non-tariff barrier, for example, market access. The tariff equivalent measure of the service trade barrier is a problem which is frequently argued. Due to model restrictions, our scenario design about service trade liberalization is only restricted to the third model of service trade, namely, the commercial presence model. This primarily relates to the government's restrictions on and interventions in foreign investor's access to the service industry. Generally speaking, by enhancing the understanding of the two trade parties toward the investment rules of the service industry, simplifying the process for the foreign businessman to invest and lowering the threshold for the foreign businessman to enter the service industry, the service trade liberalization will reduce the barriers for service trade, allow the foreign businessman a certain degree of market access so as to promote service trade, improve the service industry and the productivity of the whole society and lower the expected investment rate of return. Therefore, here we try to reflect service trade liberalization according to the improvement of the factor productivity and the reduction of the expected investment rate of return. Based on relevant studies, for our service trade liberalization scenario, we assumed that by 2010, the liberalization relating to the third model of service trade will incur an average annual increase rate of 0.3% in China's service industry and a decrease of 1.5% in the expected investment rate of return.

Investment facilitation (S3) scenario. Similar to the liberalization of the third model of service trade, investment facilitation is also reflected through the improvement of productivity and the decrease of the expected investment rate of return. According to relevant studies by Mai et al. (2005), for our investment facilitation scenario, we assumed that by 2010, the factor productivity of the service industry will improve by 0.12% and the foreign investment will decrease by 0.5% in China's expected rate of return.

Table 2 China's Tariff Equivalent Level of Goods Trade in 2005 (Unit: %)

Agriculture and Food Industry		Manufacturing Industry	
Wheat	30.0	Coal	4.7
Other grains	3.0	Natural gas	6.0
Vegetables and fruits	5.9	Other mining industries	3.0
Oil crops	15.0	Textile	9.7
Fiber crops	3.0	Clothing	16.7
Other crops	3.1	Leather industry	9.0
Other animal products	5.2	Woodware and furniture	6.6
Wool	15.0	Print - making and printing industry	4.9
Forestry products	2.2	Petroleum and coal products	6.3
Fishery	12.8	Chemical industry	9.1
Slaughtered raw meat	12.0	Non - metal mineral products	11.0
Meat products	14.0	Metal smelting and calendering processing industry	6.6
Edible fat and oil	13.0	Metal products	11.0
Diary products	9.9	Automobile and components	16.3

(contd.)

Agriculture and Food Industry		Manufacturing Industry	
Processed rice	10. 6	Other transportation equipment industry	7. 5
Sugar	25. 0	Electric and electronic industry	7. 0
Other foods	15. 8	Machinery equipment industry	8. 8
Beverage	26. 0	Other manufacturing industries	13. 5

Data source: calculated according to *China's WTO Protocol* and the customs tariff in 2005.

It should be pointed out here that our scenario design about trade liberalization hasn't specially taken the trade liberalization implication of environmental regulation into consideration. If it is introduced into the scenario design, and the situation may have changed greatly.

5. *Influence of Trade Liberalization on the Volume of Sustainable Development and Its Mechanism of Action*

After setting the baseline scenario and the three policy variation scenarios of trade specialization from 2006 to 2010, we applied China's CGE model——PRCGEM about the environment and simulated the economic and environmental influences of trade liberalization. It should be stressed that ① according to Armington's research (1969, 1970), one of the mechanisms that make trade possible is the heterogeneity of domestic products, imported products and exported products and hence the imperfect substitutability. In the environmental economy realm, such heterogeneity becomes a concrete mark of the imperfect substitutability. That is, domestic, imported and exported products differ in the cleanness and pollution level and different industries or products have different pollution coefficients. ② in terms of the environment, foreign investment and domestic investment also have heterogeneity. Foreign investment brings not only pollution transfer problems, but also low resource consumption technology and clean technology. However, owing to data restrictions, we haven't introduced different pollution coefficients for domestic products, imported and exported products in the simulation, neither have we introduced different pollution intensity assumptions for foreign investment in the simulation about service trade liberalization and investment facilitation.

Refer to Table 3-9 for the simulation outcome of the trade liberalization's influence on sustainable development from 2006 to 2010 through the application of the PRCGEM model. Table 3 offers the influences of trade liberalization on macro economic growth and relevant price indexes. Table 4, 5, 6 offers respectively, the influences of trade liberalization on GDP, export and import at the industrial or product level. Table 7, 8, 9 respectively offers the influences of trade liberalization on wastewater, waste gas and solid waste discharges at the industrial or product level. Since the model's simulation outcome relies heavily on the baseline data and relevant assumptions, therefore we must relate to the assumptions in viewing the simulation outcome.

1. Economic Influence of Trade Liberalization

(1) Macroeconomic influence

The simulation outcome (see Table 3) of the baseline prediction and trade liberalization scenario from 2006 to 2010 shows:

① Trade liberalization will simulate actual economic activities and promote GDP growth, increasing the 6.61% average annual increase rate of GDP under the baseline scenario to 7.48% under the goods trade liberalization scenario, 6.66% under the service trade liberalization scenario, and 6.64% under the investment liberalization scenario. It can be seen that the average annual increase rate of GDP respectively increased by 0.87%, 0.06% and 0.04% under the three scenarios. The average annual increase rate of investment respectively increased by 1.16%, 0.16% and 0.03% under the three scenarios; and the average annual increase rate of the residents' consumption, respectively 0.50%, 0.04% and 0.03%.

Table 3 Macro Economic Influence of Trade Liberalization (Unit: %)

	1998-2005	2006-2010			
	Actual average	Baseline scenario	Goods trade	Service trade	Investment liberalization
Actual variation rate					
GDP	7.80	6.61	7.48	6.66	6.64
GNP	7.45	6.23	6.70	6.28	6.26
Investment	8.77	6.17	7.33	6.33	6.21
Consumption	6.30	5.82	6.32	5.86	5.85

(contd.)

	1998-2005	2006-2010			
	Actual average	Baseline scenario	Goods trade	Service trade	Investment liberalization
Export	11. 30	9. 46	11. 69	9. 47	9. 49
Import	9. 98	8. 12	10. 27	8. 18	8. 13
Labor force	0. 90	0. 82	0. 82	0. 82	0. 82
Capital	8. 29	7. 86	8. 55	7. 93	7. 88
Price variation rate					
GDP deflator	-0. 92	-0. 85	-1. 72	-0. 85	-0. 87
GNP deflator	-0. 65	-0. 53	-1. 04	-0. 53	-0. 55
Investment price	-0. 54	-0. 39	-0. 85	-0. 40	-0. 40
CPI					
Import price	-1. 08	-1. 00	-1. 74	-0. 98	-1. 01
Export price	-0. 59	-0. 35	-1. 66	0. 03	0. 03
Trade condition	-0. 85	-0. 83	-1. 77	-0. 83	-0. 85
Average salary	-0. 92	-0. 89	-1. 85	-0. 89	-0. 90

Data source: baseline assumption and simulation outcome of the model.

②Trade liberalization will improve national welfare and promote GNP growth, increasing the 6. 23% average annual increase rate of GNP to 6. 70% under the goods trade liberalization scenario, 6. 28% under the service trade liberalization scenario and 6. 26% under the investment liberalization scenario. It can be seen that under these three scenarios, the average annual increase rate of GNP increased by 0. 47%, 0. 05% and 0. 03% respectively.

③ Trade liberalization will directly promote goods and service trade. As a result, the average annual increase rate of export increased from 9. 46% under the baseline scenario to 11. 69% under the goods trade liberalization scenario, 9. 47% under the service trade liberalization scenario, and 9. 49% under the investment liberalization scenario. Therefore, the average annual increase rate of export respectively increased by 2. 23%, 0. 01% and 0. 03% under the three scenarios; the average annual increase rate of import increased from 8. 12% under the baseline scenario to 10. 27% under the goods trade liberalization scenario, 8. 18% under the service trade liberalization scenario, and 8.13% under the investment liberalization scenario. Therefore, the average annual increase rate of import respectively increased by 2.15%, 0.07% and 0.02% under the three scenarios. Under the current trade pattern, this means that the goods trade liberalization and investment liberalization will expand trade surplus, but the adverse effect of service trade is not capable of changing the expanding trend of trade surplus.

④ Trade liberalization will lower production cost and bring benefits to domestic and foreign consumers. It lowered the -0.85% GDP deflator variation rate under the baseline scenario to -1.72% under the goods trade liberalization scenario, -0.85% under the service trade liberalization scenario and -0.87% under the investment liberalization scenario. Therefore, the price index of domestic consumer goods varied by -0.74%, 0.02% and -0.01% on average under the three scenarios and the trade condition, by -0.96%, 0.01% and -0.01%.

(2) Industrial influence

Since different industries have different comparative advantages and the influences of trade liberalization are based on comparative advantages, therefore, in the trade liberalization process, not all industries are able to reap benefits. Generally, industries with comparative advantages will win greater benefits while industries which need protection will suffer losses if they are not protected; it is for these reasons that trade liberalization means industries with comparative advantages have a higher level of liberalization and smaller variations in the protection rate, while industries needing protection have a lower level of liberalization and larger variations in the protection rate.

The subsector simulation outcome (Table 4, 5, 6) of the baseline prediction and trade liberalization scenario from 2006 to 2010 shows:

① According to the measurements of the influences on GDP, industries which obtain the greatest profit in trade liberalization include the clothing industry, textile industry, electric and electronic manufacturing industries, other manufacturing industries and the construction industry, while those which obtain relatively small profits include agriculture, food, beverage and tobacco industries and the transportation equipment manufacturing industry; if we further consider the influences of expanding the tariff quotas, agriculture will even suffer losses.

②In terms of the influences on exports, thanks to comparative advantages, the clothing industry, textile industry, electric and electronic manufacturing industries and other manufacturing industries increased the fastest in the trade liberalization process while agriculture, and the extractive industries would even suffer losses during the service trade process.

③In terms of the influences on imports, trade liberalization will enable a rapid growth in primary agricultural products, food, beverage and tobacco industries, metal products and the transportation equipment industry, which channels into a certain impact domestically. The textile and clothing industries, owing to the cancellation of the "multifabre agreement," would undergo structural transformation, expand modern textile and clothing imports and there even appeared negative growth in the hot water production and supply industries with electric steam.

From such simulation outcomes, the influences of trade liberalization on some departments are not consistent with the general expectations. One the one hand, this may be attributable to the baseline data problem and on the other hand, the dynamic effect, an integration of the static effect that reflects resource distributions and the growth effects that reflect economic scale expansion. The growth effect primarily comes from the investment-capital accumulation mechanism, the interdepartmental transfer mechanism of the labor force and the variations of the total factor productivity. Under the domination of the dynamic effect, unlike the static effect which only reflects the resource distribution effect, in reality, the simulation outcome reflects more of the joint outcome of many factors.

Table 4 Influence of Trade Liberalization on the Added Value of Subsectors (Unit: %)

	1998-2005	2006-2010			
	Actual Average	Baseline Scenario	Goods Trade	Service Trade	Investment Liberalization
Agriculture	3. 18	2. 57	2. 97	2. 62	2. 63
Coal Mining and Processing	7. 42	6. 3	6. 94	6. 35	6. 33
Petroleum and Natural Gas Extraction	8. 68	7. 27	7. 81	7. 28	7. 31

(contd.)

	1998-2005	2006-2010			
	Actual Average	Baseline Scenario	Goods Trade	Service Trade	Investment Liberalization
Other Mining Industries	7.43	5.62	6.38	5.7	5.66
Food, Beverage and Tobacco Industry	7.15	6.55	6.64	6.5	6.52
Textile Industry	8.61	7.39	9.54	7.38	7.42
Clothing Industry	10.08	8.11	11.11	8.08	8.13
Wood Processing Industry	9.88	8.41	9.46	8.45	8.45
Paper - Making and Printing Industry etc.	8.2	7.16	7.78	7.21	7.2
Petroleum Processing and Coking Industry	7.94	6.81	7.33	6.86	6.85
Chemical Industry	8.56	7.66	8.16	7.69	7.7
Non - Metal Mineral Products	8.61	6.53	7.48	6.65	6.57
Metal Smelting and Calendering Processing Industry	8.62	6.9	7.56	6.98	6.94
Metal Products	9.09	7.35	8.28	7.42	7.39
Transportation Equipment Manufacturing Industry	7.95	6.76	6.91	6.85	6.8
Electric and Electronic Manufacturing Industry	12.46	10.63	12.53	10.61	10.67
Common Special - Purpose Equipment Manufacturing Industry	7.72	6.02	6.71	6.11	6.06
Other Manufacturing Industries	11.05	9.01	11.23	9.02	9.05
Hot Water Production and Supply Industry with Electric Steam	8.37	7.18	7.9	7.25	7.21
Coal Production and Supply Industry	8.61	7.34	7.99	7.39	7.38
Tap Water Production and Supply Industry	8.14	6.96	7.63	7.02	6.99
Construction Industry	8.76	6.23	7.37	6.39	6.26
Trade	8.13	6.88	7.72	6.94	6.92
Transportation, Post and Telecommunications Services	9.17	8.27	9.06	8.33	8.32
Financial Industry	7.95	6.81	7.5	6.87	6.84
Insurance Industry	8.22	7.09	7.89	7.19	7.13

(contd.)

	1998-2005	2006-2010			
	Actual Average	Baseline Scenario	Goods Trade	Service Trade	Investment Liberalization
Public Utilities	7.15	6.11	6.74	6.19	6.15
Entertainment and Other Service Industries	7.91	6.66	7.51	6.74	6.7
Real Estate Industry	8.75	7.77	8.15	7.82	7.81
Administration	6.47	5.82	6.26	5.87	5.85

Data source: simulation outcome of the model.

Table 5 Influence of Trade Liberalization on the Export of Subproducts (Unit: %)

	1998-2005	2006-2010			
	Actual Average	Baseline Scenario	Goods Trade	Service Trade	Investment Liberalization
Agriculture	4.35	3.61	4.01	3.56	3.65
Coal Mining and Processing	8.93	7.44	7.85	7.39	7.46
Petroleum and Natural Gas Extraction	13.04	10.14	10.59	10.10	10.17
Other Mining Industries	11.63	9.11	10.03	9.12	9.15
Food, Beverage and Tobacco Industry	9.37	8.20	9.18	7.81	7.87
Textile Industry	7.91	6.37	8.01	6.34	6.38
Clothing Industry	11.70	8.68	12.38	8.64	8.70
Wood Processing Industry	12.96	10.77	12.11	10.76	10.82
Paper - Making and Printing Industry etc.	11.65	9.74	10.63	9.73	9.78
Petroleum Processing and Coking Industry	4.84	4.06	4.36	4.06	4.07
Chemical Industry	12.88	10.70	12.05	10.69	10.74
Non - Metal Mineral Products	8.07	6.65	7.58	6.68	6.68
Metal Smelting and Calendering Processing Industry	10.38	8.53	9.53	8.55	8.56
Metal Products	11.93	9.64	11.12	9.67	9.68
Transportation Equipment Manufacturing Industry	10.68	8.79	9.71	8.81	8.83

(contd.)

	1998-2005	2006-2010			
	Actual Average	Baseline Scenario	Goods Trade	Service Trade	Investment Liberalization
Electric and Electronic Manufacturing Industry	14. 83	11. 96	14. 37	11. 93	12. 00
Common Special - Purpose Equipment Manufacturing Industry	6. 93	5. 77	6. 53	5. 78	5. 79
Other Manufacturing Industries	13. 69	10. 30	13. 40	10. 28	10. 33
Hot Water Production and Supply Industry with Electric Steam	14. 98	12. 37	13. 55	12. 74	12. 43
Coal Production and Supply Industry	12. 81	10. 48	10. 90	10. 46	10. 54
Tap Water Production and Supply Industry	13. 83	11. 94	12. 77	11. 98	12. 01
Construction Industry	11. 49	8. 81	9. 89	8. 93	8. 86
Trade	10. 47	8. 90	9. 57	8. 96	8. 95
Transportation, Post and Telecommunications Services	11. 99	10. 68	11. 48	10. 77	10. 73
Financial Industry	11. 17	9. 59	10. 42	9. 72	9. 65
Insurance Industry	11. 88	10. 25	10. 85	10. 39	10. 31
Public Utilities	10. 14	8. 49	9. 12	8. 62	8. 54
Entertainment and Other Service Industries	10. 69	8. 85	9. 82	8. 99	8. 89
Real Estate Industry	12. 28	10. 79	11. 42	10. 86	10. 83
Administration	8. 91	7. 46	7. 41	7. 49	7. 50

Data source: simulation outcome of the model.

Table 6 Influence of Trade Liberalization on the Import of Subproducts (Unit: %)

	1998-2005	2006-2010			
	Actual Average	Baseline Scenario	Goods Trade	Service Trade	Investment Liberalization
Agriculture	7. 46	5. 31	9. 21	5. 08	5. 01
Coal Mining and Processing	8. 01	7. 61	9. 22	7. 77	7. 66
Petroleum and Natural Gas Extraction	3. 96	4. 06	4. 29	4. 10	4. 07
Other Mining Industries	7. 30	7. 36	8. 48	7. 50	7. 40

(contd.)

	1998-2005	2006-2010			
	Actual Average	Baseline Scenario	Goods Trade	Service Trade	Investment Liberalization
Food, Beverage and Tobacco Industry	10. 31	7. 37	13. 50	7. 43	7. 39
Textile Industry	11. 99	9. 45	12. 63	9. 47	9. 48
Clothing Industry	10. 40	8. 04	10. 64	8. 13	8. 06
Wood Processing Industry	11. 02	8. 20	10. 86	8. 32	8. 22
Paper - Making and Printing Industry etc.	10. 05	8. 01	9. 79	8. 09	8. 03
Petroleum Processing and Coking Industry	9. 91	9. 11	10. 06	9. 17	9. 14
Chemical Industry	8. 80	7. 46	9. 94	7. 52	7. 48
Non - Metal Mineral Products	11. 48	9. 08	11. 62	9. 17	9. 10
Metal Smelting and Calendering Processing Industry	9. 67	7. 82	9. 58	7. 92	7. 85
Metal Products	9. 70	7. 78	11. 15	7. 89	7. 80
Transportation Equipment Manufacturing Industry	10. 57	7. 21	11. 02	7. 34	7. 22
Electric and Electronic Manufacturing Industry	10. 61	8. 86	10. 69	8. 91	8. 89
Common Special - Purpose Equipment Manufacturing Industry	10. 20	7. 96	9. 62	8. 08	7. 99
Other Manufacturing Industries	9. 35	7. 23	9. 96	7. 35	7. 25
Hot Water Production and Supply Industry with Electric Steam	8. 22	7. 36	7. 11	7. 00	7. 34
Coal Production and Supply Industry	11. 05	9. 75	10. 05	9. 89	9. 74
Tap Water Production and Supply Industry	9. 31	7. 62	7. 75	7. 69	7. 60
Construction Industry	11. 09	8. 61	9. 25	8. 73	8. 61
Trade	9. 89	8. 51	8. 70	8. 54	8. 51
Transportation, Post and Telecommunications Services	8. 19	6. 97	7. 26	6. 98	6. 98
Financial Industry	10. 18	8. 77	8. 98	8. 74	8. 77
Insurance Industry	9. 16	7. 71	8. 42	7. 70	7. 72
Public Utilities	10. 22	8. 98	9. 49	8. 97	8. 99

(contd.)

	1998-2005	2006-2010			
	Actual Average	Baseline Scenario	Goods Trade	Service Trade	Investment Liberalization
Entertainment and Other Service Industries	10.84	9.48	9.87	9.45	9.49
Real Estate Industry	16.45	13.96	14.61	14.03	14.00
Administration	7.33	6.86	7.34	6.90	6.88

Data source: simulation outcome of the model.

2. *Influence of Trade Liberalization on the Environment*

In terms of environmental pollution, different industries enjoy different comparative advantages, namely, different pollution coefficients; generally, a capital-intensive industry is also a high-polluting industry while a labor-intensive industry is relatively natural and clean. With environmental pollution, exports, imports and domestic products are heterogeneous and therefore, imports, exports and domestic products should also have different pollution coefficients. Owing to different resource abundance, technological level and developmental stages, some countries and regions (mainly developed countries and regions) have comparative advantages both in capital-intensive and high-polluting industries while others (mainly developing countries and regions) have comparative advantages in both labor-intensive and clean industries. To improve efficiency and develop scale economy, countries and regions with different comparative advantages will gradually realize division of labor based on specialization in international trade patterns and thereby enable goods with different pollution levels to flow and transfer between countries through international trade. From international trade and industrial transfer, the general trend is that developed countries transfer capital-intensive high-polluting industries to labor-intensive developing countries and provide corresponding environment-unfriendly and outdated technologies to them; at the same time, since developed countries have high incomes and a strong will to make environmental payments, their environmental standards are higher, which reduces developing countries to an unfavorable position in the trade and investment of environmental products and services. To sum up, in studying the influence of trade liberalization on the environment, we should consider that not all countries can be equally professional in clean goods production and green services and investments. However, our simulation here fails to consider the heterogeneity of trade goods and domestic goods in the environmental standard and service, of foreign investment and domestic investment in environmental pollution intensity.

The simulation outcome (see Table 7, 8, 9) of the environmental influence of the subsector in the baseline prediction and trade liberalization scenario shows:

①In terms of the influence on wastewater discharge, goods trade liberalization will aggravate the discharge in tap water production and supply industries, the clothing industry, other manufacturing industries, and the wood furniture industry while the pollution condition in high-polluting industries such as non-metal mining and dressing industries, the chemical industry, paper-making and printing industries and petroleum processing and coking industries have improved more or less. For example, compared with the baseline scenario, goods trade liberalization increased the wastewater discharge increase rate of tap water production and supply industries from 469% to 514% on average, an increase of 45%. The average increase rate of the wastewater discharge in the clothing industry, other manufacturing industries, and wood furniture industry respectively increased by 28.22%, 21.09% and 9.88%; at the same time, the goods trade liberalization decreased the average increase rate of the wastewater discharge in the non-metal mineral mining and dressing industries, petroleum processing and coking industries, paper-making and printing industries and the chemical industry respectively by 5.25%, 0.66%, 0.49% and 0.47%. The service trade liberalization and investment facilitation scenario failed to reverse such a pattern.

②In terms of the influence on waste gas emissions, the goods trade liberalization will boost the increase rate of the waste gas emissions in the clothing industry, electric equipment and machinery manufacturing industries, measuring instruments and culture & office machinery industries and tap water production and supply industries, while the emission condition in other manufacturing industries, non-metal mineral mining and dressing industries, and the non-metal mineral products and metal products have improved more or less. Compared with the baseline scenario, the goods trade liberalization enabled the increase rate of waste gas emissions in the clothing industry to climb from 96.60% to

132.46% on average, an increase of 35.86%. The average increase rate of the waste gas emissions in the electric machinery and equipment manufacturing industries, measuring instruments and culture & office machinery industries and tap water production and supply industries increased by 31.47%, 17.63% and 12.14% respectively; at the same time, the goods trade liberalization decreased the average increase rate of the waste gas emissions in other manufacturing industries, non-metal mineral mining and dressing industries, and the non-metal mineral products and metal products respectively by 25.78%, 5.09%, 3.36% and 2.74%. The service trade liberalization and investment facilitation failed to reverse such a pattern.

Table 7 Variation Rate in Wastewater Discharge (Unit: %)

	2002-2003	2006-2010			
		Baseline Scenario	Goods Trade	Service Trade	Investment Liberalization
02 # Coal Mining and Processing	-7.96	-1.98	-2.18	-1.99	-1.99
03 Petroleum and Natural Gas Extraction	2.92	0.91	0.98	0.91	0.92
04 Metal Mineral Mining and Dressing Industry	-18.83	-2.89	-3.28	-2.93	-2.91
05 Non - Metal Mineral Mining and Dressing Industry	114.69	-38.78	-44.03	-39.35	-39.05
06 Food, Beverage and Tobacco Industry	26.12	8.32	8.44	8.26	8.28
07 Textile Industry	33.87	11.64	15.01	11.62	11.68
08 Clothing Industry	236.66	76.01	104.23	75.75	76.21
09 Wood Furniture	255.12	79.45	89.33	79.85	79.83
10 Paper - Making and Printing Industry etc.	-15.90	-5.70	-6.19	-5.73	-5.73
11 Petroleum Processing and Coking Industry	-35.56	-8.58	-9.23	-8.64	-8.62
12 Chemical Industry	-24.81	-7.15	-7.62	-7.18	-7.19
13 Non - Metal Mineral Products	13.47	3.13	3.58	3.18	3.15
14 Metal Smelting and Calendering Processing Industry	-24.56	-3.16	-3.46	-3.2	-3.18
15 Metal Products	89.49	6.02	6.79	6.08	6.05

(contd.)

	2002-2003	2006-2010			
		Baseline Scenario	Goods Trade	Service Trade	Investment Liberalization
16 Common Special - Purpose Equipment Manufacturing Industry	30. 57	5. 37	5. 98	5. 44	5. 40
17 Transportation Equipment Manufacturing Industry	53. 35	10. 91	11. 14	11. 05	10. 97
18 Electric Machinery and Equipment Manufacturing Industry	97. 39	37. 38	44. 07	37. 33	37. 52
19 Electronic and Communication Device Manufacturing Industry	91. 93	31. 49	37. 14	31. 46	31. 62
20 Measuring Instruments and Culture & Office Machinery	157. 54	21. 60	26. 91	21. 62	21. 68
21 Other Manufacturing Industries	-76. 22	85. 78	106. 87	85. 88	86. 11
22 Hot Water Production and Supply Industry with Electric Steam	10. 33	5. 33	5. 86	5. 38	5. 35
23 Coal Gas Production and Supply Industry	-18. 25	-3. 20	-3. 48	-3. 22	-3. 22
24 Tap Water Production and Supply Industry	779. 32	469. 02	514. 22	473. 09	471. 47
X Living	6. 33	1. 70	1. 74	1. 55	1. 54

Data source: simulation outcome of the model.

Table 8 Variation Rate of the Waste Gas Emissions (Unit: %)

	2002-2003	2006-2010			
		Baseline Scenario	Goods Trade	Service Trade	Investment Liberalization
02 # Coal Mining and Processing	11. 50	2. 85	3. 14	2. 87	2. 86
03 Petroleum and Natural Gas Extraction	-6. 70	-2. 10	-2. 26	-2. 10	-2. 11
04 Metal Mineral Mining and Dressing Industry	-3. 30	-0. 50	-0. 57	-0. 51	-0. 50
05 Non - Metal Mineral Mining and Dressing Industry	111. 20	-37. 59	-42. 68	-38. 14	-37. 85
06 Food, Beverage and Tobacco Industry	39. 80	12. 69	12. 86	12. 59	12. 63
07 Textile Industry	57. 50	19. 76	25. 48	19. 72	19. 82
08 Clothing Industry	300. 70	96. 60	132. 46	96. 26	96. 84
09 Wood Furniture	72. 9	22. 71	25. 53	22. 82	22. 82

(contd.)

	2002-2003	2006-2010			
		Baseline Scenario	Goods Trade	Service Trade	Investment Liberalization
10 Paper - Making and Printing Industry etc.	94.00	33.66	36.58	33.87	33.85
11 Petroleum Processing and Coking Industry	-99.20	-23.93	-25.76	-24.10	-24.06
12 Chemical Industry	43.80	12.62	13.46	12.67	12.69
13 Non - Metal Mineral Products	-99.40	-23.09	-26.45	-23.51	-23.22
14 Metal Smelting and Calendering Processing Industry	53.60	6.90	7.55	6.97	6.94
15 Metal Products	-45.20	-21.53	-24.26	-21.75	-21.64
16 Common Special - Purpose Equipment Manufacturing Industry	27.70	4.86	5.41	4.93	4.89
17 Transportation Equipment Manufacturing Industry	-73.60	-15.05	-15.38	-15.25	-15.15
18 Electric Machinery and Equipment Manufacturing Industry	457.80	175.70	207.17	175.49	176.38
19 Electronic and Communication Device Manufacturing Industry	90.90	25.34	29.87	25.30	25.43
20 Measuring Instruments and Culture & Office Machinery	523.10	71.70	89.34	71.80	71.99
21 Other Manufacturing Industries	93.10	-104.82	-130.59	-104.95	-105.23
22 Hot Water Production and Supply Industry with Electric Steam	13.20	6.81	7.50	6.88	6.84
23 Coal Gas Production and Supply Industry	3.60	0.62	0.68	0.63	0.63
24 Tap Water Production and Supply Industry	209.40	125.99	138.13	127.09	126.65

Data source: simulation outcome of the model.

Table 9 Variation Rate inthe Production of Solid Wastes (Unit: %)

	2002-2003	2006-2010			
		Baseline Scenario	Goods Trade	Service Trade	Investment Liberalization
02 # Coal Mining and Processing	-3.42	-0.85	-0.94	-0.86	-0.85
03 Petroleum and Natural Gas Extraction	-10.70	-3.34	-3.59	-3.34	-3.36

(contd.)

	2002-2003	2006-2010			
		Baseline Scenario	Goods Trade	Service Trade	Investment Liberalization
04 Metal Mineral Mining and Dressing Industry	-6.22	-0.96	-1.08	-0.97	-0.96
05 Non - Metal Mineral Mining and Dressing Industry	138.34	-46.78	-53.11	-47.46	-47.10
06 Food, Beverage and Tobacco Industry	33.84	10.79	10.93	10.70	10.73
07 Textile Industry	48.65	16.72	21.57	16.69	16.77
08 Clothing Industry	129.32	41.54	56.96	41.39	41.64
09 Wood Furniture	195.17	60.78	68.34	61.08	61.07
10 Paper - Making and Printing Industry etc.	-2.35	-0.84	-0.91	-0.85	-0.85
11 Petroleum Processing and Coking Industry	-12.06	-2.91	-3.13	-2.93	-2.92
12 Chemical Industry	6.25	1.80	1.92	1.81	1.81
13 Non - Metal Mineral Products	53.24	12.36	14.16	12.59	12.43
14 Metal Smelting and Calendering Processing Industry	-2.11	-0.27	-0.30	-0.27	-0.27
15 Metal Products	58.25	27.74	31.27	28.03	27.89
16 Common Special - Purpose Equipment Manufacturing Industry	64.95	11.40	12.70	11.56	11.47
17 Transportation Equipment Manufacturing Industry	15.68	3.21	3.28	3.25	3.23
18 Electric Machinery and Equipment Manufacturing Industry	64.86	24.89	29.35	24.86	24.99
19 Electronic and Communication Device Manufacturing Industry	122.03	33.99	40.08	33.95	34.13
20 Measuring Instruments and Culture & Office Machinery	409.20	56.10	69.89	56.17	56.32
21 Other Manufacturing Industries	-89.96	101.24	126.14	101.37	101.64
22 Hot Water Production and Supply Industry with Electric Steam	19.17	9.89	10.89	10.00	9.94
23 Coal Gas Production and Supply Industry	-4.33	-0.76	-0.83	-0.76	-0.76
24 Tap Water Production and Supply Industry	193.55	116.48	127.71	117.49	117.09

Data source: simulation outcome of the model.

③ In terms of the influence on the discharge of solid wastes, the goods trade liberalization will boost the increase rate of the solid wastes discharge in other manufacturing industries, the clothing industry, measuring instruments and culture & office machinery industries and the tap water production and supply industries while the solid wastes discharge condition in the non-metal mineral mining and dressing industries, petroleum and natural gas extraction industries and metal mineral mining and dressing industries have improved more or less. Compared with the baseline scenario, the goods trade liberalization increased the average increase rate of the solid wastes discharge in other manufacturing industries, the clothing industry, measuring instruments and culture & office machinery industries and tap water production and supply industries respectively by 34.90%, 15.42%, 13.79% and 11.22%; at the same time, the goods trade liberalization decreased the average increase rate of the solid wastes discharge in the non-metal mineral mining and dressing industries, petroleum and natural gas extraction industries, petroleum processing and coking industries and metal mineral mining and dressing industries respectively by 6.33%, 0.25%, 0.22% and 0.13%. The service trade liberalization and investment facilitation failed to reverse such a pattern.

As mentioned before, without considering the differences of foreign investment and domestic investment in the environment pollution intensity, therefore, here the estimations about the environmental influence of the third-model service trade liberalization and investment facilitation is very conservative. However, relevant studies by Xia Youfu (1999) have provided a good starting point.

3. Mechanism of Action of Trade Liberalization's Influence on Sustainable Development

About the mechanism of action of trade liberalization's influence on the economy, the common consensus is that trade liberalization improves trade conditions, elicits more comprehensive competition and is favorable for the improvement of scale economy and the productivity level in a larger market. The comparative advantages will promote industries to improve their professional levels and realize more effective resource distributions. Rigorous mathematical reasoning can decompose the influence of trade liberalization into the combined effect of domestic demand, import penetration and export expansion. The basic conclusion is that while facilitating economic development, trade liberalization will elicit a broadening income gap for its promotion of professionalization. However, here we will skip this problem; on the contrary, we will concentrate on the mechanism of action of trade liberalization's influences on the environment.

Since the study on the environmental influences of the North American Free Trade Agreement (NAFTA) by Grossman & Krueger (1993), generally the mechanism of trade's influences on the environment has been divided into three mutually reinforcing components: structure effect, scale effect and technology effect.

Structure Effect It originates from the professionalization and structural adjustments incurred by international trade, which refers to the environmental influence caused by trade liberalization through economic structural adjustments. Trade liberalization promotes the division of labor based on specialization and causes countries to become involved in international competition with more dependence on their own natural endowments superiority, so as to advance the economic structural adjustments of different countries. Trade liberalization can not only accelerate the transformation of a country's industrial structure from a capital-intensive one dominated by the second industry which is seriously polluted to the one dominated by the tertiary industry which is lightly polluted, which improves the environment significantly; it may also enable a country to excessively develop its resource-exporting industries and high-polluting industries, which will exacerbate the environment. Many developing countries expand their natural resource exports for the sake of development, but the small country's behavior in international trade determines that the price of their raw materials will not fully allow for their environmental cost. If a country or a region expands the export of clean or "green" goods and inhibits the import of high-polluting goods, then trade liberalization will produce a net positive effect on the local environment; contrarily, if a country or a region is unable to expand the export of clean or "green" goods but at the same time, has to expand the import of high-polluting goods, then trade liberalization will produce a net negative effect on the local environment. The structure effect has than reflected a mechanism in which trade liberalization elicits environmental changes through structural adjustments of industries or products with different comparative advantages for different environmental contents.

Scale Effect It originates from the increase of economic activities within the circumstances of given production structures and pollution coefficients which refers to the environmental influence caused by the changes in the economic scale resulting from trade liberalization. Generally speaking, trade liberalization will promote economic growth and economic scale expansion. Under the scenario of an unchanged production structure and pollution coefficient, economic growth will not only lead to overexploitation of resources and excessive pollutant discharge, which brings more pressure on the environment; it will also increase national wealth, improve people's living standards and make them more aware of and more dedicated to improving the environment. The scale effect has reflected a mechanism in which trade liberalization changes the environment through overall economic growth.

Technology Effect It originates from changes in per unit pollution production (namely pollution coefficient) elicited by increased income and enhanced environmental regulations. When the production structure and pollution coefficient remain the same, the scale effect that economic growth invariably leads to, the increase of pollutants production, is frustrating; however, a silver lining is that the income increases brought by economic growth will place a higher demand for a cleaner environment. Generally, with income increases the economy will have a stronger desire to make payments for cleaner products. Therefore, if policy decision making is not undertaken by the pollution industries and the government does not make compromises with the inaction of pollution industries, then generally, it can be predicted that with income increases, environmental standards and tax policies will be strengthened to lower the production of per unit pollutants. Trade liberalization accelerates the technological flow between countries. New technologies promote productivity and under the same output, less input is required and less pollution will be discharged; but at the same time, trade liberalization also has expanded the transfer channel of outdated and harmful technologies and crafts. Such examples are easily available in the technology transfer from developed countries to developing countries. The technology effect has reflected a mechanism in which trade liberalization leads to changes in the pollution coefficient through income increases.

Trade liberalization also influences the environment through product effect and regulation effect. It can promote the flow of innovative products and the transfer of garbage to elicit the product effect; at the same time, trade liberalization can also influence a nation's environmental regulations, promoting it to improve its environmental management, enhance environmental measures and environmental standards and strengthen the effect of environmental improvement while reining in the freedom and capability of a nation to implement environmental policies based on its national conditions with international trade regulations.

The ultimate influence of trade on the environment hinges on the combination of the structure effect, scale effect and technology effect rather than any singular effect. Any Quantified Pollutant of the Environment (QPE) can be represented with the following mathematical formula:

$$QPE = \Sigma_i QPE_i = \Sigma_i Y * \left(\frac{Y_i}{Y}\right) * \left(\frac{QPE_i}{Y_i}\right) = Y\Sigma_i (SY_i * EC_i) \quad (1)$$

In which Y represents total output (added value), $SY_i\left(=\frac{Y_i}{Y}\right)$, the structural percentage of the subsector or product i's output (added value), $EC_i\left(=\frac{QPE_i}{Y_i}\right)$, the pollution coefficient of subsector or product i, or the pollution produced by unit output of the industry or product i. With this, it is not hard to work out the corresponding variation rate of QPE as:

$$QPE = y + \Sigma_i SE_i * (y_i - y) + \Sigma_i SE_i * (QPE_i - y_i) \quad (2)$$

in which y represents the variation rate of total output (added value), $SE_i\left(\frac{QPE_i}{QPE}\right)$, the structural percentage of the environmental pollutant of subsector or product i, y_i, the variation rate of the total output (added value) of subsector or product i, QPE_i, the variation rate of QPE of subsector or product i. Obviously, the variation rate of QPE elicited by trade liberalization is the combination of scale effect (y), structure effect $(\Sigma_i SE_i * (y_i - y))$ and technology effect $(\Sigma_i SE_i * (QPE_i - y_i))$.

According to the decomposition equation (2) of QPE, we decomposed the variation rate of China's industrial pollutant discharge under the baseline scenario and goods trade liberalization scenario during the period from 2006 to 2010 and the decomposition outcome is shown in Table 10.

Table 10 Decomposition of the Variation Rate of Industrial Pollutant Discharge from 2006 to 2010

	Variation Rate and Decomposition	Wastewater Discharge	Waste Gas Emissions	Solid Wastes Discharge
Baseline scenario	Variation rate (%)	3.58	0.28	1.89
	Scale effect	7.44	7.44	7.44
	Structure effect	-0.70	-0.87	-1.31
	Technology effect	-3.17	-6.29	-4.24
Influence of trade liberalization	Variation rate (%)	5.01	0.58	2.64
	Scale effect	8.31	8.31	8.31
	Structure effect	-0.37	-0.54	-1.04
	Technology effect	-2.93	-7.19	-4.63

Data source: simulation outcome of the model.

The decomposition outcome shows:

①Goods trade liberalizationincreased the average annual increase rate of the wastewater discharge from 3.58% under the baseline scenario to 5.01% under the goods trade liberalization scenario, an increase of 1.44%. The scale effect contributed a share of 0.87%, the structure effect, 0.33% and the technology effect, 0.24%. Therefore, the scale effect, structure effect and technology effect triggered by goods trade liberalization, jointly aggravated the wastewater discharge; the percentage point increase in the average annual increase rate of wastewater discharge triggered by goods trade liberalization is more than that in the GDP average annual increase rate. Therefore, it means an enhanced marginal intensity of per unit GDP wastewater discharge.

②Goods trade liberalizationincreased the average annual increase rate of the waste gas emissions from 0.28% under the baseline scenario to 0.58% under the goods trade liberalization scenario, an increase of 0.30%. The scale effect contributed a share of 0.87%, the structure effect, 0.33% and the technology effect, -0.90%. Therefore, under the goods trade liberalization scenario, although the technology effect can totally hedge the scale effect, it cannot hedge the joint influence of the scale effect and structure effect; compared with the 0.87% increase in GDP triggered by the goods trade liberalization, the marginal intensity of waste gas emissions has decreased.

③Goods trade liberalizationincreased the average annual increase rate of the solid wastes discharge from 1.89% under the baseline scenario to 2.64% under the goods trade liberalization scenario, an increase of 0.75%. The scale effect contributed a share of 0.87%, the structure effect, 0.27% and the technology effect, - 0.39%. Therefore, under the goods trade liberalization scenario, although the technology effect can totally hedge the scale effect, it cannot hedge the joint influence of the scale effect and structure effect; compared with the 0.87% increase in GDP triggered by the goods trade liberalization, the marginal intensity of solid wastes discharge has decreased slightly.

Therefore, the basic conclusion can be summarized as: a. under an unchanged enforcement of the environmental regulations, trade liberalization will enhance the environmental pollutant discharge under the joint influence of the scale effect and structure effect. The scale effect is the root cause for the environmental degradation and the structure effect is complementary in changing the environment. They have dominated trade liberalization and increased wastewater, waste gas and solid wastes discharge by promoting economic growth. b. the technology effect is the dominant factor to improve the environment and can hedge the scale effect or structure effect so as to play a positive role in environmental changes. However, the technology effect is not capable of offsetting the joint influence of the scale effect and structure effect. Under the trade liberalization scenario, although the technology effect, closely related to environmental regulations, fails to reverse the influence of the scale effect and structure effect on waste gas and solid waste discharges, to a considerable degree, it inhibits the increase of waste gas and solid waste discharges. If without the cooperation of the environmental regulations to facilitate the technology effect in hedging the scale effect and structure effect, trade liberalization will further degrade the environment when classical comparative advantages are dominated.

Such a conclusion seems to be universal. Copeland & Taylor (1994) proved in their research on the environmental influence of trade liberalization in two groups of countries respectively in the north and south with different pollution intensities that when environmental problems are only domestic, if the environmental quality demand increases higher than income, theoretically speaking, the technology effect can offset the scale effect, but cannot offset the joint influence of the scale effect and negative structure effect. Further studies by Copeland & Taylor (1995) pointed out: when environmental problems are international rather than domestic, trade liberalization will further increase global pollution. Chichilnisky (1994) further related property right and resource management with environmental standards to explain why the north and south have different environmental comparative advantages. Therefore, the monographic study "Trade and Environment" by the WTO summarized that trade liberalization can improve developed countries' environment, but will further exacerbate developing countries' environmental problems; such an outcome is almost definitional. Because relevant studies on the relationship between trade and the environment are based on the comparative advantages theory on environmental standards and resource management, the assumption that different industries, regions or countries are heterogeneous in the environmental aspects or have different pollution coefficients is similar to the classical comparative advantages in labor and capital.

6. Some Policy Implications

Based on China's commitment to trade liberalization in the post - WTO transition period, our research simulated and analyzed the influence of trade liberalization on sustainable development through the expansion and application of China's PRCGEM model. Due to data unavailability and the limitations of the CGE model, we must be cautious in our estimation and analysis of the influence of trade liberalization on sustainable development. Even so, the research findings are still impacted by certain policy implications.

First, when the enhancement of environmental regulations remains unchanged, the environmental pollutant discharge will be enhanced owing to the trade liberalization promoted by China in the post - WTO transition period. On the one hand, the scale effect and structure effect have jointly dominated trade liberalization and increased wastewater, waste gas and solid waste discharges through economic growth and structural adjustments. The scale effect is decisive while the structure effect is complementary or nearly central. On the other hand, although the technology effect related to environmental regulations has an obvious impact on environmental improvement and can hedge the scale effect or structure effect to exert a positive influence on environmental variation, it is unable to offset the joint influence of the scale effect and negative structure effect. Therefore, if not combined with environmental regulations, the trade liberalization promised by China in the post - WTO transition period may increase the pollutant discharge.

What should be emphasized is that under trade liberalization, if the enhancement of environmental regulations remains unchanged, the classic comparative advantages will beat the environmental comparative advantages to take the dominating position in trade liberalization and the environmental pollution problem will be further aggravated; this is only one side of the "story" between trade and environment. The other side of the problem is that if we take environmental regulations into consideration, will trade liberalization still aggravate environmental pollution problems? In terms of China's reality and as is shown in the dynamic trend of China's environmental variation and industrial pollution intensity coefficient, with China's economic development and the reform and opening up, the strengthening of China's environmental regulations will decrease the industrial pollution intensity. The empirical study by Desssus & Bussolo (1998) shows: if the environmental externality is internalized through environmental regulations, trade liberalization can not only improve the environment, but also promote economic growth and social welfare. The empirical study by Lee & Roland-Holst (1997) further shows that there is a surplus of the income increase elicited by trade liberalization deducting the payment for environmental regulations (like environmental tax). Therefore, with reasonable coordination, it is absolutely possible for trade liberalization and environmental regulations to boost economic growth while improving the environmental quality. The research on the influence of environmental regulations on trade by Zheng Yuxin, Fan Mingtai and Zhang Youguo (2002) shows that if combined with effective environmental regulations, trade liberalization can serve as an essential means to realize economic growth and environmental protection and promote the sustainable development.

Second, the combination of trade liberalization and environmental regulations has two implications. One is to accentuate the environmental factors in trade liberalization and to enhance environment-related trade mechanisms under WTO regulations and multilateral environment agreements and promote the trade liberalization of the environmental products and services. In particular, to maintain domestic market order and protect human health and environment, we should refer to international norms and establish our own environmental barrier system.

We should firmly prohibit products that pose serious threats to the environment such as hazardous wastes and imported products, technologies and equipment sifted out by foreign countries for the heavy pollution they have brought to the environment and enhance the examination and quarantine inspection of imported goods to prevent products with potential threats to people's security from entering China's market. The second is to enhance the role played by trade liberalization in environmental regulations. Under WTO regulations and multilateral environment agreements, we should stand firmly in our right to make and implement environmental regulation polices on our own initiative and urge developed countries to discharge their obligations to provide fiscal and technical assistance for the sustainable development of developing countries while actively participating in the trade liberalization process in the international cooperation which promotes environmental regulations.

Third, in terms of the scientific development outlook, China's trade liberalization process must coordinate with environmental regulations for comprehensive decision-making. When the enforcement of environmental regulations remains unchanged, the result that trade liberalization will lead to the expansion of pollutant discharge shows that China cannot overemphasize trade liberalization while overlooking its environmental cost; China's trade liberalization process must be favorable to China's environmental protection and sustainable development. At the same time, environmental regulations are not only needed in the environmental protection and sustainable development, but also an important component in the international trade liberalization. Since China acceded to the WTO, China has faced increasing technological trade barriers related to the environment. Without the implementation of proper environmental policies and sustainable development strategies, trade liberalization will become an amplifier of the policy and market failure; China's opening up will also be restricted by this. To realize the target of environmental protection amidst the increase of foreign trade, China needs to upgrade its environmental standards, improves environmental legislation and enhance environmental management.

Fourth, to promote the trade liberalization process, China needs to track changes of foreign environmental barriers and enhance the capacity for building and information sharing of the environmental influences of trade liberalization.

References:

[1] Li Shantong, Zhuo Fan, et al.. *Influence of China's accession to WTO on the environment.* The report by the "WTO and Environment" Research Group in 2002. The First Session of the 3rd China Council for International Co-operation on Environment and Development.

李善同、翟凡等:《加入 WTO 对中国环境的影响》,第三届中国环境与发展国际合作委员会第一次会议"世贸组织与环境"课题组 2002 年报告。

[2] Lin Hanchuan & Tian Dongshan. Tentative study of international green trade barriers and the way to surmount them. *Review of Economic Research*, 2002.

林汉川、田东山:《国际绿色贸易壁垒及其突破对策探析》,《经济研究参考》2002 年版。

[3] [Swedish] Thomas Anderson, et al.. *Environment and Trade——Ecology, Economy, System and Policy.* Tsinghua University Press, 1998.

[瑞典]托马斯·安德森等著:《环境与贸易——生态、经济、体制和政策》,清华大学出版社 1998 年版。

[4] Xia Youfu. Study on the current situation and consequence of China's foreign-invested pollution-intensive industries and the countermeasures. *Management World*, 1999(3).

夏友富:《外商投资中国污染密集型产业现状、后果及其对策研究》,《管理世界》1999 年第 3 期。

[5] Zheng Yuxin, Fan Mingtai, et al.. *Analysis of China's CGE Model and Policy.* Social Sciences Academic Press, 1999.

郑玉歆、樊明太等著:《中国 CGE 模型及政策分析》,社会科学文献出版社 1999 年版。

[6] Zheng Yuxin, Fan Mingtai & Zhang Youguo. *Coordinated development between China's trade and environment under WTO conditions: based on the overall analysis of China's CGE model.* Research report of the national social science fund project (00BJY083) in 2002.

郑玉歆、樊明太、张友国:《WTO 条件下中国贸易与环境的协调发展:基于中国 CGE 模型的总体分析》,国家社科基金项目(00BJY083)研究报告 2002 年。

[7] Zheng Yuxin & Ma Gang. General equilibrium analysis of the influence of environmental protection objective on economic development. In: Zheng Yuxin, ed. *Economic Analysis of Environmental Influence——Theory, Method and Practice.* Social Sciences Academic Press, 2001.

郑玉歆、马纲:《环保目标对经济发展影响一般均衡分析》,郑玉歆主编:《环境影响的经济分析——理论、方法与实践》,社会科学文献出版社 2001 年版。

[8] Department of Population, Social Science and Technology Statistics, National Bureau of Statistics. *Statistic Outline on Environment in China*. China Statistics Press, 2004.

国家统计局人口和社会科技统计司:《中国环境统计概要》,中国统计出版社 2004 年版。

[9] Department of Industry and Transportation Statistics, National Bureau of Statistics. *China Industry and Economy Statistical Yearbook*. China Statistics Press, 2003.

国家统计局工业交通统计司:《中国工业经济统计年鉴》,中国统计出版社 2003 年版。

[10] National Bureau of Statistics. *China Statistical Yearbook*. China Statistics Press, 1998, 2003, 2004 and 2005.

国家统计局:《中国统计年鉴》,中国统计出版社 1998、2003、2004 和 2005 年版。

[11] Adams, Philip, Mark Horridge, Brian R. Parmenter and Xiao-Guang Zhang, Longrun Effects on China of APEC Trade Liberalisation, *Pacific Economic Review*, Vol. 5 (1), February 2000, 15-48.

[12] Anderson, K. , and R. Blackhurt. *The Greening of World Trade Issues*, Ann Arbor: University of Michigan Press, 1992;

[13] Anderson, K. , Will Martin and Dominique Van der Mensbrugghe, China, the WTO and the Doha Agenda, University of Adelaide Center for International Economic Studies Discussion Paper No. 0702, 2007.

[14] Anderson, K. and Martin, W. eds. *Agricultural Trade Reform and the Doha Development Agenda*, Palgrave Macmillan and the World Bank, 2006.

[15] Beghin, John, David Roland-Holst and Dominique vander Mensbrugghe, A Survey of the Trade and Environment Nexus; Global Dimensions, *OECD Economic Studies* 23, 1994, 167-192.

[16] Beghin, John, David Roland-Holst, and Dominique van der Mensbrugghe, Trade Liberalization and the Environment in the Pacific Basin: Coordinated Approaches to Mexican Trade and Environment Policy, *American Journal of Agricultural Economics*, 77 (3), 1995, 778-785.

[17] Beghin, John, Sèbastien Dessus, David Roland-Host and Dominique vander Mensbrugghe, General Equilibrium Modelling of Trade and The Environment, Technical Papers, No. 116, OECD Development Centre, Paris, September. , 1996.

[18] Beghin, John, Brad Bowland, and Sèbastien Dessus, David Roland-Holst, and Dominique van der Mensbrugghe, Trade Integration, Environmental Degradation and Public Health in Chile: Assessing the Linkages, *Environment and Development Economics*, 2002.

[19] Chichilnisky, G. , North-South Trade and the Global Environment, *American Economic Review*, Sep. , 1994, pp. 851-874.

[20] Copeland, B. and Scott Taylor, North-South Trade and the Environment, *Quarterly Journal of Economics.* Aug. 1994, pp. 755-787.

[21] Copeland Brian and Scott Taylor, Trade and Transboundary Pollution, *American Economic Review*, Vol. 85 (4), 1995, pp. 716-737.

[22] Cropper, Maureen, and Wallace Oates, Environmental Economics: A Survey, *Journal of Economic Literature*, June 1992.

[23] Dean, Judith M, Trade and the Environment: A Survey of the Literature, in Low, Patrick, ed. , *International Trade and the Environment*, World Bank Discussion Papers, No. 159, WorldBank, 1992,. pp. 15-28.

[24] Dean, Judith, Does Trade Liberalization Harm the Environment? A New Test, *Canadian Journal of Economics*, Vol. 35, 2002, 819-842.

[25] Dessus, Sèbastien, David Roland-Holst, and Dominique Vander Mensbrugghe, Input-Based Pollution Estimates for Environmental Assessment in Developing Countries, Technical Papers No. 101, OECD Development Centre, Sep. , 1994.

[26] Dessus, Sebastien and Maurizio Bussolo, Is there a trade-off between Trade Liberalization and Pollution Abatement? A Computable general equilibrium assessment applied to Costa Rica, *Journal of Policy Modeling*, Vol. 20, 1998.

[27] Fan, Mingtai and Yuxin Zheng. China's tariff reductions and WTO accession: A computable general equilibrium analysis, in Llyod, Peter and Xiaoguang Zhang, Models of the Chinese Economy, Edward Elgar Publishing, 2001.

[28] Grossman, Gene, and Alan Krueger, Environmental Impacts of a North American Free Trade Agreement, in Garber, Peter M. , ed. , *The Mexico-U. S. Free Trade Agreement*, Cambridge and London: MIT Press, 1993, pp. 13-56.

[29] Ianchovichina, Elean and Will Martin, Trade Impacts of China's World Trade Organization Accession, *Asian Economic Policy Review*, Vol. 1, 2006, pp. 45—65.

[30] Lee, Hiro and David Roland-Holst, The environment and welfare implications of trade and tax policy, *Journal of Development Economics*, Vol. 52 (1), 1997, pp. 65-82.

[31] Mai, Yinhua, P. Adams, Mingtai Fan, et al, Modelling the potential benefits of an Australia-China Free Trade Agreement, the official document to the Australia Department of Foreign Affairs and Trade and the China's Ministry of Commerce, 2005, see http: //www. dfat. gov. au/geo/china/fta/modelling _ benefits. doc.

[32] Martin, Paul, et al, The Industrial Pollution Projection System: Concept, Initial Development, and Critical Assessment, Mimeo, The World Bank, 1991.

[33] OECD, *The Environmental Effects of Trade*, Paris: OECD, 1994.

[34] Perroni, Carlo and Randall M. Wigle, 1994. International Trade and Environmental Quality: How Important Are the Linkages?, *Canadian Journal of Economics*, Canadian Economics Association, Vol. 27(3), pp. 551-567.

[35] World Bank, China: *Issues and Options in Greenhouse Gas Emission Control*, 1994.

[36] WTO, *Trade and Environment*, World Trade Organization, 1999.

[37] Xie, Jian, and Sidney Saltzan, An Environmental Computable General-Equilibrium Approach for Developing Countries, *Journal of Policy Modeling*, Vol. 22, No. 4, 2000, pp. 453-489.

Globalization: International Trade of China's Forestry Products and Ecological Environment Protection

By SUN Changjin, CHEN Liqiao & CHEN Lijun

I. Introduction

Economic globalization is the current trend in the world's development. As the world's largest developing country, China, after its reform and opening up, actively acceded to the WTO requirements, integrating itself into the global economic system and scoring enormous achievements. China has established industrial systems that are complete in range and form a rich set of chains, with an output of over 210 different types① of industrial products, ranking as the 1st worldwide and being renowned internationally as the "global factory." China's foreign trade turnover in 2007 exceeded 2 trillion dollars② and it became the largest global exporter in the first half of 2009. ③ China has become an essential force in the integration of the global economy.

China has also achieved rapid development in forestry and became a large manufacturer of global forest products. Most labor-intensive wood-ware processing industries have transferred to China from Western developed economies. China's forest products industry have reached or are exceeding the international standards in terms of its output of major products, market radiation, brand establishment, the scale of mainstream enterprises, equipment level and technologies. In 2006, China's total forestry output reached as high as 1,065.222 billion yuan, among which forest products manufacturing contributed 519.840 billion

① http://www.chinanews.com.cn/cj/news/2009/08-22/1830300.shtml.

② http://news.steelhome.cn/2008/01/11/n1293565.html.

③ http://news.163.com/09/1228/07/5RJSCOIP000120GR.html.

yuan (Zhang, 2007). The international trade of China's wood forest products[①] enjoyed rapid growth. On the one hand, China is the world's largest importer of industrial logs, importing wood from over 80 countries each year (Forest Trends, 2005). In 2007 it imported 155.2069 million cubic meters' of wood forest products (converted into log volume RWE), a value of 32.360 billion dollars; and on the other hand, it is also the largest global exporter of secondary wood processed goods. In 2007, it exported 68.8849 million cubic meters' of wood forest products, a value of 31.931 billion dollars (State Forestry Administration, 2008).

The emergence of China's forest products industry and the explosive increase in international trade of forest products has received tremendous international concern. In particular, the environmental problems caused by China's wood trade have been constantly raised. Some radical views are that China has obtained both economic and ecological profits from the forest's "vice industrial chain" and has left the forest damaged to the world; they blame China for "illegally felling the global forest" and "being the black hole of the global forest" and have declared that "China's wood import demand is the catalyst for rampant illegal transactions," accusing China of being "the world's largest place to dispose illegally felled trees,"[②] some people think that China's increasing demand on wood, its illegal tree felling operations will not disappear and China's development poses "serious threats to other countries' environments and the global environment."[③]

Those in support of China believe that under the current division of labor in international economic trade, China is the major venue and victim[④] of resource consumption and pollution. With the development of economic globalization, large numbers of labor-intensive, resource-intensive and pollution-intensive industries are transferred from developed countries and regions to China. Although China has obtained certain international capital and advanced technologies, and increased its income, it has paid a

---

① *China Forestry Development Report* divides the wood products into 8 categories: log, converted timber (including special-shaped wood), artificial boards (including veneer, chipboard, fiberboard, plywood and etc.), wood products, paper (including wood pulp, paper and paper products, presswork and etc.), furniture, wood chip and others (fuel wood, charcoal and etc.).

② http://info.bm.hc360.com/zt/heiguo/.

③ http://news.qq.com/a/20061113/000227.htm.

④ http://news.qq.com/a/20061113/000227.htm.

tremendous environmental cost and its domestic ecological environmental problems are increasingly pronounced. In terms of forestry, China has played the role of international forest products manufacturer. Most of its imported wood, after being processed, is exported to developed countries and regions in Europe and America. Through such industrial transfer, developed countries and regions have enjoyed cheap and quality products and transferred their resources and environmental pressures to developing countries like China. The root source for "destroying the world's forest" is the large wood products demand of developed countries and regions and China is just a scapegoat for them. China is at the low end of the global forestry industry chain and is disadvantaged in key technologies and services. It is the developed countries in Europe and America that have influenced and controlled the whole industrial chain. Therefore, rather than China, they should shoulder more responsibilities and take more actions. Such industrial transfers have brought other negative problems to China, for example, the large-scale development of the forest products processing industry has led to a series of environmental pollution problems and the overdependence on wood imports has resulted in China's wood supply security problems.

Those voices are actually concerned about the environmental problem brought about by the international trade of forest products against the globalization backdrop, rather than the attention to China's wood trade. The difference is that the former focuses on the global environmental problem, especially the negative impact brought about by wood trade to developing wood producing countries and little attention is paid to the consequence of the processing link; they focus their attention on China which is directly related to wood trade regarding it as the chief culprit for the damage to the forests and seldom notice the key power of other links in the wood trade chain. Although the latter has realized the environmental influences brought by wood trade to the world, more attention is paid to domestic industrial security and environmental problems; they stressed the inequality caused by industrial transfers and failed to cover the whole wood trade chain and its sustainability.

However, we can expect a global vision that goes beyond parochialism and emphasizes shared responsibilities. Some international organizations and scholars tried to convey objective information rather than only stress the responsibilities of a certain link. They point out, "the demand of developed countries on China's cheap products motivate the production of forestry products in China and spur China to import more wood. If China's demand on wood has aggravated the global forestry crisis, regions in Europe, America and Japan should also shoulder inescapable responsibilities" (White, et al., 2007); "no single country can solve these (environmental) problems single-handedly," "enhancing global environmental management and overcoming global market failure are the fundamental ways to solve these problems."[①] The international community has recognized the "shared responsibilities" and taken concerted action. Some wood producing countries are promulgating legislation restricting illegal wood trade and forest corruption in an attempt to shape good forestry management operations; developed countries in Europe and America are taking actions to crack down on illegal wood trade and establish "green mark;" some international organizations, such as FSC (Forest Stewardship Council) and PEFC (Program for the Endorsement of Forest Certification), are taking initiatives to promote global forestry sustainable management and aiding developing countries to improve their forestry management; the Chinese government and enterprises have also recognized their moral obligations and responsibilities and made efforts in some areas, such as signing bilateral or multilateral agreements to clamp down on illegal wood trade, promulgating business conduct to regulate the business behavior of China's foreign forestry enterprises, promoting the cooperation with international organizations to advance forestry sustainable development and providing assistance and forest training for wood producing countries. All of these have shown a positive trend.

It can be predicted that China's demand for wood imports will continue to grow for a long time. Then, during this process, what opportunities and challenges does wood trade bring to the world's and China's environments? As a responsible participator, how should China coordinate its policy arrangements and international intervention? This is the urgent topic facing us. We will use the global commodity chain theory to conduct studies on the aforementioned problems. The global commodity chain theory considers value creation as a flowing process and stresses four dimensions: the input-output structure, spatial layout, governance structure and system framework which have provided good instrumental and global perspectives for the research on trade and environmental problems. It aids in surpassing the isolated link of trade

---

① http://news.qq.com/a/20061113/000227.htm

and expands to cover many related links of the trade chain; as a result, it offers more fuller and in-depth understandings of the environmental influences brought by trade and the profound reasons causing these influences. It also provides a good framework to improve, manage and coordinate the necessary intervention.

II. Literature Review on Forest Products Trade

With the development of the international trade of forest products and the increasing exacerbation of the global environment, the environmental problems triggered by forest products trade have obtained international concern and have gradually become the hot topic in academic research. In the 1960s, changes in the tropical rainforest of Southeast Asia have received preliminary attention and in the 1970s, studies on the international trade of forest products and the environmental problems gradually emerged (Cao, et al., 2008). Since the beginning of the 21st century, trade and the environment have become an important topic in the international community. Coordinating the relationship between the international trade of forest products and the environment and promoting the sustainable operation of the forests have reached an unprecedented consensus. There are more and more relevant studies, among which the forest damage problem aggravated by trade has obtained increasing concern.

Many studies have proven that the commercial clear cutting caused by trade is an important reason for the damage to the forests. Dauvergne and Taylor proved that the international trade of forest products was highly relevant to the deforestation of the tropical rainforest in Southeast Asia (Dauvergne, 1997; Taylor, 1999); Nectoux and Kuroda thought that Japan's demand for tropical woods was the reason for the obvious damage to the forest in Southeast Asia (Nectoux and Kuroda, 1990). Angelsen and Kaimowitz proved that the international trade in forest products was an important reason for deforestation, but in different countries and regions, the reasons for deforestation are different (Angelsen and Kaimowitz, 2001). Sierra found that the tropical rainforest degradation from 1983 to 1992 in Ecuador was closely related to commercial clear cutting, but the domestic demand was also a key factor for the decrease of the tropical rainforest and the relatively low price of wood has encouraged the non-persistent looting in forests

(Sierra, 2001). Simula analyzed the influence of different trade methods on the environment and forestry development and estimated the feasibility of implementing a forest certification and eco-labeling on forest products in Latin America (Simula, 1999). Menotti took the "globalization" influence such as the free trade agreement, financial market integration and the structural adjustment plan of the international lending system as an example and proved that "globalization" has led to forest losses in developing and developed countries (Menotti, 1999). Nakazawa found that wood trade liberalization had aggravated the felling of wood exporting countries to high value-added forests and brought operational difficulties to small forest managers in wood importing countries. He thought it necessary to ban illegal wood trade and restrict wood trade liberalization unless the environmental and social value was added in the cost (Nakazawa, 2005). Duery and Vlosky analyzed the trade conditions of hardwood products and their influences on the environment and believed that the internal reasons for the over-usage of tropical woods lie primarily in felling, energy development, damaging forests to reclaim land and overexploitation while the external reasons lie in the economic and consumption growth, increasing population and land demand, backward economic policies and shortsighted administrative decisions (Duery and Vlosky, 2006).

With rapid growth in the trade of forestry products, China is becoming the focus of the international community and academic research. Some radical views accuse China's forestry products trade of posing threats to the global environment. For example, Eastin believed that China had imported large amounts of illegally felled wood, which impacted the environment of the supply country and disrupted the efforts of the international community to promote the sustainable operation of the forest; China's indirect subsidies to the wood processing industry has ruined the public's confidence in the sustainable wood trade (Eastin, 2005). Some scholars in China also tried to explore the influence of China's forest products trade on the environment from different perspectives: Xuan Linlin, et al. analyzed the unsustainability of the forest products trade based on resource abundance in the Far East and believed in the ecological development road (Xuan, et al., 2005); Mou Wanlong, et al. elaborated on the potential risk to Sino-Russian trade if we overlook the environment through their argumentation on the dialectic relationship between international trade and the environment (Mou, et al., 2005); Miu Dongling, et al. conducted relevant empirical studies on the relationship between China's forest products trade and the environment (Miu, et al., 2004); Zhu Chunquan, et al. analyzed China's demand on forest products and its ecological footprint and proposed suggestions to mitigate the environmental influence of China's wood demand (Zhu, et al., 2005); Sun Xiufang analyzed the trade condition of forest products in China and relevant countries and particularly studied the problem of illegal tree felling (Sun, 2008); Wu Guochun, et al., based on the estimation of the environmental effect of forest resources, explored the relationship between China's forest products import trade and environmental protection (Wu, et al., 2008).

Some international organizations and scholars have conducted monographic studies on China's forestry products trade, tried to convey objective and fair information and emphasized the shared responsibilities of the international community. For example, *The Influence of Chinese and International Forest Products Trade on Forest Protection and People's Livelihood* by the Forest Trends organization analyzed the total volume, structure, change and increasing trend of China's forest products import and export and their influence on people's livelihood of relevant countries and regions and proposed that measures should be adopted by importing countries, consuming countries, producing countries and processing countries. The study believed that China's rapidly growing forest products trade also has negative influences on the international society, leading to unsustainable and illegal felling, but China is only a single link in the global industrial chain and the purchasers and retailers in America, European Union and Japan also have inescapable responsibilities. China should make clear its key status in the international forest products trade, accelerate the reform in its forestry department, promote the production and supply of its forest products and realize the sustainable development of forestry.

Generally speaking, the analytical model adopted in most studies is predicated on an oversimplified framework and the influential level is obtained according to the simple factors embodied in it; there is a logical fallacy in some radical views about the assessment of China's forest products trade; the understanding of the relationship between forest products trade and the environment needs further clarification. Although some studies recognized the influence of China's forest products trade on the environment and the shared responsibilities of the international community, the essential relationship between trade and environment and the governance framework needs further argumentation.

We will use the commodity chain theory of global forest products to analyze each relevant link of the whole wood trade chain and its governance structure, and define the opportunities and challenges brought by China's forest products trade to the global and China's environment. Based on this, we will propose policy suggestions for the critical level of the commodity chain's sustainability.

III. Study on the Commodity Chain of Global Forest Products

1. Components of the Commodity Chain of Global Forest Products

The global commodity chain theory regards value creation as a flowing process and emphasizes four dimensions such as input-output structure, spatial layout, governance structure and system framework. According to different wood supply sources and product consuming destinations, the commodity chain of the global forest products with China as the processing link can be divided into four types:

Table 1 The Commodity Chain of Global Forest Products with China as the Processing Link

Commodity Chain Type	Wood Source	Product Processing	Product Consumption
1	Foreign	China	Export Market
2	Foreign	China	Domestic Market
3	Domestic	China	Export Market
4	Domestic	China	Domestic Market

We will select the first-type commodity chain for further analysis: this chain has shown typical global connections in which the import wood is processed twice before exportation and provide clues for the coordination of international intervention. In this commodity chain (see Figure 1), wood producing countries are playing the role of primary wood providers while Western developed countries in Europe and America have played the role of end consumers. China, as the intermediary wood processor, connects with the two through trade.

2. Primary Wood Supply Link: the Case of Mozambique and Russia

From China's many wood supplying countries, we choose Mozambique and Russia for detailed case analysis, primarily because:

* The two countries are abundant in forest resources, especially the virgin forest (the forest coverage rate in Russia is 45% and in Mozambique, 25%). Forestry export is extremely important for the two countries and the export volume of forest products ranks 4th in Russia's various industrial products export and also 4th in Mozambique (Zhang, et al., 2007).

* The two countries export primary wood in large quantities, mainly log and converted timber (Russia exports cork while Mozambique, valuable hardwood).

* China has rapidly become the most important import market of forest products for these two countries. In 2002, 25% of Russia's and 85% of Mozambique's forest products were exported to China (Lu, et al., 2005).

* Owing to the deficiencies in the two countries' social systems and forestry systems, there are serious problems such as illegal felling and unsustainable operations.

(1) Mozambique

In Mozambique, the land and forest are owned by the country which governs their renting. The privileged long-term manager, the short-term simple license holder and the local permanent resident can obtain the rights of forest management. However, certain companies, with good operations, have passed the recognition of three qualifications of FSC and provided wood to the target market of the Organization for Economic Cooperation and Development (OECD). Overall, Mozambique's forest operation is in a state of chaos and overexploitation, such as: most of the commercial felling is unscientific; lacks planning in felling; lacks maintenance in logging-roads; the use of heavy machinery will crush the soil; there are little oriented felling; and few measures are taken to support the regeneration of trees. The emergence of these problems primarily lies in: uncertain forest ownership and no guarantee for community interests; inconvenient transportation, insufficient investment and low efficiency which leads to an unsustainable operating

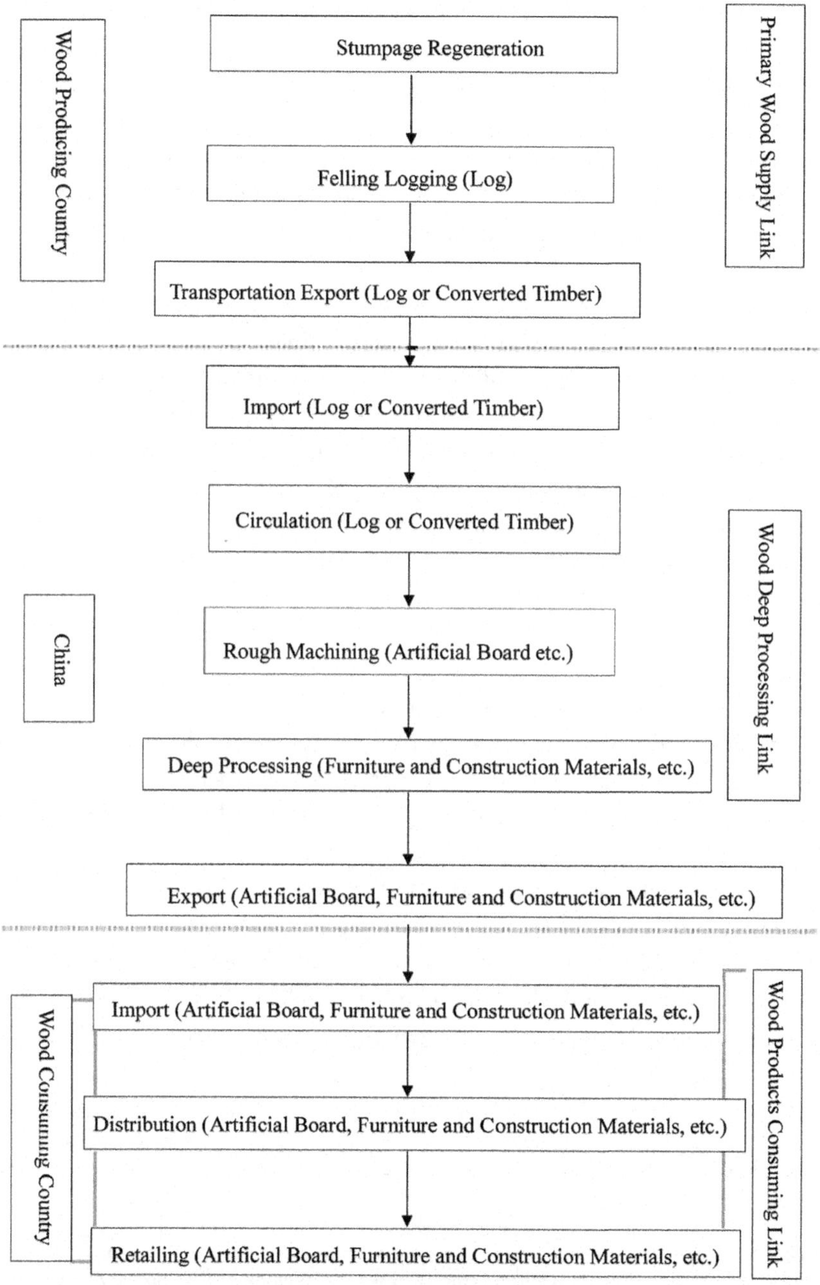

Figure 1 Typical Commodity Chain of GlobalForest Products with China as the Processing Link

environment; lacking training for the personnel in the enterprise; the forest managers lacking restrictions and a sense of social responsibilities and unable to implement sustainable forest management; rampant corruption such as rent-seeking and bribe extortion; the chaotic management of tree felling permit fostered illegal felling; the government lacking effective actions to promote sustainable management of local forests and the forest input regulations① only exist in theory and have not been put into practice.

In processing exports, Mozambique promulgated various incentive policies, such as the wood grading system, financial compensate policy and export processing policy. ② These policies have promoted Mozambique's wood rough machining to a certain degree. However, being restricted by the following factors, the scale and quality of the wood processing should be improved: the first is that the backward industrial system and governance system is incapable of supporting industrial development; there are artificial obstacles in various links such as examination and approval and even rent-seeking and bribe extortion, which have seriously jeopardized the investment environment; the second is the quality and waste problem caused by backward technologies and the low added value of products which hinders the development of a processing industry; the third is China's zero tariff import policy implemented on the log and primary wood products, which discourages the efforts made by Mozambique to develop wood processing guidelines.

At present, a large part of the log, converted timber and manufactured goods produced in Mozambique are exported to foreign countries. In 2005, about 60% the log were used for export and in the province of Cabo Delgado, the number reached 80% . China is the primary export destination for Mozambique wood. During the past six

① For example, 0. 4 dollar is levied on each cubic meter for fuel wood felling; 120 dollars for valuable timber; 50% of fines are distributed to forest management departments; a 20% forest development tax is used for the reinvestment of local communities.

② For example: divide 118 types of major commodity wood into five grades, the first must be processed domestically as a priority while others can export a small amount of logs with a special quota license; processed wood can enjoy a 40% tax preference and during the first period of wood import and supply, the tax can be exempted; the product export rate reached 85%, the enterprise enjoys a 60% tax exemption in importing goods.

years, Mozambique had about 429,710 cubic meters' of wood exported, in which 85% was exported to China (including the 25% exported to Hong Kong), with the value reaching 68.40 million dollars. The remaining 15% was primarily exported to some countries in South Africa and Europe①. It should be noted that a considerable amount of the wood was exported illegally because judging from the data, the actual cut is not consistent with the permit cut.

The major influence of the felling activity on supply chain lies in the environmental problems (destructive felling, biological attenuation, forest fires, unplanned mining and selective mining), economic problems (wood waste, low added value, a lack of input in forest management) and social problems (workers' health and security and fragile labor relations):

- Destructive Felling: for example, adopting selective cutting which damages forest ecology. The felling activity by the Mu Upua River results in flooding and hinders forest regeneration.
- Attenuation of wild fauna and flora: the operators in the forest camp usually hunt forest wildlife and sell their meat in towns.
- Forestry opening: the roads are destroyed by the felling and logging activities in the rainy season and some forests are reduced to open fields and are occupied by farms.
- Selective mining: woods with scars and wormholes and small diameters are discarded; the diameter regulations are not enforced rigorously and woods with small diameters are frequently cut.
- Wood waste: generally there remain many branches after the cutting, which have caused resource waste and fire risk.
- Low added economic value: the increases of felling activities and wood export have few positive influences on the national economy. Most profits from the wood trade are not used in the reinvestment in Mozambique. Financial and tax loss in the forestry department and low salaries and the violation of the rules of national social security will not help to improve the worker's living standard, promote consumption and increase savings.
- Health and security problem: wretched working conditions and lacking security and health guarantees.
- Backward labor relations: the standard of the international

① Germizhuizen etc., 2007 (draft).

community (Organization for Economic Co-operation and Development, FSC and International Labor Organization), the labor laws in Mozambique and the rules of national social security are totally ignored. The right and welfare of the worker has no guarantee at all.

To sum up, the supply chain in Mozambique consists of unsustainable operations. With a fragile governance structure, the illegal felling and corruption passes through all links of the chain, including production, transportation and exportation. China's participation also influences sustainable operations and aggravates the backward governance in Mozambique. However, the activities of Chinese companies also have potential influences on Mozambique—providing a comparatively advanced market, technology and investment. Currently, the intergovernmental relationship between China and Africa is improving. The new partnership is helpful to understand the comparative advantages in planting high quality hardwood and to support China's long-term demand.

(2) Russia

Russia has abundant forest resources, ranking 1st in the world; forest resources in the Far East and Siberia are very important to Russia and are also extremely important to the trade with China. However, it should be noted that the regeneration of Russia's forests also relies on natural growth (only 1% or so is artificial forests). And to a large degree, owing to the imperfect forest rights system and management, there is a long way to go if the sustainable operation of the forests is to be realized.

Since the beginning of the 1990s, illegal felling has been running rampant in Russia, with the annual illegal cutting reaching 19 million cubic meters, taking up to 10%-15% of the legal purchase quantity and the annual loss to the country reached 500 million dollars. ① Small-scale illegal felling can be done directly through unlawful tree felling without bribing governmental officials. Medium and large-scale illegal felling must obtain a permit by bribing the forestry department official who has the authorization right. Therefore, the major problem of illegal felling lies not in unlawful tree felling but in corruption.

---

① http://paper.clii.com.cn/show.asp?InfoName=%E7%8=94%AF%E5%82%9A%E6%BA%A2%E3%B7%87%E2%84%83%E4%BC? InfoType=0102&ShowID=161088.

Judging from the cost and income structure, illegal businessmen have only to pay the transaction fee of the illegal wood through market legalization without being charged with the infrastructure costs, tax and social responsibilities. The cost required is now being standardized (the cost of illegal operations consists of "cost + freight + bribes"). In 2003, in the border area of Khabarovsk, illegal businessman paid an average of 3 dollars' tax and 15 dollars' bribes for a cubic meter's illegal wood while legal businessman, paid 16 dollars' tax and 6 dollars for social security (Sun, et al., 2008).

In some regions, illegal felling has become a highly organized criminal activity. The example of hardwood trade can better illustrate such a trend because the price of hardwood is 1.5 times higher or even more than that of cork. The profit rate can reach 100% or even higher. According to the estimation of BROC (Bureau for Regional Outreach Campaigns, Vladivostok), an illegal Russian businessman can sell a cubic meter's hardwood at 140 dollars in China's Razdolnaya River market, in which a considerable part of the transaction fee is used in bribing the authorities concerned and the criminal gang (Sheingauz etc., 2005):

- US \$ 70——to Chinese wholesalers (intermediary);
- US \$ 4——to local government officials;
- US \$ 5——to municipal administration officials to obtain better sections;
- US \$ 5——to environment supervisors to avoid confiscation and upon exiting the forest;
- US \$ 3——to forest service officials to avoid confiscation;
- US \$ 5——to the military to avoid confiscation;
- US \$ 5——to customs officials;
- US \$ 10——to the timber warehouse to obtain documents;
- US \$ 5——to forest lessors for another opportunity;
- US \$ 5——to local gang leader to ensure security;
- US \$ 5——fuel charge;
- US \$ 18——divided evenly among loggers, security guards and truck drivers (US \$6 each).

In processing exports, relevant industries in Russia have been bogged down in depression and many villages and towns in the Far East are deprived of the industries for making a living. Almost all the wood-processing industries are driven by export—55% of the exported forest products are the primary forest products of logging and exported finished products are very few. In fact, Russia must import wood products to meet domestic demand. In 2003, the import of deep processing forest products reached 2.27 billion dollars. The downturn of the processing industry may originate from a series of factors, including investment shortages, the decreasing demand on processed products in the domestic market, outdated machinery equipment and decreasing government subsidies, especially China's tariff and the competition from China.

The dual influences brought by this in the wood trade include:

- Increasing employment: the forestry department has provided employment opportunities to forestry residents. With the exhaustion of the forestry in far and backward regions, local skilled workers are employed by the logging companies in other provinces.
- Income increase of forestry workers: according to the expert's estimations, the actual average monthly income of the cutting department is about 780 dollars (except the medium and high-level managers who have higher salaries), but the salary level is regionally uneven (a monthly average of 1, 100 dollars in Khabarovsk and 350 dollars in Primorsky Krai).
- The increase in local fiscal revenue: all the stages in the commodity chain require tax payments or payment to the government. ① In 2003, the commercial felling tax levied by the forestry department which is under the unified budget of Khabarovsk was 3.8 dollars per cubic meter.
- Social assistance: the logging companies and forestry department have shouldered great obligations to provide social assistance. According to the expert's estimation, the extra social expenditure of the logging companies takes up 5% of the production cost on average and in the border areas, it reaches up to 12 million dollars annually, equivalent to an annual expenditure of 40 dollars per capita for forestry residents.
- Forest damage: owing to the adoption of destructive logging methods such as selective cutting and clear cutting, valuable varieties of trees and local ecology are destroyed.
- Wood waste: as much as 40% to 60% of the wood is discarded at the cutting site, causing 4 times more waste than other countries

① Legal logging primarily pays for the following taxes: income tax; value-added tax (VAT); fund tax; land tax; social labor cost; pollution tax; other main local taxes.

(Sun, et al., 2008).

• Forest fires: the logging activity has aggravated forest fires. In the first half of 2007, there were as many as 560 cases of forest fires in the Far East of Russia, which has seriously harmed the local ecology①.

• Uneven profit distribution: the valid part of the income is distributed to the boss of the company, Chinese businessmen and managers and the federal bureaucracy while the income of local social communities and poor residents is meager.

• Tax loss: most immigrants' salaries and company profits are transferred back to foreign countries and most taxes are converted to the federal budget.

• Weak system: fragile federal legislations, decreasing financial sources, conflicts between the federation and local organizations and the rampant rent-seeking and tax evasion behaviors have dampened the government's control over forest management.

The rigid forest rights system, inefficient management abilities, corruption in the forestry department and restrictions in technologies, capital, manpower and infrastructure have greatly hindered the sustainable development of the forest management and industry in Russia. However, compared with Mozambique, Russia boasts extremely rich forest resources and needs to explore more effective techniques for the development of the forestry industry and processing industry. The Sino-Russian trade partnership has more potential which provides potential ways for Russia to construct a good forestry industry.

3. Wood Processing Link——China

The imported wood, before leaving China again, has to pass through four basic stages: import, circulation, processing and re-export. Among these, for the added value and sustainability of our concern, the wood processing stage is the most important because the physical machining has changed the wood and produced side effects.

China's wood import process is relatively transparent and standard, with a clear list of costs and no charges of excessive transaction fees, which has promoted the rapid development of China's wood import trade.

---

① Xinhuanet Moscow, June 10, http://news.qq.com/a/20070610/001487.htm.

However, with the intervention of many enterprises, unorganized competition has led to a significant profit decrease and many weak importers have quit this industry. For example, the medium and small-sized enterprises engaging in the import of Russian wood only have a profit of 35.78 RMB for per cubic meter of wood (Song, 2007).

In China, there are official or unofficial trading markets for wood circulation. In 2001, China's wood markets had reached 995, which included 344 wholesale markets and 651 retail markets. However, only less than 10% (82) wood markets were well organized and most of the others were unofficial wood markets (Foreign Agricultural Service, 2001). The large-scale wood trading market by the port is the important collecting and distributing center for wood import with standard management. Currently, the annual trading volume of the first three trading markets has reached over 1 million cubic meters. The wood trading market in Zhangjiagang is the largest, with the annual trading volume reaching over 2 million cubic meters, representing a quarter of the national total. ①

In the wood processing industry, China, with its rich cheap labor force, strong industrial foundation (including processing industries and its supporting systems such as equipment, maintenance, glue, packaging, hardware, paint and etc.), convenient logistics (transportation, road network, port facility and relevant services) and good commercial environment, has built a large-scale industry encompassing the converted timber industry, artificial board industry and furniture industry, and formed an industry agglomeration in important areas such as the Pearl River Delta, Yangtze River Delta and circum-Bohai-Sea. At present, it is recognized as the largest country for the production of medium density fiberboard and furniture export. However, accompanying the rapid growth are many problems in the wood processing industry: too small enterprise scales, insufficient capital, low technological levels, unreasonable product structures, low quality, few famous brands and low product added value.

Judging from the exports, as a newly emerging manufacturing base for forest products, China has a vigorous export market for its forest products. Professional international trade companies are still major channels for the export of China's wood forest products, but the self-

① http://218.94.123.54:8081.

support exports by production enterprises are also increasing. The large-scale wood products exhibition or trade fair held by China is regarded as the purchase center for global furniture. However, overall, the wood product export market is still in chaos, with fierce price competition and low industry profits. Take the furniture industry in Shandong as an example, although the export price is increasing, the industry profit can only be maintained at a risky level of 3%-6% and 90% of its enterprises have less than 1 million dollars of exports. ① China's major trading partners usually lodge anti-dumping charges against China with this as an excuse.

The achievements made by China are largely attributable to the implemented trade liberalization policies on forest products: after China's accession to the WTO, it has implemented zero tariffs on certain primary products——closely related to the natural forest protection projects implemented since 1998. This has promoted China's wood trade and relative forest products processing industries. However, the tariff structure gradually upgraded by the Chinese government also encouraged the over-import of logs. Although damaging the forest of the supply country, it has satisfied the expansion demand of China's wood processing industries. In recent years, the continuous accumulation of the foreign exchange reserve and the international community's concerns over the large amount of China's wood imports motivates the Chinese government to take initiatives to decrease the exports of resource commodities, such as decreasing the tax refund rate of the export and listing a batch of wood forest products in the commodities prohibited and restricted in the processing trade. Overall, these policies encourage the import of resource commodities, limit the export of resource commodities and may also be of help to decrease China's import of wood. The Chinese enterprise will be forced to face the competition of non-price relations, such as increasing the product's added value and improving the product's design and quality to promote the upgrading of China's wood products processing industries.

4. Product Consumption Link——America

China's wood products are mainly exported to America, Europe and

① http://furniture.clii.com.cn/news/show.asp?Showid=142964.

Japan, in which America is the largest purchaser during the last decade, especially the purchaser of furniture. We take America as an example to describe the consumption link of the whole supply chain.

America has a mature furniture sale network which includes wholesalers, trade and retailers. Importers/wholesalers who purchase furniture from China and sell it to domestic distributors and retailers. Major retailers include department stores, large chain stores, home centers, specialty furniture stores and interior renovation companies. Currently, they usually make direct purchases from China and through a commercial network, and even small-scale American retailers have changed the traditional way to make local purchases in America and more and more of them make direct purchases in China through online enquiry. Some brand importers usually order the products from Chinese manufacturers through OEMs (Original Equipment Manufacturers).

The following factors have influenced America's demand for China's wood products:

- The product design is the most critical market factor, especially for furniture products. Such a link is generally controlled by America's middleman or retailer and the Chinese factory works according to their orders.
- The product price is extremely important in most product markets. Large-scale distributors are highly sensitive to the market price and they are in want of a large quantity but try hard to squeeze down the prices. Large wholesalers have their own warehouses in America and are demanding in both price and quality. The brand importers offer high prices, but they only trust large-scale and high quality factories and directly order through OEMs.
- The social and environmental problems originating from the accurate production of special wood products are rapidly becoming the key problems for many retailers. For example, the American company, a member of the North American Forestry Trade Net, promised that the illegal wood trade with unclear or controversial sources should be revoked stage by stage and they would purchase the following products from designated sources: wood that is recyclable, permitted, allowed by policies, legal, veritable and certified. Although this only accounts for a small portion of the market, it is an increasing trend. According to an investigation on 100 companies by North America Fortune, 50% of the companies announced that they would sift out suppliers which failed to

live up to the sustainable standards (Kearney, 2007). In comparison, European Union countries haven't promulgated government incentive policies that motivate the retailers through government purchase policies.

Such a purchaser-driven process, to a large degree, has stipulated how Chinese factories should operate. With the ongoing transfer of the manufacturing industry to China, it also causes an enormous impact on the small-scale furniture manufacturers in America.

IV. Environmental Influence Brought by Global Commodity Chain of Forest Products

The commodity chain of forest products has embodied the global relationships of the wood trade and revealed its environmental influences on participating countries. Such influences can be both positive and negative. Against the backdrop of a degrading global environment, the negative influences are causing wide concern in the international community. The participating countries along the chain are facing important opportunities and grim challenges.

1. Environmental Influences on China

For China, the substitution effect of wood imports makes it possible to significantly cut down on domestic logging. In China, for the natural forest protection project implemented in 1998, large parts of the territory, especially the northeast region, have imposed rigorous restrictions on forest felling. China's wood cutting has decreased by half, which enabled the forest area in Asia to obtain a net increase during 2000-2005 (Liu, 2005). From 1998 to 2008, the forest industry zone in Heilongjiang Province accumulated a wood production decrease of 22.77 million cubic meters, and a forest resource consumption decrease of over 36 million cubic meters, equivalent to saving 68 million trees with a diameter at breast height of 30 cm. ① Many wood making and processing factories in the northeast region suffered from raw material shortages, but the present wood requirements of a similar tree variety can be obtained from across the nations. More and more Russian wood was used in regions outside Northeast China and transported to

① Wang Xi & Liu Jingyang, Xinhua Agency, Harbin, August 4, www. gov. cn.

Guangdong Province along the shore (Bai, 2007). At the same time, China has more motivation and energy to take active initiatives to recover the forest and vegetation in China. While the total global forest resources are declining, China eliminated the forest resource deficit at the beginning of the 1990s and began to move toward (forest area and forest growing stock) "double growth." Up to now, the construction area for the artificial forest has reached 62 million hectares with a forest coverage rate of 20.36%.[①]

Figure 2 shows the positive effect of China's wood import on domestic forest logging and forest growth. Before 1997, the upward or downward trend of China's wood production and wood forest products imports was basically the same, maintaining at a stable rate. This shows that back then, the major factors influencing the two were China's economic development and the market demand for wood. After 1997, China's wood forest products import and wood production are obviously complementary, which shows that when the domestic demand for wood is increasing, China's large-scale ecological development is on the premise of increasing wood imports. The increasing trend of the forest coverage rate and that of wood forest products imports are basically the same, which shows that wood forest products imports are favorable for China's forest protection while the protection of forest resources must be supported by importing wood forest products.

There were considerable ecological environmental effects that ensued. Taking the year 2007 as an example, the total national market supply of wood products was 382.7380 million cubic meters and the total consumption of wood products, 382.4942 million cubic meters. Among these, the imported logs and other wood forest products were converted into 155.2069 million cubic meters of wood. With the deduction of the 68.8849 million cubic meters\ of' wood converted from the exported logs and wood forest products, the actual net imported wood was 86.3219 million cubic meters (State Forestry Administration, 2008). Calculated with 72.50 cubic meters' growing stock per hectare in the commercial forest and an outturn percentage of 61% in the commercial timber (WTO and Environmental Research Group, 2004), the net import of wood in 2007 was equivalent to saving 1.9519 million hectares of

① Results of the seventh forest resource inventory, http://homw.hebei.com.cn/xwzx/jypdl/jd/200911/t20091117_706597.html.

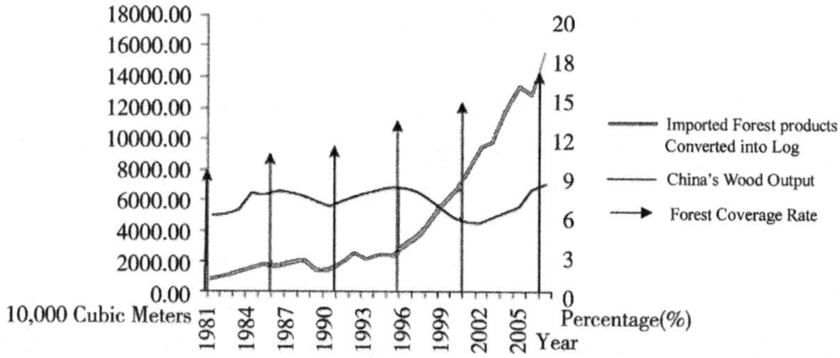

Figure 2　Relationship between China's Wood Production, Imported Forest products Converted into Log and Forest Coverage Rate

Data source: Based on*China Forestry Development Report*, *China Statistical Yearbook on Forestry* and the results of the forest resource inventory.

domestic forests. Calculated according to Jiang Zehui's research findings on the ecological function of domestic forest resources (Jiang, 2000), these saved forests could conserve 4.216 billion tons of water, save 299 million cubic meters of soil erosion, decreasing 59,700 hectares of abandoned land areas and fixating 527,900 tons of carbon dioxide. Calculated according to the mid-value① of the forest environmental benefit assessment, it was equivalent to 33.871 billion yuan's of environmental benefits, among which profits on water conservation was 4.46 billion yuan, soil conservation was 3.015 billion yuan, carbon sequestration and oxygen production were 15.951 billion yuan, air purification was 7.363 billion yuan, farmland conservation and yield increases were 1.864 billion yuan, forest recreation was 1.001 billion yuan and biological conservation was 215 million yuan.

The industrial transfer and the influx of forest capital make it possible for Chinese processing industries to upgrade their technology and develop high value-added industries. Such a upgrading has brought many benefits to China's development: for example, the establishment of

① According to Tian Minghua's *Environmental Influence Assessment of the Import Trade of China's Major Wood Forest Products*: the mid-value of the forest environmental benefit assessment is 17,352.69 yuan/hm^2, in which water conservation is 2,285.20 yuan, soil conservation is1,544.60 yuan, carbon sequestration and oxygen production are 8,171.94 yuan, air purification is 3,772.45 yuan, farmland conservation and yield increases are 955.03 yuan, forest recreation is 513.08 yuan and biological conservation is 110.40 yuan.

good systems in sustainable energy and water supply and environmental management, which is widely put into practice.

The environmental risks brought about by the forest products trade to China primarily lies in the species invasion and processing pollution. The annual economic losses caused by the invasion of a few foreign species are as high as over 50 billion yuan. According to statistics, there have been over 400 foreign harmful organisms that have invaded China, including weeds, pests, pathogenic bacteria and etc. Those that pose serious risks are: 107 weeds, 32 pests and 23 types of pathogenic bacteria. ① In 2003 alone, in China's ports, 186 harmful organisms were captured in the imported wood of 7,058 batches. ② Some foreign harmful species have invaded most of our ecological system and become a serious problem for China's sustainable development. For example, pine wood nematode is a foreign species which poses serious threats to ecological security. Since found in Nanjing's Sun Yat-sen Mausoleum in 1982, it has led to accumulative direct and indirect losses of over 100 billion yuan for China. Zhejiang Province is often plagued by it. Since the first disease outbreak in 1991 to 2005, the accumulative disease-stricken area was over 340,000 hectares, causing the death of more than 33 million pine trees. 3,400 hectares of forest land was constantly plagued by pine wilt diseases and degraded to barren mountains. The circulation and export of relative agricultural and sideline products and forest products in the epidemic area were seriously impacted (Li, 2007).

Pollutants are usually hidden in the imported forest products. Take the import of waste paper for example, waste paper is the major component in the import of paper and its import consists of 65% of China's total paper import. However, owing to complicated sources, it is listed as highly risky goods. In customs inspection, there are usually medical stuff and other pollutants hidden in it which once allowed in, will pose serious pollution to the environment and will even bring unknown viruses.

In addition, in China, the small-scale factories contain few pollution treatment facilities, and dust, noise and chemical pollution in factories and mucilage glue and paint have also aggravated the pollution risk. In the waste paper processing industries, it is easy to produce

① http://news.sciencenet.cn/html/showsbnewsl.aspx?id=174064.

② http://tieba.baidu.com/f?kz=214368800.

"secondary pollution," with many hazardous pollutants in the wastewater discharge, which, if treated improperly, will easily pollute the surrounding environment. In 2003, within some areas in the northeast, where wood processing is relatively concentrated, there were 40 or so wood processing enterprises and more than 400 drying kilns handling different woods. All year around, they produced large amounts of smoke pollutions; the local government banned over 60 factories[①] in succession, but until now, dust, noise and formaldehyde pollution are still prominent problems influencing the local environmental quality.

2. Global Environmental Influence

Due to increasing illegal logging and wood trade, to a large degree, the global forest products commodity chain is considered negative. The opportunities brought by it to other participating countries are seldom recognized by the mainstream media, but such opportunities do exist and are extremely important.

For wood producing countries, the wood trade has provided potential possibilities for the improvement of forest operations. America and New Zealand encourage a good management environment for sustainable operations, which is obviously benefiting from China's demand for wood imports. With the consolidation of this partnership, China's developing partners have potential to develop strong natural resource economies and obtain more opportunities to improve forest governance as well as their experience, technologies and capital so as to provide support for the supply of the whole wood commodity chain.

The wood consuming countries are primarily Western developed countries. Owing to China's influence, the commodity chain enables these countries to decrease domestic wood production, reduce domestic environmental pressure and give scope to other various functions of ecological systems (especially maintenance, water conservation and water source protection). While experiencing global public goods and consumption privileges, the consuming countries can establish and develop their own good forest operation orders.

Forest products trade has posed the severest challenges to wood producing countries, especially those countries without perfect

① http://www.syepb.gov.cn/data/2003_09_23/200392310422.html.

institutional structures. Overseas demand is most likely to aggravate illegal logging and hinder governance. Although commercial logging is only one factor for the denudation of the tropical forests (damaging forests to reclaim land and fuel wood cutting are the major reasons), it usually opens the forest zone and tempts forest residents to argue against the over felling of the forest. Due to China's great demands, such a trend is still intensifying and growing. At present, 12% to 17% of the global log trade, 23% to 30% of the hardwood and artificial board trade and 2% to 4% of the cork and artificial board trade may be illegal (Sun, et al., 2008); the annual trade volume of the illegal wood trade globally is about 10 billion to 15 billion dollars and the annual economic losses caused by illegal felling globally are about 150 billion dollars (Li, et al., 2009). The illegal logging rate in some wood producing countries stays high, with the most serious countries, such as Cambodia and Burma, exceeding over 80% (see Table 2).

Table 2 Percentage of Illegal Logging in Some Tropical Wood Producing Countries (Unit: %)

Country	Illegal Logging Rate	Data Source
Bolivia	80	Contreras-Hermosilla, 2001
Brazil	85	Greenpeace, 2001
Cambodia	90	World Rainforest Movement and Forest Monitor, 1998
Cameroon	50	Global Forest Watch Cameroon, 2000
Columbia	42	Contreras-Hermosilla, 2001
Ghana	34	Glastra, 1995
Indonesia	51	Scotland, 2000
Burma	80	Brunner, 1998

Data source: ITTO Tropical Forest Update, 2002.

Since over a half of the imported wood in China comes from countries where there is overcutting and illegal logging, it is often accused of being the major collecting and distributing center of illegal logging.① In 2000, the logging imported from Indonesia to China was 102 times more than that exported from Indonesia to China and the logging imported from Burma to China was 25.9 times more than that exported from Burma to China. This shows that most wood was exported illegally (see Table 3). The research of the CIFR (Center for International Forestry Research) also proves that there

① http://www.xici.net/main.asp?at=1&url=/b566764/d31837444.htm.

is a large gap between the bilateral data of the wood imported by China from Malaysia, Indonesia and Russia. Due to China's wood demand, since the beginning of the 1990s, Russia has illegally cut large amounts of virgin forests in the densely populated Far East. Some regions have suffered log losses during the process of logging and log transportation, which caused enormous waste and after the cutting, the perpetually frozen soil zone suffered from irremediable ecological system degradation. Actually, the actual felling volume of Indonesia is 75% ① higher than that allowed by the state forestry administration and most of the undeclared exported woods are cut illegally without supervision or are inconsistent with the sustainable cutting level or are under the circumstances of violating the regulations in the forest protection zone, bank reserve zone and cutting-banning steep slope. In fact, an annual amount of more than 2 million cubic meters of forest products are exported to China undeclared (Zhu, et al., 2005). In the imported wood from the west and central Africa to China, there are also serious illegal cutting problems, with the imported illegal wood and converted timber during several years exceeding 8 million and 14 million cubic meters (Eastin, 2005).

Table 3 Wood Trade Report Data and Difference between China (Import) and Major Tropical Wood Exporters (Export)
(Unit: 1,000 Cubic Meter, %)

Exporter and Product	1998			1999			2000		
	Export	Import	Difference	Export	Import	Difference	Export	Import	Difference
Cameroon(Log)	192	240	25	171	216	26	0	220	
Indonesia(Log)	28	35	25	88	382	334	6	618	10200
Indonesia(Converted Timber)	52	317	510	77	580	653	20	931	4555
Malaysia(Converted Timber)	265	399	51	140	552	294	116	495	327
Burma(Log)	40	186	365	24	335	1296	20	558	2690

Data source: ITTO Tropical Forest Update, 2002.

Illegal logging and other problems have exacerbated the loss of global forest resources. For nearly a century, the forest coverage rate of Africa decreased from 60% in the beginning of the 20th century to 10% at present; 2/3 of the tropical rainforest in South America has

① http://tech.163.com/05/0323/10/1FH97DHE00091537_2.html.

disappeared and over a half of the world's largest virgin forests in the Amazon River Basin have been cut (Li, 2007). From 1990 to 2005, the global forest area decreased by about 130 million hectares and the total area, 3%, with an average daily decrease of 20,000 hectares; also, the annual decrease in 1990-2000 was about 8.89 million hectares, and for 2000-2005, about 7.32 million hectares. The consumption rate of the forest resources in China's major wood supply countries is also alarming. From Table 4, from 1990 to 2005, except few developed countries such as America, Germany and New Zealand, the forest area in China's major wood supply countries showed different levels of shrinkage (Food and Agriculture Organization of the United Nations, 2006).

Table 4 Changes in the Forest Area of China's Major Wood Supply Countries from 1990 to 2005 (Unit: 1,000 hectares)

Country	Forest Area		
	1990	2000	2005
Russia	808950	809268	808790
Malaysia	22376	21591	20890
Indonesia	116567	97852	88495
Thailand	15965	14814	14520
Papua New Guinea	31523	30132	29437
Burma	39219	34554	32222
Democratic Republic of Congo	140531	135207	133610
Sudan	76381	70491	67546
Mozambique	20212	19512	19262
Gabon	21927	21826	21775
Paraguay	21157	19368	18475
Nigeria	17234	13137	11089
Cambodia	12946	11541	10447
America	298648	302294	303089
Germany	10741	11076	11076
New Zealand	7720	8226	8309

Data source: Food and Agriculture Organization of the United Nations, 2006.

Due to the decrease in forest resources, many impoverished regions in developing countries have suffered extremely serious problems, which not only lead to serious environmental consequences, but also consume the resources that are providing long-term employment and economic sustainable growth for rural areas. Especially for tropical wood countries, it may mean that local residents will lose their sources of livelihood. In the case of Mozambique and Russia, we have investigated these problems.

Overall, the low-efficient and unsustainable operations in the commodity chain have caused a series of global impacts. Such operations emphasize the amount of wood obtained at the cost of sacrificing forest regeneration and the forest's "supply, adjustment, cultural and support function," which usually leads to the "capital deprivation" of forest woods in the short term. The most basic challenges are the wood supply related commodity chain and sustainable problem as well as the degeneration of the survival condition and ecological systems thus ensued, especially for the residents in impoverished forest areas. Table 5 lists different environmental problems caused by the whole wood product supply chain from forest to end use:

Table 5 Forest Products Supply Chain and Environmental Problems

Link	Environmental Problems Boldface = extremely serious and typical problems
Forest Plantation Forest Management	Illegally changing natural forests Damaging soil and water body Damaging biodiversities Making local residents lose available lands (farms) and water Decreasing biodiversities (species)
Wood Logging	Illegal logging, including theft Damaging soil and water body Decreasing biodiversities (species and genes) Partial landslip
Wood Trade	Precious/endangered wood Illegal wood Species invasion/garbage
Converted Timber/ Pulp Wood	Water pollution (floating solids, chlorine) Air pollution (dioxin, furan) Energy use/climate change emissions High-water-consuming per cubic meter Using outdated techniques
Processing and Manufacturing	Air and water pollution Energy use/climate change emissions Using outdated techniques

(contd.)

Link	Environmental Problems Boldface = extremely serious and typical problems
Packaging Products	Solid wastes burden
Retailing Products	
Consumption Products	Unsustainable and abusive consumption Products waste
Disposing or Recycling Products	Methane produced from the landfill An increasing lack of safe wastes disposal sites
Transportation (Going through the whole chain)	Illegal trade [export regardless of regulations (such as log export ban and endangered species convention), tax evasion] Air and water pollution Energy use/climate change emissions

V. Conclusion and Policy Discussion

1. Conclusion

The global forest products commodity chain is of great significance to the world's sustainable development. It has absorbed large capital flow from the environmentally fragile forests in the world and hired cheap labor sources from China and other poor countries. Good forest and social governance can make the commodity chain a positive force, especially for those poor countries which can increase employment, create tax revenue and promote industrial upgrading through forest capitalization.

However, at the current time, some negative problems concentrating on the wood producing countries are assuming prominence, such as forest resource damage, ecological environmental degradation, the violation of the resident's living rights and rampant corruption, which have received special attention from the international community. The general view is: it is China that has "exported forest deforestation" to the impoverished wood supply countries in order to protect its own forests, establish a forest processing industry and import wood.

However, our research shows that the emergence of these problems, on the surface, originate from the facts that the high integration of the global forest products commodity chain has broken the boundary of a single country, increased the wood demand of economically developed countries and imposed forest cutting pressure on impoverished countries. Nevertheless, the profound reasons lie in the fact that many participators in the chain haven't adopted practical and effective measures from the perspective of sustainable development.

Western developed countries are end consumers which have shaped the market force driving the whole chain and are the key factors promoting the sustainable development of the commodity chain. The problem lies in to what degree and with what force the developed countries have shaped and guided their domestic healthy green consumption. Theoretically speaking, to ensure the product's sustainability, we must add the environmental cost in the product price and provide a comprehensive reflection of the value of sustainable wood products. At present, the green consumption policies in end consumption countries have made certain progresses, [①] but most of them lack comprehensive and in-depth governmental and social support; [②] they even show more of their purpose, which is to protect the domestic wood processing industry while enjoying low-price forest products rather than fundamentally solve the problem of environmental cost and sustainability; in selecting products, the consumer generally inclines to choose cheap products with good qualities, rather than caring too much about whether the wood source is sustainable or not.

China is the processor at the intermediate link, the bridge between the international wood demand and supply and an important force promoting the sustainable development of the commodity chain. But the reality is that while China's economy is developing rapidly, people's livelihood is improving and the domestic wood consumption is in great demand, China's forest resources are in serious shortage; after the historically scarce flood disaster in 1998, the Chinese government has implemented rigorous protection policies to protect the domestic forests. At the same time, through policies such as tariffs, the Chinese government has encouraged wood import, forest product processing and export and promoted the rapid development of the wood processing industry. China's abundant labor force supply makes its labor costs lower than the wood supply countries; its weak intellectual property rights

① 67% of Britain's imported wood has been certified. Five European Union countries and America, Japan and New Zealand have established wood purchase policies. Multinationals like IKEA also promise to use legal wood.

② Such as: imperfect public purchase policies, no established private purchase policies and no rigid division of sustainable wood and other legal wood.

protection makes it possible to copy designs and technologies for a low cost. Therefore, China's wood processing enterprises generally take a low-price strategy for competition. Here are the consequences: when the price drops (the profit rate thus dilutes), to maintain the operation of their enterprises, they must expand production. This has led to a swelling demand on imported wood in China and its dumping of forest products in the international market. This usually means that China's producers are not able to focus on sustainable wood and try to ignore the pollution caused during the processing process (too large industrial scales and low technological levels are also important reasons causing processing pollution) even if they are in confrontation of serious threats in the long-term supply security of wood, rising prices of raw materials and diluting market credits.

Countries like Russia and Mozambique are wood supply countries and their forests and social institutional arrangements have decided the sustainability of the commodity chain. In theory, as long as the forest governance of the wood supply country is sound, then external consumption demands will only bring more positive influences. For example, China also imports wood from America and New Zealand causing environmental and social impacts on these two countries, which are totally different from the influences on Mozambique and Russia. The reality lies in the fact that at the current stage, the forest system arrangement in these wood producing countries is not satisfactory and even though there are many systems and policies, it still may lead to forest deforestation with the purpose of developing agriculture and obtaining fire wood. Our research shows: in Mozambique and Russia, there is no motivation for explicating the intellectual rights and establishing a long-term healthy operation in forests and forest areas and the franchise system leads to short-term forest "exploitation," corruption is running particularly rampant in export-oriented wood production and disregards the interests of poor residents who live in the forests; the government sometimes tolerates or even encourages clear cutting to get foreign exchange and income, the income of which is transferred to high growth departments rather than returned to the forest regeneration link; forest logging and operations lack capital, equipment, technology and high-quality professional personnel, which results in destructive logging operations. These are primary problems leading to forest damage and hindering the solution of sustainability.

To sum up, the current operations of the commodity chain are deeply influenced by the European and American countries' consumption behavior, the trade policy implemented by China, some Chinese companies' socially irresponsible behaviors and the forest and social institutional arrangement of wood supply countries. To enhance the sustainability of this commodity chain is the shared responsibilities of all participators. Mutual accusation will lead nowhere. The real significance lies in the fact that each party should proceed from a global perspective, shoulder its deserved responsibilities, and take practical measures to realize the sustainable development of this supply chain to reach an ideal "win-win" situation.

2. Policy Discussion

For China, continuous wood import serves its own interests. At the same time, to some degree, it also has ensured a stable and sustainable wood supply from its trade partners. This enables China to develop its strong domestic wood processing industry and take more effective measures to protect domestic forests for their own multiple purposes. If we cease to import wood, according to the current wood consumption levels and prices, China will eliminate all its forests in 70 years (WTO and Environmental Research Group, 2004). However, if the validity and sustainability is not considered in purchasing raw materials, it will bring a series of serious problems to China: unstable raw material supply, high prices of raw materials, diluted product credits and diluted forest investment credits.

The key to realizing a sustainable commodity chain of global forest products lies in the improvement of forest governance. The collaboration of the different interest parties is very important. China follows two thinking patterns to cope with such unsustainability and to accomplish industrial upgrading. One is the transformation from acting globally to thinking globally to confronting international criticism and the adoption of effective government intervention measures to reduce illegal wood trade. At the same time, it is also important to encourage domestic enterprises to expand their industrial chain and to invest overseas in establishing artificial forests so as to be less dependent on our natural forests. The other is to reform the domestic forest rights system, including the state-owned forest rights system and significantly improve the productivity of domestic forests. In this way, we can expect a sustainable Chinese forestry industry and trade that distributes its resources globally and the security of China's wood supply can be guaranteed. We have listed the following policy considerations:

Suggestion 1: placing the solution for wood supply security on China. By promoting a domestic forest rights system (including a state-owned forest rights system) reform, we should fundamentally liberate the productivity of the forest area, improve significantly the domestic forest productivity and increase the self-sufficiency rate of domestic wood. Based on domestic forest resources, we should guarantee long-term raw material supply through global resource distribution to meet the needs of the sustainable Chinese forest products industry and trade.

Suggestion 2: establishing a sustainable forest products market. Take effective government intervention measures to decrease illegal wood trade, establish a feasible log tracking system, introduce an inspection and control mechanism, enhance bilateral and multilateral cooperation, implement a signed agreement to crack down on illegal wood trade, strengthen regional customs coordination and monitor the export of wood. Implement a sustainable forest purchase plan, encourage domestic enterprises and individuals to purchase sustainable forest products and provide tax preferential policies for the Chinese companies which purchase sustainable products or correspond to the forest sustainable operation practices that are internationally acknowledged. Meanwhile, encourage domestic enterprises to expand the industrial chain and to invest overseas in establishing artificial forests so as to be less dependable on our natural forests. Provide tax and credit incentives to foreign investment that adhere to the investment guidelines, establish and enhance sustainable conduct norms and guide the Chinese companies overseas.

Suggestion 3: promoting industrial upgrading. Revise China's trade and fiscal taxation policies which lead to unsustainable and low-efficient wood use, guard against the low-level increases in the wood processing industry, promote the transformation of China's wood processing industry to high-value production, decrease the demand of the wood processing industry on wood imports and ultimately build a wood processing industry that is more competitive, healthy, sustainable and upgraded. At the same time, be devoted to improving the added value of Chinese products and aim at sustainable production and the establishment of a high-quality

"Chinese brand" with environmental and social value. This requires Chinese factories to develop high added-value products, economize on wood use and conduct more service-oriented activities, such as product design, brand and targeted marketing.

Suggestion 4: helping developing wood producing countries to develop the capability for forest sustainable operations. Join in new national or regional partnerships for forest sustainable operations and provide financial and technical assistance to the target supply countries. Develop forest governance and operational abilities through cooperation and investment in the forest reform in local public sectors and the participation process, management structure and production ability of the stakeholders. China should particularly provide support to encourage the country which provides raw materials to abide by the laws and observe "sustainable operation practices," and follow the internationally acknowledged standards. ①

Suggestion 5: becoming a key active participator of the international forestry sustainable initiative. Participate in the international carbon sink action implementation to improve forest operations and vigorously decrease carbon emissions from forest deforestation and degradation. Join in the international cooperation on enhancing international wood product sources and trade validity. While seeking a regular FLEGT (Forest Law Enforcement, Governance and Trade) application mechanism for China's imported wood products, China should become an official member of the FLEGT plan.

References:

[1] Zhang Senlin. Reflections on problems facing the forest products industry. In: *Collected Papers of the* 6th *National Artificial Board Industry Science and Technology Development Conference.* 2007.

张森林:《林产工业当前面临问题的思考》,见《第六届全国人造板工业科技发展研讨会论文集》2007 年。

[2] Forest Trends. *China and global forest products market: beneficial to the trade transformation of forest and livelihood.* 2005.

森林趋势:《中国及全球林产品市场:有益于森林和生计的贸易转换》,2005 年。

① For example: Forest Stewardship Council, Program for Endorsement of Certification and Sustainable Forest Initiative.

[3] State Forestry Administration. *China Forestry Development Report*. China Forestry Press, 2001-2008.

国家林业局:《中国林业发展报告》,中国林业出版社 2001—2008 年版。

[4] Andy White, Sun Xiufang, Kerstin Canby, Xu Jingtao & Christopher Barr. Impact of China and global forest products trade upon forest protection and people's livelihood. *Forestry Economics*, 2007(1).

安迪・怀特、孙秀芳、克斯汀・坎比、徐晋涛、克里斯朵夫・巴:《中国和国际林产品贸易对森林保护和人民生计的影响》,《林业经济》2007 年第 1 期。

[5] Cao Yukun & Zhu Jiangmei. A review of opinions and methods on the relationship between forest products international trade and environment. *World Forestry Research*, 2008(3).

曹玉昆、朱江梅:《林产品国际贸易与环境关系研究进展》,《世界林业研究》2008 年第 3 期。

[6] Xuan Linlin & Jiang Minyuan. Enlightenment of the theory of ecotype factor endowment to forest - product trade of the Far East. *China Forestry Economy*, 2005(4).

宣琳琳、蒋敏元:《生态环境要素禀赋论对远东林产品贸易的启示》,《中国林业企业》2005 年第 4 期。

[7] Mou Wanlong, Xuan Linlin & Yang Juhong. Discussion on the influence of environmental problems on Sino-Russian Forest Products Trade. *Northern Economy and Trade*, 2005(6).

牟万龙、宣琳琳、杨菊红:《浅论环境问题对中俄林产品贸易的影响》,《北方经贸》2005 年第 6 期。

[8] Miu Dongling, Zhang Minzhao & Dang Fenglan. A literature review of empirical research on forest products trade and the environment. *World Forestry Research*, 2004(4).

缪东玲、张民照、党凤兰:《林产品贸易与环境实证研究综述》,《世界林业研究》2004 年第 4 期。

[9] Zhu Chunquan, Rodney Taylor & Feng Guoqiang. *China's Wood Market, Trade and Environment*. 2005. http://www.wwfchina.org/wwfpress/publication/forest/Chinawood_cn.pdf.

朱春全、罗德内・泰勒、奉国强:《中国木材市场、贸易和环境》,2005 年, http://www.wwfchina.org/wwfpress/publication/forest/Chinawood_cn.pdf.

[10] Wu Guochun & Sun Xiaolei. A research of forest products import trade and environmental protection problem. *Problems of Forestry Economics*, 2008(4).

吴国春、孙小蕾:《林产品进口贸易与环境保护问题研究》,《林业经济问题》2008 年第 4 期。

[11] Zhang Yukun & Li Shuhua. Import/output structure and features of forest products in Russia. *Russian Central Asian & East European Market*, 2007(2).

张昱琨、李淑华:《俄罗斯林产品进出口结构和特征》,《俄罗斯中亚和东欧市场》2007 年第 2 期。

[12] Lu Wenming & Li Jianquan. Current trade of Russia's forest products and its prospect. *World Forestry Research*, 2005(16).

陆文明、李坚全:《俄罗斯林产品贸易状况和展望》,《世界林业状况》2005 年第16期。

[13] Sun Changjin, Chen Liqiao, Chen Lijun, Han Lu & Steve Bass. *Global forest product commodity chain: defining the opportunities and challenges facing China through the analysis of the commodity chain's sustainability*, 2008. http://www.iisd.org.

孙昌金、陈立桥、陈立俊、韩璐、Steve Bass:全球林产品商品链:通过商品链可持续性分析确定中国面临的机遇与挑战,2008,http://www.iisd.org.

[14] Song Weiming. *Russian log in China: cork commodity chain and China's economic development*. Washington DC: Forest Trends, 2007.

宋维明:《俄罗斯原木在中国:软木商品链和中国经济发展》,华盛顿特区:森林趋势,2007年。

[15] Liu Jianguo. Chinese environment under globalization: how China and the rest of the world interact. *World Environment*, 2005(4).

刘建国:《全球化下的中国环境:中国与世界各地如何相互影响》,《世界环境》2005年第4期。

[16] State Forestry Administration. *China Statistical Yearbook on Forestry*. China Forestry Press, 2008.

国家林业局:《中国林业统计年鉴》,中国林业出版社2008年版。

[17] Bai Xiuping. Project and prospect on Russia's wood trade with China. *World Forestry Trend*, 2007(1).

白秀萍:《俄罗斯对华木材贸易的课题与展望》,《世界林业动态》2007年第1期。

[18] WTO and Environmental Research Group. *Research on the Environmental Influence on China's Accession to WTO*. China Environmental Science Press, 2004. WTO与环境课题组:《中国加入WTO环境影响研究》,中国环境科学出版社2004年版。

[19] Jiang Zehui. *Modern Forestry*. China Forestry Press, 2000.

江泽慧:《现代林业》,中国林业出版社2000年版。

[20] Li Lanying. *Economic Evaluation of the Environmental Influence of Pine Wilt Disease in Zhejiang Province and the Countermeasure Research*. China Forestry Press, 2007.

李兰英:《松材线虫病对浙江省环境影响经济评价及治理对策研究》,中国林业出版社2007年版。

[21] Customs statistics information website: *Annual report on the import and export of Chinese paper and paper products*. http://www.haiguan.info/UserFiles/File/Fenxibaogao/zzp.pdf.

海关统计资讯网:2007年中国纸及纸制品年度进出口报告,http://www.haiguan.info/UserFiles/File/fenxibaogao/zzp.pdf.

[22] Li Jianquan, Lu Wenming, Li Zhiyong & Duan Xinfang. International progress of forest law enforcement governance and trade to combat illegal logging in the world. *World Forestry Research*, 2007(6).

李剑泉、陆文明、李智勇、段新芳:《打击木材非法采伐的森林执法管理与贸易国际进程》,《世界林业研究》2007年第6期。

[23] Li Lianghou. *Relevant Theories and Technology Research on the Construction of Forest Vegetation*. The Yellow River Water Conservancy Press, 2007.

李良厚:《森林植被构建的有关理论与技术研究》,黄河水利出版社 2007 年版。

[24] Food and Agriculture Organization of the United Nations. *Global Forest Resources Evaluation in* 2005. 2006, http://www.fao.org.

联合国粮食及农业组织:《2005 年全球森林资源评估》,2006 年,http://www.fao.org.

[25] Peter Dauvergne. Shadows in the Forest: Japan and the Politics of Timber in Southeast Asia, MIT Press, 1997.

[26] Jonathan Taylor. Japanese Global Environmentalism: Rhetoric and Reality, *Political Geography*, 1999, 18 (5).

[27] Francois Nectoux, Yoichi Kuroda. *Timber from the South Seas: An Analysis of Japan's Tropical Timber Trade and its Environmental Impact*, AWWF International Publication, 1990.

[28] A. Angelsen, D. Kaimowitz. *Agricultural Technologies and Tropical Deforestation*, CABI Pub., 2001.

[29] Rodrigo Sierra. The Role of Domestic Timber Markets in Tropical Deforestation and Forest Degradation in Ecuador: Implications for Conservation Planning and Policy, *Ecological Economics*, 2001, 36 (2).

[30] Markku Simula. Trade and Environmental Issues in Forest Production *Environment Division Working Paper*, 1999, http://www.iadb.org/sds/doc/1306eng.pdf.

[31] Menotti, 1999. http://gogobendigo.blogspot.com/2008/06/impact-of-globalization-on.html.

[32] Kenichi Nakazawa. Timber Trade & Environment Effects, ENA-FLEG Preparatory Conference, 2005.

[33] Shadia Duery, Richard P. Vlosky. An Overview of World Tropical Hardwood Resources *Forest Product Trade and Environmental Issues*, 2006. http://www.lfpdc.lsu.edu/ publications/working papers/wp74.pdf.

[34] Ivan Eastin. *Testimony before the U. S-China Economic and Security Review Commission*, 2005. http://www.uscc.gov/hearings/2005hearings/written testimonie s/05_01_04wrts/ eastin_ivan_wrts.htm.

[35] Xiufang Sun. *Global Forest Products Trade Chain: Challenges & Opportunities*, 2008.

[36] Alexander S. Sheingauz, Anatoly V. Lebedev, Natalia Ye Antonova. *China Soft Wood-log Commodity Chain and Livelihood Analysis: From the Russian Far East to China*, 2005. http://www.forest-trends.org/documents/files/doc_101.pdf.

[37] FAS (Foreign Agricultural Service). *Timber Markets in China*, GAIN Report # CH1071, 2001, http://www.fas.usda.gov/gainfiles/200111/135682796.pdf.

[38] AT Kearney, 2007, www.globe-net.ca.

This book is the result of a co-publication agreement between China Social Sciences Press (China) and Paths International Ltd (UK)

This book is published with financial support from Innovation Project of CASS

Title: China Environment and Development Review: China's Environment and Development in the Era of Globalization
Editor in Chief: ZHANG Xiao (Chinese Academy of Social Sciences)
Translated by: JIN Jun & LIU Yusheng
ISBN: 978-1-84464-454-4
Ebook ISBN: 978-1-84464-455-1

Paths International Ltd
PO Box 4083
Reading
United Kingdom
RG8 8ZN
www.pathsinternational.com

Published in United Kingdom

CPSIA information can be obtained
at www.ICGtesting.com
Printed in the USA
LVOW03*2343221215
467539LV00025B/282/P

9 781844 644544